CAN DR. SIMON GET YOU "UNSTUCK?"
THE EXPERTS SAY, YES, HE CAN!

"SID SIMON KNOWS HOW PEOPLE FUNCTION. LIKE ALL OF US, HE'S BEEN STUCK. BUT UNLIKE MOST OF US HE KNOWS HOW TO GET GOING AGAIN."
> — **Dr. William Glasser, author of *Reality Therapy* and *Take Effecvtive Control of Your Life***

"CLEARLY SHOWS HOW TO TAKE THE RISKS TO MAKE CHANGE WHEN WE FIND OURSELVES IN STUCK SITUATIONS."
> — **Virginia M. Satir, M.A., A.C.S.W., Director of Training, Avanta Network and author of *The New People Making***

"HIS MOST IMAGINATIVE, INSIGHTFUL WORK TO DATE . . . a resource for human growth through change founded on the proposition that to be human is to behave as a free person rather than a victim."
> — **John H. Westerhoff, III, Professor of Religion Education, The Divinity School, Duke University**

"A MARVELOUS BOOK THAT WILL MAKE A REAL DIFFERENCE IN YOUR LIFE . . . . [It] will provide you with the information and practical tools necessary to stop spinning your wheels and get your life back on track."
> — **Jack Canfield, President of Self-Esteem Seminars**

"IT'S A WINNER . . . YOU CAN IDENTIFY WITH THE THOUSANDS OF PEOPLE AND EVENTS DESCRIBED. You will say, 'That's me!' Then read how wonderfully Sid Simon explains how these people, and you, can become unstuck with your life."
> — **Harry K. Wong, Ed.D., Educational Consultant and Classroom Teacher**

"GETTING UNSTUCK IS THAT DREAM THAT CAN GENTLY FALL INTO THE REALITY OF YOUR HEART. It's essential for any community that wishes to grow as individuals and as a family."
> — **Rev. Dr. Leo James Hoar, Campus Minister, Professor at Springfield College**

About the Author:

SIDNEY B. SIMON, Ed. D. is a professor of psychological education at the University of Massachusetts at Amherst. One of the founders of the Values Clarification Movement, Dr. Simon has helped develop a theory and set of practical strategies that have affected counseling practice, child rearing, education, medical care, social work, and the criminal justice system in this country and abroad. The author and co-author of sixteen books, including the bestselling *Values Clarification,* Dr. Simon lectures widely and gives seminars with his wife, Suzanne, all over the U.S., Canada, Mexico, and Europe.

GETTING UNSTUCK

BREAKING THROUGH

YOUR BARRIERS TO

CHANGE

DR. SIDNEY B. SIMON

Produced by The Philip Lief Group, Inc.

WARNER BOOKS

A Warner Communications Company

*To my wife, Suzanne Simon, for loyalty beyond
the call of love*

Copyright © 1988 by Sidney B. Simon
All rights reserved.

Produced by The Philip Lief Group, Inc.

Warner Books, Inc., 666 Fifth Avenue, New York, NY 10103

W A Warner Communications Company

Printed in the United States of America
First Trade Paperback Printing: August 1989
10 9 8 7 6 5 4 3 2 1

Library of Congress Cataloging-in-Publication Data

Simon, Sidney B.
    Getting unstuck.

    1. Change (Psychology) 2. Change (Psychology)—
Case studies. 3. Motivation (Psychology) 4. Motivation
(Psychology)—Case studies. 5. Self-realization .
6. Self-realization—Case studies. I. Title
BF471.S56   1989   158'.1   88-40092
ISBN 0-446-39024-0 (pbk.) (U.S.A.)
        0-446-39025-9 (pbk.) (Can.)

*Book design: H. Roberts
Cover design: Karen Katz*

Acknowledgments

The ideas for this book were hammered out in a hundred Values Realization Workshops and dozens of classes at the University of Massachusetts. I am grateful to all those students and workshop participants and to the myriad people on my life's bumpy path who taught me what I had to learn. I am also indebted to the people whose stories illuminate this book and whose "unstuckness" graces these pages.

I am especially grateful to those adults who used to be our children—John Simon, Douglas Simon, Julianna Simon, Matthew and Carie Lee Bernard. Unstuck themselves, they gave me bountiful inspiration.

I feel a deep gratitude to the members of the Values Realization Institute for what their commitment taught me about getting unstuck. In particular, my thanks go to Michael Wenger, the guiding star in the process that made the Institute a reality.

To Susan Meltsner, my deepest thanks for her brillance, drive, and follow-through that made the pages mount. It was just a hat full of workshop ideas until she lent her art to my craft and got this book unstuck.

A warm thanks to Cathy Hemming, a shepherd in sheep's clothing. Without her vision, support, guidance, affirmations, and hopes, I might still be on the other side of the barriers to change.

A high-energy thanks goes to Nancy Kalish, my editor. She is so wise, so ebulliently positive that one could never be less than brilliant in her care. My thanks as well to someone who was significantly supportive and who early on had a profound faith in this book, Joann Davis of Warner Books.

There were so many others. To name just a few, let me thank Howard Kirschenbaum, for his always practical insights given with full integrity, and Lee Silverstein, friend and encourager when courage was needed. Also thanks to my sister, Dorothy, who is always in my corner; to Sharon Lumbis, who manages the miscellaneous in this office with sensitivity and efficiency; and to all those other people who cared at the right time.

But let it be known that Suzanne Simon, my everloving wife-partner, never, never wobbled in her utter faith. She, noble woman, lives what GETTING UNSTUCK is all about.

Finally, let me acknowledge and thank you, the reader, who intuitively knew that something important was waiting for you when you chose to pick up this book. I pray you learn what this teacher deeply believes he has to teach.

Hadley, Mass.
April, 1988

1

What It Means to Be Stuck

STUCK IS ...

... setting goals and making plans but putting off the first step until tomorrow or next week or next year or the moment after the rest of your life is in perfect order.

... making promises—to stop drinking, quit smoking, spend more time with your family, bring down your credit card balances, exercise regularly, or be more assertive— breaking promises and feeling guilty.

... taking no action to prevent dire consequences to your health or well-being despite repeated warnings from your doctor, your boss, your family, and your friends.

... waiting for a catastrophe, a sign, an offer you can't refuse, or until you absolutely, positively cannot "take it" anymore before doing what you knew all along you should and could do.

STUCK IS NOT A COMFORTABLE, SATISFYING PLACE TO BE. When you are stuck you do not feel content. You do not think clearly. You doubt your abilities and dislike yourself. Most notably, you cannot move toward your goals or out of unpleasant, unhealthy situations.

This book is about getting *unstuck*. It will acquaint you with the psychological obstacles, emotional barriers, and practical considerations that thwart your best efforts to change. It offers guidance, ideas, and tools you can use to push through the blocks to change. By the time you reach the final page, you will be well on your way to a more satisfying and rewarding life.

However, before you begin your journey, you need a clear understanding of exactly what it means to be stuck. Your first inclination may be to avoid looking at what it means to be stuck. You may want to deny your feelings, ignore the signs and symptoms and refuse to examine what being stuck means and how it affects you. But examine it you must. Recognizing and understanding what being stuck means is a first step toward getting unstuck.

In this chapter you will find both general descriptions of being stuck and detailed profiles of people who are stuck. *You* may not be as stuck as the people whose personal stories appear here. *All* the signs and symptoms of being stuck may not apply to you, but I urge you to consider them anyway. You are embarking upon a journey that many people have taken before you. You can only benefit from their stories of getting unstuck. The ultimate destination of this odyssey is arriving at the life you truly desire and deserve. You cannot plan such a trip or begin traveling until you find the starting line. Stuck is the starting line, and you'll soon recognize that you are not the only person standing on it.

EVERYONE GETS STUCK. Everyone. There are no exceptions. Think about it. Think of the people whose lives seem to be charmed—people who have and do everything you wish for yourself. Do you honestly believe they never have a moment of doubt or insecurity? Do you think they never came upon an obstacle they believed to be insurmountable or found a frustrating, seemingly intractable barrier interrupting the path to success? Of course not. Try as you might, you will never find anyone whose life was exactly the way that person wanted it to be from the day he or she was born until death.

No matter how rich, powerful, intelligent, beautiful, famous, successful, or admired you are, you can take a wrong turn, lose your way, skid off the road, and find yourself knee-deep in quicksand and sinking fast. At least once in a lifetime, and more likely many times, you and I get stuck.

- Dynamic, talented, self-confident singer Tina Turner spent years and years married to a man who physically and emotionally abused her.

- Former first lady Betty Ford, a woman admired by millions and a role model to many, got stuck in a dangerous addiction to alcohol and prescription medicine. It took years of suffering and painful confrontations by her family to get her to change and on the road to recovery.

- A child star who grew up to be a renowned and respected actress, Patty Duke got trapped on a roller coaster ride of mental illness.

- Billy Joel, the popular music recording artist, now married to one of the most beautiful women in the world and an adoring father, once considered suicide.

Everyone gets stuck—even people who "should" know better. Even a university professor who lectures and leads workshops and writes books about getting unstuck.

In 1980 a newspaper article titled "Lifting the Barriers to Personal Success" appeared in the *Arizona Republic*. It was written by columnist Ginger Hutton, who had attended a workshop I led in Scottsdale, Arizona. In the article Ginger presented in a general way the eight blocks to change you will read about in this book, and which had been the foundation of my workshop that weekend in March. Seeing my ideas about the subject of change in print for the first time started me thinking about writing this book.

I told myself the book needed to be written and that I was the one who could and should write it. I thought a great deal about writing it and told many people of my intentions. But for seven years, I did not write it. I procrastinated. I rationalized. With my busy schedule I could not find time to write a book. I was waiting for the perfect moment; I had to be sure I had enough material. I had to see how more workshop attendees responded to the ideas. I had to be sure no other author had written a book like it.

A dozen times I started the project only to abandon it. The irony did not escape me. I wanted to write a book about change—yet *I* was stuck.

Between 1980 when I initially considered writing this book and 1987 when I finally wrote it, I reexperienced, in a very personal way, the blocks to change and rediscovered how to push through them. I was humbled by my own resistance to change—a resistance I thought I had gotten over years ago. But most importantly, I dramatically reaffirmed the principle upon which this book is based:

EVERYONE GETS STUCK AND EVERYONE CAN GET UNSTUCK

Any choice you face—from quitting smoking and getting your hair cut to accepting a marriage proposal or job offer —can confuse you, frighten you, and get you stuck. One of the most obvious and painful places to be stuck is when we have gotten ourselves into frustrating and self-destructive situations. They are all too familiar and all too painful:

• bad marriages

• dead-end jobs

• feeling alone and isolated in a new town

- experiencing physical illness or severe depression
- being unable to escape physical, emotional, or sexual abuse

All the ways you can get stuck have one element in common. Change is required—but you can't seem to make change happen. Whether you want to stop biting your nails or whether you have endured a decade of abuse from a spouse or parent, *when you are stuck your ability to do anything about your situation seems to disappear.* Nothing seems able to get you moving, not your desire to be better, not your treasured goals and aspirations, not even the pain you feel. Threats, bribes, and impassioned pleas are not enough to move you.

STUCK IS A CAR IN THE MUD
WITH ITS WHEELS SPINNING

Carla, a forty-eight-year-old social worker from Minnesota, is stuck in an unsatisfying, dead-end job.

"I don't work with people anymore," she groans. "I work with paper. Forms. Files. Memos. The name of the game is 'cover your ass.' No one cares what you do with your clients as long as the paperwork gets in on time. I took this job because I wanted to serve children, but I ended up serving the system and it's a cruddy system at that. If you started out caring, the system beats it out of you. They pile on the unreasonable demands until they bury you. Then they top it off by taking away whatever dignity you have."

Carla's tirade against the child welfare agency where she works can go on for hours. Complaining about the system is what Carla does best these days—and she does it often.

Like most people who find themselves trapped in an intolerable situation, Carla did not get to the end of her rope overnight. She had slowly painted herself into a corner by the choices she made, the real injustices and indignities of her job, and all she did and did not do to turn things around earlier in her career and in her life.

The mother of three, Carla returned to the work force when her sons were still young. She held a bachelor's degree in social work, wanted to work with children, and needed a part-time job. The county agency was the only place that offered what she thought she wanted. In the beginning, things went well, but as her children got older and more independent, she began working full-time. For unrelated reasons, Carla's husband left her, and she turned to her work and her coworkers for emotional support.

"I have such powerful ties to this place because the people here pulled me through the divorce. They are my closest friends. I made them my extended family," Carla explains. More than emotional ties bound her to the agency. The job also gave her the stability and security of a steady paycheck. "I'm not a high-risk person. I take as few risks as possible. My number one responsibility is to my kids. No matter how bad things get, leaving the job is never a serious option. I can't risk losing that paycheck."

Carla's financial needs increased as her sons became teenagers and her child support checks appeared less regularly. To increase her earning power she went to graduate school, earned her master's degree, and took the first supervisory position that became available. Ironically, as she earned more money, she stopped having direct client contact, even though working with children and families had been the only aspect of the job she liked.

"But I keep plugging away," Carla continues. "I moved right on up the paper-pushing ladder—even though I am dissatisfied and feel trapped."

Thinking that working with people again would make her feel better, Carla started a private counseling practice in addition to her full-time job. "I love counseling. But with my private practice, the agency, and raising three teenage boys, I'm giving, giving, giving, twenty-four hours a day."

It does not occur to her to leave the agency and concentrate on her private practice. "It's that paycheck thing again," she sighs. "I don't think I can make it on my own. I can't take the chance."

Feeling more and more pressured, Carla took a friend's advice and began swimming each morning to relieve stress. Carla believes the physical exercise and the "high" it produces keep her from "going over the edge."

Because Carla swam in the morning, she got to work late. Because the job made her crazy, she left early and took long lunch breaks. Because she was not the only worker suffering from burnout at the agency's expense, the agency cracked down.

"We were told to be at our desks at eight-thirty and not leave before four-thirty in the afternoon. They refuse to make any exceptions, even when I offered to work late to make up the time I spent swimming. They are totally inflexible. I have to give up the one thing that helps me survive and I'm furious.

"Then they moved me into the basement. Here I am, the most senior worker in the agency, and I'm stuck in a basement office with a smoker no less! They won't budge on anything. They won't even let me use an empty office on the first floor for the summer while the students who use it during the school year are on vacation.

"I've been with this agency for fifteen years, and believe me, I gave it a whole lot more than it gave me. But it's too late to start over. I'm forty-eight years old and two of my kids are in college. So now I'm just doing time. I do as little work as possible. I take as many sick days as I can get away with. I sneak out of the building and go shopping for a couple of hours. I bitch about the agency all the time."

Carla also notices herself yelling at her kids more, spending her weekends in bed, and having nightmares about the job. "It's a living hell, but what can I do? At this point I'm probably not capable of being anything but a powerless bureaucrat anyway."

What can I do?
I made my bed, now I have to sleep in it.
How can I risk losing what little I have?
There's nowhere to go.
I'll get by somehow.

Sound familiar? Those are the sounds of resignation, of settling for the way things are, of putting up with jobs, relationships, and circumstances that are less than you desire—or deserve. In Carla's story you can practically hear the sound of car wheels spinning in the mud. The car won't move forward, it won't back out. You're afraid to abandon it and don't know which way to walk to find help. Not strong enough to push the car out of the mud, you hold no hope of being rescued. Frustrated, you push down harder on the gas pedal and dig in deeper.

STUCK IS . . .

. . . seeing few or no alternatives to your current situation.

. . . allowing fear of failure, disappointment, rejection, loss, or change to keep you from taking risks.

. . . fatigue, depression, and decreased productivity—at first only in relation to the aspect you can't seem to change, but eventually in many areas of your life.

. . . complaining more often than you used to; seeing only the dark side, taking every opportunity to point out how bad things are; believing all available options are doomed to fail and rejecting them outright.

. . . grasping at straws; going to extremes; without careful consideration or planning, pursuing the first alternative that presents itself.

. . . starting projects, diets, exercise programs, or any other self-improvement effort and abandoning it soon after you begin, halfway through or one step before you reach your goal.

STUCK IS FINDING YOURSELF BACK AT SQUARE ONE (and wondering if you have the strength to start over).

Over a six-month period, a nationally franchised diet center's structured weight-loss program helped Karen lose thirty-five pounds. Less than a year later, the thirty-three-year-old secretary has regained all thirty-five pounds and returns to the diet center. She sits across from a reed-thin counselor whom Karen sees as a slender, condescending judge.

The counselor closes the worn manila folder and peers at Karen. "You were doing so well," she says. "What happened?"

Karen cringes. "I was completely humiliated to be in that office at all. I was back at square one. Again. I could hardly face the thought of another diet, and this lady—who probably never dieted a day in her life—wants to know what happened! The same thing that *always* happens. I diet. I lose weight. I gain it back. It wasn't the first time. Sometimes I think I should just give up, throw in the towel and resign myself to being fat for the rest of my life. I looked at that counselor, with her collarbones and her skinny legs, and I wanted to throw up my hands and admit that when it comes to dieting, I'm a big, fat failure."

Overweight since childhood, Karen has tried many diets and lost many pounds, only to regain them. Sometimes she gets back on track before too much damage is done. Sometimes she puts on more pounds than she lost. She is well aware of the health risks she faces by being overweight— as well as the damage the yo-yo effect that going up and down the scale can have. Her roller coaster ride of valiant attempts and seemingly inevitable setbacks does considerable damage to her sense of self-worth and emotional well-being.

Karen is bright, witty, and articulate, and her inability to sustain a weight loss stands in direct contrast to her other achievements. She has risen from the typing pool to being an executive secretary, consistently receives high praise from her boss, as well as large pay raises. Warm, caring, and open, Karen maintains supportive friendships, has close ties to her family, and pursues diverse interests. Her passions range from flower arranging to rock and roll music.

Yet, when she struggles to lose weight only to gain it back again, all successes are diminished in her mind. "None of the good things in my life seem as good when my weight is up. I lose my perspective. All I can see is the problem and what a weak, incompetent, unlovable person I must be because I can't get this one area under control."

Perhaps you never needed to, wanted to, or attempted unsuccessfully to lose weight, and Karen's *experience* seems foreign to you. Her *feelings* should be familiar, however. The emotions she feels crop up whenever anyone is stuck in any way. Perhaps you have tried to quit smoking, drinking, or biting your nails. You may have been determined to better manage your time, stop yelling at your children, patch up your relationship with your parents, or bring down your credit card balances. Maybe you've been telling yourself you *will* join a health club, take a course, or ask for a raise. You take the first steps toward your goal. You may even accomplish it temporarily. But for reasons that are often complicated and sometimes mysterious, you fall back into your old ways. You start smoking again, stop going to the health club, have another bitter argument with your parents (and swear hell will freeze over before you talk to them again), or get another call from the credit company because you once more exceeded your limit. You are right back where you started, and the prospect of beginning again is decidedly unappealing.

"When I'm stuck, I'm an emotional mess and hell to live with," Karen summarizes. "I look at thin people and resent them for being thin. When I see a thin person eating an ice cream cone or a huge Italian dinner while I'm munching on a dinner salad, I want to scream at them. I want to scream period. It's so unfair.

"I feel sorry for myself all the time. Poor old Karen, she doesn't deserve this. I go crazy if anyone says anything about my weight. Anyone who tries to help me is a cruel, insensitive know-it-all as far as I'm concerned. Sometimes I get very down on myself and hole up in my house for days. Other times I tell myself being overweight doesn't bother me, but I'm not very convincing. What's the matter with me? In a word—I'm miserable."

In a word, being stuck can make you feel miserable. Being stuck someplace you have been before exaggerates the feelings and often makes getting unstuck even more difficult.

You may be stuck again at square one, wondering if you have the strength to try again. Or you may have postponed and procrastinated, letting something you want slip further and further from your grasp. Or you may be contemplating new or unexpected turns of events you do not know how to manage. Regardless of your unique and personal situation, being stuck feels lousy. It always does.

STUCK IS . . .

. . . feeling helpless, hopeless, worthless, frustrated, angry, trapped, or out of control.

. . . resenting people who possess what you want (but have not attained) and rejecting anyone who happens to notice or might inadvertently hit one of your sore spots.

. . . turning into a screaming meanie when anyone has the audacity to suggest you change, anyone you can conceivably blame for your present circumstances or whoever happens to be in the vicinity when you explode.

. . . becoming a relentless self-critic, hating and berating yourself for every flaw or failure, and convincing yourself you do not have what you want because you do not deserve it.

STUCK IS COMING UP WITH AN INFINITE NUMBER OF "PERFECTLY GOOD REASONS" NOT TO CHANGE

"Basically, we stay together for the kids," says Lou, a forty-year-old restaurateur. "I know you've probably heard that a million times before, but in our case it's true. My wife and I make a good parenting team. It's the one part of our marriage that works. We form a united front when it comes to the kids. We talk about their problems and go to school conferences together and show up at their Little League games. We both love our kids and they deserve to be raised by two parents."

But what does Lou deserve? He is stuck in a loveless marriage with Lois. They sleep in separate beds. They talk to one another only when one of the children has a problem. Otherwise, their communication is restricted to bitter arguments—about money, household chores, Lou's cigarette smoking, or Lois's latest affair. Arguments are followed by the silent treatment until some trouble with one of the kids forces them to face each other. It comes as no surprise that Lou and Lois's children get into a lot of trouble.

Lou and Lois married one week after Lois's high school graduation. According to Lou, they were madly in love. According to Lois, marriage was her ticket out of her parents' home and she "might as well get it over with." She saw Lou as "a nice enough guy with plenty of ambition for someone with only a high school education."

He was working as a chef's assistant at the restaurant where Lois waitressed, but he dreamed about opening a restaurant of his own one day. It would be their restaurant, a shared venture, and they had it planned right down to the shape of the menu, the silver pattern, and the decor. Lou saw a bright future ahead of them.

"But all that got put on hold when Lois got pregnant," he explains. "We ended up having three children one right after the other. I worked two jobs and Lois stayed home with the kids."

They spent little time together. Most nights Lou got home exhausted at two A.M. and fell into bed. To make it to his day job on time, Lou left the house at six in the morning.

Lois felt trapped. She told Lou she did not appreciate having no one to talk to but three toddlers. Thinking she would be happier if she could get out of the house more, Lou bought Lois a car. She used it to go to shopping malls. The balances on their credit cards reached their limits. Lou worked harder.

"I couldn't figure out what she wanted from me," he says. "I was busting my tail to pay our bills. I'd come home dead tired and she'd want to talk or have friends over for gourmet dinners. Of course, she expected me to cook. Or she'd want to go dancing. I wanted to spend my days off sleeping late, tinkering in the yard, and hanging out with the kids."

As he had done when Lois complained about being without a car, Lou dealt with each marital crisis in a concrete manner. He realized Lois was bored and paid for her to take courses at a community college. But that wasn't enough. Lois had an affair, and Lou left home briefly to live with his brother. Finally they sought the help of a marriage counselor. During a session Lois asked what had happened to Lou's ambition. Why hadn't they opened that restaurant? Lou borrowed money from his parents and drained his savings to buy a small cafe in the New Jersey seashore town where he had spent his summers as a boy. Going into therapy and opening the restaurant made sense to Lou, but neither of these things improved his relationship with his wife.

"Your own restaurant eats up ten times as much of your time. The first year it was a headache twenty-four hours a day. In the beginning Lois was right there working with me. But after a while she lost interest. I guess I should have known she would."

Finally Lou ran out of tangible measures to please Lois and resigned himself to his fate. Three years have passed since Lou and Lois opened the restaurant. Little has changed. Lou works long hours. Lois still has affairs. They've gotten used to their life. Lou does not like it, but he sees no way to improve matters. He often wants to leave, but he always has plenty of reasons not to go.

"I guess an outsider can't understand why we stay

together, but we have our reasons," Lou explains. "The kids are one big reason, and then there's the restaurant. On paper we're partners in the business, which means all kinds of messy legal ties. And we're up to our eyeballs in debt. We couldn't afford lawyers, let alone separate houses. If we split, she might as well forget about getting child support. You can't squeeze blood from a stone. Besides, I wouldn't want to lose the kids. Lois would probably take them to California or somewhere and I'd never see them again. And hey—it's not like we're the only unhappy couple in America. After a while you get used to it. You find ways to get by."

Perhaps you are not deeply mired in a loveless marriage the way Lou is. Maybe you are just teetering on the brink of a decision about changing careers or wondering if you should move to a bigger apartment. Lou's problems seem so much bigger, but being stuck is *not* restricted to people in dire circumstances. Anytime you want or need to make a change—no matter how small—and can come up with a limitless supply of perfectly good reasons not to change, you can get stuck. Rarely do you come right out and say you do not *want* to change. Instead, you offer a perfectly logical, reasonable, legitimate argument for why you *cannot* change. Human beings have a remarkable talent for this type of circular, negative thinking, and it is one of the most obvious symptoms of being stuck.

STUCK IS . . .

. . . NEGATIVE THINKING. Your thoughts and conversations are overpopulated with phrases such as: I can't; it will never work; that won't make a difference; or I have no choice.

. . . UNDERESTIMATING YOURSELF. You believe you are not smart enough, pretty enough, strong enough, successful, powerful, rich, creative, or worthy enough to get what you really want.

. . . MINIMIZING YOUR SITUATION. You console yourself (and convince yourself not to change) with such halfhearted reassurances as: things are not so bad; other people have it worse; I should be grateful for what I have— I'll get by.

. . . MAGICAL THINKING. Magical thoughts are excuses in disguise. They usually begin with the phrase—"All my problems would be solved if only" . . . if only you could win the lottery; if only your mother wasn't in a nursing home; if only your father had never abused you; if only you had not married so young and so on.

. . . ONE-TRACK THINKING. When you are stuck, an enormous amount of your time and energy is devoted to worrying about the problem. You put it under a microscope for closer, even narrower inspection. You go over with a fine-tooth comb every single thing you have ever done or said about this problem. You desperately try to find the reason for your present condition.

All variations of "stuck" thinking conspire to keep you stalemated. Rarely do you look up long enough to see solutions. So caught up in these thought patterns, you have little will or energy to change. If you're not careful, stuck can become a way of life.

IF LIFE IS A JOURNEY, STUCK IS A DETOUR

Life is often compared to a journey, a road traveled from the day of your birth until the moment of your death. You set out on your journey intending to reach your destination. The road twists and turns, sometimes by choice, sometimes because unforeseen obstacles impede your progress. Occasionally you lose your way altogether. Everyone does.

You may get all packed and ready to go but never take the trip. You may set out hopefully but turn back at the first sign of stormy weather or get halfway to your destination and panic. Fear brings you to a standstill and you wonder if you truly want to continue the journey. You do not know exactly what lies ahead of you and worry that getting to where you are going might not make you happier. So you turn back or stay where you are. No matter which detour you take, you arrive at the same outcome. You find yourself someplace you did not plan and do not want to be—and you do not know how to get back on track. You are stuck.

How do you get off the track in the first place? Why do you turn off the main road? If life is a journey and your intention is to get to a particular place, how do you end up someplace else?

Everyone who gets stuck does so because at least one, usually several, and sometimes all of the following eight barriers cause them to reroute, postpone, or abandon their journey. By the time you finish this book you will come to recognize each of the eight barriers. You will have the opportunity to confront them and you will be given the tools to overcome them. You will be able to change if that is what you choose to do.

1. LOW SELF-ESTEEM: Negative criticism, perceived failures, and trying to measure up to other people's standards damage your sense of self-worth and lead you to believe you do not deserve better or more than you have.

2. NOT SEEING ALTERNATIVES: Without options you have no place to go. Without the decision-making skills to choose options and follow through with a plan, you spin your wheels or slide back to square one.

3. NOT KNOWING WHAT YOU REALLY WANT: Confused by conflicting messages about what you should do and be, you let parents, preachers, Madison Avenue advertisers, or "The Joneses" set priorities for you. Without a clear sense of what *you* value, you lack the vision to accomplish your goals.

4. DEFENDING THE STATUS QUO: You fritter away the energy you have. You use much of it to defend your current position. Instead of setting a goal, plotting a course, and following a plan, you find perfectly good reasons *not* to change.

5. FEAR: The prospect of changing frightens you. Change

brings with it the possibility of failure, rejection, disappointment, and pain as well as the chance that getting what you *think* you want will not solve your problems after all. Fear causes you to sacrifice probable gain so you can avoid possible pain.

6. LACK OF COOPERATION: You stoically try to go it alone because you do not know where to look for help or you are reluctant to ask for the support of people who love you.

7. PERFECTIONISM: You want a guarantee. You want a perfect solution and a perfect unobstructed road to your goal (which also must yield perfect results). For you it's perfection or nothing. With that ultimatum, you can never achieve what you want.

8. LACK OF WILL: You cannot act on your desires or summon the energy needed to get you going and keep you moving all the way to your destination.

GETTING BACK ON TRACK

If you are stuck now and particularly if you have been stuck for a while, you may not believe the ideas in this book, or for that matter, that any other ideas will help you get unstuck or lead the kind of life you want and deserve. Nothing anyone can say will convince you there is a light at the end of your tunnel.

Carla, Karen, Lou, and other people whose personal experiences are included in other parts of this book were skeptical too. However, they agreed to set aside their doubts and defenses so they could try to get unstuck. You will read about the progress they make. In a sense, they are on this journey with you.

If, at this moment, you cannot believe a light will appear at the end of your tunnel, I ask you to pretend it might. Try to remain open to the words you read. Work through the strategies for getting unstuck. If you become confused or skeptical or feel I am asking you to look at parts of yourself you'd rather not see, take a breather. Reread this chapter. Ask yourself if stuck is really what you want to be. Then try again. The brightness of that light, when it finally appears, may just surprise you.

When you are stuck, you tend to look at other people's lives with envy. You come to believe they have some special, magical, unattainable quality that allows them to get what they want out of life. You may think *they* can get unstuck, but *you* cannot. YOU CAN.

It is true that you may never sing as well as Tina Turner or be admired as much as Betty Ford. You may never be a center for the Boston Celtics, the chief executive officer of Chrysler Corporation, or as wealthy as John Paul Getty. You cannot have someone else's life, but you *can* have your life and you can make it different, more and better than it has ever been before. As Richard Bach writes in his book *Illusions*, "You are never given a wish without also being given the power to make it true. You may have to work for it, however."

You did not get stuck overnight. Life was not perfect one day and a horrible, ugly mess the next. You took your first detour a while ago, and it will take some time to wind your way back to the turning point that will take you to the road you want to travel. You may encounter your share of potholes, washed-out bridges, and fallen trees along the way, but you will be on your road and going where you want to go. You can get beyond those obstacles if you work at dismantling them. Be patient. Be resolute. Remember what stuck feels, looks, and sounds like. Ask yourself if stuck is where you want to stay.

2

Why Change?

Change. If you made a list of words easier said than done, "change" would top it. One syllable, six letters, meaning *to alter, vary, or make different,* the word "change" elicits a broad spectrum of conflicting emotions from anyone who hears it. What happens to you when you think about change? What are the first words or images that come to mind?

Several years ago, an educator at Kent State University posed that very question to a group of sophomore education majors. She asked them to jot down their immediate, uncensored reactions to the idea of change and then collected the folded slips of paper bearing their anonymous responses. She unfolded one slip of paper, then another, then another. The word she saw most gave her quite a shock. A full seventy-five percent of her students thought of death when they heard the word "change."

Why so many students associated change with something as final and frightening as death was never explained to the educator's satisfaction. However, she did learn her students believed change did happen *to them,* and that it was rarely, if ever, *chosen* by them. They adapted because they *had* to, not because they *wanted* to. In most cases change seemed to have been forced upon them, and they most frequently made changes when there was a tangible reward for their action or a punishment to avoid. All agreed that even when the result was positive, change itself was painful, and they probably would have chosen not to change if they could have gotten away with it.

These young adults viewed change dimly. I must admit at various times in my life I shared their perspective. People of all ages and from all walks of life whom I have taught, counseled, or engaged in casual conversation, almost universally believe change is difficult at best, and certainly well worth postponing or preventing if at all possible.

At first glance, change may seem to be a reasonable proposition. What could be better than abandoning unhealthy habits, altering an unfulfilling relationship, deviating from the same dull routines, accepting new challenges or work to improve the quality of your life? The results of change can only leave us better off than we were before. So why do we dread change? What is our problem with it? How did change get such a bad reputation?

We can learn something about our aversion to change by looking at what motivates people to finally change. I spoke to several friends and colleagues who had successfully changed their lives or altered specific habits and patterns. I asked them why they changed. Here are their responses:

> "I cleaned up my act the day I got out of the hospital," explains Jacob, the owner of a small, specialized publishing company based in Virginia. At the age of thirty-seven he had a heart attack.
>
> "My heart attack was one heck of an eye-opener. When the pain started, I thought for sure I was about to die, and it scared the hell out of me. I swore, if I lived, I'd change my ways and I did. No more cigarettes. No

more wolfing down fried chicken or bologna sandwiches
with extra mayonnaise. I don't work every weekend any
more or get ticked off at every little thing that goes
wrong. Hell, I'm downright mellow these days. All
because of that heart attack. You might say it scared me
right onto the straight and narrow."

"Looking back now, it's pretty obvious my life wasn't
working," Cindy, a thirty-year-old public relations
director, recalls. "Actually, I didn't have much of a life at
all. I worked sixty hours a week. If I wasn't holed up in a
moldy subbasement office listening to the people who
shared it scream at each other, I was baby-sitting clients
and recuperating from the latest crisis. Everyone was
dumping on me: coworkers, friends, my family. My love
life was the pits. You name it and it was going wrong.
But it never occurred to me to *do* anything about any
of it.

"Then, out of nowhere—or so I thought—I started
having these attacks, panic attacks I guess you'd call
them. I would hyperventilate and cry and feel like my
head was going to explode. I thought I was going crazy
and I was willing to do *anything* to stop feeling that
way."

"Anger. Anger and frustration *made* me change," Lisa
claims. "It was straight out of the movie *Network*. I was
mad as hell and I wasn't going to take it anymore."

Lisa worked as a sales representative for an office
supply company. Constantly given the most difficult
territories to cover, she received no recognition for work
well done. She was promised raises she never received.
She was not considered for promotions.

"They brought in a guy who didn't know the first thing
about office supplies and paid him twice what I was
making. He would make messes and I would clean them

up. He'd cover up his mistakes by lying and saying I had done things I not only didn't do, but didn't even know about. When I went over his head to complain, the sales manager made me look like the bad guy."

Lisa put up with the situation for over a year. It got worse and worse. She got angrier and angrier.

"God, I drove my husband crazy," she sighs. "Then one day something happened—something that wasn't even that big a deal—and I lost it. I quit on the spot. It was not the most rational, intelligent way to handle things. I was unemployed, didn't have a clue about where I would go or what I would do. The next six months were a nightmare, but eventually I got it together."

Mimi and Kerry are a married couple living in Boston, Massachusetts. She is a therapist and he is the executive director of a professional organization. They are expecting their first child. Everyone who knows them thinks theirs is the ideal relationship. Life was not always so idyllic, however.

"We came very, very close to having no relationship at all," says Mimi. "We'd been living together for seven years and Kerry wanted to get married. I still wasn't sure. We talked about going into therapy together, but I kept putting it off. I thought I wanted things to stay the way they were. Kerry didn't think the way things were was good enough. I literally did not hear what he was trying to tell me until he said he didn't see any point in staying in the relationship if it wasn't going anywhere. If I wasn't willing to work on the relationship, and if I still wanted an easy escape route, he figured we might as well end it right then and there. The possibility of losing Kerry suddenly became very real to me. The scales tipped. The idea of not being in a relationship with Kerry seemed a whole lot worse than making the changes that really did need to be made."

∎∎/////

"I *had* to change. I had no choice but to change," says Marilyn, a forty-year-old divorced registered nurse. "At the time I thought of it as 'coping.' "

When Marilyn's husband announced he was leaving her, she was taken by surprise. She was completely unprepared to go on living without him.

"I didn't have any idea of what he was up to. I didn't see it coming. I thought I'd be this happily married housewife forever. But there I was. No husband. Three children growing like weeds and eating like horses and the child-support checks coming in whenever my ex-husband felt like sending them—which needless to say was not on a regular basis. I was a mess.

"I'd been out of the work force for twelve years. Nursing had changed drastically since the last time I set foot in a hospital. But I couldn't sit around the house and mope forever, although I did do that for a while. There were bills to pay and my kids were depending on me, so I got up off my duff and put my life back together again. It wasn't easy and it wasn't fun. Things are pretty good now. But I didn't get here because I wanted to. Like I said, I had no choice. I did what I had to do."

COMMON METHODS FOR CHANGE

The experiences that Jacob, Cindy, Lisa, Mimi and Kerry, and Marilyn had represent some of the most common reasons people change. While their approaches to change work, they may not be the most healthy ways of accomplishing it. Their lives are, however, better than they were before they changed. They abandoned old habits, resolved longstanding problems, improved relationships, expanded their horizons, and regained their balance after experiencing various setbacks.

Other than the benefits they experienced, the reasons

they gave for changing have several other elements in common. In fact, when most of us deal with change, we're likely to approach it in one or more of these ways:

Scared Straight

When Jacob had his heart attack, he took the scared straight route to change. He was shocked into altering his work habits and lifestyle by a life-threatening experience.

When you change for this reason, you generally do so after years of self-defeating behavior and repeated warnings from doctors, friends, and family members—pleas and threats that fall upon deaf ears. To be scared straight is to come within an inch of losing your life, home, family, job, sanity, or freedom. The crisis—in whatever form it takes—is so big, so obvious, so painful, and so frightening, you are thrust forward from a dead stop and compelled to change.

Crying Uncle

It was not one event, but the cumulative effect of stress, overwork, and underappreciation that led to Cindy's panic attacks—she experienced physical clues that told her she needed to change, clues that caused much pain and discomfort. She reached her limit and became willing to change. Her body simply "cried uncle."

We all cry uncle eventually. We change our lives, behaviors, and attitudes because we can no longer endure the feelings or pay the physical and emotional price of staying the way we are or have always been.

The Straw That Breaks the Camel's Back

Like crying uncle, this approach to change resembles Chinese water torture. For Lisa, one unappreciated success after another filled a bucket full of anger until it overflowed. One last relatively minor upset with the sales manager triggered a chain reaction. The change Lisa avoided for so long was made impulsively and was followed by a painful period of putting back together the pieces of her life.

When you change in a burst of anger because you've experienced the proverbial straw that breaks the camel's back, you initially regret your decision—if it really was a decision rather than simply a reaction. You suffer through self-recrimination and wonder what you could have done differently before finally looking forward and improving your life.

Dreading the Alternative

Mimi summarized this approach well when she said, "The scales tipped." They tipped in the direction of change because the alternative, losing Kerry, was so unappealing.

This reason to change comes into play whenever you've trapped yourself into a corner, your back against the wall. You can no longer postpone, avoid, or resist change because the very real consequence of staying the same will cause more distress than the imagined cost of conducting your life differently. You change to avoid the dreaded alternative.

Disaster Relief, or Life Is Too Short

Marilyn said she changed because she had no other choice. When her husband left her, she saw herself as a victim of circumstance who had to cope with an event she could neither anticipate nor control. She literally was forced to change.

Perhaps you have found yourself in a similar situation. Job layoffs, natural disasters, divorces, aging parents who come to live with you, prolonged illness, car accidents—life is full of unforeseen, unprepared-for events. You rarely have any choice but to cope with the aftermath.

The students described at the beginning of this chapter immediately identified disaster relief as the reason to change. This method works, though it also is one of the most painful approaches to change.

Sometimes people change because of a disaster or loss experienced by someone other than themselves.

Let's say "good ole Joe" has a heart attack, gets a divorce, loses a loved one, or gets a serious illness. Sympathy for "good ole Joe" gives way to realizing that similar misfortune could as easily descend upon you. "Life is too short," you think, and you take action to make the positive changes you were putting off for another day.

All of these approaches to change are effective. They are the reasons most of us finally get around to improving our lives. Unfortunately, they also involve:

POSTPONING, RESISTING, AND AVOIDING CHANGE FOR AS LONG AS YOU POSSIBLY CAN. You wait to change until *not* changing is intolerable. In the interim, considerable damage is done to yourself, other people, and your relationships.

A PRECIPITATING EVENT. A tragedy, trauma, confrontation, or disaster must happen to you before you change. Your life improves, but you believe change was not *your* choice. It was an inescapable reaction to circumstances beyond your control.

PAIN AND SUFFERING. These generally—and mistakenly—are assumed to be absolutely necessary anytime a change occurs.

THE MYTH OF CHANGE

I am sure at some time in your life you have heard someone say, "You have to hit bottom before you can climb back up to the top." This widely accepted misconception implies you have to grovel, suffer, and lose all hope before you will be able to change to improve yourself and your life. The myth convinces you to wait until a situation is awful and intolerable before you do anything to make it better. And because we have such negative reactions to change, we often convince ourselves that "things really are not so bad." We create our own ready-made excuse not to change.

I have a pleasant surprise for you. Nowhere is it written that you must suffer terribly before you change. In many instances you need not to suffer at all, and you certainly do *not* have to endure prolonged pain, frustration, or uncertainty.

Hitting bottom is what *you* make it. The bottom does not have to be the gutter or the coronary care unit. It need not be a welfare line or a psychiatric ward. Bottom is the place and the moment *you* decide you want to be happier, healthier, more creative, successful, or fulfilled than you already are. When you want to get unstuck and move forward, you have to hit your own bottom line and be prepared to rise above it. You can choose to *choose* to change, and you can begin *whenever* you please.

SO . . . WHY WAIT?

Before you picked up this book, you probably had changed many times over. Perhaps you've been through a job or career change or had to readjust your life at home to the presence of your new baby. However you have experienced change, you know what it feels like. You may not have enjoyed it while you were going through it, but after it was over, you'd successfully altered your life—didn't you feel terrific? Didn't you feel a wonderful sense of satisfaction, pleasure, and pride? From your new perspective, didn't all that avoidance and resistance seem utterly ridiculous?

After I accomplish what I set out to do, I always ask myself why on earth I fought change. Why did I think I could not change? Why did I wait so long?

I tell myself, "Next time I won't wait as long." I'll find a reason to change *before* disaster strikes or my feelings become unbearable or I'm backed into a corner and think I have no choice but to change. To do that, I need some new answers to the question—"Why change?"

A LOOK AT THE REST OF YOUR LIFE

One new answer to the question "Why change?" can be found in the following values clarification strategy.

On a blank sheet of paper, draw a horizontal line from one edge of the paper to the other like this:

This line represents your life. To signify when your life began, place an X on the left end of the line and write the year of your birth underneath it.

Now let me ask you a rather threatening question. How long do you plan to live? To age seventy-five or one hundred or even older? Maybe living to the age of fifty or sixty is all you can imagine.

Whatever you decide, place an X on the right end of the line, and beneath it, write the year you plan to die.

It is not a random, casual choice of words to use the phrase "plan to die," because at some subtle level we do indeed plan our deaths—by the way we plan our living.

Now, at the appropriate spot on the line, place an X to represent the present, and underneath it, write the present year. My lifeline looks like this:

X   X   X
_____
1927   1988   ?

This book was written in 1987 when I was sixty years old and had lived over half my years, so you can see where I placed 1987 on my lifeline. Your X for the present may be at a different point on the line depending on how long you have already lived and how much longer you plan to live.

Draw a deep arc below the line between the present and the year you plan to die.

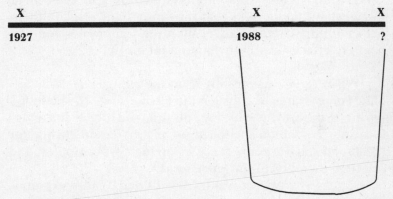

X   X   X
_____
1927   1988   ?

This arc is like a basket or net representing the years you have left to live. It can be filled with all the opportunities, challenges, joys, and experiences still ahead of you. Ask yourself the following questions and list your answers in your lifeline net. Use any other space on the page if you need it.

- What do I want to do with the life I have left to live?

- What do I want to experience?

- What do I want to witness?

• What do I want to learn?

• What do I want to be part of?

• What do I want to change, shape, leave better than I found it?

• In short, what do I want to do for the rest of my life?

I love to watch people in my workshops fill in the rest of their lives. Some have few things they can say they want to do, experience, or become. Others have many visions for the future. However they choose to fill in their lifeline baskets, I simply enjoy watching them discover or rediscover things about themselves that may eventually provide them with the impetus to change. With the lifeline net you can begin to create your own "bottom line."

When Janet, a therapist from the suburbs of Philadelphia, Pennsylvania, completed the lifeline strategy, she found her net overflowing with fun, playful, and wondrous activities, many of which she felt she'd missed out on during her childhood and the years she spent being a wife, mother, and full-time member of the work force.

"I started working when I was fifteen," Janet explains. "I thought feeling good came from keeping busy. Those times I wasn't working, when I was home with babies or towards the end of a pregnancy, I always felt sort of empty."

As the years passed and her children grew older and more self-sufficient, Janet filled her life with work and more work. She went back to school to get a master's degree in counseling while taking care of her family. She did not quit her full-time job until her private therapy practice could sustain her. Afraid she would not have enough work, she led workshops and taught courses at the local YMCA and several community colleges. Before she knew it, every minute from seven in the morning until eleven at night was scheduled and consumed by work.

"I was surprised by what I found in my lifeline net," she recalls. "Everything I wrote down had to do with fun and leisure and having space and time for myself. I wanted to laugh and play and dance and sing. I wanted to have fun and do all sorts of childlike things I'd never let myself do before. It dawned on me that working so much had less to do with feeling good than with not having time to feel anything at all. I had become a workaholic."

To experience the things in her net, Janet would have to let go of other things to make room for what she wanted to do. She decided to change her life so she could work less and play more. This would involve using her time more efficiently and saying no to work she felt obligated to do, but which neither payed well nor fulfilled her. She would have to stop seeing clients on Saturday, regardless of the loss of income, and get up the nerve to ask people to accompany her places her stay-at-home husband would not go.

"It's never too late to have a happy childhood," she decided, and she took the first step on a journey to create the life she truly wanted to live.

Regardless of what or how much you put into your lifeline net, those hopes, dreams, and plans will help you discover the answer to the question, "Why change?"

You'll want to change so you can have and do all those things you put in your net, so—from this day forward—you can live your life the way you really want to live it.

OVERALL WELLNESS

To move closer to a state of being known as overall wellness is another relatively painless reason to change.

Overall wellness is more than physical or even mental

health. It is an active process, a style of living that promotes physical, intellectual, emotional, and spiritual well-being and satisfaction. Overall wellness speaks to the *quality* of life and also to a *passion* for living.

When you work towards overall wellness, you:

1. Get enough TIME ALONE—time to meditate, relax, reflect, daydream, or be still. You manage to "stop the world" for a little while and get some distance from its frantic pace.

2. Exercise and are conscious of good NUTRITION, controlling what you consume, ingest, or inhale.

3. Have at least one GOOD LISTENER in your life. Whether a professional counselor or a close friend, this person hears what you have to say and helps you gain an objective view of the world and make decisions. A good listener offers comfort, compassion, alternatives, or a gentle push in the right direction when you are stuck.

4. EXERCISE on a regular basis.

5. Participate in a solid SUPPORT GROUP. The purpose of the support group can be professional or personal. It can meet formally and on a regular basis or casually and occasionally. A support group lets you know there are other people whose concerns are similar to your own and gives you the benefit of other people's viewpoints and experiences.

6. Have a satisfying INTIMATE RELATIONSHIP built on mutual respect and understanding.

7. Employ effective TIME MANAGEMENT techniques to avoid feeling overwhelmed and to make time for the things you want to do as well as the things you have to do.

8. Maintain a sense of PRODUCTIVITY and accomplishment by pursuing challenging work, hobbies, and/or interests.

9. Take RISKS and stretch your limits physically, intellectually, and emotionally.

10. COMMUNICATE your wants and needs as well as say no to what you do not want or need.

To determine where you stand in terms of overall wellness, take a personal inventory.

On a blank sheet of paper, draw a grid similar to the one shown on page 34 and write in the ten wellness dimensions as I have done.

In the first column, check off the items you have in your life right now.

In the second column, give yourself a rating on a one-to-ten scale (ten is high) based on the amount or quality of each item as it is included in your life right now (e.g., if you have a great deal of high-quality time alone, give that item an eight, nine, or ten. If you rarely get time alone and don't know how to use it when you have it, time alone would get a much lower rating).

In the third column, put a capital *M* beside the items you would like to have more of in your life; a lower-case *m* beside those you would like to increase slightly or improve a little; and an *S* beside those you would like to stay the same. Try not to labor over each of the points for a long time—the important thing is to be honest.

In the fourth column, rank in order all ten dimensions according to how important each item is to your feelings of overall wellness. The number one would go to the most important dimension, the number two to the next most important, and so on down to ten.

In the fifth column, choose the dimensions you would most like to change or improve. Then rank your choices—putting the letter *A* beside the area you would like to work on first, the letter *B* beside the item you would work on next, and so on until each dimension you wish to change or improve has a priority.

1. Time Alone					
2. Nutrition					
3. A Good Listener					
4. Exercise					
5. Support Group					
6. Intimate Relationship					
7. Time Management					
8. Productivity					
9. Risks					
10. Communication					

on first, the letter *B* beside the item you would work on next, and so on until each dimension you wish to change or improve has a priority.

Larry, a freelance photographer, is no stranger to change. Five years ago he sold his thriving printing and graphic design business. He packed his van and spent ten months traveling throughout North America, ultimately settling along the coast of Virginia where he bought a house and fitted it with a darkroom and studio. He creates photo-art and sells his wares during the spring and summer at art and craft festivals. Frequently, corporate officers and wealthy homeowners hire him to create dozens of pieces to decorate their offices or houses.

At the time he completed his overall wellness strategy, Larry was satisfied and comfortable with his life. He loved his work, enjoyed where he was living, and looked forward to each new day. He felt no pressing urge or painful need to change, but he did the inventory anyway.

"I must say I learned a thing or two about myself," Larry reflected afterward. "Even though I was pretty happy with the way things were going, there was still room for improvement. I saw I could be even happier if I worked on some of the areas on the inventory."

Nutrition and exercise got low rankings in terms of the amount and quality of each in Larry's life. At first glance he didn't think they were very important to his feelings of overall wellness.

"But I thought about it and realized I didn't think they were important because if I did, I would have to do something about them. I had a feeling I'd feel better physically if I quit smoking and cut down on my beer drinking and got those lazy muscles toned up again. When it came around to deciding what I wanted to change, I gave those things a high priority. I was pretty confident I could change those areas of my life."

He was less confident when it came to doing something

about the dimension he rated most important to his overall wellness and most lacking in his present life—an intimate relationship. It was the area he most wanted to change.

"I didn't see it as a problem, exactly," Larry explains. "I still don't. I mean, I'm not going to die or anything if I don't meet someone tomorrow. I have women friends and I date. But I don't have what you'd call a real love relationship with anyone. I used to say I was waiting for the right girl to come along. But I don't know exactly what I mean by 'the right girl.'

"Whoever she is, she sure isn't going to come knocking on my door. I have to get out more for one thing, meet more people, do something to get to know the women I'm attracted to instead of waiting to get hit by a bolt of lightning or something."

No dire circumstance forced Larry to change. His life was okay the way it was. However, he saw how life could be better and decided he wanted to make it that way.

By now you should have a clearer picture of what the "good life" looks like. With the overall wellness inventory you pinpointed the areas in which you can change your life for the better. Plus you've found another answer to the question "Why change?"—to enhance the quality of your life and increase your passion for living.

OVERCOMING CONFLICT AND CONFUSION

Yet another answer to the question "Why change?" is found in the conflicts and confusions that arise in your life. Areas of conflict and confusion are varied and numerous— in fact, any aspect of daily living can be puzzling, uncomfortable, or frustrating at times. Some common areas where conflict and confusion are experienced include:

family	finances
work	child rearing
marriage	diet
dependencies	aging
education	sexuality
love	friendship
race	gender

Anything posing questions with few easy answers and having the potential to produce stress and dissatisfaction is an area of conflict and confusion.

Larraine looked up from her duties as superwife and mother and saw her fortieth birthday approaching. Her three children were in school and getting more self-sufficient with each passing day. In a couple of years the oldest would be leaving the nest to attend college. Larraine's husband had just started a new business—a venture that she was neither equipped for nor interested in pursuing herself.

"I was anticipating a mid-life crisis," Larraine concludes. "I had one identity. I was wife and mommy. But my children were growing up. They didn't need a full-time mommy anymore. Pretty soon that identity was going to be obsolete altogether. I needed something else. I needed to decide who I was and what I was."

Actually, Larraine did more than stay at home with the kids. She was a volunteer counselor at a mental health center and a certified Parent Effectiveness Training (PET) instructor. These roles caused her conflict and confusion as well.

"I was limited because I didn't have a college degree," she explains. "I saw people who didn't know as much as I did doing work I knew I could do. But they got the jobs and I didn't because they had degrees. I really bought into that mentality. I started believing I wasn't good enough because I didn't have an education or a piece of paper to prove I wasn't stupid."

Before her conflict and confusion about losing her comfortable identity as a mother and being limited by her lack of education reached crisis proportions, Larraine decided to work on both issues by going back to school—to get a master's degree in social work and start a private counseling practice.

When one area of your life isn't working as well as it could—whether you realize that you're more out of shape than you thought you were or feel that you aren't communicating as well as you could with your family—you *can* take action to fix it. If you're experiencing conflict and confusion, you can act to cure what ails you. You can locate and understand the source of your discomfort and relieve that discomfort before it becomes intolerable pain, before the situation backs you into a corner and forces you to change.

Whether the reason to change is found by completing a lifeline strategy, taking an overall wellness inventory, or examining the areas of conflict and confusion in your life, you can freely choose to change and begin *now* to improve your life. You can, after considering your alternatives and their consequences, choose to do whatever is necessary to live a happier, healthier, less stressful, and more fulfilling life. You can make that choice today.

OKAY . . . THEN WHAT?

Janet, Larry, and Larraine chose to change. They made their decisions *before* fear, pain, anger, dreaded alternatives, or unforeseen and unpleasant events compelled them to change. Because desperation did not color their choices when they embarked upon the road to a better life, they were one step ahead of those people who didn't recognize that change was essential.

This one-step advantage made their journey a little bit

easier. However, they by no means experienced fair weather and smooth sailing on their voyage to change.

If making one decision was all it took to create a better life, you would never get stuck. This would be a very short book and you would not be reading it. Deciding to change, what to change, and when to change is a step in the right direction, but only the first step. You know this from past experience. Maybe you've already realized on some level that you want to change an aspect of your life, but when it comes right down to it, you can't seem to follow through.

Having made a decision, you embark upon the road to change only to find it a veritable obstacle course. Signs flash warnings of danger ahead. You begin to doubt the choice you made. Faceless monsters lurk in the shadows and tell you to turn back. Huge solid barriers block your path.

The obstacles, barriers, and monsters are of your own making. Years and years of believing change to be horribly painful and extremely difficult taught you some ingenious methods for resisting, avoiding, and blocking change. You constructed elaborate barriers to protect yourself from the suffering you believed change would bring you. You are not a bad person because you protected yourself from possible pain, and you are not the only one with self-made obstacles blocking change. Everyone has them.

However, now that you have decided to change and want to improve your life, you must push through the blocks to change. You cannot allow them to impede your progress.

The eight most common blocks to change are the focus of the remainder of this book. They are tricky and complicated obstacles, but they are not insurmountable. The most important thing to remember is that "impossible" is *not* part of the vocabulary of this book. If you think carefully about each of the barriers and determine that you can change, you'll be well on your way to a more rewarding and fulfilling life. In fact, you've already taken the first step.

3

▰▰▰▰▰▰▰▰▰▰▰▰▰▰▰▰▰▰▰▰▰▰▰

Change and Self-esteem

When introduced in the previous chapter, Larry, a Virginia Beach freelance photographer, had completed an Overall Wellness inventory and decided he wanted a satisfying love relationship. Hoping ultimately to marry and raise a family, Larry wants to meet a woman he can "trust, talk to, and be myself with. Someone I'm attracted to sexually and feel comfortable with a lot of the time." He seeks intimacy and a partner with whom to share his triumphs and tragedies.

Steven, a thirty-one-year-old Miami, Florida, plumbing contractor, also wants to find someone to love and to love him. He too hopes to marry and have children, although he expresses his desire differently than Larry does.

"I'm not very good at relationships," he says after reviewing his own Overall Wellness inventory. "My friends say I get involved with the wrong women who play on my guilt and are 'on me' all the time about everything I say or do. But I'm as much to blame. I think I hold back. I'm moody and I do spend a lot of time with my friends and my family and working on my business. If I was a different man, I'd be married by now or at least living with someone."

Both Larry and Steven want satisfying relationships. Does one have a better chance of getting what he wants? A closer look at each man reveals the answer and the effect of the first barrier to change—BELIEVING YOU DO NOT DESERVE BETTER.

LARRY

When asked to describe himself, Larry lists many positive attributes. Among other things, he believes himself to be an intelligent conversationalist, a compassionate friend, a good photographer, a socially conscious person, an avid reader, and "someone who can deal with the weirdness of freelance work—where no two days are the same. You have to discipline yourself to get the job done because no one is looking over your shoulder to make sure you produce." Additionally, Larry believes he has a good, if somewhat offbeat, sense of humor, the right amount of ambition, talent, healthy curiosity, a sense of adventure, and "a good idea of what I can accomplish and guts enough to try."

"I'm not perfect by any stretch of the imagination," he says, laughing. "I'm stuck with this short, sort of flabby body and I'm losing my hair. I get very absentminded when I'm working on a big photo assignment, and housekeeping isn't one of my strong points. Get me going on a topic I care about, and I'll talk your ear off, especially if I've had a few drinks. But even with my faults, most mornings I look in the mirror and like what I see."

There are changes Larry wants to make and ways he wants to improve himself. He wants to exercise more often, cut down on his drinking, and of course, have a satisfying, mutually supportive love relationship. He does not think less of himself for what he does not have or has not done yet. He believes he is capable of change and worthy of the best life can offer.

"I'm the guy who sold his thriving business and lived on the road in my van for ten months, remember?" Larry points out. "If I could take that risk and come out better than I was before, I figure I can do plenty of other things when I set my mind to it. No doubt about it, these changes are going to take some work, but they're doable and I owe it to myself to try."

STEVEN

To a casual observer Steven seems the more stable and successful of the two men and the better candidate for a long-term love relationship.

A tall, handsome, sensitive man, he has many close, loyal friends and owns a comfortable fifty-year-old home that he has equipped with many luxury items. He impresses others as being reasonably ambitious, levelheaded, and thoughtful—a man who has achieved financial success and personal stability at a relatively early age.

Steven sees himself differently, however, and in a far less positive light.

"I'm still waiting for the day when I'll feel like I'm good enough," Steven claims. "I'm always trying to make up for what I lack and running to catch up with myself. I've felt that way all my life. I was never as smart as my older sister. I wasn't as outgoing as my younger sister or as sure of myself as all my friends seemed to be. I did dumb things without thinking and got caught every time I screwed up.

"As far back as I can remember, I either thought everything I did was wrong or felt like I was missing something. I never measured up."

In Steven's mind, his business success is overshadowed by the opportunities he believes he missed and the mistakes he thinks he made. No matter how good things are, they could have been better if only he were more organized, efficient, decisive, or disciplined. He points to several friends who are millionaires at age thirty. He tends to forget they inherited wealth or holdings in existing companies.

Steven derives little pleasure from his achievements and often feels guilty about the good things that happen to him. When things go wrong, however, he is quick to accept the blame. There is always something he should have seen coming or done differently. He is not sure why people like him as much as they do.

"I guess I try harder to be a nice guy and do whatever they want me to," he says. "That way they put up with my moods and wishy-washiness."

Holding such a low opinion of himself, Steven is rarely content and suffers bouts of severe depression. Doubting his capabilities and questioning his self-worth, he sees every glass as half empty rather than half full, and he unwittingly creates situations that verify his doubts. His past relationships are a good example.

In the past Steven became involved with women who were needy, demanding, and whose self-esteem was even lower than his own. They wanted him to change. They wanted him to stop everything and fill the empty spaces in their own lives. They harped and nagged and told him that he wasn't good enough. As a result, Steven felt guilty. He felt more inadequate and unlovable. Yet he prolonged those relationships even though all he got from them was more evidence of his unworthiness.

"I don't know if I've got what it takes to be in a good love relationship," he sums things up. "I know exactly what kind of woman I'm looking for, but I can't believe that that kind would want me."

Both Larry and Steven want the same thing. They both have a great deal to offer another human being. Larry, however, sees himself as lovable. Steven does not. Larry thinks he can find and build a love relationship. Steven does not. Larry believes he deserves better. Steven does not.

Although Steven is more physically attractive, more settled, and more financially secure than Larry, Larry has a far better chance of finding the relationship he wants and changing in any way he chooses. Because Steven believes he does not deserve a terrific love relationship and that he is incapable of having one, it is likely that he will continue to make poor choices (when he chooses at all). He will sabotage his own happiness by seeing only what he is missing instead of what he has or could have. It is highly unlikely he will get what he wants.

Steven is stuck. To get unstuck he must deal with barrier number one—believing you do not deserve better.

BARRIER NUMBER ONE

Believing you do not deserve better is the bottom-line block to change. More debilitating than the pain and confusion of your present circumstances might be, it stands in the way of even your most sincere desire to change. It prevents you from clearing other obstacles from your path. No matter what you say you want, you will not get unstuck unless you *believe* you deserve a better life and are capable of change.

Like The Little Engine That Could in the timeless children's story of the same name, to reach any destination you must chug along chanting "I think I can, I think I can, I *know* I can." If barrier number one has a hold on you, you do not approach life or change with such positive thinking.

Barrier number one has a voice of its own. It loudly and persistently shouts a different kind of message. It insists, "No you can't. You are not good enough, smart enough, strong enough, pretty enough. You simply *are not enough*. You had better take what you can get."

That nasty little voice may sound like a parent, a teacher, a former lover, or your ex-husband or ex-wife. They were the critics who first implied you did not and would never measure up. Nowadays the voice is your own. You have come to believe you are unworthy, unlovable, and deserving of the fate life deals you—and nothing more.

This barrier's effect on your life is clearer and easier to see than any other. If you think you cannot change, you will not. If you think you are not worthy of life's riches, you will settle for the crumbs tossed your way. If you do not believe you deserve better, you will find no will, energy, or reason to try for more. By virtue of your self-proclaimed inadequacies, you think you are meant to be stuck and cannot get unstuck.

HOW THIS BARRIER WORKS

In the past few years you probably have read newspaper or magazine articles, seen movies, or watched television programs about battered spouses. You may know someone who is in an abusive relationship or have personal experience in this area.

More often than not, the battered spouse (wife *or* husband) puts up with mind-boggling physical violence and humiliation and stays with the abuser for years and years after the abuse begins. In many instances the victim never gets out of the relationship and takes no significant action to stop the attacks. Why? Often, the victim's poor economic situation will keep him or her stuck. Social scientists have many other theories, as well. But when all is said and done, it boils down to one very powerful reason. In addition to inflicting physical injury, domestic violence destroys its victim's sense of self-worth. The self-esteem of a battered spouse is so low, she comes to believe she deserves what is happening to her.

Believing you do not deserve better is most clearly seen in what you *do not do.* You do not change, and no outside force can move you to change—not even a physical threat to your survival.

Barrier number one does its dirty work in several dangerous and deceptive ways. Here are the most common outcomes of believing you do not deserve better.

1. Underestimating your capabilities and chances for success, *you persuade yourself not to attempt change.*

In the opening chapter of this book, Carla, the social worker spinning her wheels at her job, says, "Maybe I'm not capable of being anything but a little bureaucrat." For so long a cog in the bureaucratic machinery, Carla downplays her talent as a therapist and forgets her past success working with children and families. Defeated and undermined by "the system," she accepts her fate as inevitable. Each time she considers a career change, her heart races with fear. Assuming she will drown if she attempts to move through unfamiliar waters, she stands still—and stuck.

Barrier number one warps your perception of yourself and steals your self-confidence. By viewing yourself in this barrier's mirrors—which reflect only flaws and inadequacies —you become a lousy judge of your own ability. Stuck and disliking yourself for being stuck, you minimize or forget every past success while magnifying every failure, as though it had just happened. To avoid another possible failure you unwittingly sacrifice probable success.

2. Fearing others will see you the way you see yourself, *you overcompensate for your perceived inadequacies,* producing stress and stress-related illnesses.

As described in Chapter Two, Cindy, a public relations director, attempted to change her life only after she was plagued by mysterious panic attacks. A five-foot-two-inch bundle of energy, Cindy was rarely seen without a smile on her face and never uttered an unkind word about anyone. Mixing an unflappable sense of humor with perfect comic timing, Cindy won people over with her charm and wit. Creative, efficient, and hardworking, she entered the public relations field as a novice and in two years time, became the consummate professional, one highly respected by famous and powerful members of the entertainment industry. At twenty-five she bought her own home.

As far as Cindy was concerned, however, her success was a scam. Underneath those smiles, behind all that hard work and upbeat energy, she believed there lived a certifiable nothing. She was petrified people would discover she was not at all nice or creative or funny or competent.

"I worked twice as hard so no one would find out I was only half as good," she explains. "I was always cute, funny, and amusing so no one would see I wasn't particularly bright or interesting. I forced myself to be outgoing. But I was really so shy and scared of rejection that I became physically sick before press parties or show openings."

Seeking from others the approval she would not grant herself, Cindy put up with depressed, argumentative, and hypercritical colleagues who repeatedly imposed upon her, a boyfriend who took her for granted and saw her only when he felt like it, friends who dumped on her, and family members who used her as a scapegoat.

"Until I got into therapy, I never expressed a negative emotion. I never got angry. I never seriously thought anyone was treating me unfairly. I denied it all. I was just grateful to have gotten so far with the little I thought I had going for me."

The more she achieved, as the gap grew wider between how she saw herself and how other people saw Cindy, her fear of being uncovered as the fraud she believed herself to be reached overwhelming proportions. She worked twelve- to sixteen-hour days. She came home, took the phone off the hook, and stared glassy-eyed at the TV until sleep overtook her. She successfully denied how she felt until, without warning, the stress broke loose in terrifying anxiety attacks complete with hyperventilation, heart palpitations, headaches, dizzyness, and fearful thoughts about dying.

Outward success is not always an indication of inner

confidence or contentment. Many of the movers, shakers, and high achievers in business, finance, entertainment, and many other fields got so far so fast by overcompensating for feelings of inadequacy and unworthiness. Like Steven, they have obtained all the trappings of the American dream but may feel something is still missing. Happiness eludes them. Like Cindy, they cannot take pride in their accomplishments because they fear they will be unmasked as the charlatans and frauds they believe they are. So, they work harder. They smile wider. They polish and perfect the self they show the world in order to protect the "real" self they know to be flawed and inadequate.

You, too, may be a great pretender. You may feel empty in spite of your apparent success. Your efforts to cope may have turned you into a workaholic, ruined more than one relationship, or caught up with you in any number of other ways. Perhaps the stress of overcompensating and over-achieving has become overwhelming, and you have anxiety attacks, migraine headaches, ulcers, or have become dependent on addictive substances. To make matters worse, you are now stuck with these new problems as well as the old ones. You are sure you brought them on yourself, and change seems more difficult and unlikely than ever.

3. *You create and live out self-fulfilling prophecies.*

Human beings predict outcomes based on their perceptions of their own ability or worth and act accordingly.

"There's no way I'll pass this test," says the college student. So, instead of studying, he parties with his friends, and his prophecy comes true when he fails the test.

"I'll never get that raise," says the secretary. "My stingy bear of a boss wouldn't part with an extra penny if his life depended on it. Why should I work my tail off for nothing?" Her attitude shows and defeats her. She decides to meet only the minimum requirements of her job, shows no initiative, refuses to work a minute of overtime, and makes sure to use every sick day as soon as she earns it. When her job performance is reviewed, she barely makes the grade and is not offered a raise. This does not surprise her. She knew she couldn't squeeze more money from her employer.

Karen begins yet another diet she assumes will fail. Her theory is that "if I had the willpower to diet and was meant to be thin, I would be by now." She sticks to the diet at first. Then, on an exceptionally busy day, her hectic schedule prevents her from eating properly. Famished by late afternoon, she wolfs down a burger and fries. This small deviation from her diet is all the proof of weakness she needs. When she gets home at ten, she orders a pizza. This opens the gates to a three-week binge. Afterward Karen looks at herself in a mirror and says, "Let's face it. I just don't have what it takes to stick to a diet."

In countless ways, each and every day you live up to your self-image. If that image is negative, you consciously or unconsciously reinforce it. You predict failure and fulfill your own prophecy.

4. Trying desperately to boost your confidence or block painful feelings, *you develop self-defeating habits and dangerous addictions.*

People addicted to drugs or alcohol, those who are compulsive overeaters, gamblers, and money spenders, as well as those who seek solace through numerous shallow sexual encounters, have low opinions of themselves. They had low self-esteem, however, long before they lost control of their lives, dependencies, and obsessions.

Drugs, alcohol, and the short-lived adrenaline high of winning in a gambling casino offer a false sense of power, confidence, and well-being. Yet they are so appealing that you substitute the artificially induced feelings for the high sense of worth you have not been able to achieve naturally.

Steven, the Miami plumbing contractor, first tried cocaine while attending college. The attraction was immediate. Cocaine produced every feeling he had never been able to feel on his own. Energy surged through his body. He had an edge he never had before. While high on cocaine, he thought he was capable of anything. He hated to come down.

A dozen years later, Steven still uses the drug—heavily on weekends and occasionally during the week. He feels guilty about using cocaine and berates himself for not quitting. "I don't even get what I want from coke anymore," he says. "But I can't seem to stop. I try, but then I get this urge and call a friend who has some. I swear I won't touch the stuff. Then I see it at a party and go for it. I hate myself the next morning, but obviously not enough to say no to coke the next time."

In other instances, drugs, alcohol, food, sex, and spending excessive amounts of money are used not to produce feelings but to deaden them, to mask insecurity, to slow down a world that spins too fast, or to avoid facing real or imagined problems. Regardless of the reason for adopting them, these habits and dependencies inevitably lead to greater feelings of weakness and inadequacy.

Trying to fill your empty spaces with what you find in the medicine chest, liquor cabinet, gambling casino, or refrigerator may appear to work for a while. You cannot fool yourself for long, however. Instead of feeling better or liking yourself more, you are left with one more change to make, one more seemingly impossible mission to accomplish, one more place to be stuck.

5. *You get trapped in an endless cycle,* a spiral descending downward to despair.

The less you like yourself, the more you hurt yourself. The more you hurt yourself, the less you like yourself. If unbroken, this vicious cycle leaves you stuck while the good life goes on without you. You add new items to the list of things you wish you had done, but didn't. You observe your life dimly instead of living it fully. Dreams and goals for yourself fade to black. Perhaps you never even had any dreams or made any goals. Doubts and self-criticism mushroom to enormous proportions.

Are you hungry for a better life but cannot find your way to the banquet table? Do you accept only life's leftovers? If you do, you are under the spell of the most common and insidious of barriers. It grabs you and shakes the will to change out of you. It kicks you when you are down. This barrier goes to work on you when you are already suffering the fallout of low self-esteem.

SELF-ESTEEM

Self-esteem is both the image of yourself you carry with you at all times and your opinion of it. Your image of yourself and your evaluation of your worth influences everything you do or do not do. Self-esteem is built on what you feel about yourself, and to some extent, how you *think* others feel about you.

How do *you* feel about yourself? What do you like about what you are? What do you think you lack? What do you do well? What do you wish you did better? Are you competent, lovable, intelligent, funny, pretty, creative, socially adept, unique, fun, friendly, kind, responsible, or talented? Or are you inadequate, dumb, boring, clumsy, average, incapable, unlovable, shy, awkward, or apt to fail? Are other people likely to accept you, like you, respect you, admire you, converse with you, or be there for you when you need them? Or are they more likely to reject you, ignore you, laugh at you, hurt you, abandon you, or see through your facade? How many positive personal qualities can you list? On the other hand, how many sentences beginning with "I'm not very . . ." can you finish?

Your answers to such questions make up your own personal, highly subjective measure of what you think you are worth—to yourself, to the people you love, to the people you look up to, and sometimes to the world at large. Those answers shape your beliefs about what you *can* do and your chances for success in any area of life. When your self-esteem is high, you usually predict good fortune and go after the best possible results. You are more motivated, more positive, and more open to change. You are less self-destructive because the more you like yourself, the less likely you are to hurt yourself.

Low self-esteem has the exact opposite effect. It has been linked to poor school performance; overeating, alcoholism, and other addictions; aggressive and criminal behavior; promiscuity; and depression and suicide. It plays a powerful part in getting and keeping people stuck.

Yet self-esteem is not static. It changes. You see, everyone is born with high self-esteem. Infants are the positive center of their own universes, and toddlers believe themselves to be the brightest stars in the galaxy, until somehow, a little bit at a time, they learn to view themselves differently.

SELF-ESTEEM WRECKING BALLS

Since you were born with high self-esteem, how did you lose it and come to believe you deserve far less than you desire?

Picture your self-esteem as a building under construction. Based on the blueprints drawn up for you at birth, you were promised a wonderful lifelong home. Each time someone demonstrated his love or acceptance of you, the building's foundation was made stronger. Each success you experienced and each task you mastered—no matter how small—was another brick added to your building. Each risk you took, and every ounce of recognition and support you received, reinforced the idea that you were lovable and capable and made your building more livable. At the same time, each bit of negative criticism, every hurtful name, derogatory label, and term paper returned with red-pencil corrections on every page hurled a wrecking ball at your building. Unmet expectations, failed love affairs, being cut from the basketball team, rejected for a job, beaten up by the neighborhood bully, or embarrassed in any way knocked out another wall or window.

Sometimes there has been enough construction to overcome the destruction and maintain high self-esteem. Sometimes the wrecking balls strike frequent powerful blows and building blocks cannot be put into place fast enough. Then, the building's foundation begins to tremble. It's tough to find safety, security, or success when your self-esteem has been demolished.

Who propelled those wrecking balls at your brick building? The original demolition crew were people you loved and respected. Parents may have plied you with negative criticism. In moments of anger they called you hurtful names. Sometimes they wished aloud that you were different or did not exist at all. Teachers found fault in your best efforts. They compared you unfavorably to students who were smarter, stronger, or better behaved. They rapped you on the knuckles when you did not conform to their standards and gave you labels such as "slow learner," "behavior problem," "unmotivated," or "not living up to potential."

Preachers swore you would burn in hell. Bullies pummeled you and stole your lunch money. Peers laughed at you, made fun of your clothes, or picked you last for the relay-race team. Fashion magazines presented images of beauty you could not attain. You saw your home life was not like Donna Reed's or Robert Young's.

An even greater price was payed when abuse, domestic violence, or alcoholic parents were part of your childhood. It was harder still to be a member of a racial or ethnic minority group, to be poor or to be disabled in any way. All this took its toll on your self-esteem.

Steven recalls, "When I was eight or nine years old, Dad would take out a dictionary after dinner and pick words at random for my sister and me to spell. My sister, the genius, could spell anything. But I was a lousy speller and my dad knew it. I don't blame my sister, but she'd sit there waiting for me to screw up so she could spell the word right and hear Dad say how wonderful she was. Meanwhile Dad would yell at me, 'Sound out the word for Christ's sake.' Eventually I'd get so nervous I'd start to cry and he called me a sissy. So I wasn't just dumb, I was a weak little crybaby. To this day, every time I make any kind of mistake I hear my father saying, 'Come on, dummy. Think. You're not trying hard enough.' "

Steven is thirty-one years old, yet he still thinks of himself as that very sensitive young boy who could not measure up to his father's expectations and often acted impulsively with disastrous results. His father does not have to criticize him anymore. He has taken over that job himself—just as you may have.

By now you may have become your own demolition crew, able to aim and release your own wrecking balls. From well-meaning but critical role models, you learned the art of put-downs. By now you have become a brutal and unyielding judge of your own character defects. Where parents, teachers, preachers, and peers left off, you have taken up the slack with a vengeance. You can't help it, for self-criticism has become the way you talk to yourself.

Few of us see ourselves as total failures, thank goodness. Most of us reserve our most scathing self-criticism and painful self-doubts for specific areas in which we never thought we measured up. Sarah's sore spot is her physical appearance and appeal to men.

While Sarah was growing up, she often heard herself described as the "smart one," while her sisters were called the "pretty ones." She knew she had unruly brown hair and unremarkable features. She wore glasses and carried a few extra pounds around her hips and thighs. Conversely, her sisters were slender blondes, homecoming queen and head cheerleader respectively. They dated often and went out with the most popular and handsome boys. Sarah had steady boy-friends of the "nerd" variety in between long dateless stretches.

Sarah knew she had other strengths, however, and she managed to fend off the wrecking balls until a remark intended as a joke she was not meant to hear demolished a big chunk of self-esteem. Sarah was nineteen at the time and working at a summer camp for handicapped children. Her parents and two sisters came to visit and take her and a friend out for dinner. They arrived during the camp carnival, and Danny, the drama counselor, was in full clown-face makeup when Sarah first introduced him to her family. Later they were able to see he was an exceptionally attractive blond, blue-eyed man and appeared to be quite taken with Sarah.

As the group walked toward the restaurant with Sarah and Danny several yards ahead, one sister whispered, "God, he's *gorgeous!*"

"I know," sister number two agreed. "How'd she get him to go out with her? Bribe him with dinner?"

Both Sarah's sisters and her parents had a good long laugh about that one.

"That was the clincher," says Sarah. "They were only kidding and I wasn't supposed to hear what they said, but it was a big deal for me."

Now twenty-eight years old and a special education teacher working on her Ph.D., Sarah remembers the moment "as if it were yesterday. When I meet a good-looking guy and he seems attracted to me, I say, 'Nah, he couldn't be. What could he possibly find attractive about me? Do I have to bribe him with dinner?' "

We all withstand more than our fair share of put-downs, embarrassing moments, and seemingly devastating disappointments. Some we take to heart. Some we do not. Some are countered by equally persuasive successes, compliments, and triumphs. Sometimes it is not the criticism or failure that damages our self-esteem, but the feeling we are not recognized and do not belong.

Cindy's younger brother, born with a heart problem, was sick throughout his short life, required constant care, and died when Cindy was twelve years old. Cindy was shuttled from relative to relative, and when she was living at home, she might as well have been invisible. She always had to be quiet and on her best behavior, never voicing her needs and complaints. After all, she was lucky to be healthy. As a result, Cindy put on her happy face and came to believe anything she thought or felt was unimportant. She felt that her role was to please people by being cute and funny.

Cindy still had to walk on eggshells after her brother's death. Her mother was understandably despondent. Cindy tried to second-guess what her mother wanted so as not to upset her. She guessed wrong—a lot. And Cindy began to feel that her own ideas and feelings could not be trusted. This belief was reinforced when Cindy began dating the high school football hero. Everyone greatly admired him, but secretly he physically and emotionally abused her. Cindy did nothing to end the relationship, however, figuring she had done something wrong to deserve such treatment, since everyone kept telling her how she lucky she was to date such a wonderful guy.

"By the time I reached adulthood," Cindy says, "I was convinced nothing I felt was valid and nothing I did was quite right. I tried to please everyone I met and never, *ever* asserted myself."

Sometimes the self-esteem demolition derby begins later in life. The picture of yourself that you have accepted and come to like, as well as your vision of your life going on indefinitely in a certain manner, can be turned upside down by unanticipated events. For example, when Marilyn's husband left her, she temporarily lost all sense of herself and her value. The role of devoted wife and mother no longer fit her, and it would be some time before she redefined herself as a working woman and a single parent. Before she reached that point, she criticized herself for not seeing the crisis coming, blamed herself for the failure of her marriage, and examined her life intensively to see what she had done wrong and in which areas she had not been good enough.

Similarly, real accumulating problems at home, work, or in relationships can eat away at self-esteem. Lisa experienced major wrecking balls for the first time when she began working as a sales rep for an office supply company. Previously she had rarely doubted her competence and professionalism while successfully selling at another firm.

"I started working in sales right out of high school," she explains. "I worked hard and was good at my job. I moved up quickly to higher and higher levels of responsibility." Therefore, Lisa was surprised when the sales manager who interviewed her made a big deal about her lack of a college education. It put the first of many doubts in her mind. Maybe she wasn't educated or sophisticated enough to be included in planning meetings or asked for opinions or considered for promotions, she thought. In the past she had never considered her gender a disability, but as the only woman in the sales department, now she was often told she was being too emotional or acting "just like a woman." Thinking her colleagues and superiors might be right, she kept her feelings to herself. The ways in which she had always been good enough did not seem to be good enough anymore.

"These were successful professionals," Lisa comments. "They worked for the number one company in the market and were incredibly successful. They had their college degrees. How could they *not* be right? I *had* to be the one who wasn't playing the game the way it was supposed to be played. I was the one who didn't measure up."

We all experience unexpected events, life crises, and stressful situations that create self-doubt and lower self-esteem. If for the most part our basic self-image has been positive, we can bounce back and rebuild rather quickly, as both Marilyn and Lisa were able to do. Low self-esteem carried like excess baggage since childhood, as well as the damage done by being stuck in an abusive or degrading situation for many years, is more difficult to rebuild or repair. It is not impossible however.

Low self-esteem is *not* a curse, your lot in life, or an irreversible condition. Believing you do not deserve better is a barrier. Like all barriers, it can be dismantled. Consider—pretend if you must—that there is at least a remote possibility you deserve better and are capable of learning how to get it. If this is hard, pretend it is possible for a good friend of yours, someone you admire, care about, or like a great deal. Then read on. Familiarize yourself with the following self-esteem building blocks and how to use them to create a positive self-image.

DISMANTLING BARRIER #1: BUILDING SELF-ESTEEM

I do not intend to mislead you or paint a rosy, unrealistic picture of what lies ahead. This barrier is difficult to dismantle. A lifetime of experience created and fortified it, and within its walls are every belief and idea about who you are and what you can do. These images may be unproductive and unhealthy, but because they are familiar and belong to you, you may feel tense and defensive at the mere thought of altering them. If you think you are not good enough, you probably also think you don't stand a chance to become more or better. Such thinking causes pain or sadness, and so you build barricades to protect yourself from those feelings. Many of those defenses become new barriers, ones that you will read about later. But you have to deal with the problem of self-esteem first. Without raising self-esteem and starting to believe you deserve a better life, you will have no motivation to dismantle the other barrier or try to change in any way. All roads start with and lead back to self-esteem. Difficult to get rid of or not, this barrier has got to go.

This barrier is at work in your life because you believe what it tells you about yourself. As you try to dismantle it, it will talk louder, stir up more self-doubt, and cast more smoke screens. Of course all that noise and clutter occurs only in your own mind and imagination. In fact, you are in control here. You really are. It is your own voice you hear and you can have it say whatever you want.

So I ask you now to try to drum up some faith. In spite of churning stomachs, sweaty palms, and little voices crying, "No way. Not me. I can't," open your mind to the *possibility* that you might be more or better than you think you are and that what I suggest may work for you the way it has for thousands of other people.

I offer no magical formula to bring about a magnificent overnight transformation. I simply propose two logical methods for increasing positive self-esteem. The first is to add bricks to your building, and the second is to ward off the wrecking balls before they can do more damage. Both ends are achieved by accumulating self-esteem building blocks and cementing them to the foundation of your self-image.

Self-esteem Building Blocks

I have explained and given examples of self-esteem wrecking balls. Unfortunately you probably already knew a lot about them. You may not be as familiar with self-esteem building blocks. What are they? How can you get more and use them to fortify your self-image?

From my own experiences as a teacher/counselor and based on the ideas found in *Self-esteem* by Harris Clemes and Reynold Bean and *101 Ways to Enhance Self-esteem* by Jack Canfield and Harold Wells, I have chosen seven self-esteem building blocks and offer strategies to help you incorporate each into your life.

Before I get down to specifics, let me mention that your present negative self-image and low level of self-esteem may be the result of traumatic events or ongoing degradation you have blocked from your mind and are unable to consciously recall. Even with these memory gaps, the building blocks I describe will help you like yourself more and believe you deserve better. However, to fully dismantle this barrier you may want to unravel the mysteries of your past, come to terms with it, and learn how it influences your present circumstances and behavior. Professional counseling in the form of individual and/or group therapy will help you achieve that understanding.

MENTORS AND MODELS

Part of your self-image and some of your beliefs about being "good enough" came from observing the people around you. Mentors and models can be parents, older brothers and sisters, teachers, favorite aunts and uncles, the supervisor who took you under his wing on your first job, or people you admire but do not know personally. Their lives or specific actions inspire you, encourage you, and give you hope to be more or better. They have something you want. You try to learn from them to enhance self-esteem. But you should not try to *be* your mentor or model. You may lose self-esteem if you draw comparisons or imitate a model/mentor so completely that you lose yourself, becoming a second-rate copy of him or her instead of a first-rate original you.

Larry found and learned from a self-esteem model/mentor named Pat whom he met during his cross-country travels. "Pat was traveling too—by herself in a van," Larry relates. "She was older than me by at least a dozen years, and she was incredibly serene, which was downright amazing when you found out what she'd been through."

Once so poor she did not know how she would feed her children, Pat's life had been full of ups and downs. A pilot and flight instructor, she'd flown in several transcontinental air races. When Larry met her, she was forty-five. Her children, whom she had raised alone, were grown. She went where she wanted to go, camped out under the stars whenever she could, wrote poetry, studied psychology, and worked on her dissertation while she was on the road. All this, even though she had cancer.

Larry continues, "Pat wasn't going to live to be one hundred. She might not even make it to forty-six. But that didn't stop her from wanting to learn and do new things. She taught me things I'll never forget, not that she ever thought she was teaching me anything. We'd just talk. The main thing was that she thought life was a gift and that her mission was to make the most of it, to make every day worth something and never stop getting better."

Pat's words stuck with Larry, and she turned out to be a perfect self-esteem model for him. He glows as he recalls the time he spent with her. "That lady touched my life. She's the reason I try not to look backwards or dwell on what I haven't done or don't have yet. Because of her I try to get a little bit better at something every day."

Larry's model/mentor helped him be more and believe in himself. Your models and mentors can do the same for you. They can inspire and instruct, and you can build positive self-esteem when you use that inspiration and instruction to enhance *your own* strengths and attributes.

Mentor/Model Strategy

Take out a blank sheet of paper and draw five half-dollar-size circles. Scatter the circles over the page, leaving ample space between them like this:

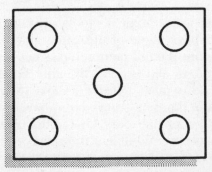

Now, think of five people whom you believe have high self-esteem, people who like themselves and have a positive opinion of their own worth. They can be people you know well or casually or people you simply know of, such as celebrities and political or religious leaders. Write each person's name in a separate circle.

Think carefully about these people.

- How do they show their self-esteem?

- How can you tell they like themselves?

- How does their self-esteem work for them?

For each way in which these mentor/models exhibit their self-esteem, attach a daisy petal to their circle and write a characteristic of their self-esteem in it, as in the diagram:

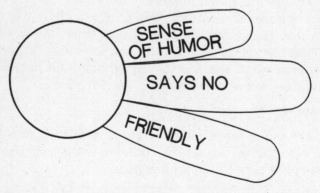

There is no set number of petals per person. Several or all people can have some of the same qualities written in their petals. Some of those common characteristics will turn out to be standard self-esteem building blocks. After you complete the daisy petals, create a daisy for yourself, with your qualities in the petals. It is often harder to do this for ourselves, but I urge you to try. One of the reasons it is hard is that we become intimidated by thoughts of all those people we know who have more petals than we do. Next list the qualities you would like to have and the ways that these high self-esteem people might serve as models and mentors for you.

Models and mentors show you how to be more, believe you deserve better, and go after what you want. They built their self-esteem with the same building blocks you will use. As I describe the remaining building blocks, think about how your models and mentors used them, as well as how you have or will fit them into your own life.

RISK

To build self-esteem, take more risks.

Take intellectual risks. Read books. Take courses. Engage in stimulating—even infuriating—conversations. Try to see the world from other points of view. Expand your horizons by gaining appreciation, skill, and understanding of art, music, theater, film, computers, or gourmet cooking. Challenge yourself to know more than you know now.

Take physical risks. Rock climb. Water-ski. Ride a dirt bike. Camp out. Take beginning aerobics, then intermediate, then advanced. Train for a ten-kilometer run, enter a race, and finish it. Push your limits of strength and endurance, and even live on the edge occasionally, but intelligently. Develop skill, practice safety, play by the rules, and then learn to hang glide, parachute, ride a hot-air baloon, or ski down the advanced slopes.

Take emotional risks. Go new places. Meet new people. Start conversations. Return a smile. Join a singles' group. Accept a blind date. Ask for a raise. Express your ideas. Assert yourself. Disagree. Be the first one to say "I love you."

Are your hands shaking, your lips quivering, your mind reeling? Are you thinking, "This man is nuts. I can't do those things"? Are you asking—"What if I fail? What if I look stupid, embarrass myself, injure myself?" Are you predicting you will be rejected, disappointed, criticized, fired, or ignored? Fear and conquering fear are what risk taking is all about. By definition, risks bring with them the possibility of failure. But what is failure anyway?

Linda Gottlieb, the author (with Carole Hyatt) of *When Smart People Fail,* describes failure as merely "a judgment about an event. Not a condemnation of character . . . not a permanent condition . . . not a contagious social disease. You lose your job, your show closes, you don't pass a crucial test. Those are events, facts. *Everything* after that is your interpretation of those events. . . . Failure makes us feel powerless and casts us into the status of victim, but it does not have to."

Instead, failure can be seen as a reason to reexamine strengths and weaknesses and an opportunity to take on new challenges. Risks offer more than chances to fail. They bring potential gain, success, pleasure, pride, and increased self-confidence. Risks embody the true meaning of "nothing ventured, nothing gained." You lose only when you do not take them.

People with high self-esteem take risks. Each risk teaches them something. If they risk and lose, they learn to risk differently in the future. If they risk and win, they learn to trust and like themselves more. A risk, well chosen and intelligently taken, stretches your limits. It makes you *more—* more agile, more informed, more sympathetic, more confident, and more sure you are lovable and capable.

A risk, carefully considered and conscientiously executed, delivers a truckload of bricks for your self-image building. Risks give you successes to savor. They give you another item to add to the list of what you *can* do. You have taken millions of risks in your lifetime already and you have succeeded. You stopped crawling and learned to walk. You left mommy and went to school. You played a tree in the kindergarten Christmas pageant.

The stakes got higher, but you continued to risk. You went out on your first date. You walked the balance beam in gym class. You tried out for the church choir, went away to summer camp, learned to drive a stick-shift car. You earned degrees, applied for jobs, got married, raised children. Of course I have not mentioned the times taking those risks ended in doom, disaster, or disappointment. You can recall those risks without my help and use them as reasons not to risk again. But you *must* continue to take risks nonetheless. The risks you take are the scale on which you measure the ways you *are* lovable and capable. If you accept no challenges, you will become a spectator in your own life instead of the active player you could be.

Risk Strategy

Risk taking is explored in more detail in the chapter on barrier #5, cold, raw fear. However, now is a good time to prepare yourself for future risk taking. This strategy will help you do that.

You came into this world helpless and totally dependent on your caregivers. On your own you could perform only the most basic bodily functions. No matter how rotten you feel about yourself today, you are more now than you were then. You know more. You can do more.

How much more? To find out, I want you to list *everything* you once could not do which you *can* do now. Start with the very basics and keep building from there, and don't worry about someone else's doing anything on your list better than you do. You'll find you have accomplished a lot in your life. For instance, once you could not walk, but now you can. Once you could not run, talk, read, write, tie your shoes, or name the pictures in your alphabet book. Once you could not drive a car, travel alone by plane or train or taxi cab. Once you couldn't cook, make a bed, iron a shirt, or open a savings account. You get my drift. There are many, many, many things you once could not do that you can do now, and each new task required a risk. You could have failed, but you took the risk and you are more today because of it.

Make a long, long list and come back to it once a day

for a week or two and add more successes to it. When you are done—temporarily, for the list will grow as you do—put your list somewhere you can find it easily. Tack it to a bulletin board or tape it to your refrigerator. Keep it in your purse, stash it in your top desk drawer, or fold it up and stick it in your wallet. Look at your list often, especially when you are considering whether a risk is worth taking. It will remind you that you have taken risks before—not once but thousands of times—and you *can* take risks again.

EMOTIONAL SUPPORT

To build self-esteem you need "a little help from your friends." As much as you might value independence, as determined as you may be to take care of yourself, as thoroughly as you may believe that needing other people is a sign of weakness or inadequacy, you will not like yourself more by isolating yourself or stand much of a chance to get unstuck by "going it alone." The absence of emotional support when you needed it in the past contributed to your present low level of self-esteem. You sought approval but received criticism. You longed for acceptance but experienced rejection. You needed sympathy but were called a crybaby. You stopped hoping to find the emotional support you needed, and so you stopped looking for it. You convinced yourself you didn't need anyone.

At her lowest point before the panic attacks began, Cindy used to say, "My life would be perfect if there were no people in it." She was tired of trying to please other people. She wanted to move into an isolated mountain cabin that had no telephone. She was also sure that no one she knew or might meet could or would do anything to help her.

Yet Cindy got back on her feet and started liking herself *because* of the emotional support she received. Her mother, who had seemed so insensitive and uncaring during Cindy's childhood, knew exactly what to do when Cindy's anxiety attacks struck. A counselor helped her understand the reasons for the attacks and taught her new ways to look at herself and behave, while her father and an old friend made her laugh. For an hour or more every night, another friend talked with Cindy on the telephone, assuring her she was not crazy and helping her relax. Then, a caring, compassionate man fell in love with her and helped her finally believe she could be herself without being rejected or abandoned.

Had Cindy remained alone with her ailing self-image and those nasty negative voices judging, criticizing, and picking at her, she might never have felt better about herself. Neither can you. Blinded by your imagined shortcomings, you may have lost your perspective. Too busy putting yourself down to build yourself up, you will need emotional support in any of the many forms it can take in order to get past this barrier.

Emotional support reminds you that you are lovable and capable and encourages you to move onward and upward. It cuddles and fusses over you when you are down and gives you a kick in the pants when you have wallowed in self-pity long enough. Emotional support shows you that you have people in your corner. Like a boxer's trainers, they can't fight the round for you, but they can cheer you on and tell you they believe in you. Emotional support can be objective advice, appreciation of your accomplishments, or respect and affection regardless of your achievements. It is knowing someone will push you to be your best and that someone will be there for you when you are at your worst.

"Oh, please!" you cry. "I don't have that and I never will. You must live in a dream world, mister. Even if I thought I needed emotional support, how am I supposed to find it? The people I know don't give a damn."

Not true. Not true at all. You think emotionally supportive people do not exist because you haven't found them yet. But they are out there. Sometimes they are right under your nose, but right now you just can't see what they have to offer.

"If you had asked me beforehand, I would have sworn I had no supportive or caring people in my life," Cindy explains. "I would have told you all counselors were idiots and I'd die before I would go to one. Nobody I knew gave a damn about me as far as I was concerned, and I never in my wildest dreams thought I'd find a man who really loved me."

The people in Cindy's life surprised her. "They were there all the time," she marvels. "Only I didn't look for them. I didn't see they cared. I never asked for their help."

Emotional Support Strategy

How to find, ask for, and receive the cooperation and emotional support you need is the subject of Chapter Eight. However, you can begin now by learning how to recognize sources of emotional support, people who are part of your life today or whom you can seek and find in the future.

The most common and deceptive mistake you can make when seeking emotional support is expecting one person to have *all* the supportive qualities you need. When you seek that kind of total support from one person, you will often be disappointed and end up overlooking what he or she *does* have to offer.

"My mother was the world's worst when it came to dealing with my feelings," claimed Lisa, the sales representative. "She actually told me *not* to feel the way I felt, as if I could turn off my emotions like a faucet."

On the other hand, Lisa's mother turned out to be a great validator. She constantly expresses her pride, appreciation, respect, love, and admiration of Lisa and her accomplishments. She brags about her children to anyone who will listen, is ready and willing to come through with financial assistance, and when Lisa was looking for a new job, she called everyone she knew to inquire about available positions. If Lisa had gone to her mother seeking solace, empathy, and a shoulder to cry on, she would have been very disappointed. But when Lisa asked her mother for the kinds of support she was capable of giving, she received more than she expected.

Cindy's mother downplayed her daughter's achievements but gave Cindy the sympathy she needed during times of crisis. Her father, on the other hand, had no concept of the stress inherent in Cindy's public relations work and could not understand Cindy's anxiety attacks. Yet he made her laugh and told her tales of times he was down as low as he thought he could get but rose above his problems, giving her hope of doing the same. Cindy found still a different type of support from her best friend. She refused to feel sorry for Cindy, but she did listen and offer wisdom and new direction.

No one person can give you all you need in the way of emotional support, and so such unrealistic expectations invariably lead you to disappointment. However, you may be surprised to find that almost everyone you know has something of a supportive nature to offer. The key is to identify the types of emotional support you want and seek that support from the people who are capable of giving it.

Below I list several types of emotional support people. Read each description and try to think of people you know who fit the description. They need not be perfect at giving that particular type of emotional support, as long as they can give you at least a little bit of what you need in that particular area. Some people will fit in several categories.

After you read each description, jot down the names of people you know who could give you that kind of support the next time you need it.

CHICKEN SOUP PEOPLE. These are people who comfort you when you feel down, saying things such as, "Poor baby. What a rotten day you had. No wonder you feel so blue." They coddle and pamper and are just what the doctor ordered when you need to wallow for a while.

COMIC-RELIEF GIVERS. These are the zany, offbeat people in your life. No matter how low you go, they can make you laugh or at least smile. They point out life's absurdities, bring over their entire collection of Three Stooges' video-tapes and watch them with you, and do hysterical "If you think you've got problems" monologues. When humor will help, these are the people you should call.

THE GREAT DISTRACTORS. Similar to comic-relief givers, these folks take your mind off your troubles. You should call them when you want to get out of the house or away from yourself for a while. They'll go with you to the movies, take you to ball games or concerts, or play gin rummy until dawn, offering you distance and a brief vacation from what ails you.

THE CRISIS CORPS. These people may or may not be much help over the long haul, but one thing's for sure, if your world should unexpectedly fall apart on you, they are capable of helping you pick up the pieces. They support you calmly, encouraging you to take control of your own life.

THE LISTENERS. They listen. They'll listen to your self-pity, anger, and the same sorry story as many times as you need to tell it. You know you can call them when you need to unload your feelings, bounce around ideas, or get a reality check.

THE ADVISERS. Problem solvers by nature, these people look objectively at your situation and give suggestions. They think of new alternatives, help you set goals, and point out plans of action that seem unrealistic. You don't have to take their advice, but their type of support gives you options and ideas so you can make your own decisions.

THE DOOR OPENERS. These are the helping-hand people. They may not have the answers, but they usually know where you can find them. They will connect you with people you want to know, refer you to a decent therapist, call when they hear about a job opening, cosign for bank loans, or write reference letters. They hold the key to doors you cannot open yourself.

I'VE BEEN DOWN AND DIRTY A FEW TIMES MYSELF PEOPLE. These are people who once had or now have problems similar to your own. As a result, they are capable of accepting you without judging you. Those further along in their recovery can become models for your own improvement efforts.

(If you do not know people like these, look for self-help groups such as Alcoholics, Overeaters, or Gamblers Anonymous, or support groups for abused women, women in transition, single parents, or other similar groups. Call your local mental health center for a list or look in the telephone book.)

UNCONDITIONAL ACCEPTERS. If you had more of these people in your life, your self-esteem would already be relatively high. You'll find more imperfect support givers in this category than any other. Flawed though they may be, however, these people forgive you, loving you even when they do not like you very much.

PROFESSIONAL HELPERS. These people are trained and paid to give you exactly the emotional support you need. They fit into almost every other category, but you rarely think of putting them there since therapy is seen as a treatment rather than a form of support. At one time or another, professionals helped many of the people described in this book, including me. Professional help is available in every corner and crossroad of this country. You can look in any telephone book, but you improve your chances of finding good professional help by asking people who have found it themselves. Your door openers can help you here.

Perhaps you can think of other kinds of emotional supporters. If you can, list those types too and try to match them with people you know or can locate. Then, hang on to your list so that when you are ready to attempt a change or dislodge an obstacle to change, you will know whom to call.

POWER

Powerlessness is a breeding ground for low self-esteem. Victims of abuse and people who view themselves as victims of circumstance usually do not like themselves and do not believe they deserve better. Low self-esteem is found in people who readily submit to peer pressure and routinely go along with the crowd. Self-esteem is also lost when people keep quiet although they have something to say, allowing others to take advantage of them or avoiding making decisions.

You could see the effect of powerlessness on Lisa, whose superiors and coworkers disregarded her feelings and opinions. Because they were more educated and experienced than she, Lisa assumed they knew what was best. The personal power that was not taken from her, she willingly gave away. She was not included in decisions that affected her and did not ask to be, and she quickly stopped expressing her opinions. She did not protest unfair treatment or even question why she did not receive the pay raise she had been promised. Instead, she swallowed her feelings and went along with other people's plans although she often did not like or agree with them. As her self-esteem plummeted, she saw herself first as a hapless pawn and ultimately as a mindless victim.

On the other hand, people with high self-esteem exercise a great deal of personal power. They don't have to be royalty or heads of state or chief executive officers in multinational corporations to do this. But they do believe they have control over their lives and use it to get more of what they want. They also believe in their ability to change. If they have no other tangible power, they always have the power to choose.

You *get* personal power by making decisions based on your personal values and desires. You *give up* that power when you allow and/or ask other people to decide for you.

When you increase personal power, you build self-esteem by claiming your choices as your own, feeling proud of your achievements and regaining control over aspects of daily living. You get personal power by asserting yourself, asking for what you need and expressing your ideas or feelings about matters that directly affect you.

You give up this power when you convince yourself other people are better, more qualified, more articulate, or need more and know more than you do. You give them the power to ignore or dismiss your ideas, take advantage of you, have their needs met at your expense, or otherwise abuse you. As Lisa discovered, not exercising personal power unleashes very dangerous wrecking balls.

You *reclaim* personal power when you say yes more often to life's challenges and possibilities and say no more often to unreasonable demands and self-defeating pursuits. You *exercise* personal power when you set a goal, make a plan, and stick to it. You increase personal power by changing bad eating patterns, breaking detrimental habits, spending money only within your budget, bringing your credit card balances down, and asking that tasks not included in your job description stop being assigned to you without your okay.

Personal Power Strategy

When you are stuck or see yourself as a victim, you cannot use personal power to build self-esteem because you do not know you have it. To increase personal power you must first identify ways to be decisive and assertive. Then you must practice, starting small and moving upward. Here are eleven ways to practice using personal power:

1. Take an assertiveness training course.
2. Stop at a service station and ask for directions.
3. Return a gift that does not suit you to the department store where it was purchased.
4. Tell a particularly verbal friend you want to end a telephone conversation. Offer to call her back later, but do not make excuses about why you want to get off the phone.

5. Tell a teenage child you will drive him to a school event, but he must find someone else to drive him home.

6. Choose *not* to cook dinner one day of the week. Ask someone else to take responsibility for that meal.

7. Suggest a work-related improvement to your supervisor.

8. Do not eat the dessert that comes with your meal the next time you travel on an airline.

9. Ask the maître d' for a different table than the one where he is about to seat you.

10. The next time anyone asks you what you want to do and you are tempted to say, "I don't know," think about what *you* really do want and answer accordingly.

11. Say no if you mean no when your coworkers pass around the doughnuts, your colleague encourages you to have a lunchtime martini, a salesperson tries to sell you an accessory, or cocaine is available at a party.

To get a clearer picture of how you personally exercise or abdicate your power, think about the week that just passed. Think of twenty instances during that week when you could have exercised personal power, made a decision, expressed ideas or opinions, asserted yourself, made a request, or said no. Write your power points on a scrap of paper.

Of those twenty opportunities to exercise personal power, how many did you actually use? In contrast, how many times did you let someone else decide, held back your opinion or said yes when you really wanted to say no? Now, think about the rest of today and all of tomorrow. Based on what you know of your schedule and routine, list at least five ways you can use your personal power. Write these as affirmations, positive statements recognizing the power you do have and confirming exactly what you will do. (I.e., "I have personal power and will use it tomorrow by driving right past the doughnut shop without stopping on my way to work.") Read your affirmations before you fall asleep tonight and again tomorrow morning, then follow through and accomplish what you have written.

UNIQUENESS

What a miracle it is that there exists no other person on this earth who is exactly like you are. Not even your twin—if you had one—would look, sound, think, and relate to the world the very same way you do all of the time. You are unique.

You may not think being unique is such a big deal, especially if being unique means you believe you are uniquely inadequate, unlovable, and unworthy. You may spend a great deal of your time trying to look more like a cover-girl model or a world-class weight lifter. You may dress for success, laugh at jokes you think are not funny, practice witty repartee in the mirror, and compare your bank account to your peers'. Perhaps you pore over the dictionary and pepper your speech with polysyllabic words so you seem more intelligent, or you force yourself to swallow more wine coolers then you should in order to be sociable at parties. Maybe you fabricate or embellish details of your job, home, love life, and sexual conquests to make them all sound more exciting than they really are. But each time you try to be like someone other than yourself, you really end up hurting yourself by relinquishing your uniqueness. You think you are not good enough the way you are, and this erodes your self-esteem. To paraphrase a point made by Dr. Leo Buscaglia in his best-selling book *Love,* if you are a plum, no matter how you try, you will never be anything but a second-rate banana. What's more, in a vain attempt to be a banana, you lose your sense of plumness.

Instead of trying to be who you are not, why not put your time and energy into being a better you? You can be a first-rate you. Such an effort enhances self-esteem, magnifying your strengths and helping you overcome your limitations.

This does not mean you can't try to change for the better. If you want for yourself the abilities or qualities you see in someone, go after them because they will make you a better you, not because they might somehow earn you someone else's life. Make them part of your life and express them as only you can.

Uniqueness Strategy

What exactly is unique about you? That's an easy question, right? You believe you are uniquely unattached, unattractive, and unimportant, the only one in the world with fat thighs, without a college education, and apt to stick your foot in your mouth every time you open it.

Stop. Let me rephrase the question. What assets, abilities, and positive attributes make you unique? That's harder to answer, isn't it, but I think you can manage a response if you try.

On a sheet of paper, I want you to write forty positive characteristics that are uniquely your own. Yes, forty of them. Break them down into three categories: twenty things you are able to do (you do not have to do them perfectly or even as well as the guy next door); ten interesting or positive physical attributes (yours—not Christie Brinkley's or Arnold Schwarzenegger's) or personality traits; and ten interests or beliefs you have. Do not give up until the list is complete. If you must, call a friend or two and ask them for help.

Remember, you are not trying to best or measure up to anyone else. This is not the time to wish you were better or different. You are simply taking stock of the assets you have—and believe me, there are many more than forty. A year from now when you have long since gotten unstuck and raised your level of self-esteem, you will be able to list forty more without trouble. But for now, spend some time coming up with the first forty and save your list. You will refer to it again while working on other self-esteem and barrier dismantling strategies, and it certainly would not hurt to consult it the next time you try to tell yourself you are not good enough.

BELONGING AND RECOGNITION

Earlier in this chapter, while discussing self-esteem wrecking balls, I mentioned that Cindy's self-esteem suffered because she did not feel as if she belonged in her family or in the fast-paced, high-pressure world of entertainment public relations. In addition, she did not believe her feelings, needs, or point of view were recognized or appreciated.

Feeling that you belong and are connected to other people, as well as having your actions and emotions recognized, builds self-esteem and validates your existence, your place in the world and your worth. Without belonging and recognition you will naturally feel isolated, unappreciated, and unlovable. You may come to the point where you mistrust your own perceptions because you have no way to test them or check them against other people's views of reality.

The quest for belonging and recognition is a lifelong project. You first sought it from your family. "Who am I?" you wanted to know. "How do I fit in? What do I do that is acceptable and likely to be rewarded in some way?" You found your answers in your relationships with family members, and those relationships had a huge impact on your self-image—for better or worse. Then you looked again for belonging and recognition when you went to school where you worked for gold stars, A grades, and nods of approval. Do you remember knowing an answer and waving your arm frantically, thinking, "Me. Me. Call on me. Look at me." If you were noticed and rewarded, you felt capable and ready to take on the next challenge. If your uniqueness and value went unrecognized for long enough, you decided you were not good enough, and sometimes you stopped trying to be more.

Your quest for belonging, connection, and recognition eventually may have led you to intimate love relationships where much of what you found depended on what you had previously learned about belonging. You may have found that nothing had ever been as close as the intimacy of a love relationship. Your experience, good or bad, shaped your image of yourself and your ability to belong.

You cannot go back and change what has already occurred. You cannot make your parents love you more than they did at the time. You cannot take back the dumb remark that caused the girls in the "in" group to laugh at you. You cannot make your ex-spouse love you again in a better way. You *can* look at how not belonging and not being recognized in the past affects your self-esteem today, and then you can move forward.

A good way to start is to look for new ways and places to belong. This time, instead of compromising who you are in order to fit in, build on your uniqueness. Look for the people, places, and activities that fit who you already are.

If you are a single parent, join a single parents' group. If you are interested in art or music or gourmet cooking, join a club or take a course. If you are a freelance professional, own your own business, or work in a particular field, become part of a network or professional association. If you like bowling, join a league. The resources for belonging and recognition are limited only by your imagination and vision.

Belonging Strategy

Using your list of unique assets as a reference and paying particular attention to your interests and activities, list groups, clubs, courses, or meeting places that complement your interests and assets. List as many as you can think of.

Then do some additional research. Check the telephone book, new neighbors' guide, or community calendar section of your local newspaper.

When you are ready to increase your supply of belonging and recognition building blocks, consult your list, choose three resources, and make a plan. Your plan can include finding the appropriate telephone number, calling for information, registering (if necessary), asking a friend to go with you (if you need moral support), and attending your first class, group meeting, or making your first connection. Be sure to set a date for each step in your plan and use affirmation statements to convince yourself you *can* belong and be recognized.

PRODUCTIVITY

When asked about people who feel they're losers and can't move on with their lives, Linda Gottlieb, coauthor of *When Smart People Fail,* suggests, "Do something in which you can succeed, accomplish something. One man built a tree house. Another person learned to swim. It really doesn't matter *what* you do. Just do something."

Her advice is well suited for people with low self-esteem. To be productive in some way—any way—is an essential self-esteem building block. Nine times out of ten, when you are asked to describe yourself, you probably start by describing something you do. This is because your self-esteem depends heavily on what you think and feel about what you achieve, accomplish, or produce. It drops noticeably when you stand still or feel stuck.

Often you can see the relationship between productivity and self-esteem in an older adult who retires from the work force. He walks out of the workplace with a gold watch in his pocket and a huge part of himself missing. If he whiles away the hours watching TV and snoozing in a retirement home, he deteriorates quickly, feeling he has little to live for and little proof he is lovable or capable anymore. Millions of senior citizens waste away from lack of productivity.

Hy could have, and he did for a time after selling the large family restaurant he had owned and operated. For the first time since he was twelve, he found himself with no job to do. He had money enough to meet his needs, a loving wife, friends, but no way to feel productive. Fortunately he blundered into a way to contribute to society and be productive by turning a charitable organization's warehouse full of donated merchandise into a thriving thrift shop. Now he earns money for a worthy cause and feels useful and rewarded. As a result, Hy's self-esteem is just fine these days.

Invariably the times you have liked yourself most were also times you have felt productive, active, busy, and creative. You can find that feeling of productivity from working, completing a course or passing a test, building a model airplane, cleaning out the garage, collecting newspapers and aluminum cans for recycling, lining the linen closet shelves, or organizing pictures in a photograph album. Choosing a task, starting it, and finishing it is the quickest and easiest way to accumulate self-esteem building blocks.

PLAN AHEAD FOR A HIGH SELF-ESTEEM YEAR

Now that you are familiar with the seven self-esteem building blocks, how will *you* use them and in what order or combination? How will *your* self-esteem urban renewal project repair the damage done by old wrecking balls?

While your unique experiences have created unique gaps in your self-esteem, your strengths are also yours alone, and you will build self-esteem differently than anyone else. However, you must take an active role in your own rebuilding project. Take inventory, create a vision, and devise a plan to enhance your self-esteem.

Taking Inventory

On a blank sheet of paper draw two vertical lines and two horizontal lines so the page looks like this:

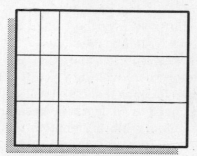

The three horizontal sections each represent a high self-esteem year in your life. Identify those years when your self-esteem was high, your outlook positive, and when you liked yourself the most. In the left-hand column of each horizontal section, write the approximate dates of your high self-esteem years. In the second column, use the numbers one, two, and three to rank in order those years, with the number one indicating the year of highest self-esteem.

Starting with the year you ranked as number one, write notes to yourself about that year in the wide third column. Then ask yourself, what went on during that year? What were you doing? Who were the important people in your life? Why do you think you liked yourself then? Think about these questions and make comments for all three high self-esteem years. Then review your self-esteem inventory and notice which self-esteem building blocks you had on hand during the years you most liked yourself.

Cindy had never seen herself as much of a risk taker, yet when she did this inventory, she immediately noticed that all three of her self-esteem years included major challenges. During each, she began a new job and turned it into more than it started out to be, learning and doing things she had never done before. Belonging played a big part, too.

Cindy says, "I was really hooked into being productive, too. I was working hard and accomplishing a lot at work. I moved into my own apartment one year, and bought my house during another year and handled repairs and renovations myself. And last year, when I was publicizing theatrical road shows all over the United States and in Japan, people were always telling me what a great job I was doing."

Compare how you felt and what you did during your high self-esteem years with how you feel and what you do now. If you plan to reach that high level of self-esteem again, what will you need to do, learn, or become? Then, for each self-esteem building block (mentors/models, risks, emotional support, power, uniqueness, belonging/recognition, and productivity) list at least one way you can get more of each.

Creating a Vision of High Self-esteem

Negative self-fulfilling prophecies were described earlier in this chapter. When you predict failure, you get it. Fortunately, you can predict success as well. To improve your chance of getting high self-esteem, visualize yourself having it already. Now think about and describe another year in your life. This time the year should not be one you have lived already, but a year you are going to live, the next year of your life.

Write a letter to the year ahead. Think of next year as a close friend and in your letter tell that friend about the success you anticipate, the risks you hope to take, the tasks you want to accomplish, and all your other goals.

Cindy wrote such a letter and allowed me to reprint it here:

Dear 1988,
I think one of the scripts Sue and I wrote will be sold this year. I know that is out of my hands, but I think we

do good work and I'd like to do more. I'd like to learn more about filmmaking too, especially the production/business end of it. I think I'll also take some college courses and get back to work on my degree. I wonder if filmmaking and psychology mix, because I'm also interested in what makes people tick.

I'll move closer to New York City. My relationship with Joe is too close and important to keep it a long distance one. Besides, the train fare is killing me! And speaking of finances, while I'm waiting to become a rich and famous screenwriter, I'd better find more freelance work or sign on with a PR agency—in New York preferably. I have some job leads already. This time around, though, I'm going to hold out for work I really want. I get by on my freelance projects. I don't have to jump on the first offer I get. I'm good enough at what I do now and have enough of a track record to pick and choose.

I'm going to travel more. I can't believe I spent so many years in a small town. Now that I've tasted travel and adventure I want more. Joe and I will take that trip to Europe. I have big plans for this year, don't I?

I will meet new, exciting people. I will make my relationship even better than it is. I might even mention the word "marriage" again—talk about risk taking! I will pay off my loans and credit card balances and get started on the children's book I've been meaning to write. Most of all, I will trust my feelings and my intuition. I'll open up and trust more, not just to Joe and Sue. Of course, I don't want to go overboard either. I'll just say what I'm thinking. Sue's not the only one who can be assertive in a business meeting. If I've learned anything, it's that people will not run the other way when I'm being something other than cute, funny, and amusing.

These exercises have helped me see all I can do. I went through a rough time financially last year, but it helped me see I am more than just an extension of my work. I used to feel lousy because I hadn't traveled much and wasn't very sophisticated, but I learned it is never too late to start. I learned to trust and open up to more people, that I can take as well as give. I definitely figured out that things *never* turn out as badly as I think they will when I let my imagination run away with me, and that I'll survive without everyone's liking me all of the time. I peeked at the rough draft of this chapter and I agree with Pat. Life really is a gift and I'd better make it count. That's exactly what I plan to do next year.

The Self-esteem Plan

How will you make next year happen the way you described it in your letter? What will you do? With your vision of a high self-esteem year in mind, once again look at each building block and determine how you will use each one to have the year you want. List at least one goal for each building block. Phrase your goal as an affirmation, positively stating what you believe will occur. Lisa wrote: "I will take intellectual risks by signing up for two college courses, completing them, learning from them, and passing them with flying colors!" Lisa sounds as if she believes she can do what she planned. How about you?

You now have the building blocks, vision, and blueprint to enhance your self-esteem. If you follow your own plan, you will soon see how much more you deserve and you will be able to accomplish the life changes that previously stymied you. You will be better equipped and more motivated to remove other obstacles from your path. You can begin this last task immediately, by learning about barrier number two—not seeing your alternatives.

4

████ ▌ █ ▌ █ ▌ ▌ ▌ ▌ ▌▌▌▌▌▌▌▌▌▌▌▌▌▌▌▌▌

Change and Options

ROADBLOCK SELF-TEST

Read the following statements carefully, many of which will sound quite familiar to you. You may have had similar thoughts or feelings the last time you were stuck in an uncomfortable, unhealthy situation or the last time you wanted to change in any way. Perhaps you feel that way right now.

After each statement you will find three comments. Circle the one that is most true for you.

" Look, there is absolutely nothing I can do about this situation. I have no choice—unless you can come up with a magic wand or a miracle, that is."

I OFTEN   I SOMETIMES   I NEVER

FEEL THIS WAY   FEEL THIS WAY   FEEL THIS WAY

"I'm caught between a rock and a hard place. The *only* thing I could do would leave me as badly or worse off than I am now."

I OFTEN   I SOMETIMES   I NEVER

FEEL THIS WAY   FEEL THIS WAY   FEEL THIS WAY

"There are alternatives, but they are not *good* alternatives. It's obvious they would never work."

I OFTEN   I SOMETIMES   I NEVER

FEEL THIS WAY   FEEL THIS WAY   FEEL THIS WAY

"I ask people what they would do if they were in my situation, and maybe their ideas would work for them, but none of their suggestions are right for *me*."

I OFTEN   I SOMETIMES   I NEVER

FEEL THIS WAY   FEEL THIS WAY   FEEL THIS WAY

"I have tried everything under the sun, but nothing ever works. I always end up right back where I started."

I OFTEN   I SOMETIMES   I NEVER

FEEL THIS WAY   FEEL THIS WAY   FEEL THIS WAY

"There are plenty of things I could do. The problem is I can't figure out which one I *should* do."

I OFTEN   I SOMETIMES   I NEVER

FEEL THIS WAY   FEEL THIS WAY   FEEL THIS WAY

"I don't want to make the wrong decision. What if I do something and still feel lousy? What if I lose what little I have?"

I OFTEN   I SOMETIMES   I NEVER

FEEL THIS WAY   FEEL THIS WAY   FEEL THIS WAY

"Ask me to make a decision on the job, ask me what to do about *your* problem, and I'm terrific. But when it comes to my own life and my own problems ... forget it!"

I OFTEN   I SOMETIMES   I NEVER

FEEL THIS WAY   FEEL THIS WAY   FEEL THIS WAY

If you have ever harbored thoughts or feelings similar to those just listed, then you have experienced the effects of the second barrier to change—NOT SEEING ALTERNATIVES. If you circled "I often feel this way" after many of the statements, it is quite likely this barrier now obstructs your path.

In a scene from the 1954 Academy Award winning motion picture, *Marty,* the title character and his friend try to decide how to spend an evening. Their dialogue goes like this:

"What do you want to do tonight, Marty?"

"I don't know. What do you want to do, Ange?"

"I don't know. What do *you* want to do?"

In this understated film about a somewhat limited man stuck in his somewhat limited world, that short scene brilliantly captures Marty's dilemma. For Marty and his friends, Saturday nights and their entire lives were full of possibilities and alternatives, but they simply could not see them.

The conversation between Marty and Ange rings true because we play the same scene over and over again in our lives. When faced with choices, too often we ask ourselves what to do, only to ultimately answer, as Marty did, "I don't know."

BARRIER #2: NOT SEEING THE ALTERNATIVES

Without realizing you have alternatives, you have no vision to guide you when a choice must be made. Without all your options, you have no destination to move toward and no *reason* to alter your course. You stay where you are because you simply cannot determine any new direction.

The following story was told to me by a suicide prevention hotline worker. It is a true story about a conversation he had with a suicidal teenager.

Gene was working an overnight shift at a crisis center in Ohio. The night had been quiet and Gene passed the time by studying for a graduate course final exam and listening to the radio. "Every half hour or so, the DJ would read the weather report," Gene relates. "It was going to be a beautiful day and he must have said a dozen times how much he was looking forward to it. I started looking forward to it too and figured if it was still quiet at dawn, I'd go out onto the fire escape and watch the sun come up.

"Around four-thirty I got a call from a girl who couldn't have been more than fifteen or sixteen years old. She didn't waste time on small talk. If I couldn't give her one good reason to live, she told me, she was going to hang up and kill herself. I tried to get her to talk about why or even how she wanted to commit suicide, but she wasn't buying. She just repeated her ultimatum—'Give me a reason to live or I'm going to kill myself.'

"Let me tell you, those are the kinds of calls nightmares are made of. But I wasn't dreaming. I was wide-awake and up against the wall. My mind was racing, trying to think of what to say. Finally I remembered the DJ and the weather report and told the caller if she killed herself she would miss seeing the sunrise.

"It wasn't a great intervention and she told me so. In fact, she said it was the stupidest thing she ever heard. I asked her to think about it anyway, and while she was at it, to think about all the other things she'd never see or do again if she killed herself. We made a list. At first she came up with all the lousy stuff in her life and all the reasons suicide was the answer to all her problems. But with a little pushing from me, she began to see the good things she'd miss and that the list got pretty long. Once I could tell she was starting to see the method behind my madness, I asked her if there wasn't something else she could do besides killing herself—seeing as she'd have to give up all this good stuff forever if she did that.

"Her first reaction was to say no. She *knew* there were no alternatives. 'Oh, you've already looked at all the options, then?' I asked. But she hadn't looked at all. She had decided right off the bat that her situation was hopeless and there couldn't possibly be anything to do about it except kill herself. As soon as she made that decision, she stopped looking for other solutions. All she had thought about for the past two weeks was suicide. She had backed herself into a corner, when, as it turned out, there were lots of other things she could do."

Gene helped the caller see the alternatives and she agreed to try them. I'm happy to report that several of her options worked out well, and two years later the caller is alive and thinking about answering phones at the crisis center. Of course, Gene was thrilled with the outcome, but he went on to say: "That story isn't the least bit unusual. Most of the people I talk to haven't considered their alternatives. Hell, they don't even see that there are alternatives."

Perhaps your job seems dull, routine, and unfulfilling, or your relationship with your children or your parents is strained and unsatisfying, or you are overwhelmed by the demands of your overflowing schedule and wish there were more hours in the day. Maybe you are constantly at odds with your supervisor or your spouse. You may spend every Saturday night at the same bar, hoping you will meet someone special—but you don't. You ask yourself what you could do differently. You wonder how to improve the situation or get out of it or how to give up a habit that is hurting you, and you come up empty-handed.

And then that helpless, hopeless, claustrophobic feeling overtakes you. You sigh, complain, pour yourself another drink, pick a fight with your spouse, or spend money at the shopping mall. You pull the covers up over your head, praying to wake up and find all your troubles magically erased. In short, you get stuck and see no alternative to being stuck.

This barrier works as well as it does because you assume that just because you can't see your options, there *are* no options. You believe you are stuck because you have no alternatives, when in fact you are stuck because you do not know how to look for alternatives. You believe you have no choices, when what actually gets you stuck is not knowing how to make choices effectively.

This block to change can be a bit tricky because it presents itself in several different forms. You may have encountered them all at one time or another, or you may have experienced only one familiar version. All work in their own ways to keep you from getting unstuck.

Alternatives Blindness

The teenager who called the suicide prevention hotline was suffering from alternatives blindness. She honestly believed she had *no* options. Her world was dark. She did not realize that all around her were switches she could flip to turn on the lights. This psychological tunnel vision can overcome you when you feel cornered, stymied, or powerless. That's when it's easy to focus all of your attention and energy on the problem and the pain. Staring so single-mindedly at the closed door, you do not notice the open ones, and convinced your situation will last forever, you are sure there is absolutely nothing you can do to change it.

Alternatives blindness is most likely to strike when an ongoing problem reaches overwhelming proportions or when a sudden, unexpected life crisis occurs. Down so low as a result of abuse, illness, or chronic depression, or thrown off balance by a death, a financial loss, job layoff or a divorce, you may lose your perspective and your ability to think clearly. As a result, you cannot see anything *but* the way things are at the moment.

Between a Rock and a Hard Place

Slightly different from alternatives blindness, although no more helpful to getting unstuck, is seeing only *one* alternative, one which is just as or more distasteful than the way things are now. Carla, the burned-out social worker described in Chapter One, has been thwarted by this version of the second barrier to change. From her perspective the only alternative to staying in a job she hates is to have no job at all. Of course, choosing this alternative usually has all sorts of negative consequences. She imagines going on welfare, losing her home, custody of her kids, and ultimately becoming a bag lady. With such a mindset, being stuck and unhappy in a job that provides a steady paycheck seems the preferable option. Even though there are dozens of other avenues open to her, Carla does not see them.

You know this version of the barrier is operating in your life when alternatives seem to be black and white, when choices seem to be either/or. *Either* stay in an abusive relationship *or* be desperately alone. *Either* go to the bar on Saturday night *or* become a couch potato who sits by herself on the sofa eating junk food and watching TV. *Either* put up with your mother's constant criticism *or* never speak to her again.

Of course, when the only course of action you can visualize taking will leave you as unhappy, unhealthy, and unfulfilled as you already are, there truly is no sense in pursuing it. But what about the rest of the spectrum, the other, less catastrophic options? They are there, but that one disastrous option on your mind is so unappealing it may distract you from the search. If that happens, you may stop looking, and you'll probably stay stuck.

Focusing on the Fatal Flaw

You can get stuck and sabotage your efforts to get unstuck by recognizing alternatives to your present situation, but rejecting them one by one. You can generate a long list of possibilities, all right. The problem is that you are struck instantly by the fatal flaw in each one. Without taking the time to pursue it, you eliminate the option because you think an imperfect alternative is a useless alternative.

April is an absolute genius when it comes to finding those fatal flaws. She can reject alternatives faster than anyone can suggest them. For example, April is firm in her belief that all forms of therapy are useless because she's been to see therapists before and they did not help her. She has also made up her mind that taking art courses is out of the question because she's too tired after a full day of work and all art majors are flaky anyway. Bars are meat markets populated by psychopaths. Getting to know men through work is impossible because her coworkers gossip and meddle. Self-help books are all the same. Personal ads, singles groups, and blind dates are for only desperate people and losers. She has a "Yeah, but" comeback for every suggestion, and what she honestly believes is a perfectly good reason not to pursue any option—not one is flawless.

Focusing on fatal flaws is the most common form of this barrier. If you are so inclined, you will always be able to find legitimate reasons why an alternative plan of action might not work for you. But you must keep in mind that while the flaw you have discovered may be real enough, it often is far from fatal. Look at the alternatives closely. It is possible that you have not looked for the potential good in the option. When you are stuck, you may not notice that the probable positive outcome of changing your situation far outweighs the possible negative consequences. When you are stuck, the flaws are all you see. As a result, you may pass up reasonable avenues for getting unstuck because smooth sailing and a direct, uninterrupted road to complete happiness cannot be guaranteed.

Grasping at Straws

Grasping at straws is the flip side of finding fatal flaws. In both instances you can see the possible alternatives to your present situation, but you do not thoroughly and conscientiously consider their true potential for getting you unstuck or weigh the potential negative *and* positive consequences. When you are grasping at straws, however, you try an alternative before you reject it. In fact, you jump on any and every alternative as soon as you find it, hoping it to be the quick fix you think you need. Invariably, however, you are disappointed when immediate, dramatic, all-encompassing results are not forthcoming, and this causes you to abandon the effort and move on to a new, equally impulsive course of action.

Lou, desperately searching for solutions to his marital problems, repeatedly tried quick fixes. He bought his wife a car, paid for her college courses, saw a marriage counselor, and even went deeply into debt buying a restaurant in hopes of rekindling the dream he and his wife had shared at the beginning of their marriage. He never looked below the surface. He just knew that he had to do *something* and went for the first solution that came to mind. He did see the alternatives. He did try them. But he did *not* achieve his goal. If anything, his marital problems got worse.

Because being stuck often causes desperation, you may be willing to try *anything* to relieve the pain and solve the problem. You may solicit advice from every imaginable source and lunge for every possible "out," like a drowning man clinging to a life preserver. That's what Jack did.

A high-level accountant for a large company, Jack feared

he was racing full steam ahead to a nervous breakdown because the stress in his life was so great and so constant. He shared his concerns with everyone he knew, hoping they would suggest a surefire remedy. His brother told him a chiropractor could relieve his stress-related aches and pains. After his first session, however, he felt worse instead of better and he stopped seeing the chiropractor. His assistant told him to meditate. He tried, but during his meditation time, he found himself obsessively worrying about work. He stopped meditating. His ex-girlfriend made an appointment for him with her psychiatrist, who prescribed medication that made Jack dizzy and lethargic. He stopped taking the medication and no longer sees the psychiatrist. He joined a health club but stopped going regularly because he got too nervous about finding time to work out. He delegated job responsibilities, but worried that they wouldn't be accomplished to his satisfaction, he took them back. He took vacations, drank strange teas, and consulted a hypnotist.

What Jack really needed was an overall stress reduction plan and the patience to follow it. Instead, he tried one "sure cure" after another, abandoning each when his stress did not disappear instantly. Consequently, he is still heading straight for a breakdown.

If this version of the second barrier to change is working its wily ways on you, you blindly pursue alternatives without thinking clearly about them. You never ask yourself if the "cure" has any connection with the "disease." Instead, you go off on a wild-goose chase only to return to square one. What's more, by trying alternatives impulsively and rejecting them before they have a chance to really work, you eliminate those that could succeed in time or under the proper conditions.

Overwhelmed by Alternatives

On any given Saturday night you could go to a play, a movie, a bar, a party, an art auction, a concert, a shopping mall, or stay at home. You could have a romantic dinner for two, meet friends at a restaurant, invite guests to a gourmet meal in your home, barbecue in the backyard, or have pizza or Chinese food delivered and rent a videotape, play charades, Trivial Pursuit, or have a sing-along. You could forgo socializing and work, pay bills, supervise your daughter's slumber party, read a Gothic novel, or give yourself a pedicure. With so many choices, how do you choose?

How *do* you choose? Unfortunately, you can have plenty of options and still get stuck. All of them may, at first glance, appear to be equal, and choosing one means not choosing another. But what if you want them all? What if you make the wrong choice? It's true that you could make the wrong choice, but becoming paralysed in your decision-making process is even worse. All your options are rendered useless if you are unable to evaluate them, prioritize them, and make a decision.

When Margaret, the public relations coordinator for a large Philadelphia-based health services organization, learned her position would be eliminated, she was stunned and confused. She loved her job. It was exactly the type of work she wanted to do. The people she worked with, the pay she received, and the creativity and freedom she was allowed met her needs perfectly. The situation upset her terribly at first, and while she was reacting to the unexpected news, she temporarily believed she had no choices. The next thing she knew, however, she was presented with more alternatives than she could handle.

"First of all, I was offered a different position with the same company," she says. "Then a friend called to tell me a position like the one I was leaving was available at her company. Another friend, who was self-employed as a publicist, had more work than she could handle and asked me to become a partner in her business. A hospital offered me some freelance public relations work, and a local newspaper asked if I would write some freelance feature stories, which got me thinking about starting my own business. The college where I got my degree was looking for an associate professor. And my husband, who makes enough money to support us, suggested it might be the right time to have a baby, which, of course, put all the other possibilities into a new light."

While you might envy Margaret because she has so many places to turn, those very viable options did her little good. They all were reasonable. They all were available. But which alternative was the right one for her? Although in the workplace Margaret made countless decisions every day, when it came to her own life and deciding on a specific course of action that could affect her for years to come, she did not know how to choose. Most of the choices were very, very appealing. She ran over each alternative in her mind, considering each from every conceivable angle, afraid she would make the wrong choice. But the more she reviewed her options, the more confused she became.

With all those doors open to her, Margaret nonetheless was frozen in her tracks. What's more, while she spun her wheels, some of the doors closed. She didn't realize that not choosing is a choice in itself. If you postpone a decision for long enough, you will be left with only one path to take, and it will not necessarily be the best path. Margaret finally decided to freelance and try to get pregnant. Although she does not regret her decision, she still wonders if it was the right one.

As a rule, the more alternatives you have, the better, *only if* you can also evaluate them, assign a priority to each, and select one. Having options without knowing what to do with them is as debilitating as seeing no options. If you cannot choose, you cannot move.

Barrier #2 takes on many disguises and cunningly keeps you from getting what you want for your life. It is a two-sided barrier—one side blinds or distracts you from seeing the alternatives, while the other keeps you from choosing an alternative to pursue. So, you stay exactly where you are—and you know where that is—stuck.

DISMANTLING THE BARRIER: HOW TO SEARCH FOR ALTERNATIVES AND MAKE EFFECTIVE DECISIONS

Alternatives *do* exist. You just get stuck when you do not know how to recognize them. You feel trapped because you have not found viable options—*yet.* But you can learn how to look for them. And you will find them. Of all the barriers to change, this one is the easiest to dismantle.

Why? Because alternatives *do* exist. There is always at least one option, and usually many more than one. There is always *something* you can do (or stop doing). Merely realizing alternatives do exist relieves stress and counteracts that desperate feeling you get whenever you believe you are trapped in a corner with nowhere to go.

The alternatives you find may not be perfect. They may not show results immediately or completely or magically alter your existence. And alternatives are not *all* you need to get unstuck or achieve your goals. However, learning to recognize all your options is a step. A step is movement, movement that can bring you closer to your chosen destination.

This barrier is also easier to tackle than most because specific, reliable tools and techniques can be used to search for alternatives, increase options, evaluate and prioritize them, and decide upon the best route to take. These tools and techniques have a proven positive track record. They are used every day by teachers and therapists. They work. You can make them work for you.

An Option for All Seasons

No matter where or why you are stuck, you always have *one* alternative. You can *ask for help*.

"No man is an island" is a phrase I'm sure you have heard. It is particularly true when applied to the *no alternatives* barrier. Ultimately you make your own choices and follow the path that is right for you. However, you do not have to grapple with each decision by yourself, nor do you have to travel your path alone. You can ask for help when you need it.

Unfortunately, people who are stuck and feeling lousy tend to isolate themselves. Think about Karen, who was described in Chapter One. She cannot maintain her weight loss. She thinks people judge her negatively because she is overweight and holes up in her house when her eating is out of control. She does not want to hear any advice, which she interprets as criticism. She wants to be left alone. So do alcoholics. So do abuse victims (and their abusers). So do people getting divorced, ending a relationship, or experiencing a great deal of stress. Just when they most need support, they push people away from them. They think they must solve their own problems and make decisions all by themselves. Yet what they need to do is ask for help.

Asking for help will not rob you of your dignity. It will not take away your independence or demonstrate that you are weak-willed or incompetent. Indeed, seeking advice prior to making a decision is a sign of levelheadedness and wisdom. Contrary to what you think when you are stuck and hurting, you are not the only person who has ever experienced that particular conflict, found yourself in a certain situation or decided to change without knowing where to begin. The fallacies in this line of thinking have been shown again and again.

Help comes in many forms. It can be professional, such as the help offered by a suicide prevention hotline or any other crisis intervention service listed in the telephone book. You can get into counseling with a trained psychiatrist, psychologist, or social worker, or find help by talking to friends, relatives, colleagues, or supervisors. Sometimes help can be found in books such as this one, inspirational tracts, or even biographies of people who have overcome adversity. Some of the very best help is offered by self-help groups (also listed in the phone book or "community calendar" sections of the newspaper). Groups such as Alcoholics Anonymous, Over-eaters Anonymous, and Al-Anon are the most well-known, but groups are available in almost every community for al-most any concern you can imagine.

You can ask for help at any time for any reason. How-ever, seeking help is particularly beneficial when you cannot see available alternatives or make decisions about the op-tions you do see. Searching for alternatives and evaluating options is easier with someone else's assistance and support. The "helper" may not always or immediately suggest alter-natives you like. However, they do have some distance from your problem and can be more objective about it. They will see the merits and drawbacks of an option before you do and may be able to shed light when all you see is darkness. At the very least, asking for help (and remaining open to the advice offered) points you in new directions and stimulates more productive thinking.

Begin to increase your alternatives by asking people what *they* would do or what *they* did when they faced similar conflicts. Read profiles of people you admire. You do not *have* to take anyone's advice. You do not *have* to follow in the footsteps of Lee Iacocca, Conrad Hilton, Shirley Mac-Laine, or anyone else. All you have to do is ask, read, listen, hear—and you will discover new options.

BRAINSTORMING

"The typical eye overlooks the ninety percent *good* in
any idea because of the ten percent *bad* that the
conventional eye never fails to see."
                                        —*Charles Kettering*

Charles Kettering's statement reminds me of every com-mittee ever assembled to tackle a problem or plan an activity. Without fail, dozens of ideas are proposed and immediately eliminated because someone instantaneously spots a flaw.

It never matters that the flaw is small and easy to correct. Conclusions are drawn prematurely and great ideas are passed over, leaving only mediocre ones.

On the other hand, you increase your alternatives when you suspend judgment during the idea-gathering stage, accumulate options, and evaluate them later. This process is called *brainstorming*.

People whose jobs require them to solve problems, make group decisions, plan for the future, or be creative are familiar with the brainstorming technique. Advertising teams commonly use it to generate ad campaign ideas. It can be seen at work in union/management meetings when ideas are needed to prevent a strike or in corporate board rooms when sales need to be increased. Therapists brainstorm with their clients; teachers brainstorm with their students; supervisors with their employees; generals with their staffs. Yet I am constantly amazed at how few people apply this proven technique to their own lives. There is no better way to increase alternatives.

To brainstorm, you turn down the volume on your inner critic and let the creative juices flow, freeing you to seek out any and all possibilities. Brainstorming asks you to identify, without evaluation, every conceivable alternative—no matter how wacky, wild, or improbable that alternative appears to be at first glance. Brainstorming can be employed to generate alternatives to any situation.

You can brainstorm:

- things to do on a Saturday night

- ways to make your job more exciting

- ways to better manage your time

- how to spend your vacation

- ways to improve a relationship

- ways to save money

- how to celebrate Thanksgiving

- things you want to accomplish in your life

- risks you want to take

- ways to make sure you stick to a diet or exercise program

- how family members can share household chores

Anytime you feel stuck and need alternatives—BRAIN-STORM!

Brainstorming can be done alone, but often it works best with other people. It is generally done in one sitting. However, if there is no time limit for resolving a problem, I like to spread my brainstorms over several sessions. Then I can take advantage of those brilliant ideas I get in between sessions while driving my car or taking a shower.

Brainstorming begins by clearly phrasing the problem or question at hand. Here are three examples:

"We have two weeks in August set aside for vacation. I want it to be a fun and worthwhile vacation for everyone. How can we have a vacation like that? Let's see how many vacation ideas we can come up with."

"All Rita and I do anymore is fight. It's getting so bad that I've been staying at work later and finding reasons to go places without her. I do love Rita and I want our relationship to work. I just don't know what to do anymore. What are my options?"

"My job is making me crazy. I am physically sick and emotionally drained because of it. I can't just quit, because I need the income. What other alternatives do I have?"

In all three examples the problem is identified and the task is clear—to discover as many alternatives as possible, *without* focusing on finding the one right and perfect solution. The person phrasing the question asks for a multitude of options, one or a combination of which will *later* be chosen as a step toward getting unstuck.

For brainstorming to work, the following rules *must* be followed:

1. NO CRITICISM. Do not judge or evaluate the alternatives at this point. Do not censor yourself in any way. Absolutely anything that comes to mind should be listed.

2. ENCOURAGE FREEWHEELING. Let those creative juices flow—the wilder the idea, the better. You can always eliminate the outrageous and trim your ideas down to size later on.

3. GO FOR QUANTITY. Make a long, long, long list. By generating lots and lots of ideas while brainstorming, you increase the probability of finding good, workable ideas when you go back over your list.

4. PIGGYBACK, EXPAND, COMBINE. Modify or spin off new ideas from old ones or combine previously listed options to create other alternatives that work.

GIVE IT A TRY

In Chapter Two you completed an Overall Wellness inventory. You examined ten aspects of daily living which contribute to your physical, emotional, intellectual, and spiritual well-being and identified those elements you personally felt needed improvement. If you are to actually improve those areas of your life, however, you will need alternatives, both as steps toward your ultimate goal and as guideposts for getting unstuck. It is easy enough to say "I'll improve my nutrition by going on a diet," but what sort of diet will you choose? Will it be a short-term low calorie diet for weight loss only, will you eliminate white sugar, processed flour, and fried foods or adopt a lifetime eating plan? How will you begin? How will you make sure you do not cheat? What will you do to keep the pounds from coming back? Will you go it alone?

You can instantly "decide" to exercise, but what form of exercise will you choose? When, where, and how often will you exercise? What can you do to make sure you stick to your program? What are your options?

If you want to better manage your time, how will you go about it? Are you aware of the many time-management tools and techniques? Have you considered which best fit your lifestyle?

Unless you ask those sorts of questions, you cannot *choose* the options that are right for you. To improve, increase, or change an aspect of overall wellness, you must first look for and list as many alternatives as possible. You must brainstorm.

To begin brainstorming:

1. CHOOSE an overall wellness area you have identified as a priority for change.

2. ASK YOURSELF—*How* can I change it? *What* can I do to have more, less, or something better in this area? *What* are my options?

3. Take out a sheet of paper, get a pencil, and ANSWER those questions by BRAINSTORMING alternatives.

4. REMEMBER— Anything goes. Be playful, zany, sarcastic, creative, or whatever it takes to make a long, long list. Go for QUANTITY not quality.

5. Try not to interrupt the flow of ideas by going back through the list to see if you already wrote down an idea or one like it. You can eliminate duplications later and variations are considered as separate options.

6. Ask for help if you need it. Explain the exercise to a friend, relative, coworker, your spouse, or your therapist. Ask them to help you generate alternatives. (Don't forget to explain the rules of brainstorming to them).

Larry's List

In Chapter Two, I introduced Larry, the Virginia Beach freelance photographer who completed the Overall Wellness inventory and selected several areas for improvement. One of his priorities was to find and nurture a love relationship. He knew that simply *wanting* a relationship was not enough to have one. He also knew that the first thing he had to do was stop isolating himself and start meeting women. This is his brainstorm list.

To meet a woman to have a relationship with I could:

- go to singles bars
- take some adult education courses
- join a singles group
- place personal ads
- answer personal ads
- sign up with a dating service
- ask friends to introduce me to single women
- ask relatives to introduce me to single women
- ask customers to introduce me to single women
- smile and say hello to women I see
- strike up conversations in the grocery store
- at the post office
- at the dry cleaners
- on the beach
- join a health club (since I need to exercise anyway)
- wear a sign saying I'm looking for a relationship

- write my number on restroom walls
- hang a "WANTED: A Relationship" poster around town
- join clubs/groups in areas that interest me
- get to know women who display things at craft shows
- be friendlier to women who stop to look at my photos
- go out more in general
- cut my hair
- tone up my body
- stop looking at the pavement when I walk places
- go on blind dates
- make a list of what I want in a woman (so I know her when I find her)
- go to workshops
- learn how to overcome shyness
- woo away my best friend's wife
- give up and become a monk
- talk to that lady I always see at the laundromat
- same for the woman who works at the bakery
- get to know other women I've noticed but never approached

Larry's list is something to behold. It is all the more impressive if you know that immediately prior to his brainstorming session, he had thought that "what I could do to meet women was limited to hanging out at singles bars or putting a classified ad in the personals section of the newspaper. Neither idea appealed to me. I never considered that some of the things I wanted to do anyway could also be social opportunities. The other thing I hadn't figured on was that I already knew women casually whom I could get to know better.

"You know it was a real relief to see the situation wasn't as hopeless as I thought," he continues. "I thought brainstorming was going to be a real pain too, like pulling teeth, but it wasn't. Actually, it was sort of fun."

Brainstorming *can* be fun. Very often you get a few good laughs about a situation you had previously seen as excruciatingly painful and completely hopeless. Brainstorming opens a door and lets ideas rush in. Brainstorming works. It is a surefire way to increase alternatives.

All options are not created equal, however. As Margaret, the woman who was overwhelmed by options when her job was eliminated, can tell you, having a plentiful supply of options is not enough to get you unstuck. Jack, who grasped at straws hoping to miraculously and immediately eliminate stress from his life, would agree that trying options just because you see them does not work either. Each option must be clearly and consciously evaluated or you will chase your tail trying to make a decision as Margaret did or waste a great deal of time and energy the way Jack did. To make your alternatives work for you, you must . . .

Narrow the Field

Use a combination of logic, gut feelings, and value judgments to evaluate and choose options from those you listed while brainstorming. As you can see from Larry's list and from your own, brainstorming leaves you with more alternatives than you can comfortably analyze in depth. You have to narrow the field.

To trim your brainstorm list to a manageable number of alternatives, you should rely primarily on "gut" instincts, using your intuition to weed out the options that just don't feel right for you. Therefore, immediately after brainstorming, prioritize each item on your list. This can be based on *general appeal* (what you most *want* to pursue); *practicality* (those options that are most doable); *immediacy* (options you could, with little difficulty, begin to pursue right away); or a combination of these criteria. Give each item on your brainstorm list an A, B, or C priority. Assign an A to items that have *high* appeal, practicality, and/or immediacy. Give a C to those that are low priority and B's to those that fall somewhere in the middle.

When you are stuck, unhappy, or unsure of yourself, it is all too easy to be indecisive, even after setting your priorities. To avoid this, try to assign *an equal number* of A, B, and C priorities. Thus, if there are twenty-four items on your list, eight should get A priority, eight should get B priority, and eight should get C priority. It may be a struggle to achieve such parity, but doing so is essential. So, take some time now to go over your brainstorm list and narrow the field by assigning A, B, and C priorities.

Carla's "A" List

"The brainstorming was really hard for me," says Carla about her attempt to find alternatives for her unsatisfying work situation. "In fact, other people came up with most of the ideas on my list. I was still being very negative when I tried to narrow the field. If I hadn't been forced to come up with A priorities, I wouldn't have any. Nothing would have gotten more than a B."

Reluctantly, Carla identified five very disparate A items from her list of fifteen alternatives. They were:

- quit my job immediately (worry later)
- take on more clients until I can afford to quit
- get a job with another agency

- pick a date to quit my job, take steps to advertise my practice, and line up consulting jobs in the meantime

- stick it out here until I can take early retirement

Now, having narrowed the field, you (and Carla) are ready to take a closer look at your A priorities. It is from these that you will choose an eventual course of action.

Evaluating Options

Although emotions and intuition come into play throughout your decision-making efforts, the evaluation of A priority alternatives requires the application of logic. Many variables can be considered when choices must be made. However, most logical analysis boils down to weighing the *positive* that can result from pursuing an option against the *negative* consequences it might produce.

Take out a separate sheet of paper for each of your A priority alternatives. Then, write the alternative across the top of the page and draw a line down the center. The left-hand column will be for POSSIBLE POSITIVE OUTCOMES and the right-hand column will be for POSSIBLE NEGATIVE CONSEQUENCES. Think of as many good results as you can and write them in the left-hand column. Do the same for negative consequences.

April stumbled and fell at this point in the decision-making process. She was so skilled and accustomed to finding fatal flaws that she drew a complete blank when asked to think of possible positive outcomes. She also countered other people's positive suggestions with matching negatives and ended up by throwing her pencil down in despair. "I told you there was nothing I could do," she moaned. "Maybe this stuff works for other people, but it isn't working for me."

I hope you do not allow yourself to fall into the same trap. Human beings *are* prone to negativity. As the earlier comment from Charles Kettering affirms, most of us zero in on what won't work and overlook what will. The tendency to find fatal flaws and reasons not to pursue perfectly good alternatives increases when self-esteem is low and being stuck has drained you mentally and emotionally. If you honestly want to get unstuck, push yourself to identify the positives. Take some time to make your own plus and minus list for each alternative. If you get stuck, call on an objective outside party to help add items to your plus column.

One of Carla's Options

"I did the pluses and minuses by myself first," Carla explains. "After that, I knew that my negative attitude was coloring my decisions, so I asked my therapist for some ideas, and then I went to a friend who had left the agency where I work and started her own business. Both women came up with good ideas, and I even came up with a few more pluses on my own once I got the hang of it."

Her analysis of the option to set a date to leave the agency and take steps to increase her private practice looked like this:

PLUSES

I would know there was an end in sight.

I would be forced to find referral sources, line up consulting jobs, get a brochure, business cards, etc., and come up with a budget for myself, (i.e., I could stop procrastinating).

If I did all those things, I wouldn't worry so much.

I would stop wasting so much time (and hating myself because of it).

My kids and my friends would stop rolling their eyes and walking away from me because of my constant complaining.

My private practice would benefit.

I wouldn't have to stay here forever.

I would feel more secure.

I would have a steady paycheck for a few more months.

MINUSES

I would have to put up with this job for a while more.

I still wouldn't know if my private practice would support me.

I'd have to give up the paycheck eventually.

Could I really work without the bureaucracy's telling me what to do?

What about health insurance and my retirement fund?

Might feel trapped if the date to quit came and I still wasn't comfortable with leaving.

Is this fair to my kids?

Carla took several weeks to complete her plus and minus lists. She asked for other people's opinions. Then she moved on to the next step:

Weighing the Consequences

The number of items in a column can be deceiving. Like alternatives, all consequences are not created equal. Some mean more to you than others, some will have a greater impact on your life than others, and some are just plain scarier than others. In essence, each consequence has its own weight or value. The next step you should take is to consciously, thoughtfully, assign weights to each consequence.

To do this, give each positive and negative consequence a numerical weight. I like to use a scale of numbers between one and five with fives assigned to consequences that matter the most. Really think hard before you assign a number. Ask yourself how much each item *really* matters and make sure fear and self-doubt are not getting in your way. Sometimes it helps to pretend there is nothing else to consider but that one consequence. If all other conditions were good, how much would that one factor influence you?

After each consequence has been given a numerical weight, review your entire list for each alternative. Cross off your list items that seem to cancel each other out. You can even add up the numbers in each column and divide by the number of items to derive total positive and negative values for each alternative. You will rarely need to go that far, however. By the time you rank consequences and eliminate items that cancel each other out, you will have a relatively clear picture of the viability of your alternative.

Carla's weighing of consequences looked like this:

PLUSES

I would know there was an end in sight. *5*

I would be forced to find referral sources, line up consulting jobs, get a brochure, business cards, etc., and come up with a budget for myself, (i.e., I could stop procrastinating). *4*

If I did all those things, I wouldn't worry so much. *1* (I'd worry anyway)

I would stop wasting so much time (and hating myself because of it). *5*

My kids and my friends would stop rolling their eyes and walking away from me because of my constant complaining. *5*

My private practice would benefit. *4*

I wouldn't have to stay here forever. *5*

I would feel more secure. *2* (no, I wouldn't)

I would have a steady paycheck for a few more months. *3*

MINUSES

I would have to put up with this job for a while more. *2*

I still wouldn't know if my private practice would support me. *4*

I'd have to give up the paycheck eventually. *5*

Could I really work without the bureaucracy's telling me what to do? *2* (this is my low self-esteem talking)

What about health insurance and my retirement fund? *5*

Might feel trapped if the date to quit came and I still wasn't comfortable with leaving. *2* (fear, just as good a chance I'll be thrilled!)

Is this fair to my kids? *1* (it isn't fair now)

Much to Carla's surprise, the possible positive outcomes of this alternative far outweighed the feared negative consequences. Such was not the case for other A priority options, such as hanging on at the agency until she could take early retirement or looking for a job with another agency. By listing and evaluating positive and negative consequences, Carla began to see a direction she could go. If you have been taking the steps described here, you too should see at least one alternative to the way things are, and at least one path clear for travel toward your goals and aspirations. Now, it is time to:

Make a Choice

Ah, the moment of truth has arrived. Even though you have searched for alternatives, used your instincts to narrow the field, racked your brain (and other people's too) to find the negative and positive consequences, weighed and measured and put a great deal of careful, clear thinking into the decision-making effort, you are once again possessed by the fear of choosing. Your hands shake. Your lower lip quivers. Your mouth is dry. Your heart pounds and your blood pressure rises. What if you make the wrong choice? Worse yet, no matter what you choose you are going to lose that good old fallback line—"I have no choice. There is nothing I can do." You might have to *do* something. What if what you choose to do does not work?

I'll deal with that last question in a moment. First, summon up some courage and rank each of your options. The most acceptable alternative should get a number one. Give the next most acceptable a two, and so on until you have given each option a different descending rank. By ordering each option rather than choosing one and discarding the rest, you leave yourself some breathing room. The number one ranked option will be the one you choose to pursue *at this time*. Yet, keep in mind that the other options remain available to you. You are not losing anything—except your unwanted "stuck" status.

You see, no decision has to be final. It is exactly this thought of finality that brings up all that anxiety and fear. If you make a choice, give it a chance to work. If it doesn't, you can always try the next option on your list or make another choice. The first alternative you choose may not turn out to be the one and only perfect answer. After all, there is more than one route to any destination.

What's more, for most of us one alternative is not all we will need. Our journey to the lives we desire and deserve will require many steps and many decisions. The choice you make now is merely the first step in the right direction. But don't forget, if you are stuck, any step in the right direction is a milestone.

Carla, who chose to set a date to quit her job and to spend the interim time preparing for a successful private practice, will still have to choose to actually quit her job when the target date arrives. She will have to decide whether to use her retirement fund to tide her over during the first months of self-employment or leave it in the bank to accrue interest. She will have to make choices about cutting living expenses, what to charge clients, how to use her time when she is her own boss, and how long to wait before deciding whether self-employment works for her or not. Yet, even with all these uncertainties ahead of her, Carla feels better because she has made that first choice and taken that first step.

"Just to know there's *something* I can do makes me feel

better," she says. "Things don't look so bleak. I have a goal to work for. I'm not just getting by. I'm going for something. I'm still scared and I'm still worried about making ends meet, but I don't feel as helpless or as trapped."

Jack, the accountant with the stress problem, practically had to be tied to a chair and forced to work through these strategies. But when he did, he discovered that many of the options he had already tried would have to be tried again, this time in some sort of logical order. He also realized that he should not expect that his stress would disappear overnight, and that he must give the option he had chosen time to work. "I'm going to have to run through all my A alternatives eventually," he says. "But I can do them one step at a time. And I'm going to think about them before I do them this time, too."

Searching for all their alternatives and taking the decision-making steps described in this chapter worked well for Carla, Jack, and Larry, and they were able to make healthy choices from viable options. You also now have the opportunity to generate alternatives and make choices. Will you?

If your answer is YES, then you can see the light at the end of the tunnel and begin to map your route toward your goals and aspirations. You may still have trouble getting started on that journey, and you will certainly encounter other barriers along your way. The following chapters describe those barriers, which I'll help you recognize and dismantle. But keep in mind that if you have begun to dismantle the NO ALTERNATIVES barrier, you have already taken a giant step toward getting unstuck.

If your answer is NO, if somewhere along the line you become queasy and confused, if you are unable to list alternatives or evaluate them, chances are you have come upon another barrier already. Perhaps it's that old low self-esteem throwing up a smoke screen in front of you, or one of the other barriers stands in your way. It might be barrier number three—the subject of the next chapter—NOT KNOWING WHAT YOU REALLY WANT.

5

███████████████████████████████

Change and Values

The other day I spent a pleasant afternoon with Mary, Peter, and Betsy. When dinnertime rolled around, we decided to order pizza. Mary went into the kitchen to boil water for tea and find the telephone number of a nearby pizza parlor.

By the time she returned to the den, I was engrossed in Peter's stories and snapshots of last summer's trip to the British Isles, and Betsy was reading a magazine article and working on a self-test from the magazine to determine if her boyfriend is as romantic as she is. Mary asked us what toppings we wanted on the pizza. Distracted, we answered quickly and barely looked up from the photo albums and magazine.

Peter said, "Don't ask me. I eat anything."

Enthralled by a breathtaking photograph of an English castle, I absentmindedly agreed, "I don't know. Whatever everybody else wants, I guess."

Betsy, too, claimed to have no preference. "Doesn't matter to me," she mumbled. "You decide."

We all went back to what we were doing. Left to her

own resources and knowing exactly what she likes on a pizza, Mary ordered two large pies with extra cheese, peppers, mushrooms, and sausage. Ravenously hungry when the pizzas finally arrived, we opened the boxes the moment Mary set them on the table. Mouths watering, we grabbed slices of piping hot pizza only to have our delight turn to disappointment.

Betsy, a vegetarian, scorched her fingers while removing bits of sausage from each slice before eating it. Concerned about cholesterol, I was dismayed to see all that extra cheese oozing grease. And it turned out that Peter hates mushrooms and peppers.

Because Peter, Betsy, and I did not consider, choose, or communicate what we actually wanted on our pizza, we got stuck with a pizza we did not like. We ate it anyway. Normally, pizza toppings are of no great significance. They certainly won't alter the course of our lives. Yet this simple story makes a powerful point.

UNLESS YOU THINK ABOUT, CHOOSE, SAY, AND DO WHAT YOU *REALLY* WANT, YOU RISK GETTING STUCK WITH A LIFE OR CIRCUMSTANCES YOU DO NOT DESIRE.

Not knowing what you *really* want is the third barrier to change. It obstructs your path whenever you:

1. make decisions without giving careful consideration to your options and their possible short- and long-term consequences.

2. make choices based on what "everybody" does, what you assume you *should* do, or because you feel guilty or inadequate.

3. give other people's preferences priority over your own or believe you do not deserve to get what you want and therefore fail to communicate your needs or speak up for yourself.

4. behave impulsively, indecisively, rebelliously, or waver back and forth.

HOW THIS BARRIER GOT YOU
STUCK IN THE FIRST PLACE

Many of the people described earlier in this book got stuck because they did not know what they really wanted. They chose the easiest, quickest, most obvious route, and it took them someplace other than where they wanted to be.

Remember the burned-out social worker, Carla? She is stuck working for a social service agency she cannot wait to leave. She had originally signed on with the agency because they were the first to offer her part-time work with children. She asked no further questions and immediately stopped exploring other options.

When Carla wanted to advance professionally and financially, she once again jumped the gun. Instead of identifying the various means to the end she desired, she automatically chose to become a supervisor within the same agency. She did not *really* want to stop working directly with children or get buried under mountains of paperwork, but that is what happened.

"At the time, it seemed like the way to go," Carla says today. "If I knew then what I know now, I would have done things differently. But to tell you the truth, I didn't give it much thought at all."

Neither did Janet, the workaholic therapist whose lifeline net in Chapter Two revealed that her days are overflowing with activities she believed she *had* to do. She describes herself as overworked and overwhelmed. She is drowning, with no time for the fun, leisure activities or the relaxation she truly desires and deserves.

"I just said yes to everything that came my way," Janet explains. "I assumed that more was better, that busy was happy, that successful people worked at success twenty-four hours a day. Those were the ideas I was raised with and I never questioned them. I honestly thought that if I slowed down, I would lose everything. You can see where those ideas got me. I'm so overcommitted that I can't get a moment's peace."

Lisa, the office supply sales representative introduced in Chapter Two, says, "I wanted to be a team player and I thought that meant going along with the program even if I didn't like it. If I was unhappy, it was my own fault. I should try harder to please people. If they brought in someone else to be sales manager, then I must not have been good enough. Who was I to question my superiors? If my opinion was worth anything, they would have asked for it."

Thinking along these lines, Lisa put up with whatever happened in the company. She did not think she was good enough to make her own decisions and thus drastically reduced her chances of getting anything she *really* wanted.

You are stuck today because of decisions you made in the past without careful consideration, and by neglecting to use your power to say and act upon what *you* really wanted. Like Carla, you may look back now and wish you had done things differently or made different choices. Like Lisa, you may have gone along with the crowd. Now you may hardly remember why or when you first got on this roller coaster ride. Like Janet, today you are paying the price for yesterday's choices. Yet, if you reviewed those choices with an open mind, you would see they had little to do with what you genuinely wanted and a great deal to do with what you thought you ought to do "under the circumstances."

Perhaps you were busy with other activities and the demands of daily living and did not take the time to consider your alternatives. It was more expedient to let someone else decide or simpler to latch onto the first available option (perhaps one that someone else suggested). At the time, you did not think that particular decision would make much difference over the long haul. Or the situation seemed so overwhelming that you gratefully headed for any port in the storm. Perhaps you can see that this barrier is also a symptom of barrier number two—the inability to recognize the alternatives available to you.

Maybe you made choices when your self-esteem was low. Already believing you did not deserve much in this life, you were more than willing to go along with the crowd. You figured that choices made by someone you saw as smarter, more creative, more assertive, or more powerful than you had to be better than the ones you could make. And because of that same low self-esteem, you believed that what someone else wanted had to be more important than what you wanted. But denying your own desires can only make you feel even more miserable and powerless. Not knowing what you want becomes a more difficult barrier to dismantle when combined with low self-esteem.

In the poem "The Road Not Taken," Robert Frost describes two roads that "diverge in a yellow wood." Frost took the road less traveled. Many of you took the other road, turning onto it automatically. You never wondered if it was the right road for you. After all, if so many other people had walked that way before you, it must be the way you too should go.

Sometimes the main thoroughfare ridden by the nameless, faceless majority took you where you did indeed want to go. More often, however, it led to another fork in the road where, once again, you went the way everyone else was going or in the direction you somehow came to believe you should go. If you are stuck now, chances are you took a few turns too many based on someone else's values instead of your own.

HOW NOT KNOWING WHAT YOU REALLY WANT SABOTAGES CHANGE EFFORTS

In today's rapidly and constantly changing world, not considering, choosing, or doing what you definitely want is a malady shared by most people.

Consider the case of the Cabbage Patch doll. Recently, many Christmas shoppers worked themselves into a frenzy in pursuit of a bundle of cloth-covered foam stuffing. At five in the morning, parents, grandparents, aunts, and uncles stood on line in front of department stores that would not open their doors until ten A.M. Once inside, they literally clawed their way through crowds of hysterical and equally determined consumers who had to get their hands on one of a limited supply of Cabbage Patch dolls. Fights broke out. People fell to the floor, and other people stepped over and sometimes on top of them. As they left the stores empty-handed, those unable to snag a doll for their children shed tears of despair.

Was this really how people wanted to spend their time and money during a holiday season intended to foster joy and goodwill? Did a doll reflect their true feelings and beliefs about Christmas? Would a doll actually tell their children how much they were loved and cherished? Did anyone stop to ask these questions? Or was the great Cabbage Patch caper the result of too little thought and too many media and Madison Avenue messages telling people that the dolls were the hot item for Christmas giving? Had they simply been convinced that children who did not have Cabbage Patch dolls would be ostracized by their peers and trau-matized for life?

Cabbage Patch capers, Transformer robot search-and-buy missions, and Rambo worship, as well as other rapidly passing and largely interchangeable passions, are relatively modern phenomena. We have become a more mobile pop-ulation and come into contact with more ideas from more sources in a few years than our ancestors did in a whole lifetime. We are influenced by more people and bombarded by media messages. As a result, there are so many possi-bilities and so many versions of the good life—so many dif-ferent ways we are *supposed* to be.

Always trying to live up to the standards put before you by parents, friends, teachers, peers, churches, and the media ultimately blocks change. You simply cannot please all of these people all of the time. When the messages received from various sources conflict—as they often do—you become confused. With so many versions of what you *should* do, how do you decide what you *will* do? All but lost and forgotten is the notion of what you might actually *want* to do.

What happens when you choose your path primarily because others have traveled it before you? What happens when you attempt to change primarily because someone else insists you should? To start with, you will not get what *you* actually want. In most instances, neither will you achieve the goal "they" convinced you to pursue. Efforts to change undertaken to satisfy someone else, options pursued because you feel obligated or guilty, and goals set so you can "keep up with the Joneses" are those most often and most quickly abandoned.

When Karen was introduced in Chapter One, she was back at square one and facing another tortuous effort to lose weight. Although she was not aware of it yet, the reasons why she chose to lose weight in the past contributed to her going up and down the scale like a yo-yo. She began all previous diets because her parents nagged and berated her, her lovers teased and sometimes humiliated her, pictures of models in fashion magazines frustrated her, or she hoped to impress former classmates at her high school reunion or an ex-boyfriend when she saw him at her cousin's wedding.

Hoping to please herself by pleasing other people did not keep Karen on track. Obesity and weight-loss research shows that dieting and maintenance of a goal weight are less likely to succeed when prompted by anything other than the dieter's sincere, inner desire to change. Karen will not achieve her goal until staying thinner is what *she* genuinely wants for her own happiness and well-being.

Consider, too, the teenage boy who performs poorly in school. He does not complete homework assignments. He daydreams during classes. He is thought to be lazy, unmotivated, and possibly learning disabled since he has such a short attention span for schoolwork. Yet this same young man spends eight uninterrupted hours each Saturday rebuilding the engine of his car (which he loves dearly and had religiously saved money to buy). When it comes to his car, he reads technical material proficiently, grasps complex ideas, and completely focuses his attention for hours at a stretch. Is this the same lazy, unmotivated, learning disabled fellow his teachers see each Monday morning? He inhabits the same body. Whether or not his teachers approve, he values engine mechanics more than English literature or ancient history. He accomplishes what he really wants to do.

With any goal or aspiration you will stick with the program you personally want to pursue, finding the time, energy, and resources to achieve what you honestly want to achieve. When you've made a personal commitment, you dismantle the barriers you find on the path you sincerely want to travel.

On the other hand, when you do not know what you clearly want, when those "should" and "ought to" messages obscure your personal vision, and when you easily, quickly choose the path of least resistance or the one everyone else travels, you get lost and you get stuck. You lack staying power. You easily find reasons to abandon the "self-improvement nonsense" that was someone else's idea instead of your own. You dissipate your energy rebelling against know-it-all authorities or scatter yourself by trying to conform to and comply with each new suggestion you are given. Wishy-washy, listless, and confused, you take one detour after another.

HOW NOT KNOWING WHAT YOU REALLY WANT
KEEPS YOU FROM GETTING UNSTUCK

This barrier does more than get you stuck. It does more than undermine your efforts to change. Abdicating your power to choose and constantly turning to others for the answers to your life's questions robs you of the ability to look for and find what you *really* want.

"All my life, other people came first," says Larraine, the Long Island mother of three who faced the conflict and confusion of no longer being needed as a full-time wife and parent. "When I was a kid, I lived to please my parents. Then I got married and lived to please my husband. Then I had children. Everyone knows a good mother puts her children's needs first, and I was a very good mother."

Then Larraine's children went off to college, her husband turned his full attention to his new business, and her parents had long since stopped influencing Larraine's daily living. In her early forties, Larraine had many years left to do what she really wanted to do, only she did not know what that was or how to find out.

"For the first time in my life I had no one to please but myself, and I didn't know how to do that. Everyone tells you what a good daughter should do and a good wife and a good mother. But no one tells you what you're supposed to do once your family doesn't need you anymore. Where was I supposed to go from there? What was I supposed to do with my life?"

Larraine's dilemma illustrates a particularly dangerous feature of the third barrier to getting unstuck. Having developed a habit of not doing what you really want, the next time you reach a fork in the road or a crisis point in your life, you do not know *how* to choose a new direction for yourself. Like the scarecrow from *The Wizard of Oz,* you dangle from a pole pointing first one way, then another, then back the other way again. All roads lead somewhere. But from your present vantage point all roads look the same.

You feel a need for change, but you do not know how to change. You wonder what you *should* do. You wish someone would tell you what to do. You ask for advice and discover people have plenty to say. Unfortunately, their opinions about what you ought to do conflict and leave you confused, ambivalent, befuddled, frustrated, and depressed. In such a state, is it any wonder you can't get unstuck?

But I Do Know What I Want

I suspect some of you have been reading this chapter and thinking barrier number three does not apply to you. After all, you do know what you want. You want to be happier or healthier; more successful or more attractive. You want to get out of a rotten marriage or into a better profession. You want to start exercising regularly or stop smoking. Furthermore, you are absolutely, positively sure you know what you want. Everyone I interviewed for this book felt the same way.

Think about Jack, the accountant who wants to reduce the stress in his life and ward off a full-fledged nervous breakdown. He impulsively tries every possible panacea but finds no lasting relief. Never once does he identify the sources of his stress, connect cause, effect, and cure, or evaluate any action's true potential to help him. He is not lying when he says he wants to feel better. But he does not stick to any one effort or get what he wants because he DOES NOT CONSIDER HIS ALTERNATIVES OR THINK ABOUT HIS CHOICES.

Likewise, Karen's every weight-loss effort ends in failure. She wants to lose weight and not gain it back, but why does she want that? She diets to please or impress other people and to avoid nagging and criticism. She frequently resents having to diet and often wishes people could just accept her for the way she is. Pressured to change, her valiant efforts always lead her back to square one. She has NEVER CHOSEN FREELY.

What about Lisa, whose self-esteem plummeted thanks to her sales job and more precisely because she failed to speak up for herself or her beliefs? She never got the respect and responsibility she wanted. In fact, with each passing day her dissatisfaction grew. Because, she DID NOT COMMU-NICATE HER DESIRES or protest her unfair treatment.

Finally there is Jacob, the heart attack survivor de-scribed in Chapter Two. He wanted to live. It was what he wanted long before he was admitted to the coronary care unit. He knew smoking, poor eating habits, and his lifestyle were dangerous to his health. He knew his alternatives and the consequences, often said he would change. Yet he did nothing differently and suffered a heart attack that nearly killed him. Jacob TOOK NO ACTION.

Jack, Karen, Lisa, and Jacob knew what they wanted, but only in a general way.

If you truly want something, you:

1. give it careful thought and consideration
2. choose it freely
3. communicate it to other people
4. put it into action

With these criteria in mind, you can see that *saying* you know what you want is different than *really knowing* what you want. If you skip a step or rush blindly after the majority, you get stuck.

But Does Knowing What I Want Really Change Anything?

After a lecture she attended, one of my colleagues chal-lenged me with the following scenario.

"Let's say I *really* want to sing like Ella Fitzgerald," my colleague began. "I want to perform in smoky bars and sold-out concert halls and read reviews about how my voice made people cry with ecstasy. But I can't carry a tune, never have been able to carry a tune, and never will be able to carry a tune. What I really want doesn't make one bit of difference, does it? If I can't sing, I can't sing, and all the desire in the world won't change that."

She was absolutely right, of course. Similarly, if you are

a five-foot-four-inch-tall forty-year-old, you will never be a center with the Boston Celtics basketball team—no matter how much you want that. If, at age thirty-two, you have never taken a dance lesson, you will not, in this lifetime, dance the lead in *Swan Lake* for the American Ballet Theater. For one thing, each of us has certain tangible and inalterable limitations. Furthermore, simply wanting something does not guarantee you will get it. Still, if you really want to sing, you can sing your little heart out at church services, rock concerts, or in the shower. You can play basketball twice a week at the YMCA. You can learn to dance, then dance at discos and parties and dance-school recitals.

Applying the four criteria for knowing what you truly want eliminates fantasies, wild-goose chases, and efforts doomed to fail. You become realistic as well as clear about what you want. Sometimes that means changing a goal or trimming a fantasy down to size. In my life, however, I have met more people who underestimated themselves than people who aimed too high. The same four criteria may help you discover you actually can do more than you previously believed you could.

BARRIER DISMANTLER #3: CLARIFYING VALUES

A Question of Values

It is time to discover what *you* really want. When I ask you what you *really* want, I am, in fact, asking what you value.

Values are guides for daily living that influence your thoughts, feelings, words, and deeds. They shape your personality and give direction to what would otherwise be an aimless, purposeless life. Your values are reflected in your goals, hopes, dreams, attitudes, interests, opinions, convictions, and behavior as well as in your problems and worries.

Traditionally, values are thought of as absolutes. If asked

to name values, you might offer words such as "honesty," "cleanliness," "freedom," "harmony," "thrift," or "brotherly love." You might recite mottos such as "Cleanliness is next to Godliness"; "A penny saved is a penny earned"; or "It is better to give than to receive." The universal principles you embraced as values were considered "good," while those you rejected were labeled "bad" or "evil."

But on a day-to-day basis, values are more difficult to name with a single word or simple saying. Values come into play every minute of every day and every time you make a decision. They are found in your answers to questions about what you *really* want.

Do you really want a hot fudge sundae with a double dip of walnut deluxe delight ice cream? Do you seriously desire higher wages for the work you do? Do you truly want to quit smoking, drinking, gambling, overeating, or compulsively spending? What about going back to school, changing careers, getting married, staying single, having children, or taking two days to a prepare a meal your family will wolf down during halftime of the Thanksgiving Day football game?

When you know what you value, such questions are easier to answer. Your course of action is clearer to you. You are more likely to follow through with plans and persevere until you reach your destination.

But I Do Have Values!

At this point in any lecture that I give about values, someone in the audience invariably asks, "Are you trying to tell me I don't have values?"

The question may be asked innocently or indignantly. The person may be slightly confused or downright angry. After all, he or she was raised to know right from wrong, and I seem to be attacking that upbringing and belief system. I do not know if you feel similarly attacked, but let me take a moment to clear up any confusion.

EVERYONE HAS VALUES. Some people simply understand their values more clearly than others—they realize values affect all aspects of their lives. Seeing the connection between values and actions, they act consistently and with commitment. This does not mean, however, that they intrinsically are better people.

People who know and live by their values took steps to consciously develop and clarify those values. You can take the same steps and they will pay off in the same ways. You will end up knowing what you *really* want, and you will improve your chances of getting it.

I do not guarantee that clarifying values will get you everything you want or remove every obstacle from the road you travel. However, from personal experience and years of observation, I can honestly say that values clarification will help you make self-enhancing rather than self-defeating decisions, gain a realistic perspective on your life, and shape a vision of the way your life can be in the future. It helps you go one step further to committing yourself to the course of action you have chosen.

VALUES CLARIFICATION

Clear values—those that make daily living both personally satisfying and socially constructive—are conscientiously and freely chosen; prized and cherished; and acted upon consistently. Choice, pride, and action, the three levels of valuing, are achieved by using seven guidelines for recognizing what you value.

Choice

All three steps under this heading were discussed in detail already. Earlier, in Chapter Four, I talked about searching for alternatives and considering consequences. And I've already discussed the impact and importance of free choice in the first half of this chapter. The three guidelines for making choices are recapped below.

You choose what you value from the available alternatives. Obviously, you cannot know or live by your values if you are blind to your alternatives or trapped by any other form of barrier number two. You must search for and understand your options *before* you make a choice, or you risk running full steam ahead into a brick wall. A valuable choice is made only after you explore all the avenues open to you.

You choose what you value after considering the consequences. Simply stated, you make a valuable choice by determining both what you might get and what you might lose by pursuing an alternative. You must also evaluate the true potential of the option to lead you to the life you truly desire and to resolve the conflicts and confusions you are experiencing. It is also time to think about whether a certain course of action could hurt the people around you or get you stuck again in the near future. And of course, at this stage you should also examine your personal strengths and limitations.

Freely choose what is valuable. A free choice is made without outside pressure or coercion; it is not based on a reward you expect someone else to give you or a punishment you hope to avoid. What other people might say or do is never a primary concern when you make a free choice. *You* are the one who must live with the choice.

Pride

Pride, commitment, and communication come into play with the next two valuing steps.

You prize and cherish what you value. A valuable choice lets you feel good about yourself and gives you a sense of accomplishment and self-worth. You feel proud of what you *really* want. Values are cherished. You are reluctant to part with them. At times you are willing to give up something else to keep what you truly value.

Unproductive, unfulfilling, or self-destructive pursuits are not prized and cherished. Automatically and habitually undertaking them, you do not feel proud of your behavior before, during, or after the fact when that behavior is not valued.

For instance, how do you feel about yourself when you wake up next to someone you met for the first time the night before—someone whose last name you do not know, someone you have no desire to know better? Have you felt this way before? Do you honestly want to feel this way again? Are you making choices you prize and cherish?

What about the Twinkies you often eat in your car on the way home from work; the overflowing ashtrays and stale cigarette smell that greet you when you awaken each morning; the money you spend on trendy Christmas toys that lie broken and abandoned by New Year's Day? You only prize and cherish what you *really* want. When values are involved, nothing can steer you off your course.

You publicly affirm what you value. When you truly value a choice or goal, you are ready and willing to talk about it. You admit your values when asked about them in public and voluntarily share them with family, friends, and acquaintances. You express treasured opinions, communicate important feelings, and proudly acknowledge valued accomplishments.

On the other hand, you are less anxious to speak out about matters you do not honestly value. You feel embarrassed, ashamed, or guilty about them. They are secrets or topics you avoid when conversation turns to them. You are not about to publicly affirm your penchant for eating Twinkies in your car. In fact, each time you leave your car at the parking garage, you pray the attendant will not notice the wrappers you shoved under the driver's seat.

Sometimes you will loudly defend actions you do not actually value. Defending a practice is not the same as affirming it. When nagged about smoking, you may claim your habit is no more risky than crossing a street where a truck might hit you. While you may offer these excuses to defend yourself, you probably wouldn't come right out and proclaim your loyalty to practices you are not proud of. For example, would you wear a button proclaiming "I smoke and I'm proud of it"? Would you tell a friend, "You should try cigarettes. They're terrific"?

Of course, public affirmations can be overdone—as anyone who encounters the newly reformed or converted can tell you. Consider others' feelings and use discretion when communicating what you value. As much as you may value parenthood, for instance, it is just plain insensitive to flash your baby pictures and gush about the joys of motherhood while dining with a couple who desperately want children but cannot conceive. Shouting your values from a rooftop is not always necessary or appropriate. However, if you feel proud about what you genuinely want and truly value, you will be willing to say so.

Action

Values must be translated into action and acted upon consistently.

A value prompts you to *take action*. You do something to get and keep what you sincerely desire. The choice you make, the pride you feel, and the words you speak become meaningful when put into action. It is then that you can move beyond fantasy and take steps to get what you want.

When you value parenthood, for example, you choose to have children. Proud of your children, you are more than willing to talk about them. Truly valuing parenthood, you go further. You act upon your value by learning and then doing what effective parents do, and you act in ways that are loving and advocate growth for all concerned. You offer guidance and discipline, encourage communication, and offer a secure, stable home. You make certain sacrifices. Your *behavior* is visible proof of what you value.

Similarly, if you value health, you take action to get and stay healthy as well as give up behaviors that are detrimental to your health. If you value learning, you continue throughout your life to take courses, read books, attend lectures, have thought-provoking conversations, and so forth. In *doing*, you are able to express and live by your values.

Furthermore, you *act consistently and repeatedly* for something you value. You make a commitment and you persevere. What you do one day, you also do the next. At the first sign of trouble, you do not turn back or give up your value. You rarely slide back to square one. Flitting from one project to another, breaking promises, and abandoning efforts to change soon after you begin are signs of *not* knowing what you actually want.

This last valuing step is the true acid test. If you act upon your beliefs again and again, you indeed will be living the life you honestly want to lead.

But I'll Never Be Able to Do All That!

By now you must think clarifying and living by your values is an impossibly tall order. It is hard work—and a lifelong process. I have yet to meet anyone who has achieved perfection when it comes to knowing and doing what they *really* want. But then, perfection is not the goal. The goal is to make progress.

You will not *always* know exactly what you want, but using these guidelines can help you know more clearly and more often what is valuable to you. You will never attain perfect clarity or be perfectly consistent, but you can be more decisive than you are now. Your life *can* have more purpose and more zest.

Working to understand and live by your values is a process that never ends. Throughout your life you will have to make choices and live with them. As a wise traveler on life's journey, you likewise will continue to strive to discover what is truly important to you. See the bibliography on page 291 for a recommended list of books that will guide you during your quest for clearer values.

You Can Start Today

Here are two values clarification strategies to do right now that will help you begin to see what is truly important to you. With a somewhat clearer perspective on your life you will be better able to tackle the remaining barriers to change. The *values grid* puts past and present efforts to change into a valuing framework, while the *planning board* lets you describe and rank what you are actually looking for in various areas of your life.

THE VALUES GRID

How are the valuing principles really working in your life? The values grid strategy helps you answer that question and identifies ways to ensure that future changes you make will reflect what you *really* want.

On a lined sheet of paper, draw a grid like the one pictured on the next page:

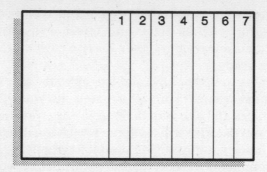

Think of six efforts to change that you have attempted in the past. Any sort of change will do. The change could involve habits you wanted to break such as nail biting or cigarette smoking; problems you tried to solve such as getting out of an abusive relationship or improving communication with your rebellious teenager; self-improvement measures such as exercising regularly or learning to speak a foreign language; or major life changes such as getting married or returning to the work force. *Three of the efforts you choose should be ones that succeeded, and three should be efforts that did not.* List all six in the wide first column of the grid.

Each narrow column has a number that corresponds to a values step listed below. Each step is followed by one or more questions. Think about those questions and answer them as honestly as possible. If your answer to each question is yes, and you did indeed complete that values step during your effort to change, check the appropriate column. If your answer is no and you did not complete the step, leave that column blank. Do this for each step and each change.

1. I CHOSE FROM THE AVAILABLE ALTERNATIVES. Did you search for alternatives and look for all open avenues before you chose a course of action?

2. I CHOSE AFTER CONSIDERING THE CONSE-QUENCES. Did you list and weigh the potential benefits as well as what, if anything, you stood to lose? Did you ask yourself if the option would get you where you wanted to go without hurting someone or getting you stuck again in the future? Did you take your strengths and limitations into consideration?

3. I CHOSE FREELY. Did you choose the route that was best for you? Did you make the choice without feeling pressured or coerced, without expecting a reward or hoping to avoid a punishment? Did you think for yourself?

4. I PRIZED AND CHERISHED MY CHOICE. Were you proud of what you did? When challenged, were you willing to fight for the change rather than readily abandon it?

5. I PUBLICLY AFFIRMED MY CHOICE. Did you express your feelings about your effort? If you did not have the actual opportunity, would you have been willing to do so?

6. I TOOK ACTION. Did you do what you set out to do? Did you translate your choice or goal into action?

7. I ACTED CONSISTENTLY AND REPEATEDLY. Did you stick to your plan? Did you persevere despite adversity? Did you take action often enough and with enough regularity to form a pattern? Did you keep going until you reached your destination? Are you still acting upon those values today?

The columns you check will form a noticeable pattern and help you answer the following questions about your past change efforts:

... How did your successes differ from your failures?
... How did what you really wanted contribute to your past successes?
... How did *not* knowing contribute to your past failures?
... Which steps seem to give you the most trouble? Why?
... Specifically, what will you do differently the next time you try to change?

Janet, the therapist who needs more time for fun and relaxation, made several discoveries. "It came as no surprise that my freely chosen column was completely blank," Janet reveals. "Even my successes weren't my idea. I guess I just followed the right person's advice those times.

"A funny thing happened when I got to the prize and cherish column. I checked it for my successes, but I found I wasn't as proud as I might have been. I wanted to say I was lucky or give someone else the credit for the success. Of course, I wasn't at all proud of my failures. I wanted to forget them and not talk about them.

"The real clinchers were the action steps. I acted when I succeeded and I'm still doing those things. But I didn't follow through on my failures, and I distinctly remember when I gave up that I was feeling pressured and angry because it wasn't what I had wanted in the first place."

Your discoveries may be similar to or different from Janet's. However, you no doubt will see that you completed more and perhaps all of the valuing steps when you succeeded and few if any when you failed. But what about future changes? How can the values grid help you get unstuck this time? Let's look at some of the changes you want to make in the future. Think back to Chapter Two and the lifeline strategy. As part of the strategy, you listed a number of things you want to do in your lifetime. Choose three of these wishes and list them several lines below the other items already on your grid. Now ask and—as honestly as possible—answer the following questions.

1. Do I need to consider more alternatives? Could there be something along the same lines that I might want *more* than the wish I listed? Do I want to give the option more thought?
IF YOU ANSWERED YES, DRAW AN "X" IN COLUMN 1.

2. Do I need to examine more closely the consequences of achieving this wish? Do I need to assess my ability real-

istically to attain this goal? Am I aiming too high or too low?
Have I overlooked anything about this wish?
IF YOU ANSWERED YES, DRAW AN "X" IN COLUMN 2.

3. Do I want this for myself or am I trying to please
someone else? Is this something I think I *should* do, and do
I resent having to do it? Will I be happy about this wish even
if no one else is?
IF YOU DO NOT KNOW, DRAW AN "X" IN COLUMN 3.

4. If I accomplished this, would I feel proud? Would I
be happy about what I'd be doing to reach my goal? Is this
important enough to me to put time, energy, and emotion
into it? Would I fight to do it?
IF YOU ANSWERED NO, DRAW AN "X" IN COLUMN 4.

5. Do I plan to keep what I'm doing a secret? Do I feel
ashamed or embarrassed by my choice? Have I thought about
not saying anything because other people won't understand
or agree with what I'm doing?
IF YOU ANSWERED YES, DRAW AN "X" IN COLUMN 5.

6. Can this desire be translated into action? Will I do
what I set out to do? Am I sure this isn't a pipe dream?
IF YOU ANSWERED NO, DRAW AN "X" IN COLUMN 6.

7. Is this going to be something else I start but do not
finish? Will I lose my resolve if I do not see immediate results? Will I give up if the going gets tough? Could something
else come along to distract me? Will I then abandon this
plan?
IF YOU ANSWERED YES, DRAW AN "X" IN COLUMN 7.

If you are to get what you want, you will have to do some
work on the steps marked with an X. You should be able to
look at your grid and make a list of things to do before
attempting that particular change effort. Ask yourself the

same questions for any goal or aspiration you hope to reach. If you filled out the grid honestly, you will better understand what you really want and act accordingly.

Lisa, the office supply sales representative, always said she wanted to earn a college degree. Her values grid helped her see why she never took the steps necessary to reach her goal. "I don't know if this was what was supposed to happen," she begins, "but I found out I wanted something different than I thought. See, I used to think getting a college degree would get me a better job and make people on the job respect me. It was one of the things I thought could solve all my work problems.

"But when I *really* thought about going back to college, it just turned my stomach. The idea of taking sales and marketing courses so professors could tell me things I had already learned through experience definitely did not appeal to me—so I didn't go, not even when my boss offered to give me time off to attend classes.

"When I did the values grid, it suddenly dawned on me that I really did want to finish college. I just didn't want a degree in marketing. Maybe I'll take communications or business management. I have to look at my options. But I do know, if I go to college, it will be to learn what I want to learn."

Lisa might have reached the same conclusions if she had asked herself which aspects or outcomes of getting her college degree were most important to her personally. That is the question the next values strategy asks about several other areas of conflict and confusion.

PLANNING BOARD

A favorite values clarification strategy of mine, a planning board is another way to find out what you *really* want.

It can be used to gain a clearer perspective on almost any topic.

A planning board requires two sheets of paper, both the same size. On one sheet, draw a board that looks like this:

1	7
2	8
3	9
4	10
5	11
6	12

Fold and tear the second sheet so you have twelve slips of paper roughly the same size as the spaces on your planning board.

Anytime you have a decision to make, are thinking about a change, or need to clarify what you actually want from a given situation, write the points to consider on slips of paper and arrange them on the planning board in order of their importance to you.

The number one space always represents the element that is *most* important to you, and number twelve is always the least important. Only one slip of paper can occupy a space. However, while trying to determine your priorities, you can move the slips around as many times as you like.

Family Planning Board

Family relationships often are a source of conflict and confusion. Since all of us are involved with families of one sort or another, examining our relationship to our families using values clarification strategies serves as a good example of how to use the planning board effectively.

You may have grown up in a two-parent family that could have been Ozzie and Harriet's or Beaver Cleaver's. Perhaps you got by with one hardworking parent or were raised by your grandmother. You might even have been abused as a child, confused by alcoholic parents, or bounced from foster home to foster home. Whatever your past experience was, today you hold a certain personal perspective of how families are supposed to be.

Your current family—whether it is traditional, single-parent with children, cohabiting adults, or any other type—may or may not live up to your expectations. You may have problems with communication, discipline, or household management. You simply may not feel as close and connected as you wish you could. You take a step toward making your family life more satisfying when you examine what you *really* want from family relationships.

Following are eleven features of family living. Each aspect is described briefly and given a key word—signified by bold capital letters. Read and think about the first item. Write the key word on a slip of paper and place the paper on your planning board. Choose the space that represents that feature's importance to you personally. Remember—number one is most important and number twelve is least important. Each element of family relationships listed below should have its own space on your planning board. Give each element careful thought. You can move a slip of paper you have already placed if its importance changes in relation to other elements.

The first feature of family living to consider is:

- The family household runs in an orderly fashion because all members understand, follow, and have a say about **RULES**.

How important are rules and an orderly household? If they are very important, place your slip of paper at the top of the planning board in the one, two or three space. If they are hardly significant, use the bottom spaces—ten, eleven, or twelve. If they are somewhat important, place the paper somewhere in the middle.

The remaining features to consider and place on the planning board in order of their importance to you are:

- **DISCIPLINE** of children is appropriate and consistent.
- Family members **TRUST** one another and feel free to share their problems and concerns.
- The family shares **RELIGIOUS VALUES** and worships together.
- The family spends **RECREATION** time together.
- **CHORES ARE SHARED** and one family member is not overwhelmed or irritated by household responsibilities.
- Family members effectively **COMMUNICATE**—really listening and allowing everyone to have their say—even when there are disagreements.
- **SAFETY** and mutual support are available along with the sense that mistakes won't lead to rejection by other family members.
- Parents present a **UNITED FRONT** on important matters so children (or anyone else) cannot play one against the other.
- Family members **VALIDATE** each other, expressing what they love, admire, appreciate, and respect about each other.
- Family **HARMONY** exists because the family has a

workable method for resolving conflict and solving problems.
- **WILD CARD**—include any aspect of family living you can think of that I did not list above.

Once you've arranged these elements on the planning board the way you want them, ask yourself about the family life you now have and the family life your planning board suggests and confirms you really want. Are the two the same?

Your planning board will measure your satisfaction or dissatisfaction. If the highest ranked items are what you already have in your family, you may be better off than you thought. Perhaps the source of your unhappiness lies somewhere else. If the highest-ranked features were those you *do not* have, you now know why you feel dissatisfied and can begin to improve the situation—one step at a time.

Your planning board can open lines of communication, particularly if you have all family members complete one. With a clearer idea of what each of you wants, you can work together to improve family relationships.

Sometimes you discover you have been upset about and wasting your energy on matters that are not really very important to you. Doug and Marsha discovered that during a family values workshop for foster parents.

"We've been arguing and worrying about discipline and rules for weeks now," says Marsha. She and Doug share their home with three teenage foster children. With backgrounds of abuse, neglect, and instability, the youngsters do need rules and discipline, but they need a few other things as well.

"Rules and discipline didn't even make the top eight on either of our boards," Doug chimes in. "Trust and communication and harmony and doing things together were a whole lot more important. Maybe those are the things we should pay more attention to."

Doug and Marsha decided to go home and do the planning board strategy with the kids. Then they would try to come up with a plan to give them more of what they all wanted.

Planning boards are excellent jumping-off points for your efforts to change. First, they help you set priorities. Then, often, you can go on to develop goals and plans for action based on the strategy's outcomes.

Family life may not be an area of conflict or confusion for you at the present time. That's why I have included a list of elements for three additional planning boards. In addition, you can always make up planning boards of your own. Simply follow the steps outlined previously to complete planning boards for the following areas of your life.

Relationship Planning Board

What is important to you in a love relationship?

- A partner who has a good sense of humor so that there is lots of **LAUGHTER** in our relationship.
- A good and satisfying **SEX** life.
- **COMMON INTERESTS** and mutual friends.
- Some **INDEPENDENT INTERESTS** and separate friends.
- A partner who is **PHYSICALLY ATTRACTIVE**.
- **COMMUNICATION** that is open and ongoing. We really talk and listen to each other.
- We should be able to **TRUST** each other with feelings and not do anything to hurt the relationship or each other.
- The relationship must include **HONESTY**.
- We should be **OPEN ABOUT OUR FEELINGS**.
- A partner who is **NOT CLINGY** or overly dependent and gives me room to breath.
- A partner who **PUTS ME FIRST** in his or her life.
- **ROMANCE**.

Job Planning Board

What do I really want from a job?

- **GOOD PAY.**
- A good job will allow me decent and somewhat flexible **HOURS.**
- I will be **CHALLENGED** and asked to use my skills and abilities.
- There will be enough variety in what I do so I feel **STIMULATED** by my job.
- My opinions are taken seriously and I'm asked for **INPUT** on decisions that affect me.
- **RESPECT** from peers and superiors.
- Enough **INDEPENDENCE/AUTONOMY** to get the job done and respect myself.
- Job **SECURITY** so I know the job will be there as long as I want it.
- Room for **ADVANCEMENT.**
- Little or **NO SEXISM** in the workplace.
- Friendly, cooperative **COWORKER RELATIONSHIPS.**
- To be **PROUD** of the work I do and have other people be proud of it too.

Free Time Planning Board

How do you really want to spend your free time?

- **LEARNING** by taking classes, reading books, or completing correspondence courses.
- **SOCIALIZING** with other people.
- **STAYING AT HOME.**
- **GOING SOMEWHERE.**
- With **PHYSICALLY CHALLENGING** activities such as rock climbing, hiking, volleyball, or hang gliding.

- **EXCITEMENT,** adventure, meeting new people, doing things I haven't done before.
- I like to **PLAN IN ADVANCE** what I will do.
- I'd rather be **SPONTANEOUS** and do things that strike my fancy at the last minute.
- To **CATCH UP** on chores and things I don't get to during the work week.
- To **FULFILL COMMITMENTS** such as visiting my parents, taking care of my nieces, or entertaining people to whom I owe invitations.
- **ALONE.**
- It doesn't matter what I do as long as it **KEEPS MY MIND OFF WORK** or other problems.

Like believing you do not deserve better and not seeing alternatives, not knowing what you *really* want is only one barrier to change. It is a powerful one and almost every other barrier gets tangled up with it at one time or another. Still, there is more to getting unstuck than discovering your values and knowing what you truly want.

6

Change and Letting Go

Renee is a colleague of mine who conducts stress management and overall wellness training seminars. In her presentations she includes the eight barriers to change. She summarizes barrier number three—not knowing what you *really* want—and introduces barrier number four by expressing the following opinion: "There are hundreds of things we do without asking ourselves *why* or if we really want to. A perfect example is watching the eleven o'clock television news every night before going to bed—a truly pointless, self-defeating practice if there ever was one.

"Think about it," Renee suggests. "The news is almost always negative. You get to see graphic video footage of fires, overturned trailer trucks, murders, and violence—your basic mayhem and madness. Do you *really* want to look at all that nasty stuff right before you go to sleep? Do you rest more comfortably knowing that, yes, indeed, the world is still one fine mess? It will all be there in the morning.

"No matter what you see on the eleven o'clock newscast,

there is NOTHING YOU CAN DO ABOUT IT! You aren't going to get out of bed, rush over to your desk, and whip off a letter to the editor. You are not going to place a telephone call to the family of a murder victim and express your condolences. Even if the news affects you directly—if rumors of massive layoffs at the factory where you work are reported, for instance—WHAT CAN YOU DO ABOUT IT, at eleven P.M., except lie awake half the night worrying? Honestly, watching the late-night TV news has got to be the most mindless, wasteful way anyone could end their day."

How do you feel about Renee's point of view? Do you think she is too darn opinionated or wonder who gave *her* the right to tell *you* what to do? As someone who views late-night newscasts on a regular basis, do you feel personally offended or attacked by Renee's words? Can you think of several perfectly good reasons to watch eleven o'clock news programs?

Renee's audience can. Her unsolicited opinion leaves them feeling offended, irritated, and argumentative. As soon as she stops talking, a heated debate begins.

"I disagree," says the first person Renee calls on. "I consider myself a well-informed person. I want to know what's going on in the world."

"I admire that," Renee replies. "But what good does it do you to be well-informed while you sleep? You can catch up on the news in the morning."

Another audience member has an answer to that point: "I don't have time to watch the morning news *or* read the morning newspaper if that's what you're going to tell me to do."

"How about listening to an all-news station while you get ready for work or on your car radio?" Renee suggests.

"What about the weather report?" someone else asks. "If it's going to snow, I want to know the night before. I'll need more time to get to work. I can't just wait to look out my window in the morning."

"You're right," Renee agrees. "Storm warnings are a valid reason to watch the late news. But certainly there are not storms pending every single night of the year."

"I watch for the sports report," another audience member claims. "I like to know how my favorite teams did."

"I do too," Renee says. "But the sportscast is at the end of any news show. It isn't worth enduring everything that comes before it, especially when I can get the same information in the morning."

"But there isn't anything else on before the Johnny Carson show. I like to watch Carson. He makes me laugh and forget about all that bad news I just saw."

"In that case, why watch it in the first place?"

Renee counters each argument with an equally convincing counterpoint. While she presents her case calmly, her audience becomes increasingly agitated. Finally one man jumps to his feet and loudly condemns her.

"This is a free country," he shouts. "I can watch what I want whenever I want to. What you are proposing is censorship, and as far as I'm concerned, you can take *all* of your ideas and shove them!"

Whether you agree or disagree with Renee's position, how important *is* the eleven o'clock news? If the TV networks discontinued late news broadcasts, would your life be irreparably damaged *or* dramatically improved? Of course not. Yet Renee's audience used a full fifteen minutes of seminar time to defend the practice—ultimately accusing the trainer of being downright un-American and discounting everything else they had already learned from her.

The issue at hand was relatively harmless and insignificant. What was not insignificant is that the audience was confronted with the possibility of change and that they recoiled at the thought. They felt threatened and mobilized their defenses—automatically. Blindly and at full speed they crashed into barrier number four—finding perfectly good reasons *not* to change.

When someone else challenges something you do rou-

tinely or habitually, barrier number four is a knee-jerk reaction to what you believe is a personal attack. You
immediately focus your attention and emotional resources
on defending the way things are—instead of considering
how things could be. You shut out all incoming messages
and look for perfectly good reasons *not* to change.

Barrier number four also defeats you when you really
do know—without anyone else's telling you—that you could
change for the better. Yet, with no one to convince but yourself, you still find perfectly good reasons not to change.

Twenty-five years ago Jennifer met George. She was a
sophomore in high school and he was a senior. She knew
immediately that he was the man she wanted to marry, and
as she puts it, she chased him until he caught her. Twenty
years ago (and two weeks after George's college graduation)
Jennifer and George got married. Her parents adored George,
gave the marriage their blessing, and bought the newlyweds
a small house in which to live. Her friends celebrated her
good fortune. George was going to be a doctor. "And in those
days, you couldn't do better than to marry a doctor," Jennifer
explains.

While George attended medical school, Jennifer worked
to support them. By the time he had completed his internship
and residency, they had three children. George joined a
thriving cardiology practice attached to a prestigious Chi-
cago hospital. They bought a huge, luxurious home in the
suburbs, sent their children to the best private schools, and
became pillars of their community. George's practice flour-
ished, and Jennifer headed charity drives, volunteered at the
hospital where George worked, and enjoyed all the privileges
accorded a doctor's wife. "I was living out my childhood fantasies," Jennifer says. "My life was exactly what I wanted it to
be and exactly how everyone said life should be."

Then, ten years ago, George had his first extramarital
affair, with an operating-room nurse. The relationship was
common knowledge among the hospital staff, and neither
participant tried to cover it up, but Jennifer was truly shocked

when another doctor's wife "did her a favor" and told her about the affair.

"I was devastated that George could be unfaithful to me and humiliated that everyone else knew about it before I did," Jennifer recalls. "I felt like a fool. I was hurt and angry. When I wasn't wondering what I did to push him into another woman's arms, I was thinking about packing up and leaving him. But I didn't. The kids were young and they loved their dad. I loved him. I'd loved him since I was fifteen years old and could not picture life without him."

Jennifer confronted George. He cried and begged her forgiveness, promising to end the affair immediately and to never again be unfaithful. "He swore he loved me and the kids more than anything in the world and never wanted to hurt us. I believed him."

She believed him again two years later and again when he had his third affair. She timidly suggested marriage counseling the fourth time he strayed, but he insisted theirs wasn't a marital problem. It was his fault alone. He again promised to stop having affairs. Jennifer did not bother to confront him the next time he was unfaithful and has convinced herself his sixth and current affair is something she can live with.

"I know that sounds crazy," she says, "but I have my reasons. George is a good father and a good provider. He is respected and admired by important people. So am I. I like that. I like what I have. I would lose it all if I got a divorce, and the kids would be devastated. I can't do that to them. When I look at it objectively, my life isn't so bad. Sharing George with his mistress isn't such an awful price to pay. . . ."

Does Jennifer's conclusion seem reasonable or does it appall you? Has she realistically assessed her situation, or is she minimizing her feelings about her husband's repeated affairs and ignoring the impact of his infidelity on the marriage, the children, and her own self-esteem? Is she someone who has learned the art of compromise, or someone who is stuck?

Sometimes you fool yourself into thinking that by *not* changing you are doing what is best for all concerned. But are you really? I think not. When your life clearly could be better but you actively work to convince yourself and others that it is good enough the way it is, you are stuck and stymied by barrier number four.

Barrier number four is there each time you rationalize a self-destructive habit such as smoking, drug use, excessive drinking, overeating, or compulsive spending. It is at work each time you abandon your hopes and dreams by deciding your physical health, your job, your relationship, your social life, or any other situation is "not so bad." It is part of every excuse you make *not* to ask for a raise, assert yourself, see a doctor about the funny-looking mole on your shoulder, start an exercise program, or sign up for a college course. It keeps you stuck by supplying a steady stream of perfectly good reasons *not* to change.

WHY YOU LOOK FOR REASONS NOT TO CHANGE

Perfectly good reasons not to change are the by-products of defensiveness. When faced with change—whether it is your own idea or someone else's—your first reaction, in almost every instance, is to defend the status quo, to protect yourself from a possible loss of self-esteem, independence, or a familiar aspect of daily living.

Think about the audience's reaction to Renee's opinion about late-night news watching. Before the first complete sentence escaped her lips, people began to feel uncomfortable. They stopped listening to her actual words. They heard instead what they *thought* she was saying about them *personally* and began to build an argument in their own defense. Why did they react this way?

First of all, when Renee claimed watching the eleven o'clock news was dumb, mindless, wasteful, and self-defeating, the audience believed she was implying that *they* were stupid, unthinking, wasteful, and self-destructive people. Her challenge of a specific behavior was a challenge to who they were as human beings. Their self-image was under attack and they did not like it. They felt threatened, hurt, and angry, and so they defended the practice of TV news watching in order to protect their self-esteem.

Often, admitting a need to change can appear to be the same as admitting you are not good enough the way you are. The premise is false, but you do not think about it logically. *Change threatens your self-esteem, so you defend your behavior to protect yourself from feelings of worthlessness or inadequacy.*

Tell a cigarette smoker that smoking is bad for his health and he hears that he is a bad person because he smokes. He replies defensively, "Give me a break. I could just as easily die tomorrow because a truck hits me while I'm crossing the street." Or he rejects the alternative: "I tried to quit once. It wasn't worth it. I gained twenty pounds and was hell to live with." Or he denounces the advice-giver: "There's nothing worse than a reformed smoker trying to convert the rest of us."

A teacher suggests to a mother that her son's schoolwork might improve if she spent thirty minutes each evening helping him with his homework. Instead of thinking about how the teacher is trying to help her son, the mother assumes that the teacher is calling her a lousy parent. So she turns the tables, saying, "If you can't do your job in the classroom, don't expect me to do it for you." Or she defends herself: "I'm a single parent and I work full-time. My kids are lucky if they have thirty minutes alone with me in a week." Or she blames the victim: "I help Joey with his homework. He's just a slow learner. He's not as bright as the other kids; never has been."

Each time change is an option, it raises the possibility that you are not good enough the way you are. After all, if you were, you would not need to change. So, you turn things around. To dodge a self-esteem wrecking ball and prove you are good enough, you convince yourself you really do not need to change.

In addition to feeling their self-esteem threatened, Renee's audience did not appreciate her telling them what they *should* do. They reacted with anger to what they believed to be her attempt to assert control over their lives. You too may react defensively and find perfectly good reasons not to change when you *feel your independence or autonomy is threatened or that outside forces are trying to control you.*

Jennifer says, "My friends tell me to leave George and get on with my life. Well, maybe that's what they would do, but they are not me. They don't know what's best for me. I'm the only one who knows that."

The alcoholic defends his drinking and asserts his independence when he says, "I can stop drinking whenever I want to. I just don't want to right now."

The lover who balks at the idea of committing herself to marriage thinks her partner is trying to control and stifle her. She says, "Don't push. I like things the way they are. Besides, I'm not going to get married just so I can impress other people with a piece of paper. It's my life, not theirs."

The rebellious teenager shouts from the bottom of the staircase, "YOU CAN'T MAKE ME DO IT!"

Barrier number four appeals to the rebellious adolescent in each of you. No one can make you change, and you put up one heck of a fight when they try.

Finally, Renee's audience reacted to a feeling that Renee was trying to take something away from them. Watching the eleven o'clock news was a practice to which they had grown accustomed. It was not a practice that actually meant much to them one way or another, but it belonged to them, they were comfortable with it, and they were not about to give it up.

You also find reasons not to change in order to *defend against the possible loss of something you already have.* Jennifer is accustomed to and enjoys the luxuries and status of being a doctor's wife. She will lose them if she divorces

George. Or, there is the worker who hates his job, but at least he knows what to expect from it. Dissatisfying as his job may be, if he quits, he gives up familiar surroundings, relationships, and routines.

Self-destructive as their habits might be, the alcoholic does not want to lose the alcohol high or the escape it provides, the overeater does not want to lose the comfort and pleasure of food, the gambler does not want to lose the risk and adrenaline rush of gambling, and the compulsive spender sees an emotional release and thrill being taken away from her.

The fear of losing what you already have is the driving force behind barrier number four. Hanging on to what you have wins out over the possibility of getting something better. No one can *guarantee* change will leave you better off than you were before. And that, my friends, is one of the all-time winners among perfectly good reasons not to change.

Whether you defend the way things are to protect self-esteem, assert your independence, or to keep yourself from losing what you have (regardless of its true value), the result is the same. You look for perfectly good reasons not to change, find them, and use them to justify staying stuck.

HOW THIS BARRIER WORKS

Barrier number four creates several negative outcomes that get you and keep you stuck.

1. *It decreases and/or eliminates viable alternatives.*

April is alone and lonely. She says she wants to change that. She wants to meet a man and have a relationship with him. Yet she offers perfectly good reasons not to pursue any avenue that could lead her to what she wants.

"A friend of mine met her husband in a yoga class," April's friend Kate mentions during a telephone conversation that began with April's claiming she would probably die without ever meeting a man she could love.

"I don't like yoga," says April.

"So don't take yoga. Take a course in something you do like."

"I don't have time."

"I thought you just said you have too much time on your hands."

"I meant I wanted something fun to do. Classes aren't fun. They're work."

"Okay, then go out. There are some great clubs down where you live."

"I hate bars. They're all meat markets."

"How about a museum, then? You're right down the street from—"

"Forget it. What am I supposed to do—walk up to some guy and say, 'Nice Picasso. Want to come home with me?' "

April goes on to say that only losers join singles groups and only weirdos answer classified ads or sign up for dating services. Her friends and relatives arrange blind dates, but the guys are never her type.

"April, you have an excuse for everything," Kate sighs.

"That's because I know the situation is hopeless," April concludes.

April uses perfectly good reasons to prove her point. By finding fatal flaws in every alternative, she ultimately convinces herself there is indeed no alternative to the way things are.

Barrier number four often leads you back to barrier number two. Like April, you have a perfectly good reason *not* to change when you reject every available option and can see no alternative to the way things are. If you have forgotten how debilitating this can be, turn back to Chapter Four.

2. *Barrier number four destroys the motivation to change by convincing you "things are not so bad" the way they are.*

In spite of her husband's infidelity and a marriage in name only, Jennifer claims her life is not so bad. She discounts the pain, humiliation, and frustration of sleeping alone most nights, making love with a man who regularly makes love to someone else, the countless petty fights she picks because she chooses not to confront the real problem, and the way her children idolize a man she knows to be far less than what they see. She instead reminds herself of the perks a doctor's wife gets, the luxuries she can afford, and the image she has in the community. By reinforcing the status quo and persuading herself that her life is not so bad, she believes she has no reason to consider marriage counseling, divorce, or any other option that would improve her own life.

Lou, as you may recall from Chapter One, also is stuck in a loveless marriage. He defends his stuckness by claiming, "We stay together for the children." He avoids change and defends his avoidance by observing that "plenty of people put up with lousy marriages." He rationalizes that if they can, he can, too. It is what he is used to, and "when you get right down to it, it really is not so bad."

By defending a behavior, habit, or way of life and conjuring up perfectly good reasons to continue on your present course, you persuade yourself change is not necessary. And when the "things are not so bad" defense develops a few leaks, you turn to the flip side of the same coin and remind yourself that "things could be worse." You defend your current position by painting a more negative and unappealing picture of changing.

You defend your decision to stay in a job you hate. "Things could be worse," you say. "I could be unemployed."

You spend Saturday nights in noisy, crowded bars and have a series of one-night stands. You console yourself, "It's better than sitting home alone, pigging out on junk food, and watching TV."

You put up with an unfaithful lover because at least he does not drink. If he drinks, at least he does not take drugs.

The money he spends on drugs is nothing compared to what your financial situation would be if he gambled. A gambler is okay as long as he does not beat you, and if he beats you once in a while, it is okay because he never lays a hand on the kids. You can always find at least one way things could be worse than they are.

In view of how bad things *could* be, you figure you are lucky to be where you are. You decide to count your blessings and stop worrying about being stuck. You draw the logical conclusion—if your life is not so bad and could be worse— YOU DO NOT NEED TO CHANGE.

3. *As you look for one perfectly good reason not to change after another, you hurt and alienate the people who care about you.*

You do not get unstuck all by yourself. Emotional support from other people builds the self-esteem you need to attempt change. Asking for help from other people increases your alternatives and dismantles barrier number two. A later chapter in this book will be devoted entirely to the matter of gaining cooperation from other people as a step toward getting unstuck. No matter how you look at it, you need people if you want a change effort to succeed. Yet barrier number four drives away the people who want to help you.

When you want a reason not to change, you may reject the person who presents the possibility of change or offers you advice. In your defensive mode you may play a hard game of "get the helper." Just as Renee's audience turned on her, you go right for the jugular when you think someone is trying to run your life or tell you what to do—even when you asked for their advice in the first place. You launch a counterattack. "What I do is none of your business," you say, or "Don't you tell me how to handle my relationship. Your marriage isn't exactly made in heaven, you know." Or "Who died and appointed you God?" Or "You could use to lose a few pounds yourself."

In an attempt to defend yourself you may make some

incredibly hurtful and accusatory statements. You reason that if the helpers are obviously flawed, so is the help they offer. Their inadequacy is your perfectly good reason *not* to change. You let them know you see right through them, so they will take their know-it-all attitude and lousy advice someplace else.

Few people will subject themselves to your wrath more than once. They will back away and become decidedly reluctant to offer their support or respond to you when you seek them out at a later date. If this happens, your need to defend yourself against change will cost you a valuable resource person.

But you need not verbally attack the well-intentioned people in your life to alienate them. You can also drive them away by burning them out. Unhappy with yourself or your circumstances, you share your feelings with people you trust and believe to be emotionally supportive. They hear your tales of woe and watch you resist change by rejecting all alternatives (for perfectly good reasons, of course). They listen to you make one excuse after another. You decide your situation is hopeless. They decide you do not really want to change. Their patience wears thin. They sympathize with your plight, but it becomes increasingly difficult to sympathize with *you.* You sing the same old tune, sometimes for years on end, but you never *do* anything except explain your perfectly good reasons not to change.

Everyone has their limit. When your emotional support people reach theirs, they turn you off, avoid you, change the subject when your problems become part of a conversation. Sometimes they lose their temper and yell at you. Like the boy who cried wolf, when you decide to really change, no one believes you. The people who could help you have been burned out by your stuckness and are nowhere to be found.

4. *Time, energy, and emotional resources that could be used to get unstuck are wasted on defending a current practice or finding perfectly good reasons not to change.*

Renee's audience spent fifteen minutes of a three-hour seminar defending the practice of watching eleven P.M. newscasts, a practice they later agreed was of relatively little importance to them. They mobilized the energy to be angry and argumentative, more energy than they had exhibited during earlier portions of the seminar. The time and energy was largely wasted, however, since no conclusion was reached and no new stress-management strategy learned. They could have used their time and energy to learn more about overall wellness or to brainstorm more peaceful, positive, or relaxing things to do before going to sleep at night.

Similarly, Carla, the Minnesota social worker dissatisfied with her job, constantly feels drained and lethargic. She uses her energy to complain about her job in one breath and convince herself to keep it in the next. She is too tired and empty to consider alternatives, set goals, or get unstuck.

If April spent half as much time testing her alternatives as she spends making excuses *not* to try them, she might have met several men by now and perhaps settled into a relationship with one of them.

I know countless therapists who wish their clients could be as focused and creative about exploring options and attempting new behaviors as they are when they defend themselves and the way things are. Every minute you devote to defending what is and creating elaborate rationales for staying the way you are, you *could be* coming up with creative solutions to your problems, pursuing new alternatives, and moving closer to the life you really want.

In case you have not yet seen yourself in the picture I have painted or still are not sure if barrier number four is impeding your progress, here are some of the most commonly used reasons *not* to change. How many have you used?

I tried that, but it didn't work.
Some people can do it, but I can't.
My situation is unique.

It's not as bad as it looks.

You're blowing this way out of proportion. It's really no big deal.

I can quit anytime I want.

I know what I'm doing.

I have it under control.

There are extenuating circumstances.

Right now I don't have the time (energy, money, freedom, etc.) to change.

I don't drink (smoke, spend, overeat, gamble, hit my kids, etc.) half as much as some people I know.

People in glass houses shouldn't throw stones.

Did I ask for your opinion?

There is absolutely nothing I can do about it.

It must be my karma.

It's not my fault.

It's just the way things are. Some things will never change.

These and other reasons not to change are used daily by you and everyone you know. They counter every imaginable reason *to* change and eliminate all avenues—except staying the same, settling for half a loaf, or putting up with the way things are. If you truly believe that is enough, then you *do* have a perfectly good reason *not* to change. But you opened this book and read this far because you wanted more. To get it, you must dismantle barrier number four and learn to let go of your defensiveness.

DISMANTLING BARRIER #4:
LETTING GO OF DEFENSIVENESS
SO YOU CAN TRY SOMETHING NEW

As Cleveland State University professor Hanoch Mc-Carty's motto goes: *"If you always do what you've always done, you will only get what you always got."*

In this statement lies the reason to dismantle barrier number four. You have a choice to make. You can settle for what you already have (and fight to the death for your right to keep it) or reach for something better. You dismantle this barrier by becoming more aware of its presence in your life and learning to counter reasons *not* to change with equally persuasive reasons *to* change.

Recognizing When Barrier #4 Has a Hold on You

Barrier number four is such a powerful obstacle to change because it comes into play *automatically* almost every time you consider the mere possibility of change. You defend the way things are without thinking about whether or not you like, value, or really want what you have. You find perfectly good reasons not to change without knowing that you are doing it. The walls go up, the drawbridge closes, the claws come out, the counterattack is plotted—involuntarily, almost unconsciously, as if an early warning device had been triggered and your normal thought processes overridden by an automatic defense system. To offer a perfectly good reason *not* to change can be as automatic and as natural as breathing.

"You don't have to take that kind of abuse," a mother tells her daughter.

Automatically her daughter replies, "I know, BUT he always apologizes. He feels really bad about it and tries to make it up to me."

"You could go to your supervisor," a husband says, suggesting a solution to his wife's work problem.

"I guess, BUT she probably wouldn't do anything about it," the wife counters immediately.

"Have you thought about telling Billy how you feel?" a counselor advises a mother having trouble disciplining her twelve-year-old son.

"Yeah, BUT he never listens to me," the mother instantly offers as a reason not to try.

You do not need someone else to trigger your defense system. You defend yourself against your own ideas about change.

"Sure, I know I should lose weight, BUT diets never work for me."

"Yeah, I know I want to exercise, BUT I don't have time."

"I suppose we could see a marriage counselor, BUT the Martins went to a counselor and now they're getting divorced."

"I know I really need a vacation, BUT there would just be more work to catch up on when I got back. Still, it would be nice, BUT money is kind of tight right now and the kids are at that awkward stage and . . ."

These examples illustrate a practice those of us in the helping professions call "yeah, but-ing." Each alternative or possible behavior change is considered for as long as it takes to say, "yeah, sure, I know," "I suppose," "I guess," or "you're right." Then an excuse is made or a perfectly good reason not to change is given. In between the grunt of agreement and the counterargument is the word BUT. A "yeah, but" is a sure sign that you are defending a practice or resisting a change.

When you "Yeah, but" every alternative, you give additional power to the obstacle to change instead of empowering yourself to succeed or get unstuck. In one way or another, you are saying that the reasons to stay the same mean more than your desire to reach your goals and aspirations. You are more committed to keeping things the way they are than to trying to make them better. You may not mean that. You may not know *why* you defend yourself and block that change. But you do it. And you do it automatically.

To begin letting go of your defenses, you must recognize when you are becoming defensive. Your "yeah, but"s serve as warning signals. The next time you hear those words coming out of your mouth—STOP!

Ask yourself—Am I looking for perfectly good reasons *not* to change? Am I defending the way things are so I can convince myself it is okay to be stuck? Do I *really* want to continue this practice and maintain the status quo? Or do I want something better than I already have?

Your body and emotions also can let you know you are getting defensive. Pay attention to your physical and emotional reactions the next time you think about or discuss change. You may feel angry, offended, confused, irritated, tense, or anxious. You might feel an urge to change the subject, criticize or verbally attack the person with whom you are talking, storm out of the room, or escape through drinking, eating, shopping, gambling, or getting into your couch potato mode. Your palms sweat or your heart beats faster. You clench your teeth so tightly that your jaw begins to ache. Perhaps you feel tears welling in your eyes or you start to hyperventilate. These feelings and physical symptoms could be signs of defensiveness. Once again, STOP!

Ask yourself—Why am I reacting this way? What am I afraid of or angry about? I feel threatened, but is there really any danger present? Why does it seem so important to protect myself and defend what I do? Do I actually need to calm down and face this issue head on?

Both your "yeah, but" statements and your automatic physical and emotional reactions tell you that your defensive walls are going up and the drawbridge is closing. If you STOP and ask yourself the questions I suggested, you can diminish the power of this barrier. Then you can counter your perfectly good reasons *not* to change with plausible reasons *to* change.

Ten "Yeah, But"s Make a Go for It!

Finding reasons *to* change is not nearly as automatic as finding reasons not to change. You will have to work at it and work hard. You must begin to counter your excuses with motivating statements. In a sense you must learn to "yeah, but" your "yeah, but" statements. Then you once again see your alternatives.

Below are ten commonly used "yeah, but" statements. They may or may not apply to your life or your present state of conflict and confusion. However, you can use them to practice the art of letting go. Counter each perfectly good reason not to change with a positively motivating statement, one also beginning with "yeah, but." I have done the first one for you.

1. I know, but if I want something done right, I have to do it myself.

I know, but as overwhelmed as I am, it won't get done at all unless I delegate it to someone else.

2. Yeah, but I don't have time to exercise . . .

3. Yeah, but the last counselor I went to was a real jerk . . .

4. Yeah, but I can't afford to take a vacation . . .

5. Yeah, but I like watching the eleven o'clock news . . .

6. I guess, but they probably want someone with a college degree . . .

7. Yeah, but he never listens to what I say . . .

8. Yeah, but I'll gain weight if I quit smoking . . .

9. I know, but nothing ever changes in this company . . .

10. You're right, but it really is not so bad . . .

Now Try It on an Actual Change You Want to Make

Choose an aspect of overall wellness or an area of conflict and confusion (from Chapter Two) or an alternative you generated as part of the strategies presented in Chapter Four.

At the top of a sheet of paper, write your choice in a sentence beginning with the words I REALLY WANT TO . . . Under that headline sentence, list every imaginable excuse and perfectly good reason not to change (or pursue the alternative). Leave several lines between each reason/excuse. When you finish, go back and cross out the excuses that are relatively meaningless (i.e., they would be highly unlikely to actually prevent you from taking action). The excuses that remain are your strongest reasons *not* to change. Contradict each with with a plausible, positive reason *to* change. Write your reason in the space you left.

If you immediately think of a "yeah but" for your newly listed reason *to* change, write it down. Then go back and "yeah, but" your "yeah, but" statements. Continue arguing with yourself until the reasons *to* change outnumber and outweigh the reasons *not* to—or until you realize what a tangled web you weave when you devote your time and energy to finding perfectly good reasons *not* to change.

Think of all you can do with the time, energy, and creative ideas you will have once you dismantle barrier number four. You can discover new alternatives, pursue different options, achieve new goals, and move ever closer to the life you truly desire and deserve.

A Success Story

As described in Chapter Two, Marilyn, a registered nurse and mother of three, was forced to change after her husband left her. She describes herself as having no choice except to change, take a nursing refresher course, get a job, and go on with her life. The demand to change was clear-cut and obvious, yet Marilyn did not change immediately. She had a number of perfectly good reasons not to.

"As soon as the shock wore off," says Marilyn, "I got

very depressed. My friends and family were understanding and sympathetic at first. But after a while they began telling me I had to 'snap out of it.' I was appalled at their insensitivity. How can you expect me to go on as if nothing happened?" she moaned. "I'm in pain. My husband left me. My life is ruined."

Then she got angry. "I'll be damned if I'm going to change my lifestyle," she growled. "I'll call my lawyer. I'll get more child support. I'll make him pay. Why should I be the one to go through hell—I didn't desert *my* family."

But Marilyn's husband refused to pay more child support, and he was not exactly the model of punctuality when it came to sending the amount he had agreed to pay. Her friends confronted her with reality, but she was not ready to accept it. "I told them I didn't have the energy to look for a job," she recalls. "That was no lie. I was so depressed I barely had enough energy to get out of bed."

Marilyn doubted her ability to get a decent job. She had been away from nursing for nearly a decade. No hospital would hire her unless she took a refresher course. She would have to work at some menial job until she passed the course. It seemed too difficult. It would also mean she would be out of the house for hours at a time, time she would normally spend with her children. She couldn't do it, she claimed, because her kids needed her.

"Your kids need to know where their next meal is coming from!" shouted her mother, who had had about as much as she could take of her daughter's excuses.

"We'll get by," Marilyn sighed.

But Marilyn and her children were not getting by. Bills went unpaid. The electric company threatened to cut off their service. Winter was coming and the children needed coats and boots. They were frightened by their mother's behavior. She rarely bothered to get dressed or comb her hair anymore. One day Marilyn's oldest daughter came to her.

"Mom," she said. "Maybe it would be better if we went

to live with Dad. You could go live with Grandma until you felt better, and you wouldn't have to worry about the bills."

Marilyn felt terrible, but still could not stop defending the way things were. "Things will be okay, honey," Marilyn reassured her. But her daughter didn't believe her any more than she believed herself.

"No, they won't. Things will not be okay and I wish you would stop saying that because it just isn't true!" Marilyn's daughter stormed out of the bedroom.

"My daughter was right," Marilyn admits now. "I was lying to myself about being able to make ends meet. When I realized that, I also saw the lies in my other excuses. I don't know what I was thinking, except that if I could fool myself into believing everything was under control, I wouldn't have to *do* anything. When I finally got my head out of the clouds, there were more reasons to get my act together than there were reasons to stay in the hole I'd dug for myself. So finally, after four months of wallowing in self-pity, I decided to climb out and rejoin the human race."

It was a struggle every step of the way, but Marilyn got an aide's job in a nursing home, completed her refresher course, and moved on to an intensive care nursing position at a hospital near her home. She works a seven A.M. to three P.M. shift, which allows her ample time with her children after school and evenings free to date occasionally.

"We're not on easy street by any means," says Marilyn. "If I had my way, my husband would never have left me, and the five of us would be living happily ever after like Donna Reed and her family. If I had my second wish, I'd fall madly in love with a very wealthy man. He would take the four of us with him to his mansion where his servants would wait on us hand and foot and I'd never have to work again. But hey, until that happens, I'll do the best I can and *never* let myself get that stuck again."

As with most people, when Marilyn recalls the time she spent being stuck, she has a hard time believing she sank so low or why she felt so afraid to let go of the way things were. I mention this feeling because cold, raw fear is a powerful obstacle to change. That change makes up barrier number five, which will be described and dismantled in the next chapter.

7

Change and Fear

Fear comes in many flavors:

Fear of failure

Fear of pain

Fear of embarrassment

Fear of hurting others

Fear of being different

Fear of seeming stupid

Fear of being
misunderstood

Fear of not measuring
up

Fear of success

Fear of rejection

Fear of being hurt

Fear of disappointment

Fear of loneliness

Fear of becoming dependent

Fear of losing what you
already have

Fear of the unknown or
unfamiliar

Nothing blocks change quite the way fear does. Cold, raw fear freezes you in your tracks. It paralyses. It keeps you from moving forward. When its power exceeds your power to push through it, fear is devastating.

Fear is a powerful and quick teacher. Its lessons are learned on the gut level—and rarely forgotten. There are no slow learners when fear is the teacher. Think of the young child who learns not to touch a hot stove. The very first time he touches the stove, he gets the message—and he does not have to think long and hard about it. He gets burned and immediately decides that he does not want to feel pain like that again. So, he stops touching hot stoves.

Throughout your lifetime you learn similar lessons in the same way. You learn to fear—and avoid—much more than physical pain, however.

MARTHA

Martha has been hurt in the past and does not want to be hurt again. She fell in love for the first time when she was sixteen, but the relationship did not last. Neither did the love relationships she had at eighteen, twenty, or twenty-one. All her relationships have followed the same pattern: She gave unselfishly to the man she loved, trusted him, and made herself vulnerable. At this point she began thinking in terms of marriage. Then in each case her lover left her for another lover, for a job three thousand miles away, or because of his need for space and freedom that baffled Martha. Her love relationships always turned out the same way, but the hurt never became easier to handle.

Martha brings her past experience to each new love relationship. As a result, the ending to the relationship is written before the affair begins. No matter how well the relationship starts off, Martha fears she will be hurt again and abandoned once more. So, at the first and slightest sign that her usual fate might be on its way, she walks away from the relationship. Without discussion or explanation she tells her lover the affair is over.

Not about to wait for her lover to hurt her, Martha wants

to "get it over with" immediately. By leaving before she is left, Martha believes that she at least retains control and her dignity even though she is hurting the men she loves. Martha followed this self-destructive pattern in six short-term relationships in two years' time before she finally stopped dating altogether. But that is not a solution either. Now she is lonely and feels isolated. But Martha also feels that she is safe, protected from the possibility of being hurt again.

WHAT ABOUT YOU?

You too have been hurt before. You have been disappointed, rejected, embarrassed, or belittled. You have lost things you cherished and failed to get what you wanted. When you remember these experiences, they stimulate all sorts of painful, negative emotions. The thought of feeling those emotions again frightens you, and you begin to avoid any situation or circumstance that presents the *possibility* of disappointment, rejection, embarrassment, belittlement, loss, failure, or anything else you fear. As a result, your fears and avoidance behaviors limit the number and kind of risks you are willing to take. Like Martha, you learn to play it safe and protect yourself. Consequently, you get less out of life and you get stuck.

Fear can be a reasonable response to a real situation. If a mugger holds a knife to your throat, if your car careens out of control at an ice-covered intersection, if the flood waters rise to the second story of your house, or if the baby's temperature reaches 102 degrees, you experience a real threat and feel fear. Indeed, in such life-threatening situations any normal human being would be frightened and traumatized. Although it feels very much the same, this kind of fear is *not* the kind that blocks change and keeps you from pursuing viable alternatives to unpleasant circumstances.

Let me illustrate the difference by telling you a very

condensed version of an old folk tale called "The Three Sillies":

Once upon a time on a fine summer's afternoon, John paid a visit to his fiancée, Mary, and her parents, Mr. and Mrs. Smith, and was invited to stay for supper.

As the foursome took their seats, Mr. Smith realized there was no wine on the table. Mary offered to correct the oversight and went to the wine cellar. Considerable time passed, but Mary did not return. Mrs. Smith went to see what was keeping her. When the two women did not return, Mr. Smith went to the wine cellar to get them. John waited and waited until he could wait no longer. He too went to the wine cellar and, much to his surprise, found Mary and her parents weeping and wailing as if their hearts would break.

"Whatever is the matter?" he asked.

All three sobbed and pointed to the ceiling. John looked up. Stuck in one of the beams, where it no doubt had been lodged for years, was an ax. John stared at the ax. Then he stared at his fiancée and future in-laws. He could not fathom why they were so upset.

Seeing John's confusion, Mary tearfully explained, "What if you and I were to marry and have a son? He would grow tall and handsome like his father and be adored by his grandparents, would he not? And they would want us to visit as often as we could and invite us to stay for supper. Our beautiful, wonderful, kind, and loving son would one day come down to this very wine cellar to fetch some wine—*and what if that ax fell and killed him?*"

The prospect of such a horrible disaster's coming to pass set off more mournful crying by Mary and her parents. Nothing John could do would console them, and they refused to leave the cellar where the imaginary son might one day meet his imaginary demise.

In exasperation John declared his belief that they were the three silliest people in the world and refused to marry

Mary until he had searched the world over to find three people more ridiculous than they were.

John found them eventually, but that is not why I told this story or why I like it so much. I tell it because it makes people laugh. How truly absurd Mary and her parents acted. Yet it is exactly what each of us do when we fear *possible* negative outcomes. We predict disaster, visualize catastrophes, and our fears about what *might* happen mushroom to outrageous proportions and block change.

CATASTROPHIZING

Carla keeps her dismal social work job because she fears the alternatives. She is afraid she will fail at any other job. She wishes she could devote herself to a full-time private therapy practice, but every time she thinks about doing that, she is plagued by fears of financial ruin. First she is sure that she will not be able to pay her bills, then she just knows she will lose her home. Her husband will then sue for custody of their children and win. Finally Carla will have to go on welfare and end up spending her old age as a homeless bag lady.

From your point of view, Carla's fears may seem as absurd as the ax's falling on the imaginary child, but to Carla they are very real. She believes she cannot risk leaving her job and persuades herself to hang on to what she has no matter how much she hates it.

As Jack's stress and anxiety increases, he becomes acutely aware of his need for professional help. He knows that he must consult a therapist, yet he is afraid of what a therapist will tell him. At best, Jack expects to hear that his life is screwed up beyond repair and he will have to give up the accounting job that he has worked so hard to get. At worst, he believes that the therapist will take one look at him, call for the men in the white coats, and commit him to the nearest mental institution. Because his fears are so strong, Jack does not call the therapist to make an appointment, and stress and anxiety continue to plague him.

You imagine your boss's reply to your request for a pay raise. "Forget it," he says. "What makes you think you deserve a raise? You are not a valued employee. In fact, I've been meaning to tell you just how disappointed I am by your work."

Because of low self-esteem combined with fear, your thoughts turn to every mistake you have made during your tenure with the company, and you figure you are lucky to have a job at all.

You worry about the party you plan to attend. You worry about what to wear. Then you worry that whatever you choose will be the exact opposite of what everyone else is wearing and you will feel embarrassed and out of place. You worry about conversing with people you do not know very well and saying something stupid or offensive or not knowing what to say at all, which will make you look like an idiot. Then you worry that no one will start a conversation with you in the first place, making you feel like a loser, just like you used to at those junior high school dances. You feel doomed to stand alone and miserable while everyone else is having fun, "as usual." As a result, you wonder why you subject yourself to such humiliation and decide not to go to the party.

In each instance you do not fear a clear and immediate danger. Instead, you fear *possibilities*—possible pain, possible rejection, possible failure, possible embarrassment. In your imagination you conjure up the worst-case scenario and fear it will become a reality. All the while, however, you overlook the *probability* that what you so desperately fear will never come to pass.

Carla is not going to become a bag lady. Jack is not going

to be committed against his will to a mental hospital or be forced to quit his job. You might actually get the raise you request or have a good time at the party. But ruled by your fears, you sacrifice probable gains to protect yourself from possible loss—a decision that is going to get you stuck.

TEN WAYS FEAR BLOCKS CHANGE

1. Fear persuades you to set easier goals and do less than you are capable of doing.

I started this book by telling you how close I came to not writing it. Fear played a role in getting me stuck. I feared every publisher in America would reject the manuscript, that no one would read the book if it was published, and that someone else had already written a better book about change. I feared criticism from book reviewers and my colleagues in academia. I was afraid that the time I spent writing the book would have a negative impact on my family and my other work and that I would run out of things to say halfway through the project. I almost convinced myself to limit my writing to journal articles.

2. Fear triggers internal defense systems and fools you into thinking that you have perfectly good reasons not to change.

In the previous chapter you met Jennifer, the doctor's wife who fears losing what she already has. If she files for divorce, insists on marital counseling, or otherwise challenges her status quo, she may end up alone and stripped of the perks, privileges, and status of a doctor's wife.

When she thinks about change, Jennifer sees a painful, unappealing picture. To counter her fear, she paints a rosy picture of her present situation, trying desperately to convince herself that marriage to an unfaithful husband is "not so bad."

3. Fear—especially fear of failure or disappointment— reduces the number of available alternatives or keeps you from pursuing them.

April fears she will be alone and lonely for the rest of her life. What she fears even more, however, is the possibility that she will try to improve her situation, be disappointed by the results of her change effort, and *still* be alone and lonely. Therefore, to reduce the chances of being disappointed, she searches for a perfect solution, rejecting any alternative she perceives to be flawed or apt to fail. The trouble is, April perceives *all* alternatives that way.

4. Fear—particularly fear of making mistakes—causes indecisiveness and confusion. It stops you from knowing what you really *want.*

After discussing his concerns with trusted friends, Steven, the Miami plumbing contractor whose problems include cocaine and women, lists several ways to feel more in control of his own life. He lists actions he could take immediately, such as organizing and computerizing his business ventures, delegating responsibility, and managing his time. He also lists options that offer long-range benefits, such as seeing a therapist, starting an exercise program, and cutting down his cocaine usage. Unfortunately, having options only increases Steven's despair.

Steven cannot decide what to do first. He does not trust his own instincts or abilities and is terrified that he will make a dumb mistake or impulsively choose the wrong alternative, as he has done so often in the past. So, he waffles and procrastinates.

5. Fear warps your perception of your life and what you can do to make it better.

A realistic assessment of her situation would show Carla that she has proven talent as a therapist, many professional contacts and potential client referral sources, valuable expertise, and a great geographic location for her private practice, which is highly likely to thrive and flourish. If she approached her financial situation rationally, she would see that she does indeed have alternatives. If she wants to leave her savings and pension fund untouched for emergencies and future retirement, she can get a small business loan to cover her initial expenses. If she could think clearly, Carla would also know that her job stress and burned-out condition could damage her health, her personal relationships, and her family. If she viewed her situation objectively, she would choose to change. But seeing only what she fears—failure, financial ruin, and humiliation—she chooses not to change.

6. Fear keeps you from asking for help when you need it or benefiting from the emotional support offered to you.

As you may recall from Chapter Three, prior to the onset of anxiety attacks that prompted her to change, Cindy's self-esteem was extremely low. She assumed she was unlovable. From childhood experiences she came to believe her acceptance by other people rested on being cute, funny, and amusing all the time. She thought people would ignore and abandon her if she let them know how she really felt. Long before her anxiety attacks began, Cindy knew she was depressed, confused, and having difficulty coping. But fearing that even the people who loved her most would reject her, criticize her, or stop caring about her, she kept her pain and her problems to herself—until an emotional crisis forced her to seek help.

It's true that to ask for help is to risk losing face or hearing something you do not want to hear (as Jack did). To delegate responsibility, seek practical assistance or emotional support, is to possibly appear weak, incompetent, dependent, or needy. You risk rejection as well. So you decide to "go it alone." But that often turns out to be the most difficult way to go.

7. *Fear keeps you from asserting yourself and persuades you to settle for what you feel you must settle for instead of going after what you want.*

Although she had years of sales experience when she began her new job, Lisa is new to the office supply business. She is the only sales representative without a college degree and the only female. In addition, Lisa's colleagues seem so smart and confident and form a tight-knit group.

Fearing she will look dumb, naive, or incompetent, Lisa is reluctant to ask questions, offer opinions, or make suggestions. She works hard and keeps her mouth shut. Soon she knows the ropes and has a sales record comparable to her male colleagues, but her fears persist. She does not communicate her needs or problems, however, or question the policy decisions made without her input. She does not complain when she does not get the raise she is promised or is not considered for promotions. Consequently, with each passing day Lisa feels more unhappy, but she is scared to do anything about the situation.

8. *To calm your fears, you develop (and get stuck with) unhealthy habits and behavior patterns.*

Melanie is painfully shy and has been since early childhood. At first her shyness was not a problem. She rather enjoyed being by herself and occupying her time with imaginative fantasies. However, once she entered high school, she realized she might be missing something, but by then she had become too shy to make friends or socialize. Then a new family moved in next door, and their fifteen-year-old daughter befriended Melanie. The girl was Melanie's opposite in every way—outgoing, confident, and never at a loss for words. Melanie's friend dragged her along to parties where Melanie always felt uncomfortable and out of place.

Sometimes beer or wine was served at these parties, and Melanie's friend suggested she drink to relax and have a good time. Melanie resisted at first, but soon gave in and discovered the power alcohol had to loosen her tongue and boost her courage. After a few drinks Melanie was not timid anymore. She was not afraid of rejection or embarrassment or long awkward silences when she ran out of things to say. In fact, she became amazingly bold and witty. To this day in any social situation, whenever she feels insecure or fearful, Melanie drinks—a lot—since it takes more alcohol to loosen her up than it did when she was fifteen.

Similarly, Steven uses cocaine to feel the rush of power and confidence. To avoid the panic she feels in public places and behind the wheel of her car, Patty rarely leaves her house. In spite of her desire to lose weight, Karen goes on eating binges while she waits to hear about a writing assignment she really wants but fears she will not get.

9. Fear often makes you give up just one step short of your goal.

Newly identified and added to the menu of fears that block change is the fear of success. It is a common fear for the achievement-oriented woman, whose power, status, and wealth sometimes threaten the man in her life. This woman has worked hard to achieve her goals and aspirations, but just as she reaches the pinnacle of success as she always envisioned it, she asks herself, "What if I get what I really want only to lose the man I really want?" It is then that her fear of success overwhelms her, and she may stop achieving, sabotage her own career goals, or leave the "rat race" to pursue less demanding and threatening interests.

Fear of success is also at work when you ask yourself, "What if I get what I want but I am no happier than I was before?" This is a question well-known to anyone who attempts a change effort in one specific area. For instance, fear of success plagues Karen each time she nears or reaches her goal weight.

"People start treating me differently," she explains. "They pay more attention to me. They are nicer. Men come on to me and I have to deal with all the complexities of male/female relationships. There seem to be a million things I have to deal with that I didn't have to deal with when I had the wall of fat to protect me. I got what I wanted and I should feel good about it, but I don't. Life isn't better, it's more complicated. At the same time I get ticked off that people can't see I'm the same person on the inside as I was when I was fat. As a result, I get myself all worked up and start overeating again."

10. Fear keeps you from taking risks.

Anything you do to change or improve yourself involves risk—the chance of injury, damage, or loss. With every step forward you risk failure, disappointment, rejection, pain, or any other feared negative outcome. When change is involved, the most common fear of all is fear of the unknown or unfamiliar.

Nine times out of ten, change leaves you better off than you were before. Nine to one are terrific odds at the racetrack, in the gambling casino, or on the stock market. However, when you attempt change, the risk you take involves *your* life and *your* future and the stakes may seem too high. In addition, you have personal choices to make (which you naturally fear will be the wrong choices), and you alone are responsible for making your effort to change work (which you naturally fear you will fail to do over the long haul). Suddenly, the nine-to-one probability of success no longer reassures you. The one in ten chance for failure, disappointment, loss, or pain frightens you. It frightens you enough to keep you from taking the risk.

Fear of unknown and unpredictable outcomes of a change effort can freeze you in your tracks. Afraid to enter unfamiliar territory, you get stuck where you are. Fear in any flavor can keep you from getting unstuck.

Fear Can Control Your Life If You Let It

In my youth, I heard President Franklin Delano Roosevelt declare, "We have nothing to fear but fear itself." At the time it made a modicum of sense to me. Over the years it has grown ever more meaningful. Fear can, and often does, take on a life of its own. As its power increases, it can take over *your* life as well.

The physical and emotional reactions to fear are extremely uncomfortable. Fear itself is frightening, escalating the pain over your situation that you already feel. Whether you fear a very real and life-threatening mugger who confronts you at knifepoint or the mere possibility of an unpleasant occurrence, your body mobilizes its energy to fend off an attack. Your muscles tighten, your breathing becomes rapid and shallow, your heart beats faster, and adrenaline rushes through your veins. Fear can also take you by surprise when no tangible threat is present.

When a physical threat passes, your body returns to "normal." However, when what you fear is intangible and relates to a problem, a pending decision that will not go away, or something of which you are not even consciously aware, fear turns into anxiety. It hangs around persistently or appears unexpectedly, perhaps blossoming into full-fledged panic or anxiety attacks, causing dizzyness, hyperventilation, tingling or numb hands and feet, pounding headaches, and other painful, frightening symptoms.

With or without panic attacks, fear and anxiety cloud your thinking and produce a sense of dread and impending doom that reduce your ability to make decisions or take action. You feel paralysed and powerless because of your fears.

The most common reaction to fear and anxiety is to avoid anything that frightens you or makes you anxious. This avoidance is most clearly and dramatically seen in people who suffer from phobias—irrational, overpowering fears of flying, closed places, crowds, heights, and many other things. The most severely afflicted phobics create specific safety zones for themselves. These may be a two-mile or two-block radius around the home, the inside of a house, or sometimes only one floor or several rooms inside the house. Agoraphobics move outside their safety zones very rarely—if at all. Their life in its entirety is turned over to their fears.

Most of you do not suffer from debilitating, life-restricting phobias. However, your reaction to fear differs only in degree. Like the phobic, you avoid what you fear. If decisions bring on anxiety, you avoid making them. If social situations frighten you, you do not socialize. If asserting yourself causes stress and tension, you keep your mouth shut and go along with what others say, even if you disagree. If lovers hurt you in the past and you fear you will be hurt like that again, you avoid intimacy. Your fears dictate how you live your life, limit your enjoyment or satisfaction, and hamper your ability to change for the better.

Quite logically you may conclude that the best way to rid yourself of fear and anxiety is to avoid the situations and abandon the behaviors that cause fear and anxiety. But the truth of the matter is that to overcome fear and get on with your life, you must FACE FEAR HEAD ON AND PUSH THROUGH IT, reclaiming the power and energy it stole from you.

DISMANTLING BARRIER #5: PUSHING THROUGH FEAR

Pioneers in the treatment of phobias, behavioral scientists often compare fear to a monster living in a cave. Periodically the monster comes out into the open to attack you and bring on the painful, panicky symptoms I described earlier. To avoid these feelings, you do anything and everything you can to make sure the monster stays in his cave— where you cannot see him and are unlikely to be hurt by him. Of course, the monster is perfectly happy to stay in his cave, because he knows he still controls your life and your behavior. In fact, he is quite pleased with himself. Without lifting so much as a finger he has you where he wants you —stuck and afraid to do anything to get unstuck.

To rid yourself of fear and regain lost control, you must

lure the monster out of his cave and whack him on the head until he can no longer harm you. You must take a good long look at your fears and see how they limit you. Then you will be able to take steps to counteract those fears, control your anxiety, and move forward once again.

Learning to Relax

As previously noted, the painful physical symptoms, thoughts, and emotions activated by fear and anxiety are themselves frightening. Often they hit you without warning, wake you in the middle of the night, or automatically escalate when you think about change. Because they seem to occur spontaneously, you may think such stress and anxiety reactions are beyond your control. This is not true.

You can learn to control your physical symptoms and actually create a state of being that is the exact opposite of distress and anxiety. You can learn how to relax your body and your mind. Relaxation techniques give immediate, measurable relief, and they contradict your beliefs about fear. If your reaction to fear can be controlled, so can anything else you do or do not do when you feel fearful. If fear is a monster, it is one of your own making. You can alter its existence or eradicate it altogether.

There are any number of resources available to teach you relaxation techniques. There are books, courses, and even anxiety-reduction clinics that use biofeedback machines to measure relaxation. I lean toward the use of audio tapes myself and recommend you get one and follow its instructions. You can also relax without electronic devices or audiovisual aids.

A PHYSICAL RELAXATION EXERCISE

Sit in a comfortable chair (recliners work well) or lie down. Close your eyes.

Focus your attention on your breathing. Think of nothing

else. Other thoughts may intrude. Acknowledge them. Let them pass through your mind, but do not focus on them. Return your attention to your breathing. Continue this until your breathing is calm and rhythmic (as opposed to rapid, tight, or strained).

Then, beginning with your toes and moving upward one muscle group at a time, *tense* the muscles—*hold* for a slow count of three—then let go and *relax* the muscles. You will feel the distinct difference between tension and relaxation. Repeat the *tense-hold-relax* sequence on the muscles in your calves, thighs, buttocks, abdomen, chest, back, shoulders, arms, hands, neck, and face. If you still notice tension anywhere, tense-hold-relax those muscles, so that your entire body is completely relaxed.

A MENTAL RELAXATION EXERCISE

Once you remove physical tension from your body, take your mind on a short vacation. Think of a place (real or imaginary) that is particularly calm and soothing for you and place yourself in it. You might be lying on a deserted beach, floating in a canoe on a calm lake, strolling through a garden, sitting on the porch swing at your grandmother's house, or any other place that symbolizes peace and serenity for you. Imagine it with all your senses. Relax and enjoy being there. Then, slowly return your attention to the here and now.

Taking only fifteen minutes, this technique offers physical and emotional relaxation. It brings anxiety down to level one or two on a scale of ten. It can be used to ward off a pending anxiety attack, prepare you to sleep through the night, or rejuvenate you to face the rest of the day or evening.

Confronting the Monster

Once you learn what relaxation feels like and how to control your level of relaxation, you can use what you learned to reduce fear's hold on your life. First make yourself relaxed and focus on your calm scene until your stress/anxiety level rates a one on a scale of one to ten. Then begin thinking about a stressful situation in your life, one that conjures up fear in the flavor of your choice. This may be asking for a pay raise, going to a party, broaching the topic of marriage counseling with your spouse, attending your first therapy session, going on a diet, or any other area of conflict and confusion.

As you think about the stressful situation, your anxiety level will rise. When it reaches a three or four level on your one to ten scale, *stop* thinking about the problem and focus once again on your breathing. Relax any muscles that feel tense and visualize your calm scene, bringing yourself back down to level one.

Over the course of several days or weeks, repeat this process. Each time, think about the situation for a longer period of time and allow your anxiety level to get higher before returning to level one. After you have worked yourself up to level ten a few times, you will make an interesting discovery. It becomes *more difficult* to reach level ten. The same catastrophic thoughts and dreaded outcomes do not frighten you *as much* as they once did. Soon they hardly frighten you at all.

More importantly, you realize *you are in control.* During these sessions, *you* create high anxiety levels and you reduce your anxiety. If you can do it during a relaxation session, you can do it as part of daily living. When you face a decision, a problem, or a possible effort to change, *you* control the amount of fear and anxiety you feel. If you notice yourself becoming fearful, you can reduce the amount of fear you feel. You can reduce it enough to push right through it and do what you really want to do.

With practice you can become sensitive to the slightest increase in fear or anxiety, and you can do something about it. The next time you fear *possible* failure, rejection, disappointment, or any other dreaded outcome—SLOW DOWN!

Take a few deep breaths. Relax your tense muscles. Take a quick peek at your calm scene and push past that fear.

Imaging for Success

Thoughts are powerful. You know that because you have watched your thoughts block change. You have seen how thinking of the worst-case scenario stirs up fear and self-doubt. You have used thoughts to reframe reality and convince yourself that things are not so bad. Your thoughts have lowered your self-esteem. All too often how you think about change blocks change and gets you stuck.

Positive thoughts are powerful too. You can visualize success as well as failure. If your mind can picture the way you really want your life to be, you vastly improve your chances of actually achieving your goals.

Once again bring yourself to a relaxed state. Visualize a success. Picture yourself shaking your boss's hand after he says, "Of course you can have a raise. You've earned it." Imagine yourself enjoying a party. See yourself ten or twenty pounds thinner. What are you wearing? How do you move? What do you do that you did not do before? Envision yourself celebrating the six-month anniversary of the day you quit smoking, receiving your college diploma, having a love relationship, crossing the finish line of a 10K road race, or achieving any other goal. Visualize each step along the way. Create a detailed image of yourself as you will be when you get what you want. Savor it and return to it at the end of each relaxation session.

Imaging predicts success and motivates you to reach for the real thing. Imaging trains you to think and act positively, to say "I can" and "I will" instead of "I can't" or "I'll never." Imaging helps you push through fear so that you stop looking at the worst possibilities and focus instead on how good life can be.

Affirmations

Imaging works best when accompanied by *affirmations*—positive statements reinforcing your beliefs about what you *can* do and how good you *can* be.

Once you have visualized achieving a goal or taking a positive step toward your goal, repeat several affirmations about that goal. Begin your affirmations with:

I can . . .

I will . . .

I deserve to . . .

I owe it to myself to . . .

Success will be sweet when I . . .

Write down your affirmations. Read them before you go to sleep at night, when you awaken in the morning, and anytime your fear monsters come calling.

Taking Action to Push Through Fear

I can fly an airplane. I learned several years ago. I did not know exactly why I wanted to fly, but the thought of being airborne behind the controls of a small plane thrilled me. If I learned to fly, I knew I would have mastered a truly marvelous skill, one that I had never done before. The challenge excited me and also frightened me.

Flying a small plane is a big risk. It involves the possibility of mechanical failures, sudden storms, gusts of wind during takeoff, and making mistakes at some crucial moment. Yes, there is a great deal of risk involved.

I did not *have* to learn to fly, but I still really wanted to risk it. I would achieve a new goal, conquer a new frontier. I knew I would feel more capable and more powerful. I was correct on all counts.

But I must admit I had my doubts when my flight instructor turned out to be just twenty years old. He assuaged some of my fears the first time I flew with him, however, flying with grace, precision, and confidence, as if flying were something he was born to do. Yes, he could fly, but could he teach? I had to be sure of that. For flying to be a reasonable risk rather than a foolish one, I had to know this young man could teach me superbly.

I had been a teacher all of my professional life, so I knew a thing or two about teaching. I knew for example that good teachers do not just teach, they teach to accomplish an objective. Half-joking and maybe a little nervous, I playfully asked what his objectives were. He took me seriously, however. "I have just one objective," he answered. "It's to teach you how to keep yourself alive."

That was exactly what I wanted to hear. It told me he understood risk. He knew about the wisdom and skill that must illuminate all risk taking, and he was well aware of the balancing act of pushing yourself to get what you want while still protecting yourself from harm. You must account for the chance of injury, damage, or loss inherent to any risk, yet you cannot become so fearful of the possibilities that you do not risk at all.

MORE ABOUT RISK TAKING

To be healthier and happier as well as to get what you really want, you must push through fear by taking well-chosen, carefully considered, and wisely executed risks. Let me review four types of risks, three of which were presented as self-esteem building blocks in Chapter Three. All four promote growth and change, and all produce an exhilaration that gives life a certain spice.

INTELLECTUAL RISKS expand awareness, acquaint you with new ideas, reactivate your brain cells, make you more open to the world around you and more accepting of the positive possibilities life offers. To risk intellectually, read more demanding books, see more challenging films, drive miles if need be to hear a provocative speaker, subscribe to magazines and newspapers that stretch you intellectually and sometimes even threaten your opinions.

PHYSICAL RISKS push your body to its limit, increase your endurance, test your agility, your courage, and your survival instincts. Physical risks are tangible proof of your current capabilities and your potential to do more today than you did yesterday.

Included in the physical risk category are those activities that present some physical danger, activities where injuries can occur unless skill, knowledge, and wisdom are employed. When done correctly and responsibly, these "edge sports" let you experience the thrill, sense of accomplishment, and sheer exhilaration that comes from successful risk taking. Edge sports include everything from rugby to rock climbing, from hang gliding to waterskiing. My edge sport may not be yours. There are countless areas of physical risk from which to choose, including learning to drive a stick-shift car, dirt biking, running a mini-marathon, or diving from the high board at the community swimming pool.

SPIRITUAL RISKS ask you to explore your faith and dare you to meet your God in ever more meaningful ways—ways that go beyond the boundaries of traditional religion. By exercising faith and discovering the realm unexplainable by your five senses or the marvels of modern technology, you expand your world tremendously and conquer fear. When you live your life by faith instead of fear, you make no excuses. You do whatever it takes to be the best you can be.

EMOTIONAL RISKS are the most frightening. So many fears are reactions to the possibility of emotional pain. Emotional risks are taken when you dare to meet new people, deepen existing friendships, ask for emotional support or seek counseling, repair broken family ties, face conflicts head-on, or ask brave questions about the future of a relationship. The greatest emotional risk of them all is to move toward genuine intimacy, to allow another person to see all of you, including your fears and vulnerability.

LISA'S RISK

Risking genuine intimacy was something Lisa and Bob were afraid to do. They met at a social function sponsored by a company to which Lisa sold office supplies. There was real chemistry between them, and by the end of the party they had plans to see each other again in the near future.

Dinner and a concert led to more dates. Soon they were spending every weekend together, then weekends and two or three nights each week. After a year Lisa wondered why she rented her own apartment, but Bob had never mentioned living together, and marriage seemed to be an off-limits topic.

"When I met Bob, he was dating several other women," says Lisa. "They were tall, gorgeous, and sophisticated. Bob's friends never failed to mention how I was not his usual type, and it got to me. He was this rich, powerful lawyer who had traveled all over the world and knew lots of important and famous people. I loved to listen to his stories, but at the same time they made me feel insecure. What was this hotshot doing with a boring sales rep from a one-horse town on Long Island?"

Further fueling Lisa's fears was the fact that Bob did not have a terrific track record when it came to relationships. "By the third month we were dating, I had heard about all his old girlfriends," Lisa continues. "And there were plenty of them. They came with the same basic story. In the end they all turned into clingy, demanding shrews. Bob tried to let them down nicely but eventually had to hurt them to free himself."

Determined *not* to be like her predecessors, Lisa made no demands. She was supportive and understanding and flexible. She never shared her problems with Bob, seeking emotional support from her girlfriends instead. Whatever time they spent together was at Bob's suggestion, not Lisa's.

"It was easy to let him call the shots, because he was really good to me. We had a great time together and I loved him dearly. Besides, even if he did not say it, I was pretty sure he was in love with me, too. But after about nine months it started to get to me. I couldn't go on pretending what I needed did not matter or keep things from him because I did not want to look demanding or dependent. And I needed to know if the relationship was going anywhere, if it had a future and what the future was."

It took Lisa three more months to "get up the nerve" to say anything. She was afraid he would reject her, abandon her, or hurt her. Finally she told him what she had been doing and why she had done it. Then she took a deep breath and asked him where he saw their relationship going.

"I braced myself for the response I expected," Lisa recalls. "I thought he would say 'Why does it have to be going anywhere?' and launch into a lecture about freedom and no commitments and going with the flow. Instead, he said he would have asked me to marry him six months ago, but he didn't think I was interested."

Fearing rejection and the possibility of being hurt, Lisa had behaved with calculated nonchalance. Responding only to what Bob wanted, she had asked for nothing and gave no indication that she wanted anything of significance from the relationship. Fearing the same possibilities, Bob thought Lisa did not need him, that she could take or leave their relationship and would indeed walk away one day. He assumed she would say no to a marriage proposal or an offer to live together, so he did not ask either. For at least six months they both allowed their fears to convince them to settle for what they had and reach for no more.

Then, fortunately, Lisa took a huge emotional risk. Everything she believed about Bob told her he would run as fast and as far as he could if she used words such as "future" or "commitment." Asking her brave question *could have* turned her fears into reality. On the other hand, she could have settled for less than she wanted and *still* been hurt if their relationship had ended one day.

"The biggest risk I ever took had the best results," says Lisa, who has been married to Bob for two years now. "I don't know if risk taking always works out that way, but I can't imagine what my life would be like today if I had not taken that risk when I did."

Lisa took a risk and came out ahead. Much of the time, risks work out that way. You may not get all you want, but you generally get more than you had before. And you give that fear-monster a hefty whack on the head, reducing fear's control over you.

TO PUSH THROUGH FEAR—TAKE MORE RISKS

WE ALL TAKE RISKS. If you think *you* do not, reread the list of successes you compiled while reading Chapter Three. You *have* taken risks before. You will take them again. To get unstuck, you must. Risks teach valuable lessons, not the least of which is how to risk successfully in the future.

Five Risks Already Taken

On a sheet of paper, list five risks you have taken in the past. Remember, a risk is anything that includes the chance of physical or emotional injury, damage, or loss. Your risk could have been taken at work, in your family, or as part of a love relationship. The risk might have been intellectual, physical, spiritual, or emotional. Leave seven or eight blank lines between each risk.

Now think about how you felt *before* you took that risk. What did you fear? Directly below each risk, list your fears.

In spite of those fears, you went ahead and took the risk. What did you do to push through fear? What did you think, say, and do to get yourself to take the risk? Write your answers in the remaining space below each fear.

Five Risks You Want to Take

Of course, there are many other risks you will take during your lifetime. The next risks you take may result from your desire to move closer to overall wellness, get something in your lifeline net, clear up an area of conflict and confusion, or pursue an alternative to a specific problem. Using your ideas about change found in the strategies you did in Chapter Two or the alternatives you listed in Chapter Four, select five risks you need to or want to take now or in the near future. List them on another sheet of paper. As you did before, leave space between each risk.

What fears come to mind or well up in your gut when you think about taking the risks you have listed? What possible physical or emotional danger, injury, or loss do you fear? List those fears. How will you push through your fears and actually take those risks? Using what you have learned from past risk taking as well as ideas you found in this chapter, make notes to yourself about how to push through fear.

Creative Worrying

You may want to go one step further and do some *creative worrying* about the risks you want to take. When you worry creatively, you let your imagination run wild, catastrophize prolifically, and think of all those worst-case scenarios.

List *everything* that could go wrong.

For every potential disaster, ask yourself what you can do to make sure the catastrophe you fear does *not* happen.

List one or more contingency plans for each imagined disaster. Then—like the flight instructor whose objective was
to teach me how to keep myself alive—you will be able to
risk wisely, with your eyes open wide and your anxiety under
control.

Whenever you risk, pushing through fear is easier if you
have the cooperation and support you need. Without other
people's help, support, validation, and cooperation, you will
get stuck again. Chapter Eight describes this next barrier
and shows you how to dismantle it.

8

███████████████████████████████

Change and
Cooperation

In previous chapters I have described Carla, who is stuck in a job she detests, and Marilyn, who returned to the work force after her husband unexpectedly left her. Both are divorced working mothers and have three children living at home. Carla's sons are nineteen, sixteen, and thirteen years old. Marilyn has sixteen- and fourteen-year-old daughters and a twelve-year-old son. With a full-time job and a part-time private therapy practice, Carla spends as many hours outside the home as Marilyn, who works full-time and takes nursing refresher courses. Yet, although their basic situations are quite similar, Marilyn and Carla run their households very differently.

Once Marilyn was no longer immobilized by depression, she tried to be superwoman. She works, goes to school, takes care of all homemaking chores, and is an active, involved parent. "The demands are endless," she sighs. "I have to be mom, dad, housekeeper, cook, dishwasher, chauffeur, cheerleader, seamstress, and breadwinner."

Marilyn's days begin at five-thirty A.M. She straightens

the house, does a load of laundry, and irons school clothes and nursing uniforms. Then she wakes the kids, makes breakfast, checks homework, packs lunches, and sends the children off to school. After that, she showers, dresses, drives to work, works her shift, runs errands, starts dinner, drives the kids to afterschool activities, helps with homework, serves dinner, and cleans up after the meal. She also goes to class three nights a week, invariably returning to find her house a mess or her children in the midst of some crisis. After they go to bed, she studies, pays bills, does more laundry, and falls into bed by midnight.

Weekends offer little relief. She must catch up on all the housekeeping and errands she could not get to during the week as well as spend as much "quality" time as possible with her children. "I don't know how other single working mothers handle it," she groans. "Being all things to all people is making me crazy. I'm running myself ragged.

"But it all *has* to get done somehow. Asking the kids to help is more trouble than it's worth. They moan and groan and never do things the way I like them done. Most of the time I have to go back and redo what they've done. Then they moan and groan some more, asking why I didn't just do the job myself in the first place.

"I used to be too depressed to do anything. Now I do it all and I'm a raving maniac. Instead of whining and crying, I yell and criticize. I lie in bed after the alarm rings each morning and don't know how I'm going to make it through another day. I pray that things won't be like this forever, but I don't see any end in sight."

On the other hand, Carla has worked and single-handedly raised her children for close to a decade. At first she handled her many roles and responsibilities in the same way Marilyn does and also felt overwhelmed and resentful. Now, Carla and her sons work together to complete household chores and coordinate their hectic schedules.

"It's a matter of survival," Carla explains. "If you want clean clothes, a house that isn't a pigsty, food to eat, and a clean fork to eat it with, you have to pitch in. It isn't fair to expect me to do it all just because I'm the mother.

"It's also about family harmony," she continues. "We each have things we have to do and things we want to do. The boys have sports and dates. They want to hang out at the shopping mall. The oldest has a part-time job. I have work and friends and errands to run, clients to see. Three of us can drive, but there are only two cars. If any of us are going to get at least some of what we want, we have to join forces and work together."

In Carla's house, each family member has several permanently assigned responsibilities. Particularly distasteful chores, such as vacuuming, dishwashing, and cleaning bathrooms, are assigned on a rotating basis. A multicolored housework schedule hangs on the kitchen wall so that everyone can see who is supposed to do what. Next to the work schedule is a large calendar. As soon as any family member learns of a scheduled appointment or activity, he or she writes it on the calendar.

Once a week a family meeting is held at which the calendar is reviewed and transportation arrangements made. Failure to complete assigned tasks is also discussed, and conflicts between two or more family members are resolved.

"We talk about fun things, too," Carla explains. "Like how to spend money left over from the household budget and where to go on vacations. The point of everything we do is to avoid turning minor disagreements into major arguments and prevent any one person from feeling abused or unappreciated."

Disagreements do occur, of course. Plans or schedules are not always followed to the letter. One family member can ask another to do his chore—usually in exchange for cash, a ride, or some other favor. The bartering system occasionally gets out of hand, however, and inequities must be corrected at the next family meeting.

"There are always little crises," Carla admits. "Someone decides they just *have* to go somewhere right away, or that an item of clothing they neglected to put in the clothes hamper needs to be washed and ironed immediately because it is the *only* thing they can wear that day. We're not perfect. But our system works for us. Everything that needs doing gets done, and no one feels overburdened or taken for granted."

The difference between Carla's family harmony and Marilyn's family chaos can be summed up in one word—COOPERATION.

BARRIER #6: A LACK OF COOPERATION

To cooperate is to act or work *together* with another person or other people. People who cooperate join forces to reach a common goal or solve a mutual problem. They unite to emotionally support one another, share wisdom, and benefit from each other's experiences. Cooperation creates partnerships. Each partner brings something into the cooperative effort and gets something out of it. They pull together and as a result achieve more than they could if they worked alone.

Carla gets cooperation. With each person contributing to an effort that benefits them all, Carla's household runs smoothly and to everyone's satisfaction most of the time. Marilyn, however, lacks cooperation. Household chores get done only because Marilyn overextends herself to do them all. She feels overwhelmed, resentful, and trapped—feelings that detract from her relationship with her children and her ability to enjoy life.

Barrier number six—a lack of cooperation—slows and complicates change efforts. It does this by preventing you from getting the help you need, creating new problems or unexpected obstacles. It may also strain relationships with people who matter to you, sometimes prompting them to work *against* you rather than *with* you.

Why You Need Cooperation

Change does not occur in a vacuum. From the moment you decide to change, while you progress toward your goal, and after you reach it, people are drawn into your change effort. Some participate at your request. Some become allies, encouraging and supporting you. Some are automatically affected by what you do, such as friends, family, coworkers, and others who feel the impact of your effort to change and must adjust accordingly.

With cooperation you get more of what you need and move steadily toward your destination. Without cooperation you get less help, support, or encouragement, make much slower progress, or get stuck altogether.

COOPERATION gets you the emotional support or practical assistance you need to succeed. A LACK OF COOPERATION limits the help you receive and the success you are able to achieve.

In many cases, in order to succeed, you *must* act or work together with other people. Simply put, you may need help. You need the services of a professionally trained therapist or the emotional support and advice of other recovering alcoholics, addicts, overeaters, or compulsive gamblers. Or you may need a "change partner" who goes on a diet with you, attends the same aerobics class, runs with you each morning, or edits the great American novel you have always wanted to write. Cooperation may also take the form of practical assistance—help with household chores, transportation, child care, typing, finances, or the planning of your father's sixtieth birthday party.

When you know how to cooperate, you get the help that allows you to change successfully. If, for reasons I will present later, you try to change without cooperation, you are liable to fail or get stuck.

COOPERATION supplies encouragement or backing from allies. A LACK OF COOPERATION leaves you with discouragement and more problems.

Jack, the accountant, has started a step-by-step stress management plan and is pleased with the progress he has made. He assumes other people will be pleased too, but finds that just the opposite is true. Jack's friend and drinking buddy, Kevin, tries to get Jack to "loosen up and party." He says the new, improved Jack is boring and less fun than he used to be. Jack sometimes believes Kevin's assessment, and it takes all his strength to *not* get plastered with Kevin on a Saturday night or keep his therapy appointments instead of "playing" with his friends.

Jack's business colleagues also notice the change in Jack. They too are put off by his new mellow approach because they still run around like chickens with their heads cut off and feel their blood pressure rise each time a work-related problem presents itself. Although Jack expects his cohorts to admire and respect his self-improvement and perhaps ask how they too can reduce stress, he instead hears put-downs and comments about how he is "losing his competitive edge and killer instinct."

"Other people's reactions are a whole new source of stress for me," Jack says. "I'm sticking to my program, but it would be a whole lot easier if people didn't give me such a hard time about it."

The amount of cooperation you ask for and receive influences the level of success you achieve and your desire to continue moving forward. Cooperative people say, "Go for it. You can do it. We're behind you all the way." Hearing these enouraging words, you want more than ever to forge ahead and reach your destination. When you lack cooperation, however, you hear, "Give it up. It isn't worth it. Why can't you leave well enough alone? Your ridiculous notions are ruining our lives." Understandably, your desire wanes and your determination wavers. You are quite likely to give in, give up, and get stuck.

COOPERATION helps you contend with new or unexpected obstacles and problems. A LACK OF COOPERATION often prompts you to turn back at the first sign of resistance.

Change can create unanticipated problems or present unexpected obstacles. Any goal you pursue, bad habit you alter, or self-improvement effort you undertake touches the lives of the people around you. Accepting the job you *really* want means you will have to relocate, travel extensively, or work longer hours. Now your family faces the prospect of uprooting their lives to relocate with you, or your lover must adjust to seeing you less often.

Similarly, a return to the work force alters relationships with your spouse and your children. Newfound assertiveness confounds your friends and coworkers. Giving up drugs or drinking alters your social relationships. Getting involved in a love relationship threatens friends who see you spending more time with your lover and less time with them.

In these examples you can see change's domino effect. Altering and improving *your* life starts a chain reaction. Your success or a step toward it will subtly or dramatically change your relationships with the people around you. They must adjust, and you, in turn, must adapt to their adjustment.

When you approach change cooperatively, other people have a better idea of what to expect from the change effort and are more willing to work together to resolve the resulting problems or obstacles. On the other hand, a lack of cooperation turns obstacles into barriers and problems into crises. Working through the conflicts can become so painful and complicated that you abandon your effort.

COOPERATION is the difference between being supported or being sabotaged.

Sometimes people who are stuck themselves feel threatened by your self-improvement efforts. Your time-management plan may work brilliantly for you. Unfortunately, your coworkers feel your efficiency makes them look bad, and they decide to give you the silent treatment.

Your diet may be a terrific success. Compliments on your appearance abound. As a result, your spouse cannot help but notice your renewed desirability to other men. This consciously or unconsciously frightens him, and the next thing you know, he brings home devil's food cakes and ice cream. He finds ingenious reasons to celebrate by taking you to fancy restaurants that serve rich, tempting foods. He decides to learn to cook and appoints you his chief taste-tester. A day does not pass without his asking when the diet will end or mentioning how much he misses having "love handles" to grab.

Or perhaps, for the first time in years, your life seems to be going the way you want it to. You work part-time, take courses at the local community college, and date or socialize with friends on Saturday nights. Unexpectedly, however, your son begins to suffer headaches of unknown origin, your daughter misbehaves at school, both children's grades drop, and they complain every time you leave the house. They enlist grandma as an ally and she heaps on the guilt. Feeling bad, you limit nights out to once a month. Then you drop your night courses. Finally you quit your job. Without knowing how you got there, you find yourself back at square one.

When you lack cooperation, your best-laid plans get you nowhere. Instead, your best efforts run you smack into a brick wall of resistance from the people who matter to you. They want to reinstitute the old you—the person they were used to and comfortable with, the person they could relate to without having to change themselves in any way. In this way they are subtly or obviously sabotaging your change efforts.

**But It's Their Fault, Not Mine. The People in My Life
Are Not About to Cooperate!**

Barrier number six comes with a ready-made reason *not* to change. When you take a quick inventory of your friends, family, lovers, and coworkers, you easily see that most of them are completely uncooperative. You believe that because they have their own problems or they are set in their ways or they never really understood you, you cannot force them to cooperate.

Each year, Thanksgiving Day is a disaster. Your mother criticizes your cooking. She argues with your mother-in-law, who thinks you should have used *her* recipes. Children, screaming like wild banshees, race through your home knocking over furniture and breaking things. The meal is wolfed down during the halftime of TV football games. Even so, there is enough time to start a vicious political discussion or bitterly rehash a wrong done by one family member to another. Someone leaves the table in tears, someone spills red wine on your antique oriental carpet, and as soon as you finish washing dishes and wrapping leftovers, someone walks into the kitchen and asks to take home some turkey, stuffing, and pumpkin pie. Each year, the best you can say about Thanksgiving is that it is over. You dearly wish you could do things differently, but sadly sigh, "It will never happen. *They*'ll never go for it."

Although you want more from your marriage and you and your husband have reached an impasse, you reject counseling as an alternative. "He would never agree to it," you claim.

You do not present your plan to improve job satisfaction because your boss "is not open to employee suggestions" and your coworkers "would never get behind the idea."

You want to go into business for yourself and know you can succeed. All you need is five thousand dollars in start-up funds, but you do not ask your father for it because "he doesn't loan money to his children, never has and never will."

You want to start a support group for working mothers, but you can't seem to get it off the ground. You decide the women you want to join your group "are all too busy for something like this. They'd never get it together."

I could go on endlessly about the dreams and goals that fall by the wayside because you assume you cannot get the cooperation you need from the people you know and/or love. You honestly believe they will *never* agree to cooperate. Of course, *you* do not actually ask for their cooperation. Instead, you blame a lack of cooperation on the people whose co-operation you need, assume you will not get what you want, and give up without trying to change. Consequently, *you* give barrier number six the power to get you and keep you stuck.

Now, before you discount what I'm saying because I don't know your friends, family, or coworkers, let me re-assure you that their lack of cooperation is not entirely *your* fault either. But the real reason barrier number six impedes your progress is because you DO NOT KNOW HOW to get the cooperation you need. Few of us have mastered the art of cooperation.

WHY YOU DO NOT KNOW HOW TO COOPERATE: MYTHS ABOUT SUCCESS AND SELF-RELIANCE

MYTH NUMBER ONE—I don't need anybody.

"I used to think there were two kinds of people in the world," Cindy explains. "Givers and takers. I was a giver.

Givers are strong, independent, and reliable. We're like cactus plants—we survive without much care or attention. Givers never take," she says, relating the details of the belief system that contributed to her downfall and brought on her anxiety attacks. "We never ask for anything. We think we don't need much, and to tell you the truth, we'd rather suffer in silence than let other people think for a second that we are weak or needy. No matter what the problem is, we think we should be able to handle it ourselves."

You may not divide people into two mutually exclusive categories the way Cindy does, but I suspect you agree with the basic point she makes—that to ask for help is to admit weakness, failure, or inadequacy.

It is almost universally accepted that a "good" and strong person succeeds and gets unstuck on his own. This philosophy works better in principle than in practice, however. While working as a public relations director, Cindy was in pain. She doubted her ability and was confused about her identity and where she belonged. No one knew about her feelings, however, because she kept them well-hidden, giving the impression that she needed no one's help, support, or cooperation. In fact, she resented even minor suggestions. To Cindy, input was the same as criticism.

"Whenever anyone was sensitive enough to ask if something was wrong, I denied it," Cindy recalls. "I cut them off, changed the subject, or told them to mind their own business. I really thought I had to get my act together all alone." Of course, Cindy did not get better by herself. In fact, she got worse.

When you cling to the myth that only the weak and inadequate ask for help, you make the mistake of deciding to go it alone. You do not actually go anywhere, however. You are stuck without emotional support—other people's knowledge, optimism, and life experience. You reject people who could help you and sincerely want to cooperate, all because you believe you do not need anybody.

MYTH NUMBER TWO—If you want something done right, do it yourself.

This popular misconception is wreaking havoc on Marilyn's household. Like Cindy, Marilyn wants to manage without assistance. In addition to thinking she does not need anybody, she believes no one's help can meet her standards. The few times she has delegated responsibility, she has been dissatisfied with the result. More aggravated and overwhelmed than ever, she redid the job and decided not to bother asking for help again.

How many of you have fallen into the same trap? You could delegate tasks to the workers you supervise. You could ask your husband to do laundry, grocery shop, or prepare meals. Your kids could vacuum, dust, or make their own lunches. Each relative coming to your house for Thanksgiving dinner could bring part of the meal. You do not have to handle all the details for your father's sixtieth birthday party. You could ask your siblings to help or hire professionals.

You do not do any of these things or seek cooperation in countless other ways because you believe you will not get *exactly* what you want unless you get it yourself. By believing myth number two, you are unwilling to compromise or give up the smallest bit of control. Determined to do it all, do it right, and do it yourself, you become more overwhelmed and experience more stress, and of course, such a state is not conducive for starting or sticking to a self-improvement plan.

MYTH NUMBER THREE—I shouldn't have to ask.

Marilyn believes that if her children really cared about her, they would know she is overworked and would volunteer to help with the housework. She believes that she should not have to ask for their help.

Likewise, on more than one occasion, Cindy thinks her friends and family should sense her life is not all she makes it out to be. Even if she denies her feelings, she believes they should keep trying to get to the root of her problem. She believes that she should not have to ask.

You think you should not have to tell your lover you want more intimacy and communication. He thinks he should not have to tell you he needs space after a hard day at work. You think your boss should know you want positive feedback on a job well done. You believe your mother should be sensitive to your weight-loss efforts and know not to tempt you with fattening food. Your relatives should realize Thanksgiving dinner at your house every year is a tremendous burden. You think that someone should volunteer to have the family come to their house for a change. But you also believe that you shouldn't have to ask for any of those things.

So many of us honestly believe the people we love, respect, and work beside week in and week out *should* know what we need and *should* cooperate without being asked. Whether they should or should not is irrelevant—usually, they do not. And expecting to get cooperation without asking for it almost guarantees disappointment.

As a rule, human beings are lousy mind readers. Other people simply won't understand how you feel or what they can do to help you feel better—*unless you tell them.* They cannot give you what you need—*unless you request it.* Even if they try to be cooperative and supportive, they will continue to miss the mark—*unless you clearly communicate your desires.*

Of course, asking for cooperation does not guarantee that you will get the exact amount and kind of cooperation you *want.* However, *not* asking assures you of getting less cooperation than you *need* and, in most instances, no cooperation at all.

MYTH NUMBER FOUR—Success is achieved through COMPETITION.

To COOPERATE is to act or work together.

To COMPETE is to be in a rivalry, participate in a contest, or vie for a prize.

When you COOPERATE you join forces and combine strengths to achieve a common or mutually beneficial end. Everybody gains something. When you COMPETE, on the other hand, you win only when your opponent loses. You both want the same thing, but only one of you can have it. When you compete, getting what you want depends upon your ability to beat, overpower, outwit, or eliminate the other guy. The last thing you want to do is cooperate with him.

From preschool playground games to insider trading on the stock market, from outperforming the next kid on the geography quiz to outselling the next guy in order to win a trip to Hawaii, from making the best birthday card for your mother to getting your toddler into the "best" nursery school, the belief that success comes through competition is deeply ingrained in our culture and characters.

Throughout your life you hone your competitive abilities and reinforce the belief that being your best means proving that you are better than someone else. Unfortunately, this killer instinct and your competitive edge are not very helpful when you need cooperation. The deep-seated desire to win, win, win, stifles your ability to cooperate. Indeed, it keeps you from seeing cooperation as a viable alternative for reaching your goal.

But you must remember that you do not get emotional support or practical assistance by competing against the person whose help you need. Someone you try to outwit, outdo, beat, or eliminate is not about to work with you to achieve a mutually beneficial goal or willingly adapt to life with the new you. Competition is not conducive to personal growth and self-improvement—cooperation is.

To get the cooperation you need, you must compete less and cooperate more. You must counteract your own misconceptions about self-reliance, competition, and going it alone. Then you can learn new skills and approaches that promote cooperation and help you work *with* other people to attain the kind of life you desire and deserve.

DISMANTLING BARRIER #6:
GETTING MORE COOPERATION

Just as you learned to compete, you can learn to cooperate. The following suggestions and strategies help you get
more cooperation than you get now or have gotten in the past.
But *please*, do not think for an instant that you will get *all* the
cooperation you want each and every time you seek it.

We live in an imperfect world populated by individuals
who do not always speak or act precisely as we wish they
would. That will not change. People who know little or less
than you do about cooperation will be uncooperative at times.
Well-intentioned friends and relatives will do the best they
can and still fail to fully meet your expectations. And people
accustomed to hearing you say that you don't need anybody,
or people whose help you previously rejected, may hold back
when you attempt to gain their cooperation now. But that is
reality, and if you learn to work within its limits, you will
get the cooperation you need to improve your life.

So, please remember, you must dismantle barrier number six in order to get *more* cooperation, but that cooperation
does not necessarily have to be *perfect* and *complete* in order
to work for you.

Eight Ways to Get More Cooperation

Let's assume that one reason you lack cooperation today
is because, in the past, you did not cooperate often or easily.
You may be the product of a family that valued achievement
and competition. Perhaps your educational experiences included rewards for getting the highest marks in the class or
winning athletic competitions. Or you may be a perfectionist
or a control artist who does not trust other people to do things
the way you want them done, or you may be a loner who

prefers to keep some distance between yourself and other people. Whatever the reason, your past behavior did not foster cooperation.

Consequently, the people around you may be surprised by your present attempt to cooperate. Questioning your "real" motives or thinking that you are going through some kind of "phase," they may disregard your overtures and continue their old uncooperative ways. As a result, both you and the people who matter to you have to get used to the idea of cooperation before you embark upon cooperative change efforts. The first three ways to foster cooperation, listed below, lay the groundwork and set the stage for working together harmoniously.

1. Be open to suggestions and support when they are offered.

You must immediately begin to overcome success myth #1, I don't need anybody, and success myth #2, If I want something done right, I have to do it myself. Try not to be so hell-bent on getting unstuck *your* way that you reject or alienate people who sincerely want to cooperate. Do not bite the hand that brings you alternatives, advice, encouragement, or assistance—even if the unsolicited support is not exactly what you want at that moment.

In addition, listen for ideas that have not occurred to you and ignore the devilish voices that tell you accepting help is the same as admitting weakness. These are the people in your life who want to cooperate. Let them help you.

Maybe they are making their approach at the wrong time. Maybe the suggestion they are giving isn't really the right one for you. Perhaps you are getting advice when you want sympathy, or friends want to talk when you want something more tangible. Poor timing or an offer that misses the mark is no reason to callously dismiss someone who wants to be your ally and your friend.

You must lay the groundwork for cooperation by remaining open to emotional support, practical assistance, and advice when it is given voluntarily. If you cannot take the advice or follow their lead at the present time, let them know you appreciate them for caring. They may surprise you by adapting to your real needs now, and they certainly will be more likely to cooperate in the future.

2. Give cooperation.

This approach is so logical that it ought to occur to each and every one of us. In biblical terms, you reap what you sow. You get cooperation from the people with whom you cooperate.

Start looking for opportunities to help other people. Find the time to listen to their concerns. Carla did. From experience, her children knew that their mother was available to them—to hear their problems, answer their questions, and help them to make decisions. She gave her support without expecting to be paid back someday. She gave them concern and cooperation for its own sake. As a result, when, out of necessity, she asked for concern and cooperation from her children, they were willing to give it.

There are countless small ways you can cooperate. You can help with the housework even though it is not traditionally your primary responsibility. You can allow a co-worker to run ideas past you, watch your neighbor's children, offer a ride when a friend's car is being repaired, bring dessert or wine or the turkey to Thanksgiving dinner, accompany someone to an Alcoholics Anonymous meeting, or listen to the speech your husband has to give the next day.

Don't keep a tally sheet or fill a green stamp book full of favors. I know I am not the only one who cooperates reluctantly with people who remind me of everything they did for me in the past. Cooperate for cooperation's sake, to model and experience the joys and benefits of working together. Once partnership and harmonious relationships become familiar and comfortable for all involved, cooperation becomes easier to obtain. You will pave the way for future cooperation by being cooperative today.

3. **Decrease negative criticism and increase valida-tion.**

You undermine cooperation with negative criticism and all the nagging, harping, and nit-picking you do in the name of building character and improving performance.

Negative criticism erodes self-esteem. Someone who feels unloved, unworthy, or inadequate whenever he is around you is not going to stick around to cooperate with you. In addition, someone regularly subjected to your negative criticism may come to believe that your efforts to better yourself are, in fact, thinly disguised attempts to make him look worse. This may lead to sabotage instead of cooperation, and your put-downs and "constructive" feedback will only set an example of noncooperation. If you habitually criticize and complain about the help you *are* given, you will convince others nothing they can do will satisfy you. Why should they even try to cooperate?

Cooperation increases when your criticism decreases. If negative criticism worked, you would not spend so much of your time nagging, complaining, and repeating yourself. The next time you feel the urge to criticize—STOP. Instead, ask yourself: Will what I am about to say *really* help the other person? Will it *really* get me more of what I want? Is the damage it might do to my relationship in the long run worth the short-term benefit of being right or feeling superior to the person I am about to criticize?

If the answer to even one of these questions is no, bite your tongue and keep the peace. Try a little validation instead.

Validation is the opposite of negative criticism. When you validate someone, you tell him what you admire, appreciate, respect, love, celebrate, applaud, and enjoy about him as a unique and worthwhile human being. Look for opportunities to show that you value the people in your life and stay away from those validations that can be construed as backhanded compliments or poorly hidden criticisms, such as "It makes me so happy when you put your socks in the hamper" or "What a thrill to see you here on time." Start small if you must, but give the people you value at least three validations a day, preferably more.

You will be amazed to see how far a true validation goes to create bonds between people and foster cooperation. Think how much *you* would like to hear someone say, "I love seeing your smiling face in the morning" or "I appreciate how thoughtful you are. You always remember to ask how I'm feeling" or "I know how much work you put into that proposal. I really do admire your creativity and stick-to-itiveness."

A validated person is less likely to resist your efforts to change. Unlike the overly criticized person, someone who is validated has healthy self-esteem and is less threatened by your change effort. If you knew someone truly valued you, wouldn't you want to support and cooperate with him?

Accepting suggestions and support when offered, giving your cooperation willingly, reducing negative criticism and increasing validation, all set the stage for cooperation for your change efforts. Cooperation itself becomes an integral part of your life and the lives of those around you. Consequently, asking for help, support, encouragement, or adjustment to the new you fits you and your lifestyle, and because it does, it is much easier to come by.

4. Account for change's domino effect.

Consider in advance how your change effort will affect the people around you. If you can anticipate resistance or sabotage, you may be able to prevent it.

On a sheet of paper, make a list of people who play a significant role in your life. They can be family, friends, lovers, colleagues, or anyone else. For the most part they should be people you come in contact with at least once a month.

Which of these people will have to change in some way as a result of your change effort? Put a capital *C* beside their names.

Which of these people seem to be stuck themselves and

may feel threatened by your attempt to get unstuck? Put a capital *T* beside their names.

Who might try to sabotage you? Put a capital *S* beside their names.

Who are the adaptable people on your list? Even though your change effort may present them with an unexpected need to change, who will nonetheless try to cooperate? Put a double asterisk (**) beside their names.

This inventory of people in your life helps you in several ways. "C" people need to know from the outset what you plan to do and what impact it may have on them. Then you can work together to iron out the details. "T" people can also be informed of your intentions. But keep in mind that, for the most part, these are people whom you cannot expect to give you encouragement or praise and you must learn to accept that. People marked with a double asterisk (**), however, are your front line for cooperation. They have demonstrated their willingness to cooperate with and support you and should be the first people you consider when you want to ask for cooperation.

On the other hand, "S" people pose a tangible threat to your self-improvement effort, and their reaction or behavior has the potential to halt your progress or send you back to square one. As you did when you were "creative worrying" at the end of Chapter Seven, think about potential problems or possible sabotage and come up with contingency plans.

For example, after Lisa quit her second sales job, she was hired by another firm as a sales manager. She knew she was brought in to reorganize a department. The people she would supervise knew changes were coming, and one person—who wanted the job Lisa got—was particularly unhappy and vocal about it. But Lisa anticipated resistance and resentment and expected to be sabotaged. After consulting people who had been in similar situations, she decided that her best bet was to make change a group effort. So, she brought her group together, outlined the goals she was given by her superiors, asked for input, and formed committees, making sure to have the disgruntled employee head one of those committees.

By getting everyone actively involved in the effort, Lisa gave them a feeling of ownership. As she realized, people are less likely to undermine something they "own." What Lisa did to prevent sabotage is only one kind of contingency plan and it may not be the one you choose. However, you must try in some way to anticipate how change will affect the people in your life and plan to overcome problematic reactions.

5. Know what you want from whom.

In order to dismantle other barriers you have on several occasions reviewed the strategies found in Chapter Two (Why Change?). By now you have identified one or several benefits from your lifeline net you want to get or areas of conflict and confusion you would like to resolve. Now, from these possible change efforts, choose one you *really* want to pursue.

To improve the odds that you will get enough cooperation to succeed, before you begin a change effort, think about the cooperation you *wish* you could have. Luckily, what you wish is generally more than you absolutely need and almost always more than you will get, but it is nonetheless a good place to start identifying *kinds* of cooperation your change effort will require.

KINDS OF COOPERATION include:

Emotional Support (in the many forms described beginning on page 68 of Chapter Three)

Change Partners (people who will undertake the same self-improvement effort along with you)

Practical Assistance (help with tasks that are overwhelming or frustrating you)

Instruction (formal or informal)

Advice or Alternatives

Self-help/Support Groups

Professional Services
Adaptation to the New You
Encouragement/Gentle Pushes
Honoring Specific Time-Limited Requests (such as
keeping quiet while you study for an exam or loaning
you fifty dollars until payday)

Thinking about the change effort you intend to pursue, list every imaginable kind of cooperation you *wish* you could have. Be as specific as you can. For instance, if you are a wife and mother of three children who wants to return to college for paralegal training in hopes of returning to the work force, you may want, among other things—

—your husband to encourage you and let you use a portion of your savings to pay tuition;
—your children to give up part of their playroom for you to set up a desk;
—your neighbor to keep an eye on your children on afternoons you must attend classes;
—your family to cook dinner and clean up afterward several evenings a week;
—to be left alone to study whenever you ask.

For whatever change you hope to make, try to anticipate the kinds of cooperation you will want and make an extensive cooperation *wish list.*

As you may recall from Chapter Three (Self-esteem), you will rarely get all the support or cooperation you need from a single person. Some people in your life can give emotional support but are unreliable when it comes to helping with child care or transportation. Others will drive, cook, watch your kids, or loan you money, as long as they do not have to hear you say you are hurting. Still others are great cheerleaders or great brainstormers.

After reviewing the emotional-support-people strategy found in Chapter Three, identify a minimum of three people you know or could find to cooperate in each of the ways written on your wish list. Each person can be listed beside more than one kind of cooperation.

Give each of your three potential cooperators an A, B, or C rating. An A person is the most likely to cooperate and the person whose assistance you will request first. Bs and Cs are backup people or those who could do part of what you ask, if not all.

You may have difficulty completing this task. You may rack your brain but be able to think of no one who can cooperate in just the way you want. This is a clue that your standards and/or expectations are too high. Remember, you cannot expect all your desires of cooperation to be fulfilled. Now is as good a time as any to start seeing things more realistically.

6. Be realistic.

Karen really wants to develop healthy eating and exercise habits so she can lose thirty pounds and maintain her weight loss. Previously, in all her other attempts to achieve her goal, she never considered cooperation. At most she got help from a medically supervised weight-loss program, relying on one weight-loss counselor to meet all her needs. This time, however, she is making a cooperation wish list and immediately notices she cannot get all she wants in several areas. Particularly unrealistic is her wish that someone commit to walk with her for one hour every day, and her wish that no one tempt her with sweets or fattening foods. To get what she needs, however, she has to alter her idea of what she wants. She has to be more realistic.

DIVIDE AND CONQUER: To make expectations more realistic, consider getting *all* of what you want by combining the contributions of several people. It is easier to get a little cooperation from a number of different people than to get a great deal of cooperation from one person.

With this in mind, Karen, who wants to walk every day

and wants a walking partner, lines up several friends to walk with her on different days. Having the more flexible schedule, Karen walks at the time each friend wants to and goes to the location of *their* choice. Through compromise, therefore, Karen gets all of what she wants—although not in the exact way she originally expected to get it.

Are there ways *you* can divide and conquer? Could you rotate responsibility for distasteful chores the way Carla does? Could you get emotional support by discussing some concerns with friends, some with your spouse, and some with the members of a support group? If you reach an impasse when seeking cooperation, consider asking more people to do less rather than expecting a few people to do more than makes them comfortable.

COME DOWN FROM THE CLOUDS: Karen wishes no one would ever tempt her with sweets or fattening foods, which is obviously an unrealistic expectation. In order for that to work, she would have to inform everyone in her life (family, friends, and coworkers) of her goal and her wish for cooperation and that everyone would keep her diet in mind when serving food. Not even dividing to conquer could get Karen all of what she wants. She has to come down from the clouds and look at her need for cooperation realistically.

In order to look at cooperation realistically, you first need to be more specific about your needs. Break the cooperation you want into smaller pieces. When you say you want more help with housework, specify the help you need—someone to cook dinner twice a week, someone to do the laundry, someone to wash dinner dishes, someone to vacuum three times a week, someone to clean the bathrooms, someone to take out the garbage each morning, and so on. If you want Thanksgiving dinner to be more harmonious, specify what you want from your family—each person to bring a covered dish, to go to a different home each year, direct supervision of the children, a cleanup crew, and requests for leftovers made before leaving the table. List your exact wishes as clearly as you can.

On another sheet of paper, write numbers down the left side of the page, beginning with number one and continuing until you get to the number of items on your list of exact wishes. Then rank each item. Write the cooperative act you *need* the most to succeed beside number one, the next most *needed* item next to the number two, and so forth.

Next, review your list. At what point would you actually have what you need to change successfully? If items one, two, and three would be enough, draw a line across the page under item number three. If the top five are essential, draw a line under item number five. Anything *above* your line represents cooperation you *really* need and should be the cooperation you request from the people you previously identified as likely to give it.

7. Ask for what you need.

Sadly, most of you have a horrible time asking for what you need. The thought of revealing that you need anything, no less asking for help, is terrifying. I recommend you use what you learned about conquering fear (Chapter Seven) to reduce your anxiety level about asking for cooperation.

How to ask for what you need is an assertiveness skill. If asking for cooperation is very new to you, in addition to using the approach described below, I suggest you consult one of the many books about assertiveness that are available in most libraries or bookstores.

When you ask for cooperation, also help people understand *why* you need their cooperation. Tell them what you want to accomplish and how much achieving your goal means to you, as well as explaining what you actually need from them. You can clarify this for yourself by finishing the following sentence stems:

I want to . . .
It is important to me because . . .
I need you to . . .

Be specific and honest. And use what you have written as the basic for what you will say when you make your actual request. It also may help you to *rehearse,* especially if you fear you will get a negative response. Have someone you trust play the part of the person whose cooperation you seek. Make your request and have the actor respond in several different ways so you can work out contingency plans.

Remember, other people will not know what you need unless you tell them. Even if what you want is something you *think* you should be getting already—if you are not getting it, you have to ask. Remember, too, that asking *does not* guarantee your request will be granted. If you get a negative response on your first attempt, you need not allow the situation to be a total loss.

8. Be willing to negotiate.

Always, always, always approach cooperation with an open mind. Accept that other people will not meet your every need simply because you want them to. Do not *demand* cooperation or you will not get it. Instead, present your needs and discuss various alternatives until you arrive at a mutually agreeable solution. The process will not be painless, and it may be time consuming, but in the end you will have something you did not have before and might never have had if your concept of cooperation remained nonnegotiable. So, be willing to negotiate, to compromise, to trade favors, make concessions, and receive only *some* of what you need. That's still better than getting nothing.

One way to approach negotiation is to sit down with another person or other people and exchange descriptions of what each person sees as the optimal outcome to a particular situation. Each person asking or being asked for cooperation should complete the following sentence stems:

In my opinion the best possible outcome would occur if I would . . .

You would . . .
We would . . .

Each response defines the distance between individual positions and reveals points of compromise or potential to trade favors. For instance, a husband and wife, having reached an impasse in their marriage, complete the sentence stems in the following manner.

In the wife's opinion, the best possible outcome would occur if she asks her husband to get counseling, if he hears what she has to say and agrees, and if they go to a counselor together. In the husband's opinion, the best possible outcome would occur if he does not have to involve strangers (i.e., a counselor) in his private affairs, if his wife would spend weekends at home with him instead of working or socializing, and if they could work through their problems by talking honestly with each other.

After some negotiation the wife agrees to reserve one weekend a month exclusively for her husband. They also both agree to spend one hour twice a week discussing their problems and feelings the way they would if they were seeing a counselor. And the husband agrees to go into therapy with his wife six months from now if the situation has not improved. By negotiating, both get part of what they want and build a foundation for future cooperation.

Can Someone Who Gets Little or No Cooperation Really Improve the Situation?

Marilyn did. Using the same ideas you read about in this chapter, Marilyn got the cooperation she needed to get unstuck. She sought out other single working mothers and solicited their advice and suggestions. She also made a list of household chores she wanted her children to perform and held her first family meeting. Each child accepted two permanent chores and the rest were rotated weekly, with Marilyn included on the schedule. When her children complained that she was never satisfied with their work, Marilyn agreed to show them how she wanted things done. If they still did not perform to her standards, however, she would not criticize. Instead, she would bring it up for discussion at the next family meeting and promised to seriously consider being less of a perfectionist.

At first, Marilyn did not know quite what to do about constantly having to drive her children to afterschool activities or attend all of their school or extracurricular functions. Then her oldest daughter suggested asking Marilyn's father to help. It turned out that grandpa, recently retired and restless, was thrilled to oblige.

"We haven't worked all the bugs out of the system yet," Marilyn reports. "There are still things I need help with and things the kids want that I cannot give them. But life in our house is one hundred percent better than it used to be—and six months ago you could never have convinced me it was possible."

As Marilyn learned, you can't always get exactly what you want. But if you try, you may be able to get what you need. The truth of that premise was demonstrated throughout this chapter. It applies to cooperation *and* every other facet of any effort to change. Unfortunately, when we cannot get what we want, many of us give up without trying to get what we need. We see change as an all or nothing proposition. Why? Because we are plagued by the curse of perfectionism—barrier number seven and the subject of the next chapter.

9

![decorative bar]

Change and Perfection

Dave, a thirty-two-year-old architect, and his wife, Alison, a thirty-year-old graphic artist, are a two-career couple planning a family and looking for their dream house. Both work in the city of San Francisco and want to live within a reasonable commuting distance in a community that is attractive, has a small-town feel to it, and offers superior schools for the children they hope to have. Real estate is quite expensive in communities meeting this description, however, and saving money to buy their first house took longer than they had originally expected.

The years of scrimping, saving, and tripping over each other in their one-bedroom apartment gave Dave and Alison plenty of time to visualize every detail of the house they would one day own. Now they have finally begun house hunting in earnest and have a long list of requirements for their perfect home. They are determined to find a house that matches their description exactly.

After explaining to the real estate agent where they want to live and how much they want to spend, Dave and Alison present their list of nonnegotiable criteria. Unfortunately, the real estate agent looks at the list and shakes her head. She does not think she can find a house they can afford that has *all* of these features, and she asks if there is anything on the list they would be willing to do without. But Dave and Alison insist that the list describes the home they *really* want. They ask the real estate agent to find *that* home—no matter how long it takes.

The real estate agent does the best she can, and over the next few months she shows Dave and Alison dozens of wonderful homes, but none is *exactly* what they envisioned. Finally they grow impatient and try a different real estate agent, who reacts in much the same way as the first. He too cannot seem to locate the house of their dreams. Dave and Alison are upset and disappointed. Still, they will not settle for less than their original vision.

By the time they move on to their third real estate agent, Alison is pregnant and the prospect of bringing a baby home to their already cramped quarters is very unappealing. The third real estate agent knows this, and unlike her predecessors, she convinces Dave and Alison at least to consider a compromise. She hands them a pad of lined paper and asks them, just for the sake of argument, to list their bottom-line requirements for a home: those features that make a home safe, comfortable, and functional.

Dave and Alison struggle with the task but eventually draw up a list describing a simple four-bedroom home with those features that are actually essential for a young couple starting a family. The real estate agent looks over the list and smiles. She can think of half a dozen houses that meet their basic needs *and* include over half of the extras found on their first list. In addition, many of the special features these homes now lack can be added at a later date.

It is only after making that list that Dave and Alison discuss the matter and decide that, in fact, they can live with the compromise. Ironically, they end up buying a home quite similar to one the first agent showed them and are able to move into it long before the baby is born. They do add a few extras, but forgo others. The funny thing is that they can't imagine why they ever thought they could not live without them.

Based on what you have read in earlier chapters of this book, I bet you think I am going to tell you Dave and Alison are still stuck because they settled for less than they *really* wanted. But if you guessed that, you would be wrong.

Dave and Alison were stuck when they would not compromise on *any* aspect of their perfect house, holding firm to their stubborn decision that they would buy the exact home they wanted or no home at all. If the third real estate agent had not pushed them to be more realistic, they still would be living in a one-bedroom apartment and desperately looking for their dream house, no better off than they were before they started house hunting.

BARRIER #7: THE CURSE OF PERFECTIONISM

Dave and Alison were plagued by the curse of perfectionism. The curse of perfectionism sets up all-or-nothing propositions. Either you achieve your ultimate goal or you do nothing. Of course, this would not be a problem if your goal was attainable and realistic. However, when cursed by perfectionism, you set goals that are inordinately high and standards that are impossible to meet, expecting more of yourself than is humanly possible or insisting that everything else in your life must be in perfect order before you change. While under this curse, you will not even consider smaller steps toward a larger goal, and you reject opportunities to be better off than you are. You want it all or you want nothing—and nothing is what you get.

You may be confused by this idea. After all, I was the one who told you to go after the best life has to offer. I still think you should. When I speak of the best life has to offer, however, I am referring to your personal best, something that is—in a specific way—exceptional and very, very good, yet not necessarily perfect in all respects all of the time. True perfection is rarely, if ever, attainable. The chances of achieving it are so slim that the pursuit of perfection is a waste of your time and energy, particularly if you postpone the pursuit of goodness or excellence while you wait around for the perfect answer, the perfect change effort, or the perfect moment to begin that change effort.

THE PERFECT ANSWER

Once Larry made up his mind to exercise regularly, he was determined to find the perfect exercise program. Thinking the most hassle-free exercise program would be the one he sticks with, Larry did some creative worrying and listed criteria for a program that presents no obstacles at all.

He wants to exercise indoors, so that he does not have to battle the weather, and he wants to exercise with other people so he can make new friends and meet women. In addition, the facility must be near his home because he does not want to waste time driving, and the program must not be too expensive or require that he buy costly equipment or sportswear. It must also be noncompetitive, take no more than forty-five minutes to complete, and be something he can do when he is on the road peddling his photographs. Instructors—if he needs them at all—cannot be pushy or hypercritical.

As you can see, Larry gave his exercise program a good deal of thought and covered all contingencies. His list is long and detailed and describes what he *really* wants. Unfortunately, his requirements are so stringent and inflexible that no exercise program can live up to them. He has searched high and low for the perfect program, but there is always something missing, some criterion unmet. His quest has continued for several months—during which time he has not exercised at all.

April has not always been alone and lonely. At one time she was in a terrific relationship with a kind, attentive man who was deeply in love with her. Brian was a few years younger, attractive, intelligent, sensitive, and quite ambitious. At the age of twenty-four he was the general manager of a very successful restaurant. He earned a handsome salary, much of which he was saving to open his own restaurant and nightclub before he turned thirty.

At first April was in seventh heaven. Brian was wonderful. He made her laugh, listened to her concerns, and accepted her for who she was. He spent all of his precious free time with her and even rearranged his work schedule and made as many adjustments as humanly possible to be with her as often as he could. Not one to try to impress April with lavish gifts, extravagant dates, or expensive getaway weekends, he still went out of his way to make their time together adventurous and romantic. He got along with her friends and was not intimidated by her mother or her wealth. He was even good in bed. Indeed, Brian was as close to April's ideal as any man she had ever known.

But he was not perfect. April cared for Brian and enjoyed his company, but she could not help thinking that there might be someone better out there somewhere, someone with a little bit more of Brian's good qualities who also had a less demanding job or more money and the desire to spend it to pamper her. The more April thought about how nice the perfect man would be, the more she began to dwell on Brian's imperfections.

The fact that Brian worked Friday and Saturday nights began to seem like a bigger and bigger problem. She wondered what good it did her to have a boyfriend if she still had to amuse herself on the weekends. He was consumed by his ambition, she thought, forgetting how she had complained about her previous boyfriends' lack of ambition. And she was unhappy that he rarely had the energy to go dancing or stay until the end of a party.

Eventually Brian's flaws, although few in number and minor in comparison to his positive attributes, were all April could see. She nagged and criticized him incessantly. And when Brian called to say business was slow and he could leave work early, April had worked herself into such a state that she refused to see him.

"Why should I go running whenever he calls?" she asked.

"Because you want to be with him," her mother suggested.

"That's not the point!" April groaned.

The real point is that April managed to sabotage her relationship by refusing to compromise on any matter or discuss ways to resolve their problems. In April's mind the problem was that Brian was not perfect, and if she could not have all and exactly what she wanted, then she wanted nothing at all. Consequently, she ended the most satisfying love relationship she ever had and returned to complaining about being alone and lonely.

For a moment, think of what you miss when you live by all-or-nothing propositions. While you wait for the perfect job, you stay in a job you hate even though you are offered jobs that are better in countless ways than your present job. But you reject them because they do not meet every one of your exact requirements. Or you look for the perfect college—one near your home and offering *all* the courses you want to take. But not finding that perfect school, you take *no* courses and get no closer to earning your degree. Or you seek the perfect therapist. That therapist must be the right age and gender, come from the same socio-economic background as your own, have a perfect track record for treating problems like yours, and not charge a lot of money. You search, but you can't seem to find him. In the meantime, you receive no therapy and your emotional problems are no closer to being resolved.

You are looking for the perfect answer to your prayers. Being better off than you already are is simply not good enough for you. When you hold out for the unattainable, however, you get no further on life's journeys than you would have if you had set no goals whatsoever. You are still stuck and you stay that way because you stubbornly refuse to take a single step forward unless you can "have it all."

I truly believe you deserve to "have it all"—as long as "all" falls within the boundaries of reality, does not become part of an all-or-nothing proposition, and does not prevent you from getting something here and now. Letting life pass you by while you wait for the one right and perfect solution to all your problems is the essence of the curse of perfectionism.

THE PERFECT CHANGE EFFORT

When Karen diets, she accepts nothing less than perfect adherence to her food plan. Unfortunately, she makes this extremely difficult for herself by choosing an extremely restrictive diet of one thousand calories or less per day. She sees the slightest deviation as a complete dieting failure, and her disappointment with herself leads to brutal self-criticism that in turn leads to frustration and despair. She sighs and asks herself why she bothers to diet at all since it seems that she can never do it right. The trouble is that for Karen "right" means perfectly.

Thus, if Karen eats so much as one saltine cracker she had not planned to eat, she declares the entire day of dieting a failure. She does not consider that the few extra calories will have no meaningful effect on her weight loss if she otherwise adheres to her diet or compensates by eating fewer calories at another meal. No, eating that cracker means her effort is imperfect and imperfection is unacceptable. Her day is ruined and she might as well eat whatever she wants and start over tomorrow. Unfortunately, her one-day binge turns into a two-, three-, or four-day binge, and as a result, she finds it even more difficult to get back on track. When she does, her perfect effort lasts a few days. But invariably she slips up and starts the cycle once more.

In another overzealous attempt to manage stress, Jack follows the advice he finds in a magazine article. He accepts the idea that improving his physical health will automatically improve his mental health, and—all on the same day —he stops smoking cigarettes, gives up drinking, starts a macrobiotic diet, and begins a rigorous exercise program. Like Karen, Jack embarks upon this drastically altered lifestyle fully expecting to adhere perfectly to his new regimen. He wants to rid himself completely of every unhealthy habit, make all these changes at once, and do so perfectly on his first attempt.

But unfortunately, Jack trips over his own expectations, by trying to do too much too quickly and leaving no room for human error. His life becomes a hell while he simultaneously contends with nicotine cravings, refusing alcohol at social functions, and scheduling time to exercise during his impossibly busy workday. During frequent business lunches in restaurants, he agonizes over what to eat. In addition, he has to learn to shop for and cook macrobiotic meals. Ironically, instead of reducing stress, his change effort and unrealistic demand for perfection place additional pressure on him. Jack does not get what he wants. But instead of stepping back and taking one change at a time, he decides the entire effort is too stressful and abandons it completely. Cursed by perfectionism, he wants all or nothing—and gets nothing.

Cindy's anxiety attacks are barely under control and her recovery is just beginning when she takes a new job. Not quite ready for the stress of a new job, she finds her first day of work leaves her disheartened and panicky. She arrives at her therapist's office and immediately bursts into tears.

"I can't do the job," she claims. "I don't know why I took it in the first place. It looked so easy. I thought I could handle it, but I can't. I've never felt so confused and incompetent. You wouldn't believe all the mistakes I made today—at least a dozen major ones before I stopped counting."

"Only a dozen?" Her therapist chuckles. "Listen to yourself. Did you really expect to learn everything you need to know and do a brand-new job perfectly on your very first day?"

But Cindy believes that if you cannot do something right, you should not do it at all. And like Jack and Karen, Cindy thinks doing something "right" means doing it perfectly, the first and every time. While Karen could not accept a single deviation from a diet program that was probably too restrictive to begin with, and Jack tried to do too much at one time, Cindy expects to immediately (and flawlessly) master all facets of a new job and instantly adapt to a new situation. After a rough and imperfect first day she is ready to quit. All or nothing, the curse of perfectionism, strikes again.

Perhaps you too apply all-or-nothing standards to change efforts, demanding perfection right away and all the time. In doing so, you invite disappointment, disillusionment, and disaster. When you cannot adhere *perfectly* to a self-improvement program, break a habit *completely* the first time you try, or adjust *flawlessly* to a new situation or lifestyle, you throw the baby out with the bathwater. Instead of slightly altering your course or modifying your expectations, you abandon the change effort entirely. Consequently you end up back at square one—no better off than you were before. This is the second way the curse of perfectionism gets you stuck.

THE PERFECT TIME AND THE PERFECT CONDITIONS FOR CHANGE

"As soon as I lose ten more pounds, I'll quit smoking."

"These holiday parties are just too tempting. I'll go on a diet after the new year begins."

"Things will settle down at work soon. Then I'll sign up for those business courses, take that vacation, move to a new apartment, etc."

"Let's give this time to work itself out. If the relationship isn't better six months from now, *then* we can see a counselor."

"I can't leave him now. The kids are too young. When they get a little older, then I'll leave."

"If only I didn't spend so much time on the road. I'll get a promotion to management soon. Then I'll have more time to spend with my kids."

"This project is all I can think about right now. I'll worry about a social life and getting into a love relationship later."

"If I had . . . the money
the time
the freedom
a better job
fewer problems at home . . . I would change."

"When I . . . am more financially stable
get over this cold
know my kids are okay
find a better apartment
turn twenty-five, thirty, forty, etc.
. . . then I will change."

These are the sounds of procrastination. These are the reasons you do NOT take action *today*. Something always happens *today* that proves change should wait until another day, until you think the time is right and the conditions are perfect. You believe that a perfect time is one that guarantees success. At the perfect moment there will be no temptations, no interruptions, no unanticipated events, nothing to disrupt or undermine your change effort. Unfortunately, there will never be such a perfect moment, but you nonetheless wait for it to arrive. And it is just that waiting for perfect conditions that gets you stuck.

While you postpone and procrastinate, your life does not

get better. Often, it gets worse. The ten pounds you wanted to lose become twenty pounds or thirty. You withstand *more* criticism and abuse from your spouse. With each passing day it becomes more difficult to see how you—an obviously unworthy and unlovable person—can improve your life. Your coworkers become accustomed to your nonassertiveness and take advantage of you at every opportunity, and you put up with it until you can no longer stand it. Then, without trying to improve the situation, you walk off the job.

Procrastination erodes your motivation to change. If you have hung on for this long, you figure, what is another day or month or year? So, you spin your wheels, digging a hole so deep that the prospect of climbing out of it seems all the more difficult—maybe even impossible. You become paralyzed, impotent, unable to do anything more or better than the dissatisfying status quo—all because you refuse to take a single step forward until the perfect moment arrives and the rest of your life is in perfect order.

The curse of perfectionism turns you into a modern-day Scarlett O'Hara. "I'll worry about this tomorrow," you say. But the perfect tomorrow never comes and you never take action. You do not get out of the starting blocks. You cannot get unstuck.

THE PERFECT BARRIER

The curse of perfectionism undermines change so brilliantly because this barrier never works alone. It teams up with other barriers to more efficiently get you and keep you stuck.

This barrier invites the return of barrier number one, believing you do not deserve better. If you look for the PERFECT spouse, job, exercise program, house, social life, or answer, you will not find it. If you expect your change effort to be completely flawless every moment of every day, you will fail to achieve the perfection you want. You fail to get what you think you want, and you decide that a failure is a failure. You believe you failed because you personally were not good enough and therefore do not deserve success. Self-esteem takes a nosedive and stops you cold. The sad thing is that, because of your obsessive attitude toward perfectionism, you were doomed before you even began your effort.

Barrier number seven is almost always tangled up with barrier number two—not seeing your alternatives. In the same way you look for perfect moments and perfect conditions for change, you seek perfect alternatives. Excellent alternatives are not good enough and not worth pursuing. You want one right and perfect solution to your problem or one right and perfect path to your destination. You cannot find it because you spend so much time rejecting all the "imperfect" alternatives you do find. The end result is that you do not change.

Barrier number seven reactivates barrier number four—finding perfectly good reasons not to change. The curse of perfectionism demands a perfect rationale for why you should change. It asks for proof that self-improvement is actually needed and accepts only an airtight case in favor of change.

You may really want to change jobs, go back to school, fall in love, or lose ten pounds. You may really want to stop hurting yourself or other people. You may be as close to the end of your rope as you want to get. But unless the arguments are perfect and cannot be countered in any way, you decide that they are not good enough. If you can find one reason, no matter how lame, NOT to change, the curse of perfectionism tells you not to bother trying.

Barrier seven would be insignificant without barrier number five—cold, raw fear. Fear and anxiety run rampant when you set up all-or-nothing propositions. The curse of perfectionism with its unrealistic expectations sets you up for a fall. You reach for something you may not be able to attain in a lifetime and expect to get it immediately and flawlessly on the first attempt. In your heart you know you can't succeed perfectly, and so fear steps in to prevent the failure, disappointment, rejection, or loss you have practically guaranteed by such unrealistic expectations.

You fear the disappointment you will feel if you cannot find the perfect job, spouse, social life, or any other perfect answer you seek. You fear you will fail to change perfectly. You fear you will choose the wrong moment to start a self-improvement effort. Perfectionism leads to procrastination, and fear turns procrastination to paralysis. It is a deadly one-two punch.

ARE YOU PLAGUED BY THE CURSE OF PERFECTIONISM?

Perfectionism is puzzling. At first glance you may be unable to distinguish perfectionism from high standards. You may think your expectation to go for the best life has to offer is realistic, when in fact you are seeking the unattainable. You may claim you are carefully, conscientiously planning the change effort most likely to succeed for you, when what you are really doing is procrastinating and perpetually waiting for perfection.

How do you tell the difference? How do you know if you are cursed by perfectionism? LOOK AT WHERE YOU ARE.

Are you still in the same dissatisfying job, hanging on to what you have until you find another job that meets every single one of your exacting requirements? Have you rejected options that offered more than you now have because they were not perfect? Are you still looking for the perfect spouse, exercise program, diet, social life, home, or alternative? Have you maintained the status quo in the meantime? Has anything about your life gotten better?

Are you back at square one? Did you attempt change but fail to flawlessly adhere to your self-improvement program? Did a single setback convince you that the entire effort was not worth the time and energy? Did you try to do too much too quickly and give up when you did not succeed immediately?

Are you still waiting to take the first step? Do you know exactly what you want to do but have yet to do anything? Can you list all the little things that have happened to keep you from starting your change effort?

If what you want, how you expect to get it, and when you will take the first step have kept you from moving forward at all, then you are cursed by perfectionism. You set your sights TOO high, asked TOO much of yourself, and wanted TOO many conditions to be met before you would change.

LOOK AT WHERE YOU ARE. If your original expectations had been realistic and attainable, by now you would be at least a step or two closer to your destination. On the other hand, you will know perfectionism and procrastination are blocking change *when you know what you want but are NOT a single step closer to getting it.*

DISMANTLING BARRIER #7: AIMING FOR EXCELLENCE

To open this chapter I described Dave and Alison's search for the perfect house. They looked everywhere for the exact replica of their dream house. Unfortunately, no such house existed. Now, there *was* a remote possibility that if they waited long enough, a house meeting all of their requirements would be put on the market at a price they could afford. But there was a much greater chance that no matter how long they waited they would never find the perfect house of their dreams. They had a choice. They could hold out for perfection or they could compromise. Fortunately, they chose the latter option and bought a home that met their basic needs and included most—but not all—of the features they wanted. It was a wise and realistic choice. Now Dave and Alison love their new home and hardly miss the extras they once believed they could not live without.

Dave and Alison escaped the all-or-nothing trap set by the curse of perfectionism. By lowering their expectations slightly and becoming more flexible about what they would accept, they opened themselves up to all the possibilities that lie between all or nothing. Yes, they settled for less than perfection. But they got a great deal more than nothing.

PERFECTION VERSUS EXCELLENCE

According to the dictionary definition, to be perfect is to be *"complete and flawless in all respects."* If you ever become perfect by this definition, pull off a change effort that is perfect by this definition, or find an answer, a time, or a condition for change that is perfect by this definition, I want you to write me a letter and tell me about it. I will be the first one to celebrate your good fortune. In the meantime, I hope you do not mind it if I do not hold my breath.

Excellence is defined as something *"outstandingly good or of exceptional merit."* Each and every one of you have the potential to achieve excellence as it personally applies to you. The first difference between perfection and excellence is that excellence is a realistic expectation and a worthy goal. Perfection is neither.

Perfection is a condition that neither you nor anyone else in the entire world can find fault with or criticize in any way. It is a state described by absolutes. A perfect person *never* errs in his own eyes or anyone else's. A perfect job *never* gets boring, stressful, overwhelming, or frustrating. The person who holds the perfect job loves going to work *every single day* of his life, *never* disagrees with a coworker or a policy, and gets paid the *exact* amount of money he wants, as well as automatically receiving pay raises whenever he asks for them. The perfect couple *never* argues or disagrees about *anything*. Each partner anticipates and meets the other's *every* need. Neither one *ever* squeezes the wrong end of the toothpaste tube, steals the blankets in the middle of the night, or sleeps with the window open if his partner wants it closed. They *never* feel grouchy, insecure, frustrated, or confused. No remark is ever misinterpreted. No hurt is ever felt. And of course, the couple's parents, children, and home are perfect, too.

The perfect person, job, and couple are figments of my imagination—and always will be.

Excellence, however, does exist in the real world. An excellent human being conducts his life to the best of his ability—but he sometimes makes mistakes. An excellent job has a few bad days mixed in with the good. It has a few flaws. However, for the person whose job it is, even with its flaws the job is outstanding and exceptional. Any couple who get along half as well as the imaginary perfect couple I described have an excellent relationship. That very same relationship might not work for you or me, but for the people in it, it is wonderful and satisfying—even though it is not complete and flawless in all respects.

Perfection is an end state, while excellence leaves room for growth. You can achieve excellence and decide you want to be even better. You can create an excellent career, then go on to develop an excellent love relationship. You can continue to grow and experience success.

In addition, aiming for excellence allows forgiveness. When you seek excellence, you accept the fact that there are no absolutes. There will be bad days and you will make mistakes. There will be setbacks and temptations you should, but do not, resist. The perfectionist focuses on the flaw and rejects the whole. The seeker of excellence looks at the big picture, recalls the good already done, forgives the error, and gets back on track.

Perfectionism is rigid and uncompromising, while excellence is flexible. Sometimes everything you want simply is not available, so you adjust, compromising and negotiating. But if you cannot have it all, you give up what you must to get most of what you want. The result may not be perfect. Instead, it is outstanding, exceptional, and much, much more than you already have—a great deal if there ever was one.

Perfectionism negates the value of progress, while aiming for excellence rewards progress. To achieve your personal best you simply try to get a little better each day. You may be a long way from your destination, but each time you master a step and achieve excellence at that level, you have cause for celebration. You have progressed and progress is excellent. What might have happened to some of the people I described earlier if they had aimed for excellence instead of demanding perfection?

If he had aimed for excellence, Larry would have been exercising regularly. Instead of waiting until he found a program that met all of his stringent requirements, he would have chosen the option that met all of his basic needs and some of his preferences. And most importantly, he would have discovered that even though the program was not perfect, it suited him well and he could stick to it.

Karen would have been well on her way to losing weight. She would have chosen a more flexible eating plan, one that fit her lifestyle. She would have kept her eye on the big picture, noting progress as she made it and reminding herself of it when she deviated from her diet. And instead of going on a binge each time she dieted imperfectly, she would have looked at what she did right and been motivated to stick with her eating program.

Jack would have chosen one self-defeating habit to conquer at a time and persevered until he achieved his goal. Then, with one success under his belt, he would have attempted to rid himself of the next unhealthy habit on his list, and so on until he achieved excellence in each of the four areas he had failed to change when he demanded perfection.

Cindy would have avoided the agony she felt when she could not master a new job immediately. She would have seen what she did right on her first day and have set realistic goals to improve her performance one day at a time until she achieved excellence.

If you had not been procrastinating, you would have taken your first step by now. An excellent time to change is the present—before matters get worse or stuck becomes a lifestyle.

In each case described above as well as in Dave and Alison's, something had to be sacrificed in order for change to be set in motion. Dave and Alison's house did not have everything they originally wanted. The exercise program Larry eventually chose did not satisfy his every desire. And Karen ended up losing weight at a slower pace than if she had adhered perfectly to a very restrictive diet. It also took Jack longer to "get clean." And Cindy had to admit she was not perfect.

COMPROMISING VERSUS CAVING IN

Throughout this book I have told you to pursue what you *really* want and go after the best life has to offer. By lowering your standards and aiming for excellence instead of perfection, aren't you doing exactly what I've been saying you should not do?

No. No. No. If you review the chapter on knowing what you really want, you will recall that you should only choose what you want after considering the consequences. One consequence you must consider is your ability to achieve your goal, given the resources available to you. If you honestly evaluate perfection as a goal, you will see it is unrealistic. Are you doing what you *really* want when you pursue something you cannot get? I think you are doing yourself a disservice and setting yourself up for failure when you expect to achieve perfection. That is NOT a consequence you *really* want.

As far as the best life has to offer is concerned, life offers many things, but perfection is not one of them. What's more, while you sit around waiting for your perfect dream to come true, countless pleasures and opportunities are escaping you. If compromising your vision means getting *some* of life's goodness—while refusing to accept less than perfect answers, change efforts, or conditions for change means you get *nothing*—which will you choose? I hope you will choose to compromise.

When I suggest compromise, I do not mean caving in or giving up or settling for something you do not want. I do mean toning down your expectations and seeking excellence instead of perfection. You must set goals that are realistic and attainable. Yes, you can reach for more than you now have, but you should not reach so far beyond your grasp that you fall flat on your face. Instead, consider your own uniqueness and take one step at a time toward your ultimate destination.

Compromise is a nebulous concept and a bit frightening. It requires you to sacrifice something in order to get something else. How do you know when you are giving up too much or getting too little in return? The third real estate agent Dave and Alison consulted showed them how to achieve the balance between holding on and letting go. Perhaps a similar exercise will show you how to compromise and free you from the all-or-nothing trap of the curse of perfectionism.

Compromise Strategy

On a sheet of paper draw a four-column chart. Leaving the first column blank, label the second column "Perfection," the third column "Bottom Line," and the fourth column "Excellence"—as I have done on the next page.

	Perfection	Bottom Line	Excellence

On the first line of the blank first column, write the word HOME. In the "Perfect" column, list five to ten words or phrases that describe the perfect home. When you finish the list, draw a line across the page, write the word CAR in the first column, and list five to ten attributes of the perfect car. Repeat the process for the perfect RELATIONSHIP and the perfect JOB.

Now go back to the top of the page and consider the *least* you would accept in a HOME, a CAR, a RELATIONSHIP, and a JOB. This is your "Bottom Line." It can be exactly what you have now or a little more. It should *not* be less than you already have. List five to ten bottom-line standards in each area.

Review your descriptions of perfection and your minimum bottom-line requirements. Somewhere between the two lies "excellence." Give the matter some thought and then realistically describe a HOME, a CAR, a RELATION-SHIP, and a JOB that is *more* than the least you would accept and *less* than perfect.

By setting goals that exceed your bottom line but are less than perfect, you can overcome the curse of perfectionism. Your expectations will be more realistic, and you can give up those awful all-or-nothing propositions, opting for reasonable gains attained one step at a time.

Approaching change one step at a time makes compromise easier to swallow. Once you reach the level of excellence you have defined by compromising, you can take new steps forward to obtain things you gave up when you first compromised.

Aiming for Excellence in a Change Effort You Want to Make

Let's apply the same compromise process to a change you personally want to attempt. First, review the overall wellness strategy in Chapter Two and choose an area that you would like to improve. Use one you have used in other chapters, if you'd like, or choose a new area. What is your ultimate goal and the perfect outcome of improving this area of overall wellness? Write your answer in as much detail as possible.

On the other hand, what is the *least* you would accept in this area? Remember, your bottom line should *not* be less than you already have. Describe your bare minimum in this overall wellness area.

Now compare your idea of perfection with your bottom line. Consider what you *really* want and what is realistic to expect to achieve in this area *in the next year*. Write a goal for achieving excellence in this area.

This same process can be used to tone down your expectations of any effort you're making to change. First, list what you would do if you were to adhere to your self-improvement effort perfectly. Then set a bottom line, and finally, identify a middle ground, leaving room for flexibility and human fallibility.

A Realistic Goal is Not Enough

The curse of perfectionism affects more than the out-come you have come to expect from a change effort, how-ever. It also influences the conditions that you decide must be met before you take your first step.

List the PERFECT CONDITIONS for change. Include any task you want to complete before initiating a change effort, any personal or professional matters you want to have in order, any upcoming events you want to get through, and any requirements for the change effort itself (such as Larry's conditions for his exercise program). You are describing the best possible circumstances for self-improvement, those which you believe will ensure a successful change effort.

When your list is complete, give each item on it an A, B, or C priority. "A" priority items are those that are abso-lutely essential, items that you will *not* sacrifice for the sake of compromise. It is in your best interest to also make sure that all "A" priority items are realistic and attainable in the foreseeable future. Waiting for someone else to change be-fore changing yourself or finding a diet that allows you to eat unlimited quantities of everything you love are both un-realistic and unattainable conditions. They should not be given "A" priorities—no matter how much you would like such conditions to be met. "B" priority items are those you really want but could live without if you had to. "C" priority items are the least significant and easiest to give up in order to make real gains. As you did with your alternatives in Chapter Four, code all the items on your list so that you have an *equal number* of A, B, and C items. This forces you to seriously consider compromise and shake the curse of per-fectionism.

When you look for a self-improvement program or the right moment to change, you must willingly sacrifice your "C" priority requirements and be prepared to give up a few "B" priority items (or all, if need be). Remember that an excellent time to change is as soon as possible, and that the fewer conditions for change you set, the less likely you will be to postpone, delay, or procrastinate.

Once you learn to reject all-or-nothing propositions, your need for procrastination will naturally decrease. You will become less likely to slide back to square one. Sometimes, however, you will be tempted to do both. Those are the times when you must depend on the will and energy to change. They are also the moments in which you may encounter the eighth and final barrier—a shortage of will and energy. The next chapter tackles this ultimate barrier to change.

10

██▅▅▅▅▅▅▅▅▅▅▅▅▅▅▅▅▅▅▅▅▅▅▅▅▅▅██

The Will to Change

Karen feels terrific. Alone in her parents' seashore apartment while they are out of town, Karen has completed the chores she promised she would do in time to watch a magnificent sunset. Now, in the comforting quiet of the apartment, she settles into a reclining chair and reaches for the magazine section of the Sunday *New York Times*. She will work on the crossword puzzle, watch some TV . . .

Suddenly, however, thoughts of rocky road ice cream intrude upon her serenity. She visualizes the brand-new carton tucked behind the bagels and Thanksgiving leftovers in her mother's freezer, and it is calling her name.

"Stop that," she tells herself. "Don't ruin what you've got going."

What Karen has going is a sensible nutrition program. Having considered the alternatives, she decided to strive for overall wellness instead of quick weight loss. She has stopped eating sweets and fried or fatty foods. As a result, she is losing weight and sees a dramatic improvement in her overall disposition. She has every reason to continue her change effort and no reason to go back to her former habits. Yet she feels an overwhelming urge to eat the rocky road ice cream.

Karen tries to focus her attention on the crossword puzzle, but she is distracted by the battle raging in her mind. The voice of temptation bombards and tries to seduce her. "A little bit of ice cream won't hurt just this once," the temptress argues. "You've been so good. You deserve a treat. You worked hard today. Reward yourself. You really want that ice cream. You know you're going to eat some before the night is over. Why torture yourself? You can get right back on track tomorrow, can't you?"

The more Karen tries to resist, the stronger her craving becomes. She cannot stop thinking about the ice cream. She can practically taste its sweet deliciousness melting on her tongue . . .

In another part of the country, Larry's alarm clock wakes him at six on a winter morning. His bed is warm and cozy. From it he sees that a thin layer of ice has formed on the windowpane. According to the radio announcer, it is a chilly thirty-three degrees outside. Larry groans.

Last August, Larry began a program of regular exercise. After several false starts, he settled into a routine of working out at the gym three times a week and running two miles every morning. But this particular morning is a cold and dreary one. The sun has not yet risen, and Larry's bed feels like a warm, comforting cocoon. He is not thrilled by the idea of throwing off the covers, donning layers of clothing, lacing up his running shoes, and logging his daily miles. He wants to roll over, yank the blankets over his head, and go back to sleep.

Larry's inner dialogue goes like this:

"One day off won't kill me."

"But I made a commitment."

"But I'm not perfect. It's not like I'm in training to run a marathon or anything. I only run for my health."

"And it's working. Look at how much better I feel."

"But it's cold out there. I'll probably catch pneumonia. I was sniffling last night and my throat feels scratchy. It really does."

To prove his point, Larry coughs. Then he sighs, lifts the covers, and slides one leg toward the floor. Then he changes his mind, lifts his leg back onto the bed, replaces the covers, and sighs again.

It took some doing, but Jack found a therapist who specializes in stress-related problems. He is scheduled to see the therapist for the first time at seven o'clock tonight. All day Jack has second thoughts about keeping his appointment. His resolve fades. He figures that a man of his age and position should be able to handle his problems without outside help. He argues with himself until his motivation returns, realizing that being a successful accountant does not necessarily qualify him to figure out new directions for his own life. He knows that his previous single-handed efforts failed miserably. Yes, he concludes, therapy is the right first step and he is ready to take it.

At six o'clock Jack's will to change wavers again. He paces in his living room, wringing his hands and chain-smoking cigarettes. He tries to strengthen his resolve. He gives himself pep talks. Therapy may not be easy or painless, he argues, but it will help him in the long run. He is reluctant to take the step now, but one day he will be glad he did.

The telephone rings. Jack's friend Kevin tells him he has an extra ticket to a sold-out Lakers game and a six-pack of beer chilling in the refrigerator.

"Come on over," Kevin says. "We'll kick back, drink some beer, and go to the game. It will take your mind off business. You haven't cut loose for a while. It will do you good."

Kevin has a point, Jack thinks. He reminds himself that he hardly ever gets a chance to unwind. A Lakers game and Kevin's good-humored company sound great right now. The therapy appointment *could* be rescheduled.

"I can see a therapist anytime," Jack thinks. "But tickets to a sold-out basketball game come along once in a blue moon. I could go to the game tonight and start therapy next week—unless I have to work late on that audit next week. Okay, so I'll make an appointment for the week after that ..."

Karen, Larry, and Jack are beginning to get unstuck. They understand the first seven barriers to change and work to dismantle the ones that influence them. Karen gives up old eating habits. Larry starts a new exercise program. Jack considers his options and devises a step-by-step plan to manage stress. Now each faces a moment of truth—and one last barrier.

Torn between a powerful craving for rocky road ice cream and her commitment to better nutrition and control over her eating habits, can Karen find the will and energy to resist temptation? Or will she slip back into old behavior patterns?

As part of his commitment to exercise regularly, Larry runs two miles daily. He wants to continue what he started, but does he have the will and energy to leave a warm bed on a cold day? One day without running may not hurt him, but Larry will face the same choice every morning all winter long. Does he have the inner strength and discipline to stick to his plan over the long haul?

Seeing the immediate benefits of a night out with his friend and having his doubts about therapy anyway, Jack is tempted to procrastinate. Can he find the resolve and inner resources to take a step in the right direction today? Or will he postpone change until a later date?

Change is not easy. Life's journey presents an endless array of choices and dilemmas to divert you from the route you have chosen. That's why you must reach deep inside yourself for the force to propel you toward your goals. If you find that inner strength, you can leap the hurdle and surge ahead. If you come up empty-handed, you will give in to temptation or postpone the action you planned to take. You have reached barrier number eight—a shortage of resolve and energy.

A MATTER OF WILL

Every change effort leads to a moment of truth. Many moments of truth, actually, moments when you act upon your choices or do not act, when you move forward or turn back, when you take a step or postpone it. You may know what you really want and believe you deserve it. You may conquer your fears and disarm your defenses. You may clear all other obstacles from your path. But when all is said and done, at a moment of truth change becomes a matter of will.

You muster resolve to take your first step and stay on course. You exercise resolve so you can adopt a new behavior or way of living and stick with it over the long haul. You activate resolve to resist temptations to return to old habits. When it is far easier not to, resolve is what gets you to actually DO what must be done.

But What Is Resolve, Anyway?

Resolve, or will (the two are interchangeable), is an invisible hand pushing you forward. It is a jumper cable feeding power to a dead battery. You need will to start your engine and keep it running.

Will is the commitment that turns a pipe dream into a plan. It supplies the energy to turn visions into reality. Resolve is a fire burning inside you. With it, you ignite new fires and begin new change efforts. You produce enough energy to stay with any course of action you choose. Without it, you give in, give up, procrastinate, and get stuck.

Resolve is the deciding factor each time you face a mo-

ment of truth, stopping you from slipping backward. A moment of truth arrives each time you feel an urge to return to old ways of thinking or acting. Temptations present themselves. Someone offers you cocaine. You walk past the same store every day, wanting to spend five hundred dollars you don't have on the leather coat on display in the window. For your birthday your mother bakes your very favorite banana cream cake just after you tell her you are on a diet. You hear the winner of next week's lottery drawing will rake in six million dollars and feel the urge to blow one hundred dollars on tickets. Having made a commitment to be drug-free, stay within a budget, not eat sweets, or abstain from gambling, it takes will to say no to such temptations.

Old habits and behaviors offer comfort and escape when you are tired, lonely, angry, or sad. In the midst of a work crisis you crave a cigarette. Your lover leaves you and you want a drink. Your child throws a tantrum and you want to hit him. You wreck your car and want to feel the shelter of someone's arms, anyone's arms. You previously stopped smoking, drinking, hitting your children, or settling for one-night stands with strangers. However, in stressful situations you need extra will and inner strength to keep from going back to old behaviors or losing the ground you gained.

Will helps you stay on any new path you choose for yourself. Having adopted a new behavior pattern or way of life that requires discipline and stick-to-itiveness, you will face many moments of truth when NOT sticking to your commitment seems easy and appealing. There are those hectic, harried days when you have been one step behind from the moment your alarm clock rang. So, you think about not going to a support group meeting or a therapy session. With a party you could attend or a great movie you could watch, you feel like skipping a weekly class. But you don't. Instead you go to your therapy session or class because you've resolved not to fall back into your old, destructive behavior patterns.

Whenever you come to a crossroad where you can keep moving forward or turn back, your will to change is what keeps you on track.

Will pushes you to take the first step in a new direction. The greatest moments of truth are those that confront you when the time comes to actually do what you have planned. Today is the day you planned to go on a diet, quit smoking, or stop drinking. Will counters those "perfectly good" reasons not to change and makes you take action. You drive to the support group meeting location. Resolve opens the car door, walks you to the building, and carries you to your seat. It stops you from turning your car around or convincing yourself to attend next week's meeting instead of this one. You have updated your résumé, read the want ads, and composed a letter of resignation. When the time comes to leave your job, resolve helps you do it. Without sufficient resolve you are likely to decide to give the job another month or six more months to become fulfilling (even though you already gave it twelve of the best years of your life). The first step of any change effort is a real killer, and you need resolve to take it.

Do You Have the Will to Change?

I suspect by now all this talk about the will to change is making you uncomfortable. When I say will or resolve, you think about your old nemesis—willpower. Just the thought pushes your panic buttons and tears open old wounds. References to willpower dredge up some decidedly unpleasant memories of all the times you needed willpower but did not have it.

Karen's reaction is typical. "Oh, that's just terrific!" she groans. "I work my tail off trying to get unstuck, go through all those strategies, reorganize my life, my thinking, my priorities, and *now* you tell me that what I need is willpower.

If I *had* willpower, I wouldn't be in this mess in the first place!

"I hear willpower and I think failure," Karen continues. "Show me someone who says dieting only takes a little will-power and I'll show you someone who never dieted a day in her life. I wish I had a dollar for every time my mother got that pained expression on her face and asked, 'Where's your willpower?'

"I don't know where it is. It sure isn't around when the Christmas cookies are. It takes a leave of absence at mid-night when I want to raid the refrigerator. It goes on vacation every time I do—which is why I gained seven pounds on a six-day cruise last year. You'll never see willpower hit the highway faster than mine does when there's chocolate cake in the cupboard or rocky road ice cream in the freezer."

Obviously Karen knows what it feels like to look inside herself for the will to change and not find it. In the past she has reached for the strength she needs and watched it slip through her fingers.

Resolve *is* slippery. Perhaps it has eluded you in the past. Resolve has an infuriating tendency to evaporate into thin air at the precise moment you most need it. Perhaps you think you have no willpower at all. I think you do, however. You have merely forgotten how to awaken it and use it.

WILLPOWERLESSNESS

Will is like a muscle. It gets stronger when you exercise it regularly. It lifts more, pushes harder, and carries you further than a muscle weakened and limp from long periods of inactivity. If you only use your legs to carry you from the car to the garage door or from the TV to the refrigerator, you cannot expect to run a four-minute mile (or make it even once around the track for that matter). Similarly, if you have not exercised your will in a while, you cannot expect it to be available at full strength and in plentiful supply when you face a moment of truth.

Most of the time it seems to be easier and faster *not* to exercise your will, so you choose not to. Or sometimes you muster the will to start a change effort but run out of steam somewhere down the line. In either case you fall into a trap set by barrier number eight and get into the habit of not exercising your will often enough or at all.

Exercising your will pays long-term dividends, but you want immediate rewards. Ours is an instant gratification society. We want it all and we want it now. So, we look for the easiest, shortest, fastest route to our goals. We feel a pain, we take a pill advertised to produce instant relief. We drink instant coffee, eat fast food, play "instant lottery" games, buy diet products that promise fast, effortless weight loss.

If resolve was needed for an effort that guaranteed instant results and immediate rewards, you would rarely experience a shortage of it. But most efforts requiring willpower are efforts that promise future rewards or gains that are not immediately apparent. The payoff will come eventually, the relief will be longer lasting, and the benefits will be greater in the long run. Still, more often than not, you opt for immediate, albeit temporary, relief.

Think about Jack's dilemma. He can keep his therapy appointment and begin a change effort that six weeks, six months or a year from now will have dramatically improved his life and his ability to manage stress. Or he can drink beer with his buddy and go to a Lakers game, a form of immediate relief because Jack won't think about his problems at the game. Instead, he will laugh, relax, and have a good time. But what about when the game is over?

In general, Jack leans toward instant gratification. As you may recall, when Jack first felt stress overpowering him, he looked for quick fixes, easy answers, and fast cures. When an action did not bring instant benefits, he abandoned it.

With conscious effort Jack has reoriented his thinking about change. He accepts that real relief and a better life will require time and effort and has devised a step-by-step plan to achieve stress management. But old habits die hard and slow deaths. Each step of his plan brings him to a moment of truth. Will he take action today to receive benefits in the future? Or will he, out of habit, postpone a step, take an easier route, and go for an immediate pleasure?

If you seek immediate relief and instant gratification or want your rewards right away, you probably choose not to exercise your will. Unfortunately, quick and easy is not necessarily healthy or better. The long haul is a rough road to travel, and a better life somewhere down the line is not as motivating as instant gratification of an immediate need, especially when easy answers and fast relief are close at hand. In addition, you may have forgotten what willpower feels like and how to find it. From lack of exercise your resolve weakens and eludes you the next time you really want to change.

Maybe you can *mount will to start a change effort—but can you maintain the energy to see it through?* Will is like a furnace. It needs constant refueling. You get stuck when you stoke up the fire to take a first step and then forget to tend the flame. Uncared for, it flickers and dies. To move forward again you have to start a new fire from scratch.

"I started managing my time with a vengeance," says Janet, who was determined to have more time to do what she really wanted. "I made lists, delegated responsibility, turned over one of my groups to another therapist and stopped teaching courses at the Y for a pitiful ten dollars an hour. I discontinued Saturday hours. I even hired a secretary to help with the paperwork. Things were going great."

Janet pursued new interests. A portion of her time was devoted to learning new therapy methods, and she could hardly wait to put her new ideas into practice. If she received a call from someone who had a problem in her new specialty area, she automatically scheduled an appointment—even if it meant working one of her free evenings or on Saturday. Then she began to lead a new group on the night her old one used to meet and began teaching a college class about her new area of expertise.

"I was flattered by the university's offer," she says. "I was excited about my new clients and my new approach. But the next time I stopped to catch my breath, I realized I was as overcommitted and overworked as I had been before. Again I had no time to relax, go to movies, dance, see my friends, or do anything else on my list of fun things to do. I had to start my time-management plan all over again."

Janet found the will and energy to start a time-management program, but she could not sustain that energy. Instead, she lost track of her commitment and slid back to square one. It happens to us all.

You start diets fearlessly and begin to lose weight immediately. Basking in the success of a rapid ten-pound loss, you figure you can get away with some extra dressing on your salad. You continue to lose weight, so you decide dessert once a week would be okay, and a day off your diet completely now and then wouldn't hurt. You might even treat yourself to one binge day each week. As a result, your weight loss slows to a halt. You cannot understand it. It must be the diet. You abandon it, find a new diet, and start over again.

In the beginning you and your partner worked hard on your relationship. You communicated and did little things to surprise and please one another. You each bent a little bit to accommodate the other. You even rearranged your schedules so you could spend more time together. Once you felt comfortable, loved, and secure, however, one by one those special efforts fell by the wayside. You believed love conquered all, and that rationale allowed you not to devote as much will and energy to the relationship or work as hard to demonstrate your caring and commitment. Then one morning you discovered your relationship no longer felt close, comfortable, or satisfying.

Life promises goodness but does not deliver it automatically. Any pleasure, achievement, or change worth pursuing requires work and sustained effort. Your initial burst of will and energy may get you moving in the right direction, and you may even reach your destination, but you will not stay there or continue to grow unless you continue to exercise resolve and tap your internal energy supply.

The times you chose instant gratification instead of committing yourself to long-range, lasting benefits, and the times you got yourself moving on the right track only to run out of steam, may have convinced you that will is elusive and largely unavailable to you. Like Karen, you may believe you simply do not have enough willpower to face your moments of truth and take action to get unstuck. If this is the case, your willpower failures have become self-esteem wrecking balls.

The Ultimate Barrier

Barrier number eight is the ultimate obstacle to change because it impedes your progress at the most crucial point in your journey. You face a moment of truth and you do or you do not take action. You will or you will not continue on the course you have chosen. You are or you are not able to get unstuck.

If you exercise your will and mobilize energy, all the work you did to clear other obstacles from your path will pay off, and you will truly be on your way to the life you desire and deserve. If barrier number eight appears and you experience a shortage of will and energy, however, it will make no difference that your road is clear of obstacles. You will not move forward.

Logically speaking, if you cannot move, you are stuck. Those old stuck feelings, thoughts, and behaviors reappear. This barrier is the ultimate block to change because it reconstructs the other barriers, most notably barrier number one—believing you do not deserve or have what it takes to be better.

Each time Karen tries to lose weight but her willpower evaporates into thin air, she likes herself a little less. She feels like a failure.

Each time Carla thinks about changing jobs but doubts she has the inner resources and does not mobilize the energy to take action, her self-esteem suffers. She feels inadequate.

Each time Steven swears he will stop using cocaine but cannot muster the will to resist it, he damages his self-image. He feels weak and unworthy.

Each time Janet tries to manage her time but sees her resolve and control slip away, she feels the full force of a self-esteem wrecking ball. She feels powerless.

Each time *you* say you will—but you don't—you think less of yourself. You come to believe you do not have what it takes to get what you want and that you personally do not deserve better. Allowing your inner resources to remain untapped, and letting resolve elude you when you need it most, can send you directly back to the starting line where you find barrier number one waiting for you.

Don't Turn Back Now

Regardless of the reason you come up short in the will and energy department, the outcome is the same. A moment of truth arrives. You know where you want to go, but you DO NOT GO. You know what you must do, but you DO NOT DO IT.

But you have worked long and hard to decide what you want and plot the course to your goals and aspirations. Why see the effort wasted? Having come so far, you do not *really* want to turn back, do you? I hope not. Instead, let's work together to dismantle barrier number eight right now and finally send you on your way to your desired destination.

BARRIER DISMANTLER #8:
TRICKS AND TREATS TO STRENGTHEN WILL

Will makes or breaks a change effort. The work already done and the barriers already dismantled put you back on the main road and set the course you will travel. Resolve is what gets you out of the starting blocks and pushes you onward to the life you really want for yourself. But how do you find the will to change, and having found it, how do you use it?

Remember, will is mysterious and elusive. It is as slippery as an eel and as wily as a con artist. It hides from you and dodges your attempts to grasp it, and so you must draw it from its hiding places and tease it into working for you. You can do this by employing several "tricks of the trade" to mobilize your resolve and then "treat" it well so it does not slip away from you.

First, You Practice

Let's compare will to a muscle. Let's also say that you are a runner intent on competing in the next New York City marathon. You do not rush out, register, and simply show up on the day of the race. There is no way you could reach the finish line if you did that. Instead, you must practice running, building your strength, stamina, and endurance a little more each day. You start on flat ground and run a single mile. Then you add miles slowly and start running up hills. What's more, you do not just jump out of bed and hit the pavement for your daily practice runs. You do warm-up exercises, loosening and stretching your muscles so they can tackle your effort without injury.

The same holds true for mobilizing your resolve. You do not go straight to the moment of truth, reach down inside yourself, and hope for the best—especially if you cannot remember the last time you exercised your will. Instead you nurture and fortify your inner resources through practice, practice, practice.

If you doubt you have the will to change, practice proves otherwise. If will has eluded you in the past and left you feeling like a failure, practice lets you rediscover success, build confidence, and identify your personal trouble spots so you can overcome them.

Practicing exercising your will is a hands-on lesson. You can't just *think* about using willpower—you have to actually *use* it. You have to take every opportunity to experience will-power in action. Sometimes you have to create opportunities. That way you recognize the factors that sap your will—and learn to compensate. You become familiar with the dialogue between your little devil on one shoulder and your little angel on the other. The little devil, using tricks he has learned from other barriers, tries to convince you that you do not need to change and do not really want to, while the little angel reinforces your honest desire to change and encour-ages you to exercise your will. Sometimes you may feel like a ping-pong ball in a table tennis match. Do it. Don't do it. Do it. Don't. Do.

With less at stake, practice lets you feel the pull of op-posing forces and make a choice. If your will eludes you, you practice some more—until you get it right. And what tremendous joy and excitement you feel when you do get it right. Taste it, savor it, remember every detail. The small successes will persuade you to try more difficult tests of will.

WARM-UP EXERCISES

I sometimes ask my students at the University of Mas-sachusetts to test their willpower by participating in a group experience I arrange. One such test of their resolve has stu-dents walk to a nearby doughnut shop. Baking is done on the premises, and the aroma reaches them while they are still a block away from the shop. I encourage them to let the smell of fresh-baked doughnuts tease and entice them.

Then they enter the doughnut shop and stare into the glass cases at all those glazed doughnuts, jelly doughnuts, doughnuts covered with powdered sugar, cinnamon doughnuts, chocolate-coated doughnuts with sprinkles on top, and every other imaginable kind of doughnut. If they could buy five different doughnuts, which five would they choose, I ask them. They talk about their very favorite kind of doughnut and take one last fond look at the doughnuts before they file out of the shop—without buying anything.

Now, doughnut shops may or may not test *your* will. But had you been on the field trip with my students, I'll bet you would have heard a few choice words from your will-weakening devil and few desperate pleas from your will-strengthening angel. Ultimately you would have walked out of that doughnut shop savoring a sweet willpower victory.

Here are six additional will warm-up exercises followed by a series of thought-provoking questions to help you maximize the benefits of your willpower practice sessions.

1. Attend a Friday "happy hour" at a bar or cocktail lounge of your choice with coworkers or friends—BUT DO NOT DRINK an alcoholic beverage. Stay at the bar for at least one hour.

2. Go to the grocery store and purchase a box of cookies, a carton of ice cream, a bag of potato chips, or some other munchie-type item that you really like. Bring it home, put it in the freezer or cupboard, but DO NOT OPEN OR EAT any of it for at least forty-eight hours.

3. The next time someone comes to you with a piece of juicy gossip, tell him NOT TO TELL YOU THE RUMOR until at least twenty-four hours have passed.

4. Go to a department store and try on clothes until you find an outfit that fits well, looks terrific on you, and that you would really like to buy. DO NOT BUY IT that day.

5. Spend an evening at home and DO NOT TURN ON

THE TELEVISION SET. If you get through one evening without watching television, try two days or an entire weekend.

6. Practice developing a new behavior pattern. Each night before you go to bed, empty the coins from your pockets, wallet, or purse and put them into a quart jar. Do this every night until the jar is full.

After you finish some willpower warm-up exercises (and you may have to make several attempts before you succeed), answer the following questions:

—How did you feel right before you tested your will; while you were testing it; after you passed the test?
—What part of the will test was most difficult for you?
—When, if at all, did it seem as if will would elude you?
—What did you do or say to strengthen your will?
—What discouraging words/thoughts tried to sap your will?
—If you were faced with this temptation again, what could you do to make it easier to resist?
—On a scale of one to ten (with one being least tempting and ten being most tempting) how would you rate the will test the exercise provided?
—In the same kind of situation, what circumstances would test your will a bit more?
—Next, test yourself under those conditions.

Taking One Step at a Time

Three years ago Eleanor lost fifty pounds and has maintained the weight loss ever since. Karen, seeing Eleanor has done something she too wants to do, chose Eleanor as a mentor. Karen asked about willpower and this is what Eleanor told her:

"Finding enough willpower to lose fifty pounds was practically impossible. The goal seemed so big and so far away that I couldn't believe I would ever do it. But finding the willpower to lose ten pounds seemed easy enough; to lose one pound was simpler still. Willing myself to stick to the diet for twenty-four hours seemed like a cinch, and I figured anyone could wait an hour before digging into the leftover lasagna. So that's how I looked at it—one step at a time. When I thought I was going to lose my willpower, I moved back and looked at the smallest possible step—a teeny tiny baby step. I took it. Then I took another and another until I'd gotten through the day."

Eleanor's advice is similar to the suggestion made by twelve-step recovery programs such as Alcoholics Anonymous, Overeaters Anonymous, or Al-Anon. Participants are encouraged to progress one day at a time.

The idea of looking at a major change effort as a series of smaller, more manageable steps is a sound one. The philosophy of succeeding "just for today" teaches a valuable lesson. Why are change efforts easier and more likely to succeed when taken one step at a time? Well, remember your need for immediate results and instant satisfaction? It is not about to disappear. Dividends payable in the distant future will never be enough to entice your resolve out of hiding or persuade it to stick around. But when you accomplish a little bit at a time and stick to your change effort for one day at a time, you feel pride and experience success often enough to gain momentum for the next leg of your journey. As twelve-step recovery program participants discover, eventually it is easier and more satisfying to stay on course than to go astray.

Additionally, looking only at the big picture can be frightening and stir up self-doubt. To be completely drug-free for the rest of your life seems impossible. That you one day will find the right partner, marry, and raise a family seems doubtful. To manage stress under all circumstances seems more than you can handle. To get out from under all the debts you have accrued over years of uncontrolled spending seems beyond your capabilities. Just at the thought of all the changing you have to do, your confidence wavers and your will weakens.

However, you know you can abstain from using cocaine or drinking alcohol for one day. You can start a simple conversation with someone or attend a singles group function. You can learn and use a new relaxation technique. You can cut up your credit cards or use coupons when you grocery shop and immediately put the amount of money you saved into a special savings account. These steps take willpower too, but they take less of it. These steps do have long-term benefits, yet you also see the short-term results. You did *something,* and no matter how small that something might be, it is better than nothing and proof you can do more.

BREAKING DOWN THE BIG PICTURE

Think about a change you want to make. It can be an item on your Overall Wellness inventory, something in your lifeline net, or an alternative you identified when you confronted barrier number two.

State your ultimate goal and put it in writing. For example, Janet's goal is "to manage my time so I have three evenings a week and the entire weekend available to do things I want to do." Karen's goal is to "figure out and stick to a lifelong nutrition program that brings me to my goal weight, keeps me there, and helps me be healthier and happier."

Think about all the steps you must take to reach your ultimate goal. What is the first step you must take; the second; the third; and so on? Write each step on an index card.

Janet decided her first step would be to move all her Saturday clients to appointment times during the week. Karen's first step was to eliminate foods containing white sugar from her diet. It was a step requiring stick-to-itiveness, one she would have to take every day, so she phrased what she put on her index card like this: "For today I will not eat anything with white sugar in it."

Put away all index cards but the one with your first step on it and keep that first-step card with you as a willpower reminder. If your first step is a one-time step such as "ask friends to recommend a therapist" or "cut up credit cards," when you complete the step, write "DONE" across the card and hang it somewhere to remind you of your success. Then, when you are ready for the next step, go to your index cards and repeat the process with the card for the next step.

Offer Rewards for Willpower Achievements

Like anyone else, I experience willpower shortages. I most often notice them when I am in the middle of a project—such as when I was writing this book—or when I have to complete a task I find particularly unappealing—such as paying bills or answering the mail I have allowed to accumulate on my desk. From such experiences I have learned that resolve sometimes needs to be poked, prodded, or outright bribed.

Exercising will, regaining control over your life, or completing a project is its own reward. So is losing weight, earning a college degree, finishing a writing assignment, or running a 10K road race. There can be no doubt about the inner satisfaction and sense of accomplishment you feel when you finally reach your destination. It is a wonderful natural high. Unfortunately, the promise of future gains and the pleasant feelings produced by achieving a long-term goal are not enough to counter willpower shortages you are experiencing here and now. Sometimes even the pride and confidence boost found in completing a small step toward your goal is not enough either. In those instances your will must be pushed into action by offering yourself tangible rewards for progress made.

For instance, on a bright, beautiful day such as today I have difficulty disciplining myself to work on this book. I just do not feel like writing. At this particular moment I am bored or frustrated by the project. The right words do not come to mind immediately, and I am not in the mood to push myself to find them. It is such a lovely day. I would rather be riding my bicycle, hiking through the woods, or rowing my canoe on the lake.

But, I have to write. I committed myself to the project. There are deadlines to meet. The time I scheduled for writing is the only time I have available for the next few days. I cannot postpone or procrastinate any longer. Besides, I really want to write this book, and I knew when I started it that I would have days like this.

Reminding myself of my commitment, the deadlines, and my schedule, however, is not enough to restore my willpower. So, I make a deal with myself. If I have a chapter to finish, I promise myself I can go to the movies after I finish it. If I want to organize my notes and outline the next chapter, I offer myself a bicycle ride as a reward. Sometimes I put in two solid hours of work so I can relax in an easy chair and listen to my favorite record for the next twenty minutes. I keep a whole list of tangible rewards and willpower enticements, and the payoffs I promise and give myself push me forward when inner discipline is nowhere to be found.

Tangible rewards bolster shaky willpower and get you beyond the rough spots in any change effort. Perhaps you *should* be able to force yourself forward without external rewards or bribery. Yet, realistically speaking, there will always be times when you just cannot find the inner strength and willpower you need. Those are the times to call for reinforcements in the form of tangible rewards.

Willpower rewards can be *things* you give yourself—a paperback novel, a new hat or pair of shoes, a cassette tape, a new piece for your collection of glass miniatures, or some gizmo or gadget you want. The item often is something you already want and plan to get. So, to strengthen willpower, wait to buy these little luxury items until you need a willpower reward.

What are some gifts you would like to give yourself that could also reward a willpower success?

Willpower rewards can be *activities* you enjoy—hot bubble baths, long walks in the woods, viewing a videotape of an old movie, listening to music, visiting a friend, reading part of a mystery novel, or taking a nap. When you feel your will weakening, set an achievable goal and offer yourself this activity as a reward.

What activities pamper and please you that can be used as willpower rewards?

Rewards can also be words of praise, encouragement, and support delivered by friends, family, colleagues, or bosses. Go public with a step toward improvement that you have taken. Tell one of your emotionally supportive people (see Chapter Three) about it. Or call one of your support people and ask them for encouragement or to help you celebrate your success.

What people can you call upon to deliver a well-timed pat on the back or encouraging words?

Temptation Alternatives

Temptation alternatives are similar to willpower rewards. Both work when inner resources dwindle. While rewards get you to do something you cannot find the resolve to do, temptation alternatives stop you from doing something you have an irresistible urge to do. Rewards are delivered after you complete a task, while temptation alternatives are employed as soon as you realize you are at a moment of truth.

Perhaps you feel stressed, fatigued, angry, or sad, and those old negative self-esteem messages are echoing through your mind. Hoping to silence them, you think about smoking cigarettes or marijuana, taking a drink, picking up a stranger, or buying something you do not need and cannot afford.

Or maybe you are bored. Eating ice cream, wandering through shopping malls, or going to see your abusive former boyfriend seems better than boredom. Or on a special occasion you might want to treat yourself to a drink, a slice of German chocolate cake, or a day off from running, therapy, or night school. Perhaps an unexpected opportunity to indulge presents itself.

Temptation taunts you and the more you try to resist, the harder it tugs at you. At times like these you need alternatives to switch your focus from the temptation to something else. Distraction often works where sheer will cannot. So, take your mind off the battle of will and occupy yourself with another activity. By the time you complete your temptation alternative, you may find the urge to cheat, indulge, or break training has passed.

Instead of giving in to temptation, you can make a telephone call, go for a walk, write in your journal, go to the library, visit a friend, clean a closet, sort through old photographs, do a crossword puzzle, watch a movie, or play a cassette tape and dance until you drop. The activity you choose must meet one basic requirement, however. It must occupy your mind and/or body sufficiently to distract you from thinking about the temptation you want to resist. It also does not hurt to choose temptation alternatives that take thirty minutes or more to complete, or ones that strengthen one of the seven self-esteem building blocks described in Chapter Three. In addition, be prepared at times to employ a second or third temptation alternative if the first does not completely squelch the urge to "cheat."

What can you do to resist temptation and call a temporary cease-fire in your willpower war?

When it comes to temptation alternatives, it is best to think ahead. Identify the potential trouble spots in any change effort and plan your own detours and diversions. For help in planning your temptation alternatives, turn back to Chapter Three and consult your list of support people. You can ask one of them to help you brainstorm temptation alternatives.

Then make a list and memorize it. Then when you feel willpower weakening, do something on your list. If the urge persists, try another temptation alternative and another. Eventually, either the urge will leave you or you will get tired of distracting yourself. Your resolve will return when you say, "Enough already. This compulsion is ruining my day and I won't put up with it for one more minute!"

Forgive Yourself

The final will booster I suggest is forgiveness. Forgiveness prevents a single willpower failure from ruining an entire change effort.

No one is perfect. Indeed, expecting perfection is a barrier itself. Because you are human, you will make mistakes. Because you have not exercised will regularly in the past, you can expect it to elude you at least once and possibly many times.

When it does, you can view your willpower shortages and imperfect efforts as evidence of your own unworthiness and inadequacy. When you falter or fall, you can say to yourself, "You weak, incompetent son of a gun, look what you did. Things were getting better—but could you hang on? No. You blew it. You always blow it. You'll never change."

Expertly beating yourself for an indiscretion and reminding yourself that you obviously do not deserve a better life, you polish off the whole carton of rocky road ice cream, go on a three-day binge, abandon your diet completely, and regain the weight you lost. Not only do you not run today, but you do not run tomorrow or the next day or the day after that, until you give up running altogether—all because you could not forgive one little mistake.

Or, when you're at the exact same crossroad, you can

FORGIVE YOURSELF. Grant yourself the right to be human and therefore imperfect. Acknowledge where you went wrong, but also remind yourself of all the right moves you made before. And let go of those negative messages and self-propelled wrecking balls. Tell yourself you succeeded before and can succeed again. Instead of taking a long, self-destructive detour back to square one, forgive yourself and get right back on track.

Without forgiveness you see every misstep as evidence of inadequacy. When that happens, your self-esteem drops and barrier number one halts your progress. You get stuck —again.

But you do not want to be stuck anymore. So, do the very best you can. Practice will. Take one step at a time and reward willpower successes. Employ temptation alternatives and *still* be prepared to mess up once in a while. Also be prepared to forgive yourself, restart your engine, and get moving once more on the road to change.

What Now?

You have read about eight barriers to change and how to dismantle them. Now you have all the pieces of the puzzle. If you also have the resolve and desire to change, the next and final chapter will help you put the pieces together and actually plan the change effort *you* really want to undertake.

11

║▌▌▌▌▌▌▌▌▌▌▌▌▌▌▌║║║║║║║║║║║║║║║║

Getting Unstuck

You now know a great deal about change and the eight barriers to change. You have plenty of information about getting stuck as well as tools and ideas you need to get unstuck. Will you do it? Will you change? Will you go after the life you desire and deserve?

I cannot answer that question for you. The choice is yours. Others before you have faced the same choice. Some chose to get unstuck. Some did not.

Before adding the final touches to a blueprint for change, let's catch up with some of the people whose lives and struggles appeared as examples throughout this book.

Carla no longer works for the Minnesota child welfare bureaucracy. Instead, she serves as a consultant to smaller, privately run organizations, conducts training seminars for social workers, and is writing a textbook on child sexual abuse. She shares an office with two other therapists and conducts a modest but profitable private counseling practice.

Once doubtful about her ability to be anything but a petty

bureaucrat and fearful of financial ruin, Carla is thrilled with her accomplishments. "For the first few months I was in a constant state of panic," she admits. "New clients were not coming in fast enough, and I really thought all my fears were going to come true. But I was determined not to let them get the best of me. I pounded the pavement, knocked on doors, and called everyone I had ever worked with to try to get consulting contracts. When I finally got my first contract and knew I had at least one source of steady income, I relaxed, and one thing after another fell into place."

Karen has yet to lose all the weight she originally set out to lose. She is proud of the progress she *has* made, however. "I'm down twenty pounds so far," she reveals. "I'll lose the last ten eventually. I don't make myself crazy about it the way I used to. The pounds are not as important as the program, and I'm really sticking to that."

Karen created her change by obtaining valuable information about nutrition and using it to create an eating plan that suited her. She has eliminated sugar from her diet and rarely eats red meat or foods that are fried or have a high fat content. She takes one hour walks at least five times a week and works out with an exercise videotape on the days the weather keeps her from walking outdoors.

"I think I'm proudest about not eating as an emotional outlet anymore. It's not my main form of recreation either," she says. "I eat at mealtimes and I eat what's good for me. Oh, I blow it every once in a while. But I stop before I go on a true binge. I ask myself if I really want to go back to the way I used to be. I don't, so I make sure to get right back on track. It's amazing how much happier I am, and I now have the energy to follow through with other plans that have nothing to do with dieting."

Cindy worked as a freelance publicist for a while before returning to full-time employment with an established public relations firm. "Hustling for clients and bidding against other people to get a contract wasn't my cup of tea," she explains. "I don't count it as a failure though, just something I learned I didn't actually want to do."

Cindy no longer sees her therapist, but she would return for counseling if she reached another impasse in her life. She is involved in a "terrific" love relationship, has deepened old friendships and made new ones. Job offers poured in as soon as word got out that she was looking for employment.

When asked why people are drawn to her professionally and personally, Cindy—who once wondered if there was anything about her anyone could ever love or appreciate— replies, "Hey, what's *not* to like?"

Larry now gives himself an "A in exercise and a B-plus in relationships." He continues to work out three times a week and runs daily, although he admits he does not stick to his program religiously when he is on the road. And yes, on some winter mornings, he rolls over and goes back to sleep.

He grins sheepishly and says, "What can I say? Nobody's perfect."

But boy, has he progressed. He even thinks about entering some mini-marathons and imagines winning one someday. "The headlines will read: 'Former Couch Potato Makes Good,' " he says, laughing.

Larry has not found a lasting love relationship—yet. "But I will," he states confidently. "In the meantime I am meeting a lot of great people—male and female—and I have a whole lot of fun."

"I'm working on self-esteem mostly," Steven reports. "There's more stuff for me to work out than I thought."

Steven is in therapy. Where his business and life are concerned, he is taking "small steps in the right direction." He is more organized than he once was and more apt to initiate things rather than simply drift into them. "I guess I'm better," he admits. "Yeah, I *am* better. There's a long way I have to go yet, but at least now I think I have a chance to come out ahead."

After taking time off to have a baby, Lisa now works part-time as a sales rep. "Just to keep my hand in, and I want to hang on to my business contacts," she explains. "So that when I return to work full-time, I can be even more successful. I have it all mapped out. It's going to happen, you'll see."

Confidence to reach for ever higher goals has been an unexpected benefit of getting unstuck for Lisa, who once was too timid and intimidated to express an independent idea in the workplace.

Marilyn lives with two of her three children (the oldest is away at college most of the year) and supervises a hospital intensive care unit. She is amazed at how much she enjoys working. She also dates a high school teacher who is ten years younger than she is.

"I met him at one of my son's soccer games," Marilyn explains. "Our relationship caused quite an uproar with my kids and parents at first. But we worked it out. I deserve a little happiness, right? And I am pretty happy. Not every minute of every day—but when I think about how I used to be . . ."

Thinking about how he or she used to be is something everyone who got unstuck has in common. When Jack thinks about how he used to be, he is "surprised I *lived* long enough to get it together."

Jack has reached step six on his twelve-step stress management plan. He sees a therapist, no longer drinks or uses drugs, and tries to exercise three times a week. He uses relaxation techniques each morning and whenever he feels his stress level start to soar. Instead of treating every decision or dilemma as if it were a crisis, he carefully evaluates the situations he encounters at work and at home. His most recent change effort was to cut his coffee intake to one cup a day.

Jack recalls, "I had to figure out new ways to have fun, which was tough at first. Still is sometimes. I lost a few friends. But all things considered, it was a small price to pay."

Not everyone who attempted change succeeded, and some folks chose not to take a single step forward. Larraine, at age forty, earned her master's degree and became a family therapist. However, she got stuck when her husband suffered a heart attack and his computer software business failed. The last time I spoke to her, she could not see any alternatives to her painful situation and was very depressed and waiting for a job with a school system to become available.

Having chosen not to do anything about his marriage, Lou is in the same place he was in Chapter One. And April, still pursuing stuck as a lifestyle, has gotten worse. Her desperate search for the perfect man has led to numerous casual sexual encounters, jeopardizing her physical health as well as her emotional well-being.

Everyone you read about in this book had a choice to make. Those who got unstuck chose to take the first step forward. Then they chose to keep moving in their new direction.

"The first step was the killer," Carla recalls. "I started to take it so many times but always lost my nerve. Finally I got sick of myself and my excuses. It just got to the point where I was going to do it now—or never do it. So I *made* myself do it."

Larry adds, "It's not like I jumped in with my eyes closed. I thought it through and worked out the details ahead of time. Or as you put it, I plotted my course, figured out which barriers were in my way, and dismantled them—either up front or when I got to them. Then I kick-started the old engine and took off down the road."

Larry and others "took off down the road" even though

no one guaranteed they would reach their ultimate destination. They moved forward even though they knew they would hit a few bumps and encounter a few obstacles along the way.

"Movement is movement," says Janet, who judges herself to be halfway to her goal of having enough time to enjoy life. "As long as I'm moving, I'm not stuck. I'd rather change my course along the way than have to start over again from a dead stop."

The points made by Larry, Carla, and Janet are worth repeating. *The first step IS a "killer."* However, if you want to get unstuck, you have to take it. But taking the first step and continuing to move forward is easier when you plan for self-improvement, identify potential barriers, and begin to dismantle them. Finally, *imperfect movement is better than perfect paralysis.* You cannot completely dismantle every barrier before you take your first step, and if you wait for perfect conditions to change, you may never actually start to change. And keep in mind, once you start moving, it's easier to alter your course a little than to stop and start over. With these points in mind you can pull together information about change and barriers to plan the change effort most likely to succeed.

Set a Goal

What do you *really* want to do? Once again, state your goal in a positive manner, beginning with an affirmative— "I will . . ."

Review the Barriers

There are eight barriers to change. Each has the potential to keep you from getting out of the starting gates or to impede your progress once you get moving. All eight do not necessarily operate in *your* life, however, and the impact a barrier has on you may be quite different from how it affects someone else. As I review the eight barriers, think about their potential influence on *your* proposed change effort.

BARRIER #1 is believing you do not deserve better. It is a by-product of low self-esteem. You know barrier #1 is at work when you believe you are not good enough to have what you want, think you *cannot* accomplish change, or see yourself as lacking the qualities necessary for success.

BARRIER #2 is not seeing your alternatives. When this barrier appears in your life, you think you have no choice except to stay the same, see only the one option that does not appeal to you, reject every available alternative because it is flawed in some way, or cannot decide which avenue of change to pursue. Since you do not know which way to go, you go nowhere.

BARRIER #3 is not knowing what you *really* want and value. When you are stymied by this barrier, you go along with the crowd, let other people choose the direction you travel, or do not communicate your needs and desires. You get stuck because you pursue a goal you do not choose or do not even consider choosing an alternative. When in the grips of barrier #3, you do not prize and cherish or publicly affirm those types of aspirations, and you do not take action at all or do not act repeatedly and consistently.

BARRIER #4 supplies perfectly good reasons *not* to change and encompasses all the "yeah, but"s and excuses you offer to defend the way things are and convince yourself that change is unnecessary. You know you are finding perfectly good reasons *not* to change when you claim things are not so bad or could be worse, build an airtight case for staying the same, or counter every suggestion with a "yeah, but" statement.

BARRIER #5 is cold, raw fear. Like the Three Sillies you read about, you dread a negative outcome that may never come to pass and ignore the probable good that would occur if you did change. You fear possible failure, disappointment, rejection, pain, and a host of other horrors—all of which freeze you in your tracks. In an effort to protect yourself from what you fear, you pass on probable success, accomplishment, acceptance, pleasure, and all the other riches life offers.

BARRIER #6 is a lack of cooperation. When obstructed by this barrier, you try to change alone, think you have to get what you want without anyone else's help, fail to ask for the assistance you need, compete instead of cooperate, and find that your successes have been sabotaged by the people around you. Change can occur without cooperation, but it is slower, and more difficult and painful to achieve.

BARRIER #7 is the curse of perfectionism. Under this barrier's influence you make change an all-or-nothing proposition. You expect perfect answers, perfect change efforts, perfect times and conditions for change, or an ironclad guarantee of perfect results. Your impossibly high expectations cannot be met, but you refuse to accept anything less than exactly what and all you want. Consequently you do and get nothing—when you could achieve excellence.

BARRIER #8 is a shortage of resolve or energy that saps the inner life force you need to take the first step, keep from returning to old habits, or stick to your self-improvement program. Too little will or energy leads you to procrastinate, give in to temptations, or slide back to square one.

Which of the eight barriers stand in *your* way? What kind of and how much impact can you expect them to have on *your* change effort?

THE OVERALL BARRIER INVENTORY

On a sheet of paper, draw a chart like the one you drew for the Overall Wellness inventory presented in Chapter Two—with one wide column on the left-hand side of the page and seven skinny columns on the right side of the page.

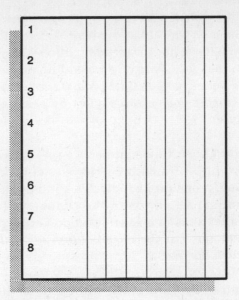

In the wide left column, write key words for each road-block:

#1 – SELF-ESTEEM
#2 – ALTERNATIVES
#3 – VALUES
#4 – EXCUSES
#5 – FEAR
#6 – COOPERATION
#7 – PERFECTION
#8 – WILLPOWER

With your personal goal in mind, answer the following questions:

Column One: Which barriers are present in your life RIGHT NOW? *In the narrow first column, place a check mark across from each barrier you feel influences you today.*

Column Two: Which barriers do you think will impede your progress *during* your change effort? These may be the same barriers you checked in column one or they may be different. (I.e., you may have the *will* to get started, so barrier #8 is not in your way at the moment. Yet you feel your will could fail you if you had to face temptation somewhere down the line. In that case, barrier #8 could be expected to affect you during your change effort.) *Mark the barriers you may encounter during your change effort by putting an X in the second column.*

Column Three: How significant a role does each barrier play in your life? Give each barrier a one, two, three, four, or five rating. A one rating indicates a minimal or relatively insignificant impact on you or the change you plan. A five rating signifies a major obstacle that powerfully blocks your ability to change. *Use the third column for your numerical rating of each barrier.*

Column Four: How much will each barrier affect *this particular change effort*? Using the letters *A* through *H,* rank the barriers according to their potential to keep you from getting what you want (based on the goal you have put into writing). An "A" barrier is the one that most powerfully blocks this particular change effort, while an "H" wields the least influence. Each barrier should have a different letter grade. *Use column four to rank them this way.*

Column Five: Which barriers must be at least partially dismantled *before* you can take your first step? Do not allow fear or perfectionism to cloud your judgment. Taking into consideration that there are never perfect conditions for change, which barriers do you *really* need to work on before you actually embark upon your change effort? *In the fifth column, mark these with the letter N (for "now").*

Column Six: Which barriers must you continue to confront and dismantle *throughout* your change effort? Will you have to confront fear/anxiety again and again? Or once you push through your initial fear will barrier #5 stop influencing you? Will you be done with barrier #2 as soon as you choose your course of action from the available alternatives? Or will you come to numerous crossroads where new alternatives are needed?

If you expect a barrier to reappear periodically during your journey, *write the letter* O *(for "ongoing") in the sixth column.*

Column Seven: If there is any barrier you feel you need to know more about, *place an asterisk (*) in the seventh column* next to it. To learn more about a barrier or how to dismantle it, you can reread the chapter about it and redo the strategies you find there. Or you can do additional research and learn other skills by reading books, listening to audiotapes, or consulting experts.

This Overall Barrier inventory shows you how each of the barriers to change affects you personally. The degree to which each influences your life, the kinds and severity of problems it creates, as well as when and how you will dismantle a barrier, are different for each individual.

For many people, self-esteem is the most powerful obstacle blocking success. Like Steven, you may delay major life changes until you like yourself enough to believe you deserve better. In that case, before conquering a big problem, you should actively build self-esteem and take small steps forward so you can experience some success.

For Jack, on the other hand, perfectionism is a major impediment. He wants it all and he wants it now. So, before he can change, he has to redefine his expectations, break down his ultimate goal into manageable steps, and reward himself for the progress he does make.

Willpower is a significant issue for Karen and continues to be every step of the way. So she has learned to cope by using temptation alternatives she designed herself. In this way she tries to recognize and overcome temptation each time it threatens to halt her progress.

Before Marilyn takes her first step, she needs to stop finding perfectly good reasons *not* to change. To stay on course, she needs cooperation. Therefore, her change effort began by tackling barrier #4. It was only then that she was able to move forward and begin dismantling barrier #6.

From *your* Overall Barrier inventory you too can get a general overview of what you need to do to get unstuck.

DO/GET/BE/ACT

Once you recognize the impact of the eight barriers to change, you can reaffirm your goal and fill in the details of your personal blueprint for change. My longtime friend and colleague Merrill Harmin uses the following strategy to paint a crystal-clear picture of change.

On a sheet of paper held horizontally, draw a four-column chart. From left to right, the columns should be labeled DO, GET, BE, and ACT.

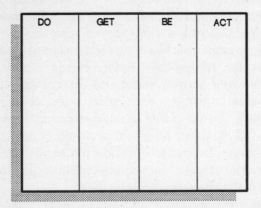

DO	GET	BE	ACT

In the DO column, write your goal.

Ask yourself what you hope to GET by pursuing and achieving your goal. Your GETs represent your reasons *to* change. List your hopes and expectations in the GET column.

Ask yourself how you will have to BE in order to do and get what you want. The bottom line here is that you have to BE more powerful than the barriers you identify as significant to your change effort. You must BE able to push through your fear of failure. Or you must BE able to see alternatives and choose one to pursue. Or you must BE sure that going back to school is what you want to do and not merely what others are pushing you to do. Using that sort of phrasing, list the barriers to be dismantled in the BE column.

At this point I have added a new item to Harmin's original Do/Get/Be strategy, and that is the word ACT. To do and get what you really want and to be more powerful than the obstacles you face, you must take certain actions. What are they?

If you want to be able to see alternatives and choose one to pursue, your possible actions would include brainstorming, asking three friends for suggestions, calling a meeting of your business colleagues, or using the decision-making strategies found in Chapter Four.

If you want to be able to get more cooperation, your possible actions should include defining what you need, deciding who you need it from, writing out a request, rehearsing, and actually asking for cooperation. Or you might act by validating the people around you or being more open to their ideas and offers.

For each BE you listed, jot down the actions you want to take to do, get, and be what you want.

My Do/Get/Be/Act Chart

My goal was to write a book about getting unstuck, so that is what I wrote in my DO column.

If you looked at my GET column, you would see the following hopes and expectations. I wanted to get:

... the book published and a sense of accomplishment from achieving this goal.

... money from the sale of the book (I wouldn't mind if it turned out to be a best-seller).

... recognition of the ideas in the book and the work I've devoted myself to for many years.

... praise and positive strokes from university colleagues, book reviewers, and readers.

... pride and satisfaction from hearing that the book has helped people create better lives for themselves.

How would I have to BE? Well, I had to be able to overcome my fears of rejection and negative criticism. I had to be able to find reasons *to* do what I wanted and counter the excuses I kept making. I had to be able to get cooperation because writing the book would consume time I usually spent with my family and my students. And I had to be able to find the will to persevere with a *big* project. My BEs are listed here in the order of their relative power to keep me from getting and doing what I wanted.

My ACT column was crammed with ways to successfully do, get, and be what I wanted. The work I listed to do on fear alone will give you a good idea of what can go in this column.

I felt I could assuage many of my fears by finding out in advance if the book might "work." Actions in this area included: asking people if they would read a book about getting unstuck; researching what sorts of books on the topic of change had been published recently; and preparing an outline and content summary to elicit the interest of publishers.

I also thought I would work on fear by writing a dozen affirmations about what I was capable of doing and reading them when I got up in the morning and before I went to sleep at night, as well as repeating them after my daily meditation session. If my fears cropped up while I was writing the book, I felt that I could have my wife or a colleague read some of what I had written and reassure me.

All of these steps were ones I ultimately took—and since you are reading the finished product, obviously my plan worked! Do/Get/Be/Act charts can work for you, too.

The Do/Get/Be/Act strategy pulls together the pieces of your change puzzle. It reminds you that barriers do exist and influence you, but it also reveals the actions you can take to keep from getting stuck again at some point in your change effort.

I like to make a typed copy of my Do/Get/Be/Act chart and hang it on the bulletin board in my office. When the going gets tough, I consult my chart, figure out what is happening, and do something about it.

THE GOAL SQUEEZE

The desire to change becomes a plan when you identify the specific steps you will take to reach your goal and set a tentative deadline for each step. The GOAL SQUEEZE strategy helps you do this and also serves to prevent procrastination.

Once again, state your goal. What do you really want to achieve? Then list *everything* you have to do to achieve your goal. And I do mean everything.

If you want to paint watercolor pictures, for example, your task list should include *everything* you will do, beginning with buying a box of paints, paper, and paintbrushes. My list for writing this book included tasks as seemingly insignificant as buying an ample supply of number two pencils and asking colleagues for contacts in the publishing world, as well as obviously essential actions such as getting lecture tapes transcribed or going through the letters workshop participants had sent me.

From your list, pull out all the items you can and want to do over the next *six months*. Then make a six-month list, and from that, pull items you can do during the next *month* and make a one-month list. Then, from your one-month list, select tasks you can complete in the next *week* and make a one-week list.

Rank the items on your one-week list according to what you will do first, second, third, and so forth. If you desire, you can assign a day and/or time to each task.

THEN—ONE BY ONE—DO THE TASKS ON YOUR ONE-WEEK LIST.

As each week passes, return to your one-month list and make a new week list. When a month passes, develop a new month list from your six-month list (and take that month week by week). GOAL SQUEEZES really pay off. Before you know it, you will have climbed all the way to your goal.

SELF-CONTRACTS

Any way you look at it, change requires commitment. You have to commit yourself to take the first step *and* you have to commit yourself to pursue your goal until you reach it *and* you have to commit yourself to maintain your new way of life.

A self-contract reinforces that commitment. Even though it is not a legal document and no one will sue you if you do not keep your end of the bargain, a self-contract bolsters your will to change and reminds you of your commitment to change. It encourages you to do the best you can to get what you really want.

If you were indeed entering into a legal contract, you would consider certain questions before drawing up the actual agreement. Going through such preliminaries helps clarify self-contracts, too. Honestly and *realistically* answer the following questions. Then, based on your answers, complete the self-contract form I provide.

1. What is your goal?
2. By what date do you hope to achieve it? (If your goal is a lifestyle change, this date represents the date you hope to adopt your new way of life. It is a given that you will maintain the effort beyond that date.)
3. What steps must you take?
4. When will you take your first step?
5. Will you need to ... build self-esteem ... increase alternatives ... clarify values ... let go of excuses ... push through fear ... obtain cooperation ... overcome perfectionism ... mount resolve/mobilize energy?
6. Have you started to or made plans to dismantle the barriers in your way?
7. What tangible rewards can you give yourself when you make progress?
8. Will you forgive yourself and get right back on track if, for any reason, you are unable to perfectly comply with your self-contract?

Self-Contract

I (your name) _____

will (your goal) _____

_____

This contract affirms my commitment to accomplish this goal by (date) _____. I plan to honor my commitment one step at a time. If I should make a mistake or give in to temptation, I promise to forgive myself and get right back on track.

My signature below confirms my intention to get unstuck and go after the life I sincerely desire and richly deserve.

Signed _____

Dated _____

A FEW MORE ENCOURAGING WORDS

Here you are at the end of the book, facing the question you faced when you read the first word. I could write one hundred more pages without answering that question for you. It is your choice. Will *you* get unstuck?

Before having the last word myself, I will let others who have been where you are now offer you some encouraging words about getting unstuck.

"So much has happened to me since I took my first steps to change," says Cindy. "Not all of it has been good. A year after I got help and got better, my father became ill and then died. I'm not sure the person I used to be would have gotten through that experience in one piece. I know I wouldn't have made peace with my father or understood that he always did the best he could. I wouldn't have been able to be there for my mom or my younger sister.

"Wonderful things have happened to me, too. The old me would never have been open to them. In the past year I've fallen in love, traveled, written a screenplay. I've met new people and had all kinds of new experiences, and none of it would have been possible if I had not made that first move to get unstuck and change my life for the better."

"Life is pretty darn good," Carla claims. "I wake up in the morning smiling. Okay, not every morning, but some mornings. And that's something when you figure I used to go into the bathroom and cry because I didn't want to face another day at the agency. I actually enjoy my work now. I can't believe I was so scared or that I let myself get so stuck. The only regret I have is that I didn't do something sooner."

"I'm not going to lie about this change business," Jack begins. "It ain't easy. I'm still waiting to get through a whole day without once thinking about chucking the whole program and going back to my old ways. I *can* say I think about giving up less and less these days. The better I get, the worse the old Jack looks to me. Basically I'm happy not to be back where I used to be."

"Do it. Do it. Do it," Larry cheers. "What have you *really* got to lose? If you like what you've got now, then you aren't stuck. If you don't like it, do something. As a buddy of mine likes to say, 'Better to try for *something* and fail, than to try for *nothing* and succeed.' So go for it!"

Karen laughs at Larry's enthusiasm and says, "I'm not *that* gung ho. But I do agree if what you are doing isn't working, you have to try something else. And give it a chance. Don't be too hard on yourself either. It all comes down to believing in yourself. And as long as we're trading quotations about success, here's one a guy I know gave me. 'Whether you think you *can* or you think you *can't*—you are right.' "

Let *me* leave you with the words of America's dean of psychology, William James. He suggests three steps to take if you honestly want to change. They are:

1. START IMMEDIATELY.
2. START FLAMBOYANTLY.
3. MAKE NO EXCEPTIONS (or excuses).

Because you can recognize the barriers to change and know how to dismantle them, you are now able to do exactly what James suggests. Will you?

I hope you will and that your journey brings you to the places found in your fondest dreams. The possibilities for a better life are out there waiting for you. They are within your grasp as soon as you take your first step to get unstuck. Life is a banquet. Sample its goodness. Life is a gift. Enjoy it. Strive to be more and better. You CAN do it.

Recommended Reading

Helping Your Children Learn Right From Wrong. Sidney B. Simon and Sally Olds. McGraw-Hill, 1976. (Ideas and exercises for the entire family.)

Meeting Yourself Halfway. Sidney B. Simon. Hadley, MA: Values Associates, 1974. (A month's worth of values strategies.)

Values Clarification: A Handbook of Practical Strategies for Teachers and Students. Sidney B. Simon, Leland Howe, and Howard Kirschenbaum. New York: Dodd Mead 1972. (The original strategy workbook, used in classrooms, counselors' offices, and meeting halls throughout the United States and Europe.)

Index

FATAL
ERROR

A NOVEL

J. A. JANCE

Pocket Books

New York   London   Toronto   Sydney   New Delhi

Pocket Books
A Division of Simon & Schuster, Inc.
1230 Avenue of the Americas
New York, NY 10020

This book is a work of fiction. Any references to historical events, real people, or real places are used fictitiously. Other names, characters, places, and events are products of the author's imagination, and any resemblance to actual events or places or persons, living or dead, is entirely coincidental.

This Pocket Books trade paperback edition January 2013

POCKET and colophon are registered trademarks of Simon & Schuster, Inc.

For information about special discounts for bulk purchases, please contact Simon & Schuster Special Sales at 1-866-506-1949 or business@simonandschuster.com.

The Simon & Schuster Speakers Bureau can bring authors to your live event. For more information or to book an event contact the Simon & Schuster Speakers Bureau at 1-866-248-3049 or visit our website at www.simonspeakers.com.

Manufactured in the United States of America

10 9 8 7 6 5 4 3 2 1

Library of Congress Cataloging-in-Publication Data
Jance, Judith A.
    Fatal error : a mystery / J. A. Jance.
        p.   cm.
    "A Touchstone book."
    1. Reynolds, Ali (Fictitious character)—Fiction. 2. Police recruits—Fiction. 3. Arizona—Fiction. I. Title.
PS3560.A44F56 2011
813'.54—dc22
            2010025091
ISBN 978–1–4767–2647–2
ISBN 978–1–4165–6389–1 (ebook)

For Pat S.

FATAL
ERROR

1

Peoria, Arizona
August

G et on the ground," Ali Reynolds ordered. "On the ground now!"

"Make me," Jose Reyes said, glaring back at her with a withering sneer. "Try and make me, bitch."

Jose Reyes was a stocky Hispanic guy in his early thirties, tough as nails, with the muscle tone of a serious weight lifter. A guy with attitude, one who could toss out schoolyard taunts and make them sound deadly.

"I gave you an order."

"And I told you to go to hell."

Ali moved in then, grabbing his arm and setting up for the hip toss. Only it didn't work the way it was supposed to. Jose spun out of the way and suddenly Ali was the one flying through the air. She landed hard on the gym mat and with him right on top of her. The blow knocked the wind out of her and left her seeing stars. By the time Ali got her breath back, she was face down on the floor, with her wrists at her back, imprisoned in her own handcuffs. Lying there under Jose's full weight, she felt a rage of impotent fury flood through her. She was still there, helpless but furious, when a pair of highly polished shoes appeared in her line of vision.

"My, my, little lady," Sergeant Bill Pettit said. "I don't believe that's the way takedowns are supposed to work. He's the one who's supposed to be wearing *your* handcuffs."

Ali Reynolds was in week four of a six-week-long course at the Arizona Police Academy. Of all the instructors there, Pettit was her hands-down least favorite. The class had started out on the fourth of August with an enrollment of one hundred seven recruits, five of whom had been women. Now they were down to a total of seventy-nine. Two of the original females had dropped out.

"Uncuff her," Pettit told Jose. "Good job."

The restraints came off. Jose tossed them to her, then he grabbed Ali by the elbow and helped her up.

"No hard feelings, Oma," he said with a sly Cheshire grin that said he was lying. He had done it with malice and had hit her far harder than necessary, to prove a point and because he could.

To begin with, Ali's fellow classmates had called her "Oma" behind her back. Originally the word came from one of the other young recruits, a blond-haired, ruddy-faced guy whose family hailed from South Africa. In Afrikaans *oma* evidently meant something like "old woman" or maybe even "grandma." There it probably had an air of respect about it. Here in the academy, however, most of Ali's classmates were fifteen to twenty years younger than she was. In context, the word was intended as an insult, meant to keep Ali in her place. To her knowledge, this was the first time she had been called that in front of one of the instructors.

"That's why female officers end up having to resort to weapons so often," Pettit said. "They don't know how to use their bodies properly. By the way, what's that he called you?"

Ali's face flushed. "Old Lady," she answered.

"What?"

"Old Lady, sir!" she corrected.

"That's better. Now get your butt over to first aid. You should probably have a Band-Aid on that cut over your eye. And have them give you an ice pack. Looks to me like you're gonna have yourself a real shiner."

It was a long walk through the sweaty, overheated gym. The Phoenix metropolitan area was roasting in triple-digit heat. Although the gym's AC was running at full strength, it couldn't do more than thirty degrees below the outside temp of 116.

Ali's classmates stopped what they were doing and stood on their own mats to watch her walk of shame. Some of them were sympathetic, but more shared Jose's opinion that no self-respecting fortysomething female had any business being there, and they wanted her to quit. Blood dribbled down the side of her cheek and onto the neck of her T-shirt. She made no effort to wipe it away. If her classmates were looking for blood, she'd give it to them.

She stepped out of the gym into glaring sunshine and brutal afternoon heat. The mountains in the distance were obscured by a haze of earth-brown smog. August was supposed to be the rainy season with monsoon rains drenching the thirsty Sonoran Desert, but so far the much-needed rains were absent although the rising humidity was not.

By the time Ali arrived at the administration office, she had made herself a promise: sometime in the next two weeks, Jose Reyes was looking at a takedown of his own.

BettyJo Hamilton, the academy's office manager, was also in charge of first aid. "Oh, my," she said, peering at Ali over a pair of horn-rimmed spectacles. "What do we have here?"

3

"Just a little bump," Ali said.

After determining that no stitches were required, BettyJo applied a butterfly Band-Aid to the cut and then brought out an ice pack. "If I were you," she said, "I'd take it pretty easy for the rest of the afternoon. Let me know if you feel faint or experience any nausea."

Ali was glad to comply. She wasn't used to losing, and she didn't need to go back to the gym to revisit her ignominious defeat. Instead, she returned to the dorm, shut herself in her room, and lay down on the bed, with the ice pack over her eye.

Most of the academy attendees from the Phoenix area made the nightly trip home. The out-of-towners, recruits who lived too far away for a daily commute, made use of the dorm facilities. The three remaining women had rooms to themselves. Ali was especially grateful for that now. She needed some privacy to lick her wounds.

Months earlier Ali had been serving as an interim media relations consultant for the Yavapai County Sheriff's Department when Sheriff Gordon Maxwell had broached the idea of sending her to the academy. Once a well-known TV news anchor in L.A., Ali had returned to her hometown of Sedona, Arizona, after both her career and marriage came to sudden ends. Paul Grayson, Ali's philandering, late, and very much unlamented second husband, had been murdered the day before their divorce would have been final. As a divorcée, Ali would have been in somewhat straitened financial circumstances. As Paul's widow, however, and through no fault of her own, she was now an extremely wealthy former anchor and aspiring cop.

After her life-changing pair of crises, Ali had spent a year or two back in her hometown, getting used to the idea of being on her own. Her parents, Bob and Edie Larson, owners of the Sugarloaf Café, lived there in Sedona, as did Ali's son, Christopher,

4

and his fairly new and now newly pregnant bride, Athena, both of whom taught at Sedona High School.

For a while it was okay to be Bob and Edie's daughter and Chris's mom, but Ali was used to working, used to being busy. Finding herself bored to distraction, she took on the project of purchasing and remodeling the house on Manzanita Hills Road, which she shared with Leland Brooks. Mr. Brooks was her aging but entirely capable personal assistant or, as she liked to call him, her majordomo, since both he and the word seemed to hail from a more gracious, bygone era. Ali had had a boyfriend, but at her age the word *boyfriend* rankled. She liked to think of B. Simpson as her "lover." When speaking to others, she referred to him as her "significant other."

Ali was lying on the bed, wondering what B. would think about her showing up for Labor Day weekend with a shiner, when her cell phone rang. She checked the caller ID.

"Hi, Mom," Ali said to her mother, Edie Larson. "What's up?"

"One of your friends dropped by the Sugarloaf this afternoon, looking for you."

"Really," Ali said. "Who was it?"

"Dad said her name was Brenda Riley. She used to work with you in L.A."

"Not exactly worked with," Ali replied. "She was the anchor for a sister station in Sacramento when I was in L.A. So we were acquaintances and colleagues rather than friends. She got booted off the air about the same time I did for approximately the same reason. They thought she was too old. I haven't heard from her in years. What did she want?"

"She told Dad that she really needed to see you—that it was urgent. You know your father. He's such a softie, he falls for every sob story on the planet."

"What kind of sob story?"

5

"Just that she needed to see you—that she was looking for help. From what he said, I wouldn't be surprised if she was really looking for money."

Ali had found that old acquaintances did have a way of doing that, of showing up on her doorstep and asking for a loan or an outright handout. They seemed to think that since she had money and they didn't, she was obligated to give them some of hers.

"Did Dad give her my number?"

"I chewed him out for it, but yes, he did. Worse than that, he also told her where you were and what you were doing. He said she seemed shocked that you were in the process of becoming a police officer."

Ali ran a finger over her rapidly swelling eye. "I'm shocked by that myself sometimes," she said with a laugh.

"Anyway," Edie Larson continued. "From what he said, she may very well be on her way down to Phoenix to see you right now."

Ali suppressed a groan. Brenda Riley was pretty much the last person she needed to see right now—especially with a cut on her eyebrow and with a black eye coming on. Brenda had been one of those irksome women who never went anywhere without being perfectly put together—hair, makeup, and clothing. She had been almost as tall as Ali—five ten or so—but as far as Ali was concerned, Brenda was better-looking in every way.

"Thanks for the heads-up, Mom," Ali said. "Tell Dad not to worry about it. Whatever Brenda wants, I'm sure I can handle it."

"Are you coming home for the weekend?" Edie asked.

Ali knew that B. Simpson was flying in from his most recent business trip and was due to arrive at Sky Harbor late the next morning. Ali had been looking forward to going home for the long Labor Day weekend and escaping the August heat in the Valley

6

of the Sun. There would be socializing and barbecues galore, but knowing she'd be showing up with a black eye made Ali think twice.

Small towns were small towns, and Sedona was no exception. If Ali appeared in public with B. Simpson and a black eye, tongues were bound to wag. She could try explaining that her injury was a result of her police academy training, but she doubted anyone would listen. In fact, the more she protested, the more they would talk behind her back.

"I'm still planning on being home," Ali said, finally, "but I've got a whole lot of studying to do this weekend. I may have to bail on the barbecue end of things."

"I hope you don't dodge out on everything," Edie said. "Chris and Athena would be so disappointed. I know they're planning on having everyone over on Sunday afternoon."

"We'll see," Ali said.

The call waiting signal buzzed in Ali's ear. The number was one she recognized as having a Sacramento area code.

"Gotta go now, Mom," Ali said. "I have another call."

"Ali?" a woman said when Ali switched over. "Is that you?"

"Yes, Brenda," Ali said. She might not have recognized the voice without the benefit of her mother's advance warning. "How are you doing? My parents said you might call. Where are you?"

"I'm in a place called Black Canyon City, although it doesn't look like much of a city to me."

"Coming from California, it wouldn't."

"Could we get together for a while tonight? Is there someplace where we could meet near where you are, like a bar or something?"

"There's a joint called the Rimrock Inn," Ali said. "It's off Grand Avenue here in Peoria. If you're on the 101, exit to the right and turn right. That's only a couple of miles from here. I've heard some of the guys here at the academy talking about it. According to them, the Rimrock has great burgers."

Ali had also heard that the Rimrock was something of a dive—cheap and relatively dingy. Maybe in the dim light Ali's bruised and swollen eye wouldn't show up quite so much.

"How long will it take me to get there?" Brenda asked.

"Probably forty-five minutes." Ali glanced at her watch. "It's coming up on rush hour. So maybe a little longer than that."

"Okay," Brenda said. "See you there."

Ali got off the bed, stripped off her bloodied T-shirt and shorts and made her way into the bathroom. She was grateful she didn't have to share the bath with anyone else. The half-inch cut over her eye was no longer bleeding, so she peeled off the Band-Aid before she got in the shower. After blow-drying her hair, she used makeup to repair as much of the damage as possible. It wasn't great, but it was better than nothing. By the time she left the dorm, classes were getting out for the day. She managed to dodge her returning classmates as she headed for her car.

She had no intention of running into Jose Reyes and giving him a chance to rub her nose in it.

2

Peoria, Arizona

It was a little more than an hour later when Ali pulled into the lot at the Rimrock Inn. She'd expected to arrive before Brenda, but what looked like Brenda's signature vehicle, a BMW with California plates, was parked just to the right of the front door.

Ali remembered that Brenda had always taken great pride in her vehicles. This one was shabby and more than a little the worse for wear. For one thing, it was covered with grime and a film of reddish road dust. The rear bumper and trunk were both dented in as though they'd made contact with something substantial, like a bollard. There were smaller dents in the side panels too, and some of the chrome trim had disappeared. The window in the rear driver's side door was missing, and the empty space had been covered over with a combination of clear plastic and duct tape.

As Ali walked past the car, she glanced inside. The Beamer looked lived in. It was full of trash—empty food containers, soda cans, and more than a few empty booze bottles as well. None of this fit with the Brenda Riley Ali knew.

Things went downhill from there. Ali stepped inside and looked around. It was late afternoon, so there were plenty of men lounging around the long bar—plenty of men and only one woman. At first Ali didn't believe it was Brenda. Even in the tavern's dim lights it was possible to see that Brenda's trademark long, straight blond locks were gone. The hair was still there, but it stood out around her head like a fright wig. She had evidently tried a do-it-yourself dye job/permanent kit, and it hadn't worked out very well. Most of her hair was a very convincing shade of pink, fluffed atop an inch of brown roots. Cotton candy immediately came to mind.

As Ali walked up to the bar, Brenda was chatting with the guy next to her, joking and laughing. Only when Ali was a few steps away did she see the set of three shot glasses sitting in front of Brenda. There was also a plate of lime sections and a salt shaker, so Brenda Riley was doing shots of tequila at four thirty in the afternoon.

"Hello, Brenda," Ali said. "How's it going?"

Brenda spun around and studied her. "Ali?" she asked. "You look like hell. What did you do to your eye?"

"Ran into a door," Ali said.

As if Brenda had any room to talk. Ali could have asked her the same question, because Brenda Riley really did look like hell. The perky smile that had greeted Sacramento viewers for more than a decade was long gone. Brenda looked haggard and careworn. She wore no makeup of any kind. None. There were dark circles under her red-rimmed eyes. She appeared to be years older than Ali knew her to be. Her clothing was grimy and wrinkled and looked as though it had been slept in. And she had put on weight—forty pounds at least, more weight than even her relatively tall frame could handle.

The guy on the stool next to Brenda's moved away, clearing a place for Ali to sit. The bartender came forward. "What can I get you?" he asked.

"Do you have any coffee?" Ali asked.

Making a face, Brenda salted the side of her fist, licked off the salt, downed one of the shots of tequila, and then sucked on a lime wedge as she pushed the shot glass back across the bar. There wasn't anything about this that was genteel cocktail-hour-type sipping, and Ali recognized it for what it was—serious drinking.

The bartender nodded in Ali's direction. "Give me a few minutes," he said. "I'll make a new pot."

"And maybe a menu," Ali said. "We should probably have something to eat."

The bartender picked up the empty shot glass. "Got it," he said. "Coming right up."

Brenda gave Ali a sly, squint-eyed look. "Are you really a cop?" she asked.

"Not yet," Ali said. "But I'm going to be. What about you? My dad said something about your needing my help."

Brenda nodded. "I do need your help," she said, slurring her words ever so slightly. "It's a long story, a very, very long story. I was engaged to a guy named Richard, Richard Lattimer. He dumped me."

Which meant it was also an old story. As Brenda began to recount her tale of woe, some of Ali's classmates from the academy, including Jose Reyes, wandered into the bar. Wanting to avoid them if at all possible, Ali steered Brenda and her latest shot glass into a sheltering booth in the back corner of the room, beyond the bank of pool tables. Once in that airless section of the room, Ali realized how much Brenda reeked of booze—not just what she was drinking now but what she had most likely been imbibing for the past weeks and months. This was way more than recreational drinking.

"What happened?" Ali asked, trying to seem interested but not intrusive.

"Richard was working down in San Diego. Things just seemed funny, out of sorts. I thought we needed to see each other face-to-face to get things sorted out. So I drove all the way down there to see him, and he was gone. I went by the place where he supposedly lived, but they had never heard of him. The same thing happened when I went by the place where he told me he worked. They said they had another man named Richard who worked for them once, but his last name wasn't Lattimer. I was just frantic. I didn't know what to think."

Unlike Brenda, Ali had a pretty definite idea of what to think. In her current guise, Brenda Riley was clearly a very troubled person. Under those circumstances it made perfect sense that most right-thinking men would have done the same thing Richard Lattimer had done—run like hell in the opposite direction.

Their food came, along with another cup of coffee for Ali. She was starved and lit into her burger. Brenda picked at her fries and ordered another shot of tequila. Keeping count, Ali was astonished at her capacity.

"So anyway," Brenda continued. "Like I said, he'd been acting all weird for weeks—sort of distant, like something was bothering him. That's why I went down to see him—to surprise him. When I got back from San Diego, I called Richard and told him I knew he had left San Diego and that I knew he had lied to me."

"What happened then?"

"He hung up on me. I tried sending him text messages and e-mails, but he blocked them. I haven't heard from him since. That's why I'm here. I need you to help me find him," Brenda said miserably. "Even if he doesn't love me anymore, even if he lied to me, I still love him. I need to be sure he's okay. Finding him should be easy, right? I mean, especially now that you're a cop."

That was when Ali finally understood what Brenda wanted and why she was here. Ali also knew the ramifications. Using law enforcement tools and sources to track down personal information on someone who was not a suspect in a specific crime is illegal. Yes, cops did that kind of thing occasionally, but it was also grounds for instant dismissal if the snooping was discovered.

"Tell me about him," Ali said.

The floodgates opened. "Like I said, his name is Richard," Brenda said. "Richard Lattimer. He grew up in Grass Valley, California. We met in an Internet chat room, a support group for abandoned spouses. My husband had left me and his wife had left him. Once we met, we just clicked. I know it sounds trite, but it seemed like we had always been meant to be together. For one thing, we had so much in common. We both had cheating spouses in our backgrounds. Our fathers died at an early age when we were both in high school. His father committed suicide. Mine had a heart attack and died.

"Richard and I talked about everything, and he was always there for me. When the station fired me, he was the only one who stood by me. We spent hours on the phone, talking, texting, e-mailing. Whenever I felt like I was falling apart, he was there to bolster me up and help me get a grip. At least he was for a while. Once I wasn't working any longer, there was no reason I couldn't drive down to see him on occasion, but every time I made plans to go, something seemed to come up at the last minute. Once his daughter, Suzanne, was sick; once he got called out of town on a job-related problem; once he got called in to work on some kind of emergency and was there for five solid days, fixing some problem or another."

"What does he do?" Ali asked.

"He's an electronics engineer," Brenda said. "He said he did highly classified work for a small defense contractor down in

Southern California. He told me they really counted on him. He was always on call, even on the weekends. He had to have a suitcase packed and ready to go in case he had to take off at a moment's notice."

"So he was part of an AOG team?" Ali asked.

Brenda gave her a mystified look. "A what?"

"The way my ex explained it to me, it's a term used by airplane companies, and it means 'aircraft on the ground.' Team members have to be ready to go wherever that broken plane is, repair the problem, and get it back in the air. Paul Grayson always had his own AOG bag packed. It took me a long time to realize that when he took off at a moment's notice, it turned out he wasn't fixing problems; he was making them."

Brenda nodded, but she was so caught up in her tale of woe, Ali doubted if what she said had penetrated.

"I didn't mind him being on call like that," she said. "I know what it's like to have a demanding job. I didn't worry about it. I was patient. I didn't want to rush him. We were supposed to get engaged on my birthday in May. He sent me links to a couple of jewelry websites. He showed me three different rings and asked me to choose which one I wanted. I did, and I didn't even choose the most expensive one, but when he went to order it, that one was already sold out. We talked about what kind of wedding we'd have, where we'd go on our honeymoon, the kind of apartment we'd have . . ."

Brenda's voice drifted away into silence.

"But you didn't get a ring," Ali supplied.

"No, I didn't," Brenda said sadly. "I had made the mistake of telling my mother and my sister that I thought a ring was coming. They haven't given me a moment's peace about it since, especially my sister. She said I had to be out of my mind to get engaged to someone I had never met. That's why I finally decided

I had to go see him no matter what. I drove to San Diego without letting him know I was coming, and that's when I found out he was gone.

"You have to believe me, Ali, this is all so out of character," Brenda continued, barely pausing for breath. "Richard would never do something like this—especially like cutting me off without any reason. Something must be terribly wrong. I'm sure of it. What if he has cancer or something? What if he's dying? What if he has only a few months to live and doesn't want to drag me through it with him?"

"Wait a minute," Ali said in dismay as something Brenda had said earlier finally penetrated. "You're saying you were practically engaged to a man you'd actually never met?"

"You don't have to be standing next to somebody to know him," Brenda said. "We talked on the phone for hours almost every day. Now that I can't talk to him anymore, I miss him so much. I just need to know he's all right—that he's not sick or dying."

For a time Ali was stunned into silence. Brenda was a well-educated professional woman. How was it possible that she could fall in love and be virtually engaged to someone she had never met? Clearly *virtually* was the operant word. The man Brenda Riley supposedly loved wasn't a person at all. What she knew about Richard Lattimer was what he had told her in a stream of words typed on a computer screen, endearments uttered over a cell phone. The whole idea was beyond bizarre. It made no sense.

Ali found herself in full agreement with Brenda's mother and sister. Richard whoever-he-might-be was a lying son of a bitch, and he most definitely had been stringing Brenda along.

"Have you ever thought about running a background check on him?" Ali asked.

Brenda frowned. "You mean the kind of thing employers do when they're getting ready to hire someone?"

Ali nodded.

"It sounds expensive," Brenda said. "I probably couldn't afford . . ."

"The people who handle my computer security issues do background checks all the time," Ali said. "I'm sure they'd be happy to look into it for you."

"Really?" Brenda grasped at this slender thread of hope with heartbreaking eagerness.

"Really."

"All I want is to know that Richard is okay. If he doesn't want me in his life, that's fine, but I need to know for sure that he's not sick or dying."

"I understand."

"What do you need?"

"Just his e-mail address." Ali knew that once the people at B. Simpson's High Noon Enterprises had Richard Lattimer's IP address, they could go from there and find all kinds of things Richard might prefer to leave unfound.

Brenda's sad face was suddenly radiant with hope. She reached into her purse and dug around for a piece of paper and a pen. While doing so, she placed her car keys on the table. Ali quietly slipped them into her pocket, although what she was going to do from there was anyone's guess.

Brenda was still scribbling down Richard's e-mail address when a broad shadow loomed over their table. Ali looked up and was astonished to see Jose Reyes standing there. In one hand he held a cup of coffee. In the other another shot. "This is for you," he said, setting the coffee cup in front of Ali. "And this is for your friend." He handed the shot glass to Brenda.

"Peace offering," he said to Ali. "Thanks for not raising hell about today," he said. "You could have. I was out of line."

Brenda downed the drink and then gave Jose a bleary-eyed smile.

"I'm willing to let bygones be bygones," Ali said, "on one condition."

"What's that?" Jose said.

"I need some help. My friend here is drunk out of her gourd and is in no condition to drive. There's a motel next door. Would you please help me get her there?"

"How much has she had?" Jose asked.

"Too much," Ali said.

Jose nodded. "Sure," he said, then he held out his hand to Brenda.

"What's going on?" Brenda asked.

"We're moving the party," he said.

"Really? What fun."

Jose guided Brenda across the two adjoining parking lots while Ali hurried on ahead. Fortunately the VACANCY sign was still lit. Inside the office, Ali rented a room and told the clerk, "My friend's had a little too much to drink. I'm keeping her car keys. Tell her to call me in the morning."

When she went back outside, Ali discovered that Brenda was violently sick. If Jose hadn't been holding her up, she might have fallen in her own mess. Ali opened the door to the room. After the spasm passed, Jose picked Brenda up and carried her into the room.

"On the bed?" Ali asked.

Jose shook his head. "She'll be better off on the floor in the bathroom."

He propped Brenda against the wall beside the toilet. Ali threw a couple of bath towels in her direction. On the way out she turned the wall AC unit on high.

Jose was waiting for her out in the parking lot. "Thanks," she said. "I appreciate the help."

"You're welcome."

They shook hands. As they did so, it occurred to Ali that she might pull off a hip toss right now. Jose wasn't expecting it, but he also didn't deserve it. She had needed his help with Brenda. She couldn't have gotten the almost comatose woman out of the bar, across the parking lot, and into the room by herself.

"See you tomorrow," she told him and walked away.

Ali took herself back to her dorm room at the academy and climbed into bed. The fall she had taken had hurt more than her ego and her eye. Her whole body ached, and the several cups of coffee she had drunk in the bar earlier in the evening kept her from going to sleep at a reasonable hour that night. Instead, she lay awake and thought about Brenda Riley, about what she had been once, and what she was now.

The difference between the two was nothing short of astonishing.

3

Grass Valley, California
August

By 4:30 a.m. Richard Lowensdale was up, had made his first pot of coffee, and was at his computer. It was ironic that he worked harder now than when he had been working and that he put in far longer hours. Thank God he had cut back to just two fiancées at the moment. Trying to juggle three of them had been a killer. If it hadn't been for his storyboard file, he never would have managed.

There had been a time in Richard's life when he had thought about being a writer. He had even gone so far as to take a correspondence course taught by Gavin Marcus Hornsby, a once-published but relatively obscure novelist who, in his old age, supported himself by teaching his "craft" to flocks of deluded wannabe authors. Richard figured it must have been as easy as taking candy from a baby. No doubt Hornsby had kept his "students" on the string for years, assuring them that they were each writing and rewriting the great American novel.

That's what the writing instructor had told Richard about his first paltry attempt, that it had the potential of being "great literature." Since Richard was an expert at dishing out BS, he recognized that comment for what it was. He deleted his novel file and never sent another rewrite, but what he had learned in that creative writing class hadn't been a total loss. Richard had hung around long enough to learn about storyboards. Gavin Marcus Hornsby was a big believer in storyboards. After that Richard had never again tried his hand at fiction, other than what he did each time he re-created his own next persona, but the storyboard suggestion had appealed to him. Over time he had made good use of it.

He located Lynn Martinson's storyboard. Forty-one years old. PhD in secondary education. Divorced for three years. Superintendent of schools in Iowa City, Iowa. Richard liked targeting high-profile women. They often didn't want to spill their guts or their troubles too close to home. When they needed to vent, they needed to do so with someone far away, someone who didn't know where all their personal bodies were buried. After his troublesome breakup with Brenda, being from out of state was first and foremost on Richard's list of requirements. The women in his life all had to be from out of state.

When Richard was working in San Diego and had been involved with someone else, having Brenda Riley as a side dish safely stowed in Sacramento had been ideal. For a long time the distance thing had worked in his favor, right up until Brenda lost her own job. After that, she had started harping about coming down to visit and spending some time together. Richard knew that wouldn't do. He had spun some wild stories about who he was and what he did, and he didn't need Brenda Riley showing up at his office and blowing the whistle on him.

With that in mind, Richard kept stalling with one excuse after another. It worked for a while, but then Richard's own carefully constructed real world imploded. Mark and Mina Blaylock gave him his walking papers. They said it was all about losing the defense department contract and the economy and all that other crap, but Richard didn't believe that was all there was to it. He suspected that Mark Blaylock had finally wised up to the fact that maybe his sweet little wife liked some of their employees—and Richard in particular—just a little more than she should have.

But the point was, Richard was out of a job. He needed a place to stay—a cheap place to stay. He had always despised Grass Valley and had sworn he would never go back there. When his mother and stepfather died and he had inherited their house, he had rented it out, furnished. Now though, even though Grass Valley was alarmingly close to Brenda's Sacramento home, Richard wasn't stupid enough to walk away from a free house. The renters weren't happy about leaving, and the eviction process had taken time. But while Richard was getting rid of the renters, he was also getting rid of Brenda.

At that point he was still under the impression that breaking up was hard to do. Now that he'd had some practice, he realized it wasn't difficult at all and that he could have dumped Brenda much faster. That's what he did these days, but back then, during his first time out, he had enjoyed playing her and watching her squirm. Faced with losing him, she had exhibited the whole entertaining gamut of reactions from anger to despair, from raging to resigned, from hopeful to devastated. She had begged him not to leave her and pleaded with him to take her back. The more she groveled, the more he liked it.

Brenda Riley had willingly given him a kind of control over her life that he had never experienced before. She had been putty in Richard's hands, and he had loved every minute of it. Wielding that power had hit his system like some incredibly addictive drug. Once he started on that path, he couldn't let go. He had strung Brenda along for months, making promises he never intended to keep because it was fun to put her through her emotional paces.

Richard Lowensdale was almost fifty years old. He was out of a job, living off the insurance settlement that had come to him after the drunk-driving incident that had claimed the lives of his mother and stepfather. He understood that much of the rest of the world might look at him and see a loser, but not Brenda Riley and not the women who had followed her either. To them, Richard was the ultimate prize—the most wonderful man in the world.

In a strange way, he owed much of his newfound happiness to two very different women—Mina Blaylock, who appeared to know more about sex and how to use it than anyone Richard had ever met, and Brenda Riley, who taught him exactly how stupid women could be, stupid and pitiful.

So back to Lynn Martinson. Her sixteen-year-old son, Lucas, had just gotten sent to juvie for drug dealing. How embarrassing it must be for her to be the top educator in her small town while at the same time having a kid who was totally out of control. No doubt every parent who had a child in that district was looking to Lynn to lead by example when it came to parenting skills, yet here was her son, totally off the charts and into drugs in a big way. That was where Richard had met Lynn in the first place, in a chat room for parents dealing with out-of-control kids and trying to survive the hell of tough love.

Richard—Richard Lewis in this case—understood every nuance of how that kind of family disaster felt. He had told Lynn how his own life had devolved, with an ex who married a drug dealer after their divorce and who took his kids along for the ride. For a moment, Richard had to go back to his storyboard file to verify the exes' names and details. Lynn's former husband's name was John. Rather than working as an electronics engineer as he had in San Diego, the newly minted Richard Lewis was a well-respected executive with a Silicon Valley software company. His former wife's name was Andrea and the teenaged daughter who had just gotten out of rehab was Nicole. Happily for Richard Lewis's fictional existence, seventeen-year-old Nicole had managed to make a seamless transition from being a druggie to being clean and sober, thank you very much.

Over time Richard had learned that it was easy to keep his own background story hazy and out of focus. After all, these desperately needy women weren't really interested in him. They were totally self-absorbed. What they really wanted was someone to listen to them while they bared their souls.

Richard was always glad to oblige in that regard, but only up to the point when he was ready to stop being glad to do it. Once that happened, he sent his poor ladyloves packing. He thought of it as a kind of "catch and release." Or else maybe "shock and awe," depending on his mood at the time. First he went to the trouble of reeling them in, then he let them go. Not kindly. Not gently. No, he took pains to tell the losers they were losers and that they needed to do the world and him a favor and get lost.

He was getting close to doing that with Lynn. She was starting to bore him. She was so focused on that damn prick of a kid of hers that she just wasn't fun anymore. Phone sex didn't count for much when one of the partners was totally preoccupied.

Richard had asked Lynn his customary trick question by sending her to the links with diamond engagement rings. He told her he had a ring in mind for her, but he didn't tell her which one he preferred. If she lucked out and picked that one—the one he regarded as the right one—then he'd let her hang around for a while longer. If she picked the other one, the wrong one? Too bad. It was time for a quick dose of "So long, babe. Have a nice life."

So far, with the notable exception of Brenda Riley, there hadn't been any blowback from any of his breakups. Why would there be? What could the women do about it? They couldn't very well go around crying on the shoulders of their friends and relations because they had been dumped by a fiancé they had never met. Telling that story was bound to be a winner. People would laugh their heads off.

And what other recourse did Richard's lovelorn victims have? They couldn't go to the cops either, because Richard Lowensdale had committed no crime. Unlike breaking into somebody's house and stealing someone's stuff, breaking somebody's heart wasn't against the law. As far as Richard was concerned, this whole thing was like playing a very complicated video game, only better because he got to do it with real people.

"Morning, sweetie," he said cheerfully to Lynn Martinson over his VoIP connection when she picked up the bedside telephone receiver at her home in Iowa City. Richard sometimes teased her about still clinging to her guns and religion as well as to her landline. He was firmly entrenched in the camp of Voice over Internet Protocol users. For someone with his particular brand of hobby, not having to pay long distance charges was a major money-saving consideration.

"I didn't wake you, did I?" he asked. "How are things? I wanted to hear the sound of your voice and wish you good morning before you have to go off to work."

4

Peoria, Arizona

When Ali's phone rang at six the next morning, she assumed it was B. calling her. He was spending a lot of time doing consulting work in Japan these days. The sixteen-hour time difference meant that early mornings for Ali and just before B. went to sleep were the best times for them to talk on the phone. At other times they made do with text messages and e-mail. The phone was still ringing by the time Ali realized that he was probably on a plane somewhere over the Pacific. When Ali finally answered, Brenda Riley was on the phone and she was outraged.

"What the hell do you mean stowing me in this fleabag hotel and taking my car keys?" she demanded.

No good deed goes unpunished, Ali thought.

"You were drunk," she said calmly. "You were in no condition to drive. Would you like me to bring your keys?"

"You're damned right I want you to bring me my keys."

"I have to be in class by eight, but between now and then, I'll treat you to breakfast. There's a Denny's just up the street."

Brenda started to say something else and then stifled. "All right," she said grudgingly. "I'll meet you there."

By the time Ali got out of the shower, she saw the text message from B. that she had missed earlier when the phone rang.

Bordng now. CU at home. Dinner? LV. B.

By the time Ali reached the restaurant, Brenda, dressed in an oversized man's shirt and a pair of ragged jeans, was already seated in a booth, drinking coffee and sulking. She had evidently showered in the motel room. Her hair was still damp and smelled of shampoo, but a cloud that reeked of tequila still lingered around her.

Ali remembered a friend of hers who had gone into AA after he got tired of what he called "drinking and stinking." Ali wondered if Brenda was there yet. If she wasn't, she ought to be.

Ali put the car keys down on the table and then slid them across to Brenda. "I couldn't let you drive," Ali explained. "You were an accident waiting to happen, a danger to yourself and others. What if you'd had a wreck? What if you had ended up in a hospital or if you had killed someone else?"

Brenda closed her fist around the key fob. "Thank you, I guess," she muttered, but she sounded mutinous rather than grateful.

Ali slid into the booth and picked up her menu. The waitress was there with a coffeepot before Ali found the breakfast pages.

"Coffee?"

Ali nodded. The waitress slapped a mug on the table, filled the mug with coffee, and then took off. Efficient? Yes. Personable? No. The service made Ali long for the down-home comfort of her parents' Sugarloaf Café.

"So," she said, for openers and hoping to break the ice. "Last night you told me about your boyfriend, Richard Lattimer, and your difficulties with him. Do you still want me to have someone run a background check on him for you?"

Brenda looked surprised. "You'd still do that? Even after . . . well . . . you know."

"You mean after you made a complete fool of yourself?"

Brenda made a face and nodded. "Yes," she said meekly. "I guess I just got carried away."

To Ali's relief it sounded as though Brenda was genuinely sorry.

"So yes, I'll still do it because I told you I would," Ali said. "I'll need an address so I can send you the report."

"But . . ." Brenda began, then she stopped. "I don't have an address right now," she admitted. "I don't have a computer either. I guess you can send it to my mom's house."

Ali located the piece of paper Brenda had used the night before to jot down her missing fiancé's e-mail address. "Use this," Ali said. "That way I'll have all the information in one place."

Brenda scribbled an address on the paper. The waitress came, took their order, and disappeared again.

"I don't have much money," Brenda said, as she handed the paper back to Ali. "How can I possibly pay for a background check?"

As a customer of High Noon Enterprises, Ali knew she could ask for a routine background check with no charge, but Brenda didn't need to know that.

"I'll tell you how you can pay for it," Ali said.

On the way to the restaurant, Ali had decided that she wasn't going to pull any punches. "You're a mess right now, Brenda—a wholesale mess. Yes, your fiancé dumped you, but considering the way you look and act right now, I'm not surprised. If you don't believe me, you might take a gander at yourself in a mirror."

Two bright angry splotches appeared on the surface of

Brenda's once-narrow cheekbones. "How can you talk to me like that?" Brenda demanded, as tears of self-pity welled in her eyes. "I thought you were my friend!"

Ali didn't relent. "I am your friend," she declared. "And that's the very reason I'm telling you this. Your broken-down wreck of a BMW is parked outside. It looks like you're living in it."

At least Brenda had the good grace to look embarrassed. "I lost my apartment," she said. "Living in my car beats living on the street. What was I supposed to do?"

"You're supposed to pull yourself together," Ali told her. "Find a job, any kind of job. You say you don't have money, but you had enough money to buy tequila last night."

"My mother gives me an allowance," Brenda said.

"That allowance isn't helping you, Brenda. It's enabling you," Ali said. "Stop using your mother and stop using whatever else you're on. I don't know if it's just booze or if it's something more than that. You told me Richard dropped you. I don't blame him. He probably didn't want to be involved with an addict. He's not the one who's sick or dying. You are. The amount of tequila you put away just last night should have been enough to kill you."

Brenda stared into her coffee cup and said nothing.

"If booze is all you're on, go to AA," Ali continued. "If you're on drugs, go to Narcotics Anonymous. Put yourself in a treatment center if you have to. Get your life back on track. Once you're clean and sober, if Richard Lattimer is the kind of empathetic guy you seem to think he is, maybe he'll take you back."

Their order came. Instead of touching it, Brenda shoved the plate across the table. Then she stood up and stormed out of the restaurant without touching a bite.

The waitress came back over. "Something the matter with the food?" she asked, picking up Brenda's abandoned plate.

"No," Ali said. "Something's the matter with her."

The waitress shook her head. "Some people don't have a lick of sense."

A few minutes later, when the waitress brought Ali the bill, the charge for Brenda's food had been removed. Ali left enough cash on the counter to cover Brenda's breakfast along with a generous tip. Outside in the parking lot, Brenda's BMW was long gone.

At least I tried, Ali told herself. *It was the best I could do.*

5

Peoria, Arizona

Ali headed back to the academy. She was there in plenty of time to get into her uniform for the early morning session. Some of the swelling had gone down, but the bruise on her cheek was still purple. Ali thought about trying to cover it with makeup but decided against it. She had earned it the hard way; she might as well show it off.

Cell phones were forbidden during class. The last thing before she went out the door, she turned on her cell phone and called B.'s number. "You're still in the air," she said. "I won't have access to my phone again until after four. You had said something about going out for dinner. I'm ready to stay home. I'm going to call Leland and ask him to pull together a light dinner for tonight. Hope you don't mind."

Then she called Leland and asked him to do just that. "Very good, madam," he said. "I think a nice chilled fusilli pesto salad would fill the bill. Sam will be glad to have you home. I think she much prefers your company to mine."

Sam was Ali's aging cat, a one-eyed, one-eared, sixteen-pound tabby who had come to Ali on a supposedly temporary basis, which was now comfortably permanent for all concerned.

"I miss her too," Ali said with a laugh.

Off the phone, Ali hurried to the parade ground, where she was dismayed to find Jose Reyes waiting for her.

"Morning, Oma," he said with a cheerful grin. "How's it going today?"

Jose's friendly overture, made in public, sent a clear message to those around them that whatever problem he'd had with Ali before was over—at least on his part. She understood that he was enough of a ringleader that if he buried the hatchet, the others would follow suit.

But that didn't mean it was completely over. That day, when they went to the shooting range, Ali made sure she had the slot next to Jose's. When target practice was over, she had beaten him six ways to Sunday. She knew it. He knew it. Neither said a word. They signed off on their respective targets and handed them over to the range instructor.

On her way to the next class, Ali wondered if the antagonism between them had really been put to rest.

All things considered, Ali thought, *it doesn't seem likely.*

Barstow, California

In an unreasoning rage, Brenda Riley slammed out of the Denny's parking lot with her tires squealing. Her speeding BMW left behind a rooster tail of gravel as she roared into traffic. She missed the entrance to the 101 and decided to stick it out on surface roads rather than taking a freeway. Somewhere along Grand Avenue she finally caught sight of a drive-in liquor store. She stopped at the drive-up window and filled her purse with a collection of three-ounce bottles of tequila—a little hair of the dog.

Ali Reynolds wanted Brenda to stop drinking? Big deal. Who had appointed Ali Reynolds as the ruler of the universe? What business was it of hers? What right did she have to go around pointing fingers? Brenda Riley would stop drinking when she got around to it—and only when she was good and ready.

Then since her mother's credit card was still working, Brenda decided to take the scenic road back home. She stopped for lunch in Wickenburg and ended up having to spend the night when an alert bartender in the Hassayampa River Inn took away her car keys. For Brenda, having her car keys confiscated twice in as many days was something of a record.

On Saturday morning, Brenda was up bright and early—well, ten o'clock, which was bright and early for her. She ate half a bagel and some cream cheese from the breakfast buffet at the hotel and was on the road as soon as she got her car keys back. She was doing just fine until she made pit stops in Kingman and again in Needles. By the time she was outside Barstow, she was feeling no pain. That was when she drifted off the highway. Without even noticing the rumble strips, she slammed into a bridge abutment and rolled over several times into a dry riverbed.

Brenda was knocked unconscious. Her seat belt kept her from being ejected from the vehicle, but the sudden force exerted by the belt broke her collarbone in two places. By the time rescuers reached her, she had regained consciousness and was screaming at the top of her lungs. Her nose was broken, as was a bone in her right wrist. There were several cuts on her body as well, some from flying debris from the windshield but others from glass from numerous broken booze bottles, most of them empty, that had gone flying around the passenger compartment of the battered BMW as it finally rolled to a stop.

One of the early first responders was a San Bernardino deputy sheriff who noticed the all-pervading odor of tequila and took charge. He summoned an ambulance. Once Brenda was loaded into it, he followed the ambulance to Barstow Community Hospital, where he saw to it that the doctors caring for the patient also administered a blood alcohol test, which came back at more than three times the legal limit. That was enough to maintain the deputy's interest and make his paperwork easier. It was also enough for the alert ER doc to admit her to the hospital for treatment of her injuries as well as medically supervised detox.

Afterward, Brenda Riley would recall little about her three-day bout with DTs. The acronym DT stands for "delirium tremens," and Brenda was delirious most of the time. Even with IV drips of medication and fluids, the nightmares were horrendous. When the lights in the room were on, they hurt her eyes, but when she turned them off, invisible bugs scrambled all over her body. And she shook constantly. She trembled, as though in the grip of a terrible chill.

During her stay at Barstow Community Hospital, Brenda Riley wasn't under arrest; she was under sedation. She wasn't held incommunicado, but there was no phone in her room. Besides, when she finally started coming back to her senses, she had no idea who she should call. She sure as hell wasn't going to call her mother or Ali Reynolds.

Finally, on day four, the doctor came around and pronounced her fit enough to sign release forms. Once he did so, however, there was a deputy waiting outside her room with an arrest warrant in hand along with a pair of handcuffs. Brenda left the hospital in the back of a squad car, once again dressed in what was left of the still-bloodied clothing she'd been wearing when she was taken from her wrecked BMW—her totaled BMW, her former BMW.

It didn't matter how the press found out about any of it, but they did. There were reporters stationed outside the sally port to the jail, snapping photos of her as the patrol car with her inside it drove into the jail complex.

Sometime during that hot, uncomfortable ride from the hospital to the county jail with her hands cuffed firmly behind her back Brenda Riley finally figured out that maybe Ali Reynolds was right after all. Maybe she really did need to do something about her drinking.

First the cops booked her. They took her mug shot. They took her fingerprints. They dressed her in orange jail coveralls and hauled her before a judge, where her bail was set at five thousand dollars. That was when they took her into a room and told her she could make one phone call. It was the worst phone call of Brenda's life. She had to call her mother, collect, and ask to be bailed out of jail.

Yes, it was high time she, Brenda Riley, did something about her drinking.

Peoria, Arizona

Back in Peoria that Friday, Ali Reynolds knew nothing of Brenda's misadventures in going home. At noon Ali went back to her dorm room to check her cell for messages. Ali understood that the major purpose of academy training was to give recruits the tools they would need to use once they were sworn officers operating out on the street. Weapons training and physical training were necessary, life-and-death components of that process. The rules of evidence and suspect handling procedures would mean the difference between a conviction or a miscarriage of justice.

Drills on the parade ground were designed to instill discipline and a sense of professional pride. That sense of professionalism was, in a very real sense, the foundation of the thin blue line. Still, some of the rules rankled. There was a blanket prohibition against carrying cell phones during academy classes, to say nothing of using them. In the first three weeks, instructors had confiscated two telephones and kept them for several days as punishment and also as an object lesson for other members of the class.

Ali had definitely gotten the message. She had taken to returning to her room for a few minutes at lunchtime to make and take calls. That Friday, there was only one text message awaiting her. B. said that he had landed in Phoenix, picked up his vehicle, was on his way to Sedona, and would see her at dinner. That was all Ali really wanted to know.

On her way back to class, Ali encountered one of her fellow recruits, Donnatelle Craig, out in the hallway. Donnatelle was an African-American woman, a single mother, who hailed from Yuma. She was standing in front of the door to her room, weeping, and struggling through her tears to insert her room key into the lock.

Ali stopped behind her. "Donnatelle, is something wrong?"

"I flunked the evidence handling test," she said. "Sergeant Pettit just told me if I screw up again, I'm out. I can't lose this chance," she sobbed. "I can't."

When she finally managed to push open the door to her room, Ali followed her inside uninvited. Donnatelle heaved herself down on the bed, still weeping. Looking around, Ali noticed that, unlike the comfortable messiness of her own room, this one was eerily neat. Nothing was out of place. The only personalization consisted of a framed photo on the small study desk—a picture of Donnatelle flanked by three smiling youngsters, two boys and a girl. The girl, clearly the youngest, was missing her two front teeth.

"Are these your kids?" Ali asked.

Donnatelle nodded but didn't answer.

"Who takes care of them while you're here?"

"My mom," Donnatelle said.

Ali didn't ask about the children's father. He wasn't in the photo, and he probably wasn't in the picture anywhere else either.

"What did you do before you came to the academy?" Ali asked.

Sniffling, Donnatelle sat up. "I was a maid, in a hotel," she said. "But I wanted to do more. I wanted to do something that would make my kids proud of me—something besides making other people's beds. So I went back to school and got my GED. The sheriff said he'd give me a chance, but I'm not good at taking tests, I'm scared of guns, and Sergeant Pettit has it in for me."

School had always been easy for Ali. She aced written exams at the academy in the same way she had aced exams in high school and college. And she had come here with a more than nodding acquaintance with her own handgun and how to use it. Her notable failure with Jose Reyes was the first real black mark on her academy record.

Donnatelle, on the other hand, had come to the academy with a school record that was less than exemplary, but Ali found her determination to improve herself for the sake of her children nothing short of inspiring.

"That may be true," Ali said ruefully, "but I seem to remember you were fine in the hip toss. You threw your guy down and you don't have a black eye either. Besides I think Sergeant Pettit has a problem with women—any women."

Donnatelle sat up and gave Ali a halfhearted smile. "But my guy wasn't as big or as tough as yours was."

"Are you going home this weekend?" Ali asked.

Donnatelle shook her head. "It's too far. I'm going to stay here and work on the evidence handling material. They're going to let me retake the exam next week. As for the gun thing?" She shrugged hopelessly. "I don't know what to do about that."

"Had you ever handled a gun before you got here?"

Donnatelle shook her head. "No," she said. "Not ever."

"You need to practice," Ali said. "Spend as much time on the range this weekend as you can."

"I was going to, but now I can't," Donnatelle said. "They told me the range here is going to be closed because it's a holiday."

"Use a private one then," Ali said. "Go practice somewhere else."

"But where?"

"Just a minute," Ali said. She returned to her room and woke up her iPhone. She returned to Donnatelle's room a few minutes later with a list of five shooting ranges in the nearby area.

"Try one of these," she said. "And next week, when I get back, maybe I can help you with some of the written material."

"You'd do that?" Donnatelle asked.

"Absolutely," Ali told her with a smile. "After all, the girls on the thin blue line have to stick together, don't we?"

Rising from the bed, Donnatelle went into the bathroom and washed her face. Then rushing to keep from being late, they hurried to their next class. When the recruits were finally dismissed at four o'clock on that scorching Friday afternoon, Ali joined what seemed like most of Peoria in migrating north on I-17 in hopes of escaping the valley's crushing heat. On the way Ali speed-dialed High Noon Enterprises and spoke to Stuart Ramey, B.'s second in command about doing a background check on Richard Lattimer, originally from Grass Valley, California. Ali could have gone directly to B. with her request for information, but she had grown accustomed to dealing with Stuart during B.'s many absences. Besides, Ali assumed B. was probably dealing with a killer case of jet lag and there was a very good chance he was napping. She gave Stuart all the information she could remember from what Brenda had told her. She even dragged out the scrap of paper with the addresses on it and gave that information to Stuart as well.

"You want me to mail this to that address in Sacramento?" Stuart confirmed. "Do you want a copy too?"

"Why not?" Ali said. "I'm a little curious about this guy. The idea that he could get a fairly intelligent, accomplished woman to fall for him sight unseen is a little over the top." Of course, Ali realized that Brenda had severe "issues," but she was nonetheless baffled. Brenda had, after all, worked as a journalist, albeit the eye candy variety.

Stuart laughed aloud. "You'd be surprised," he said. "And you'd also be surprised at the number of requests we get these days that are just like this—somebody checking out the real deal of the new person who's supposed to be the love of his or her life."

"How long does it take?" Ali asked.

"The background check? Not long," Stuart said. "A couple of days at most, but this is a three-day weekend, so some of my sources may not be back online until Tuesday."

"That's all right," Ali said. "No rush."

As far as she was concerned, there was no big hurry. Yes, she had agreed to order the background check on Brenda's behalf, and she was doing so because Ali Reynolds was a woman of her word. But Ali could see that Brenda's problems went far beyond her simply being dumped by a boyfriend. Somehow, in the last few years of troubles, Brenda Riley had lost herself.

That could have been me, Ali thought. *If it hadn't been for the people around me, I might have gone down the tubes the same way.*

6

Sedona, Arizona

One of the people who had helped keep Ali on track was B. Simpson and his considerable charms. Ali and Bartholomew Quentin Simpson had both been born and raised in Sedona, but Ali was enough older than he was that they hadn't been friends or even acquaintances during grade school and high school. They weren't formally introduced until years later, when as adults and in the aftermath of failed marriages, they had both returned to their mutual hometown to recover their equilibrium.

Due to unmerciful teasing from his classmates, B. had shed his first name in junior high. The other kids had ragged on him constantly about that "other" Bart Simpson until he had abandoned his given name entirely. B.'s nerdy interest in computer science may have made him the butt of jokes in small-town Arizona, but it had translated into two successful careers—the first one in the computer gaming industry and his current gig as an internationally recognized computer security guru.

After a rancorous divorce, B. had returned to Sedona as a

reluctant bachelor with no particular interest in cooking. For months he had survived by eating two meals a day at the Sugarloaf Café. Over time he had struck up a friendship with Ali's father. It was Bob Larson who had suggested to Ali that she might want to turn to B.'s start-up computer security company, High Noon Enterprises, to safeguard her computers.

From shortly after they met, B. had made it clear that he was interested in more than a client-only relationship, and the man should have qualified as a good catch. He was an eligible bachelor with plenty of money and a beautiful custom-built home. He was tall, good-looking, and had a pair of gray-green eyes that seemed to send female hearts into spasms. He functioned well under difficult circumstances. He wasn't needy. He didn't whine.

But even with all those things going for him, Ali had been immune to his entreaties for several reasons, one of which was their similarly checkered marital pasts. Ali had lost her first husband to cancer. Her second husband, Paul Grayson, who had cheated on her repeatedly, had been a terrible mistake. B.'s wife had divorced him and was already remarried to someone B. had once regarded as a good friend. In other words, they'd both been burned on the happily-ever-after score, and that meant that more than a bit of wariness was well in order.

For Ali, though, the biggest stumbling block had been and continued to be B.'s age. It didn't help that there was now a specific epithet—"cougar"—for a woman in her situation, an older woman involved with a younger man. It was worrisome to Ali that B. was fifteen years younger than she was. She didn't like thinking about the fact that B. was closer in age to Chris and Athena and to most of Ali's police academy classmates than he was to Ali herself.

In a weak moment, she had finally let down her defenses enough to succumb to his charms, and now she was glad she had. She enjoyed spending time with him. They were having fun; they were devoted to one another, but they also weren't in any hurry to take the relationship to another level. On the other hand, Ali was occasionally troubled by the questioning looks that were leveled at them when they were out together in public.

Ali drove up the driveway from Manzanita Hills Road to her remodeled house. By the time she finished parking in the garage, Leland Brooks appeared in the kitchen doorway to collect her luggage.

"Oh, my," he said, peering at her face. "It looks like you ended up in a pub fight and lost."

"You're right," Ali said. "I did lose, but it happened in the academy gym, not in a bar."

"If you say so, madam," he said. "And, if you don't mind my asking, how does the other fellow look?"

"I'm sorry to say he's fine," Ali said.

"So most likely you'll be dining at home this weekend?"

Leland's question made Ali smile. It was a very nice way of saying she looked like crap. It also meant that he was back to his old mind-reading tricks.

"Yes, please," she said.

"I'll probably need to go out and find some more food, then," he said. "I was under the impression that you and Mr. Simpson would be going out a good deal of the time, but apparently that's not in anyone's best interest."

"Thank you, Leland," Ali said. "I don't know what I'd do without you."

Initially Ali had wondered about the advisability of keeping Leland around after the demise of his previous employer, who had also been the previous owner of Ali's home. He was a godsend.

B. arrived in time for dinner at eight. Afterward, they sat outside on the patio and watched as a late-summer thunderstorm rumbled away off in the west without ever dropping any rain on

Sedona proper. They talked about lots of things including Brenda Riley's visit and Ali's encounter with Jose Reyes.

"So nobody at the academy is giving you a free ride," B. said. "Have your parents seen your shiner yet?"

Ali shook her head.

"No guts, no glory," he said. "We'd better go have breakfast at the Sugarloaf tomorrow morning and give your mother a shot at you. Otherwise you're never going to hear the end of it, and neither will I. Now what say we go to bed?"

They went to bed early but not necessarily to sleep. When Ali woke up the next morning, B. was sitting in the love seat, shuffling through a set of papers. A tray with a pot of coffee and two cups sat on the side table.

Ali scrambled out of bed, pulled on a robe, and poured herself a cup of coffee. She would have sat down on the love seat, but the spot next to B. was already occupied by Sam. Rather than move Samantha, Ali went back and perched on the end of the bed.

"What's that?" she asked.

"The background check you ordered," B. replied.

"It's already here?"

"Stu's been a busy little bee. And he gets things done. He must have dropped it off last night. Leland found it just inside the gate when he went down this morning to collect the newspaper. From the looks of this, your friend's ex-boyfriend is a pretty interesting character."

With that, B. handed Ali the first of several pages.

"But wait," Ali said as soon as she read the top line of the header. "This is about somebody named Richard Lowensdale. I'm sure Brenda told me Richard's last name was Lattimer."

"That may be what he *told* her," B. corrected, "but if you keep reading, you'll learn that Richard Lattimer is a figment of someone's imagination. Richard Lowensdale is the guy who was raised in Grass Valley, California, and worked for Rutherford International in San Diego. As far as Stu can discover, Richard Lattimer doesn't exist."

Continuing to read the report, Ali was appalled. "It looks like everything Richard Lowensdale told Brenda is a lie."

"Pretty much," B. agreed.

Yes, Richard had worked for a defense contractor, but as a minor player, not a big one. It turned out that Rutherford International was a small, minority-owned company with a niche market that supplied drone controllers. Lowensdale had a degree in electrical engineering from UCLA, but his career wasn't exactly stellar. For one thing, he had spent time bouncing from one employer to another. For another, Stuart Ramey's search of various databases revealed no patents issued in his name and no scientific papers listing him as author. His only listed hobby included a lifelong interest in model airplanes—remote-control model airplanes.

"Model planes," B commented. "That fits."

"What fits?" asked Ali.

"He's worked on drones. UAVs. Unmanned aerial vehicles—like the ones our troops are using in the Middle East."

"Aren't those a lot bigger?" Ali asked. "Like Piper Cubs?"

"Some are," B. agreed. "The ones they're using in Afghanistan, the Predators that fire the big missiles, are about that big, but the ones Rutherford was working on are much smaller. The most they could possibly carry would be a forty-pound payload, and some not even that much."

"So what's the big deal then?" Ali asked.

"There's an even smaller variety that's about the size of those remote-control helicopters that were such a hit at Christmas a couple of years ago. They can look in a window of a building and take out a single target sitting in the room without damaging anyone else."

"So there's less chance of collateral damage," Ali said.

"Exactly," B. agreed. "They cost a lot less because of size. They can go places where it would be too dangerous to have a piloted aircraft. Regardless of size, drones are relatively silent. They fly low enough to avoid radar detection. They can do precision targeting, and if you release enough of them at once, you can create a swarm.

"Think about it. If you have a single offensive weapon flying at any given target, chances are you've got a missile defense of some sort that has a good chance of taking that one missile transport device down. If you've got several hundred tiny drones heading in all at the same time, defenders can probably take out some, but not all of them."

"Like trying to chase off a swarm of killer bees with a fly swatter."

"Exactly."

"So Lowensdale worked for Rutherford and then he stopped," Ali said. "How come?"

"Because the bottom dropped out of the drone market," B. explained. "For a long time it looked like Rutherford was going to snag one of the big cushy military contracts. When that didn't happen, when those opportunities went away, so did most of Rutherford's employees, including Richard. The only people left working there are the owner and her husband, Ermina and Mark Blaylock and maybe a secretary. Definitely a skeleton crew."

"Richard Lattimer or Lowensdale or whoever he is told Brenda that he was an integral part of the design team. Was he?"

"I think it's more likely that he was just a cog in the wheel. When the layoffs hit, Lowensdale was let go right along with everyone else."

Ali studied a line in the report. "It says here that he was laid off in February of last year."

"That's right."

"But that's over a year before Brenda had any inkling he was no longer working in San Diego. Every time she made plans to go down there to see him, he came up with some phony excuse or another as to why she shouldn't come to visit. They were in this supposedly serious relationship without ever laying eyes on one another. How on earth could he deceive her like that for so long?"

"You tell me," B. said with a smile. "On paper, at least, he's nothing special. He has two degrees to his credit—a BS from UCLA and an MBA from Phoenix University. He also routinely signed documents with the PE designation, even though there's no record of his ever having earned it."

"Physical education?" Ali asked.

"Professional engineer. Requirements vary from state to state, but you have to take and pass exams that demonstrate an understanding of all kinds of engineering principles with an emphasis on your own specialty. I suspect he's an adequate kind of guy."

"Adequate but not brilliant," Ali said.

"And with a real tendency to inflate his accomplishments. I'm thinking his BS was totally appropriate."

Ali agreed and went back to reading. After being laid off in San Diego, Lowensdale had moved back to Grass Valley. His parents—his mother and stepfather—had died in a car crash more than two years earlier, leaving Richard as their sole heir. For a while he had renters living in the house, but after he lost his job and needed a less expensive place to live, he got rid of the renters—evicted them, actually—and then had moved back to Grass Valley in July.

"What a creep," Ali said. "He's spent the past year living forty miles or so from Brenda, all the while claiming he was still in San Diego."

"Right. Since he was no longer there, no wonder he needed to find one excuse after another to explain why Brenda shouldn't go to San Diego to visit him."

"What's this house in Grass Valley like?" Ali asked.

After shuffling through some extra papers, B. plucked a single sheet out of the bunch.

"According to his Zillow report, Lowensdale's place on Jan Road is valued at two hundred eighty-five thousand."

"That's pretty reasonable," Ali said. "Especially for California real estate. Must be fairly modest, but still, if he hasn't worked in more than a year, what does he do for money?"

"He doesn't appear to need much," B. said. "He was on unemployment for a while, but there was also some kind of insurance settlement—with an undisclosed amount—that came as a result of the drunk-driving incident that killed his mother and stepfather. His ride is a ten-year-old Cadillac, which, like the house, he inherited from his mother. He apparently orders online and has everything delivered—food, clothing, books, electronics, you name it. His medications come from an online pharmacy in Canada. Oh, and as far as Stu can tell, he doesn't have garbage service, or at least he doesn't pay for it."

"What about his father?" Ali asked.

B. gave Ali a puzzled look. "Did his father have garbage service?"

"No," she said with a laugh. "Richard told Brenda that his father committed suicide. Did he?"

"That part was true. His father blew his brains out in his office at the Grass Valley Group/Tektronix plant while Richard was a junior in high school. His mother remarried two days after her first husband's funeral. She married a guy who was supposedly one of the father's best friends, which sounds all too familiar to me," B. added.

"If the wife was screwing around behind his back, that might account for the father's suicide," Ali offered. "And look here. It says Richard has never been married and has no kids, but I distinctly remember Brenda saying that one time when she was

46

planning on going to visit him, he told her she couldn't come because his daughter was sick. His nonexistent daughter."

"There you go," B. said. "So yes, we know that he lied about that—or at least, according to Brenda he lied about it—but he has no criminal record, no pending lawsuits, and no bankruptcies. He's coming through this downturn with an excellent credit rating. On paper the guy looks solid."

"Which is how he must have looked to Brenda too," Ali said. "What happens now?"

"You told Stuart to mail the report to her," B. said. "I'm sure he will, but it probably won't go out until Tuesday."

Ali emptied her coffee cup. "That'll be plenty of time," she said. "He's kept the wool pulled over Brenda's eyes for this long. I'm sure an extra day or two isn't going to matter. Let's go have breakfast and show my parents what having a daughter in a police academy really means."

When the long weekend was over, Ali gave B. a ride to Sky Harbor to catch a plane for D.C. after which would be another trip back to Taiwan. From the airport, she headed back to the academy.

For the next two weeks, Ali Reynolds threw herself headlong into the program and worked her butt off. In a way she hadn't anticipated, helping Brenda had inarguably helped her. The antagonism from Jose Reyes and some of his cronies that had been the bane of her existence during the earlier weeks faded into the background, sort of like the bruising and swelling around her eye.

Donnatelle had taken Ali's advice and had spent much of the weekend on the practice range and hitting the books. By the middle of the week, she had managed to retake and pass the evidence handling test and had eked out a qualifying score on the target range as well. Each evening that week, there were impromptu study sessions in the common room of the women's dormitory, with Jose and some of his pals in attendance.

There were no e-mails from Brenda Riley and no calls either. Ali took that to mean that her well-intended advice about seeking treatment had come to nothing. The same thing must have been true about the background check. Richard Lattimer/Lowensdale may have turned out to be a liar and a cheat, but Ali resigned herself to the idea that Brenda would do what Brenda would do regardless.

On the last Friday afternoon just before graduation, Sergeant Pettit once again paired Ali and Jose for what would be her final attempt at a hip toss try with a wily adversary. Ali figured the instructor was looking for a repeat of their previous performance. What the instructor didn't see as Ali approached Jose was the wink he sent in her direction.

When the confrontation started, instead of the expected hip toss, Ali surprised both Jose and Pettit by taking him down with a simple leg sweep. Once Jose was on the ground, she cuffed him and it was over. The fact that he had put up zero resistance made Ali feel like she was cheating the system, but when Sergeant Pettit came over to slap her on the back and tell her "Good job," she didn't tell the instructor otherwise. She just reached down and helped Jose up.

"We're even now?" Jose asked her with a grin.

She nodded and smiled back. "Even," she said.

When she removed the cuffs and shook hands with Jose, Ali knew it really was over. She was ready to go home and be a police officer, and so was he.

7

San Diego, California
September

On Friday afternoon, Mark Blaylock made his way through the deserted administrative offices of Rutherford International. They had finally let Mina's secretary go, so now it was just the two of them. They'd hung on to the office space in hopes that things would turn around, but that wasn't happening. They had gotten a hell of a deal by paying the lease in advance, but time was up. The landlord had someone who was interested in moving in.

Renters for the warehouse/manufacturing spaces in the office park complex were few and far between at the moment, so he was letting them hang on to their storage space at a greatly reduced rent. That gave Mark and Mina a place to store the office equipment and furniture they had been unable to unload. How much longer they'd be able to manage even that paltry amount of space was a question for which Mark had no easy answer.

Mark slammed open the door to his wife's office, then he went inside and collapsed into the nearest chair.

"How'd it go?" Mina asked.

Mark shook his head. "I don't know," he said. "There's something wrong with the controls. The drone flew fine for a while, like there was nothing at all the matter with it. I was putting it through its paces and it was perfect, but when I tried to land it, everything went to hell."

"It crashed?" Mina asked.

"I'll say," Mark said with a nod. "And I don't know why—no idea."

"What about the wreckage?" she asked.

"Don't worry," Mark said. "That's the only good thing about all this. It went into the water. No one will ever find it."

The water in this instance was the Salton Sea, near Mark's rustic cabin. It was possible that someday if the lake dried up, someone might find the wreckage, but it wouldn't happen anytime soon.

"Good," Mina said.

That was all she said. She could have said a lot more. When Mark had insisted on doing the test run himself, she had worried about how capable he was, but right then there really wasn't anyone else to do the critical flight. They'd let everyone go, and Mina sure as hell couldn't fly one of the damned things herself. When Mark said he could do it—that it was "dead simple"—she had believed him. Evidently she'd been wrong about that, but playing the blame game wasn't going to serve any purpose. Ermina Blaylock was nothing if not absolutely practical.

"What can we do to fix this?"

"I'm no engineer," Mark said, shaking his head. "And I don't have the technical skills to sort it out. We need help, Mina, and we need it fast. If we're going to make this deal work, we're going to have to bring back someone from engineering."

That was a risk and they both knew it. When the military contract went away, they had bought up an entire warehouse of UAVs as scrap and for pennies on the dollar with the understanding that the UAVs would all be destroyed. Rutherford International had been paid a princely sum to make sure they were. The powers that be were concerned that if one of the UAVs happened to fall into the wrong hands, people unfriendly to the United States might manage to reverse engineer the product and come up with a workable drone design of their own.

Together Mark and Mina had falsified records showing the scrapped UAVs had all been destroyed and a helpful inspector had signed off on the paperwork. Now after months of putting out discreet feelers, Mina had finally stumbled across a potential customer, one Enrique Gallegos, who wanted to buy several working UAVs, for which he was prepared to pay an astonishing amount of money into a numbered account in the Cayman Islands. Before anything could happen, however, Mark and Mina needed to put on a successful demo flight. Mina was grateful that Enrique Gallegos hadn't been on hand to witness this afternoon's show-and-tell disaster.

It was easy to see that once they made the sale to Gallegos, they'd be financially whole again, but all of that depended on their having a working product. Right now they didn't.

"We need it to work," Mark said desperately, giving voice to what Mina herself already knew to be true. "We're going down for the third time."

Mina couldn't help feeling a little sorry for the man. She slept easily each night while he lay awake trying to find a way around their disastrous cash flow problems. Gallegos had been very specific in his request. He needed his UAVs capable of making an hourlong flight. He also wanted them equipped with some kind of self-destruct application.

Mina was good at playing stupid, but she wasn't stupid. She

understood that Gallegos's principals intended to use the UAVs to smuggle illicit cargo—drugs most likely—from somewhere in northern Mexico to predetermined landing areas in the United States well north of the last Border Patrol checkpoints. If each drone was capable of carrying a valuable ten-kilogram payload, she was a little puzzled by the need for a self-destruct mechanism, but she had agreed that any UAVs they sold would be so equipped.

"What about Richard Lowensdale?" Mina asked Mark casually. "Maybe we could bring him in on a consulting basis."

Mark let his breath out. "I never liked Richard," he said. "I'm not sure he can be trusted."

"Yes, but he's a good engineer, and he knows the product," Mina said.

"But how the hell are we going to pay him?"

"Let me see what I can do," Mina said. "Maybe I can get him to defer payment until after he gets us up and running. To bring him on board, though, I'll have to go see him. We can't risk sending him an e-mail about any of this. I don't want to put anything in writing."

"Yes, definitely," Mark agreed. "Nothing in writing."

He stood up and stretched. "I'm going to go home and shower. It was hot as hell out there today, but by now the ATVers are all showing up for their long weekend. I was glad to come back to town."

Once Mark left, a worried Mina paced the small confines of her office. If the feds could pull a wrecked 747 out of the ocean and reassemble it, they could do the same thing to a drone that had gone down in the Salton Sea. All the parts, even the smallest integrated circuits, had source codes that would come straight back to Rutherford and to her. There were laws, federal laws, against selling supposedly scrapped equipment to unauthorized purchasers. Enrique Gallegos was definitely not authorized.

Mina wanted to be rich again—she liked being rich—but she most definitely didn't want to go to jail.

Two nights later, she sat in a darkened bar in the Morongo Casino outside Palm Springs. She sipped a tonic with lime and waited for Enrique to pull himself away from the baccarat table. The casino was far enough out of the way for Mina to meet him there without raising any San Diego eyebrows.

"Is there a problem?" he asked.

She nodded. "My husband is hung up on the idea of blowing up the hardware," she said. "It's possible, of course, but in order to make sure it works, we'd have to take another drone out of our inventory. And there's always the very real danger of an event like that leaving a debris trail. We'll need to do a test run."

"What are you saying?"

"If you want us to use two UAVs—one for us to blow up and the other for you to own—then you'll need to pay us in advance for two UAVs."

Enrique lifted his glass to his lips. "Sounds expensive," he said. "I don't know if I can make that work."

"We're the ones taking all the risks," Mina said. "If we get caught, Mark and I could end up in jail for a very long time."

That's what Mina said, even though she had already decided that she would disappear long before any possible fallout hit. She'd be gone; the money would be gone; and Mark—poor old Mark—would be the one left holding the bag.

Without another word, Gallegos stood up and walked away. He didn't say he'd be back, but Mina was sure he would be, and she was right. He returned twenty minutes later.

"All right," he said. "We'll buy two of them up front."

Mina was impressed. Twenty minutes wasn't very long to get the go-ahead on that kind of expenditure. Whoever was behind this was someone with very deep pockets.

"We've already paid a quarter of that amount as an advance on the other drone, with another quarter due after a successful demo and the remainder on delivery," Gallegos continued. "We'll buy the second one at half price on the same terms—a quarter now and the rest on completion of a successful demonstration."

All of which means they really want this, Mina told herself.

"Seventy-five percent, not fifty," Mina said. "And I'm going to need that first quarter up front in cash. I need operating capital."

And running money.

8

Barstow, California

Valerie Gastellum Sandoz, Brenda's older sister, was the member of the family drafted by their mother to make the seven-and-a-half-hour, almost four-hundred-mile trip from San Francisco to Barstow in order to bail Brenda out of jail. She'd had to use one of her precious vacation days. So when it came time to sign Brenda out of the jail, Valerie was not a happy camper.

She and Brenda were sisters; they had never been pals. Brenda had been the golden child, from grade school on. She had been an exemplary student, a cheerleader, a star, while Valerie merely plugged along in the background. Val had been a late bloomer who married for the first time at age thirty-seven. While her younger sibling had embarked on her high-flying broadcasting career, Valerie had labored away in school, changing majors several times before finally settling in to become an architect. She had worked her way up from several lowly drafting positions until she landed herself a decent position in a commercial architectural firm in the Bay Area.

Now that their situations were reversed, with Valerie in the catbird seat and Brenda on her uppers, Valerie was not amused by her younger sister's plight, and she wasn't very sympathetic either.

"What the hell were you thinking?" Valerie demanded as they headed west on California Highway 58. "Mom's been frantic. Where the hell have you been all this time?"

"I went to Sedona," Brenda answered. "I went to see a friend from L.A., Ali Reynolds. I thought she might help me, but she didn't. She's becoming a cop."

"Too bad she didn't arrest you before you wrecked your damned car. Did you talk to the insurance adjuster?"

Brenda shook her head. She didn't want to say there was no insurance adjuster. Her auto insurance had been canceled two months ago, after her second DUI. Not canceled really, but they had raised the premium so much that she couldn't afford the payments. Her insurance stopped when the premiums stopped. The remains of her wrecked car had been towed to the impound lot and they were going to stay there.

"Thank you for coming to get me," Brenda said contritely sometime later.

"If it had been up to me, I would have left you to rot in jail or else walk home," Valerie continued. "Mom has been beyond upset. You were gone for a week and a half. Did it ever cross your mind that she was worried? Would it have killed you to take out your cell phone and call her?"

There was nothing Brenda could say in response to Val's tirade. Before the wreck she hadn't wanted to call and hadn't answered her mother's calls. Since the wreck her phone had been MIA and was probably even now toasting its circuit boards in the impound lot. As for her other reason for not calling? Telling Val that she'd been hospitalized for four days with DTs didn't seem to strike just the right note. Besides, Val was on a roll. She wasn't interested in any response.

"The only reason I agreed to come get you is that I was afraid Mom would try to do it on her own. She can't drive anymore. At least, with her macular degeneration, she *shouldn't* drive anymore, but she still does. And since you're her favorite, she would've tried to come riding to your rescue herself if I hadn't told her I'd do it."

Brenda said nothing. Had she been drinking, she would have fought back. But if being sober meant sitting there and having to take this kind of bitching out, she didn't think it was worth it.

"With three DUIs, you are *not* under any circumstances to drive Mom's car, understand?" Valerie added.

Brenda nodded. That pretty much went without saying. Besides, the cops had just confiscated her driver's license.

"I won't," she said. "Just take me to Mom's."

"What about your apartment?"

Brenda didn't want to admit to her sister that three weeks ago she'd been evicted from her apartment because she hadn't paid the rent. For months. That was one of the reasons she'd hit the road. She'd been living out of her car, but she was still afraid that someone might see her and recognize her.

Was that what hitting bottom really meant—living out of your car or not caring if people knew you were living out of your car? Which was worse? And did it really matter? Whatever possessions she'd had left had been in the car with her. Now the car was gone and so was everything else.

She tried to lighten the somber mood. "It's like they say in that old song: 'I figure whenever you're down and out, the only way is up.'"

"Don't even start," Valerie said. "Give me a break."

After that they pretty much stopped talking. By the time Valerie stopped in front of their mother's faux Victorian house on P Street in Sacramento, it was well after dark. A single lamp was lit in the living room, and Brenda caught sight of her mother sitting in the halo of light. She was just sitting there, waiting. There was no television set glowing in the background. There was no book on her lap. She was simply waiting.

Brenda looked at her sister. "Are you coming in?"

"I guess," Valerie said. "But only for a minute. If I stay any longer than that, I might say something I'd regret."

"Thank you for the ride."

"You're welcome," Valerie replied. She didn't say the rest of it, but she was sure Brenda got the message—just don't let it happen again.

Palm Springs, California

One week later, again on a Friday afternoon, Mina made another trip to the casino, where she found Enrique Gallegos waiting for her in the bar. He sat in a corner booth with an athletic bag on the banquette between them. After a brief chat, Gallegos walked away, leaving the bag behind.

As Mina drove out of the parking lot, she called Mark. "Did they spring with the cash?" he asked.

"Some," she said. "Not as much as I wanted but enough to bring Richard Lowensdale on board." The truth was they had given her exactly what she'd asked for in terms of the cash advance, but she wasn't going to tell Mark the whole truth about that. He'd find a way to fritter away the money on things he felt were essential— like bringing their mortgage payments up to date.

Mark sighed with relief. "So you're off to see Richard?" It had taken some talking, but she had finally convinced Mark that

Richard was their only hope of resolving their technical problems without bringing in a lot more people.

Mina glanced at her watch. "Yes," she said. "I'm on my way to the airport. If I can get a flight to Sacramento tonight, I'll go see Richard in the morning. The sooner we get him started working on this, the sooner we get the rest of our money."

She couldn't help feeling just a little sorry for Mark. The man was incredibly transparent. He was afraid of losing what they had, and by most standards, they had a lot. Generally speaking, having was better than not having, but Mina wasn't nearly as hung up on that prospect as Mark was.

Losing possessions held no particular terror for Ermina Vlasic Blaylock. She'd already been through that once. She'd lost everything and everyone she'd held dear as a thirteen-year-old child during the Bosnian war. A Croat by birth, she had hidden in a barn while her entire family was slaughtered—her parents, her grandparents, her brothers and sisters. Of all those people, she was the only one to survive. More than survive, she had thrived. She had been adopted by an older couple from America, Sam and Lola Cunningham. Lola had wanted a daughter. Sam had wanted something else, but that had been her ticket to the American dream, one she had made her own.

She had been working as a minimum wage server for a caterer at what turned out to be the memorial reception for Mark Blaylock's first wife, Christine. Mina had seen Mark looking brokenhearted and handsome and needy—to say nothing of rich—and had sought him out like a heat-seeking missile. She had managed to put herself in his way, and he had taken the bait. They had been married now for seven years.

Somewhere along the line Mark had been given what was supposedly an inside track on getting a military contract for guidance systems on a particular class of UAVs. It had the potential of turning into a financial gold mine. Mark had mortgaged everything they owned to buy Rutherford International. They had put Mina at the helm of the new entity so it would qualify as a woman-owned company in terms of government contracts. Had they managed to get the drone contract, they would have been millionaires several times over, but the drone contract had gone away completely, and now they were broke.

One thing was certain, however. Ermina Vlasic Cunningham Blaylock was nothing if not resourceful. She was pretty sure she'd be able to bring Richard Lowensdale to heel just as she had Mark Blaylock and Enrique Gallegos. Instead of heading directly to the airport, she drove east past the Palm Springs exits, toward Indio. With the bag of money safely in her trunk, she turned south on California 86.

She had changed clothes at the office, slipping out of her work clothes and into a golf shirt, jeans, and sandals. Dressed like any other weekender, she drove to Mark's cabin. She was glad to be coming from the north. That meant she could turn off toward the cabin miles before the Border Patrol checkpoint. The cash was most likely in unmarked hundred-dollar bills. She knew, however, that far too many of those bills might have come into contact with the drug trade in one guise or another. She didn't need a drug-sniffing dog to point out the cash.

The property on the outskirts of Salton City had been in Mark's family for generations. The cabin was a stout clapboard affair that decades after being built still somehow managed to hold together and remain upright in the face of howling desert winds and scorching dust. Nothing if not austere, it included a single multipurpose room that was kitchen, dining room, and living room combined, a tiny bedroom with a minuscule closet, and a bathroom that was functional but definitely not deluxe. When the AC was on, the place was comfortable enough. There was

running water, but the brownish stuff that came out of the taps
tasted and smelled like dirt—salty dirt. There was no real furniture, only a collection of odd mismatched outdoor chairs and
lounges that were stored inside and then dragged outside and to
the sandy beach as needed.

Mina knew how much Mark had appreciated the fact that
she understood his need to hang on to the derelict old wreck. It
had escaped being mortgaged along with everything else, because
the lending officer from the bank had claimed it was essentially
worthless.

Sometime earlier—during that terrible year the fish in the
Salton Sea all died for no apparent reason—there had been a
period of months when almost no one had been able to use their
cabins owing to the fierce odor of dead fish. While the owners
were mostly absent, someone had broken into Mark's cabin and
most of the others and vandalized them all. As a consequence
and at great expense, Mark had insisted on installing a system of
roll-down metal shutters that covered the cabin's windows and
doors.

It had been an expensive process, not unlike putting lipstick
on a pig, but the shutters made the cabin, humble as it was, impervious to intrusion. Once the shutters were in place, Mina had
made her own contribution. She had hired a workman to install a
fireproof safe concealed behind what appeared to be an electrical
box in the cabin's only closet. The safe made a perfect hidey-hole
for Mina's private hoard of cash, not just Gallegos's cash but other
monies she had accumulated over the years by skimming funds
off the top and hiding them without Mark's ever being the wiser.

Mark Blaylock was under the impression they were going
broke. Mina knew that wasn't entirely true. Mark would be
broke; Mina would be fine. She would see to it.

Driving to the Salton City cabin early that evening, Mina

threaded her way through various campsites with their outdoor bonfires and their amazing collections of ATV rolling stock parked outside massive motor homes and fifth-wheel campers. Using her remote control, Mina opened only the shutter that covered the front door, then she let herself inside with a key. Without the AC on, the place was like an oven. She held back only as much cash as she thought Richard might demand. She stuffed that into her Gucci bag and then put the remainder in the safe.

She was in the cabin for only a matter of minutes, but by the time she left, she was dripping with sweat. She paused outside long enough to relock the front door and close the shutter. With the now-empty athletic bag safely stowed in the trunk of her car, she headed for the airport.

Mina knew that she was cutting it close, but she didn't need to check any luggage. Besides, with this new influx of cash, she was once again flying first-class. That meant security wouldn't be a problem. She'd be there in plenty of time to board her plane.

9

Grass Valley, California
September

Richard Lowensdale was busy chatting with Lynn Martinson that Saturday morning, trying to prop her up in the face of that day's so-called family meeting, which was part of her son Lucas's incarceration process. Lynn, her ex-husband, the ex's new wife, the druggie sixteen-year-old, Lucas's court-appointed attorney, and his counselor would all be in attendance. Lynn was expecting the session to be one of blame-game finger-pointing, and Lynn's devoted listener, Richard Lewis, allowed as how that would probably be true.

He read Lynn's messages and sent back what he hoped sounded like sympathetic one-word comments—encouraging words, as it were. The truth is, committee meetings of any kind bored the hell out of him, so listening to Lynn going on and on about a meeting that was going to take place half a continent away was not high on Richard's agenda. The more she blathered on about her problems, the more he knew it was time to take her off his list. She just wasn't fun anymore, and any woman who wasn't fun wasn't worth having around.

So when there was an early-morning doorbell ring at his front door—a totally unexpected doorbell ring—Richard was grateful for the interruption and was glad to tell Lynn someone was there, that he had to go to the door.

Richard was smart enough about home security to have a CCTV camera on his front porch, one with a video feed that went directly into his computer. Before leaving his desk, he switched over to that screen and was pleased to see Mina Blaylock—the beautiful Mina—waiting there for him to open the door. He wasn't surprised to see her. He knew exactly why she had come and what she would need. The only thing that did surprise him was how long it had taken for her to show up on his doorstep.

As he started toward the door, however, he looked around the room and had a glimpse of how bad it was. The house was a mess. When his mother and Ron had lived here, you could have eaten off the floor. Now you couldn't eat off the dining room table. For one thing, Richard had turned that into his primary assembly station for model airplanes. His own collection, layered with dust, covered the bookshelves where his mother had once kept her collection of murder mysteries. Those had been banished to the trash heap at the bottom of the basement stairs.

There were plenty of people who wanted to fly model airplanes but didn't have brains enough to put them together properly. In addition to building his own planes, he made several hundred bucks a month on the side by doing the assembly work for those dunderheads. They sent him their kits and their money; he sent them their planes.

Doing that, however, meant he needed packing material. That was also in the dining room. The packing station was his mother's old buffet, where instead of good china, packing boxes and tape and shipping labels held sway. To the side of the buffet, on the floor, a huge plastic bag spilled a scatter of foam peanuts in every direction.

Richard spent most of his waking hours either working at the dining room table or at his computer at the far end of the small living room. Over time, there had come to be trails from the computer station and the dining room table that led through the debris field to other rooms in the house—the bathroom, bedroom, and kitchen. Most of the time he didn't worry about any of this.

The string of women he romanced over his VoIP connection had no idea how dirty his house was or how long it had been since he'd had a haircut—or a shower. The delivery guys who handed him packages or dropped them on the front porch or picked up the outgoing ones didn't mind how Richard or his house looked. It wasn't their business, and it wasn't their problem.

Now, though, with Mina standing out on the front porch, Richard realized how the house would look through her eyes— how he would look—and he was embarrassed. He spent a few minutes clearing a spot on the couch so she'd have a place to sit down. Finally, when she rang the doorbell again, Richard made his way to the door.

"Hey," he said. "What's up?"

"Hello, Richard," Mina said. "Can I come in?"

"Sure," he said. "What brings you to these parts?"

He pushed open the screen door. Mina looked great, but then she always looked great. He often wondered why she put up with Mark. He seemed so . . . well . . . ordinary. Boring and old. Mark had to be pushing sixty, probably twice Mina's age.

Richard led her through the entry and into the living room. He gestured her to a place on the couch while he resumed his place on the chair in front of the computer. On the screen, Lynn

Martinson was leaving him a long text message. More whining, no doubt.

"I need some help," Mina said, then she corrected that statement. "We need some help."

Clearing a path through the mess on the floor, Richard rolled his desk chair closer to the couch. "With what?" he asked.

That was disingenuous. Richard knew exactly what Mina needed help with—a problem with the drone guidance system. The reason Richard knew all about that problem and how to fix it was that the problem was his own creation. One of his last acts when leaving Rutherford International was a bit of "gotcha" sabotage. He had inserted the problem, a single set of rogue commands, buried deep in the thousands of commands it took to run the supposedly scrapped drone and make it work on GPS coordinates.

Richard knew that a sharp programmer might be able to locate and fix the problem, but a search like that would take time and money—lots of money. He also understood why it had taken so long for the problem to come to light. That had to do with the fact that no one had bothered to do a drone test flight for well over a year. No test flights meant that RI had no customers.

If Mark and Mina knew about the problem now, that meant they had needed and tested a working model—for someone. A customer of some kind must have come out of the woodwork. Richard knew it sure as hell wasn't the military, because as far as they knew the drones were history. Besides, if it had been someone on the up-and-up, Mina wouldn't have come skulking up here unannounced to ask Richard for help.

As far as Richard was concerned, a customer who was interested in staying under the radar was very good news. It meant money was in play—lots of money, for the Blaylocks and, if Richard played his cards right, for him as well.

"What do you think is the problem?" he asked.

Mina shrugged. "I have no idea," she said. "Neither does Mark. We need someone who can troubleshoot for us. We're not in any condition to start bringing people back on a permanent basis," she added, "but since you're so familiar with the project, we were hoping you'd agree to come on board on a consulting basis."

"What happened?" Richard asked.

"We put a drone up in the air, or rather, Mark put it up in the air. He's flown them before with no trouble, but this time it crashed and burned."

Which, Richard thought, *is exactly what I programmed it to do: take off, fly flawlessly for a while, and then drop out of the sky for no apparent reason.*

Richard let the silence between them stretch for some time before he shook his head. "I just don't see how I can do it, Mina," he said reluctantly. "Not after what I hoped would happen between us. There's too much history. Just seeing you again is enough to break my heart."

Lying to someone's face was a lot more difficult than telling lies over the phone, but between the last time Richard had seen Mina and now, he'd had a whole lot more practice in the art of prevarication. And he had to admit that she was a pretty capable liar herself. Ignoring the mess around her, she watched him with a kind of almost breathless, bright-eyed attention. That was how she made men sit up and take notice.

"I'm so sorry, Richard," she said. "Please understand. I had to let you go along with everyone else. Otherwise Mark would have figured it out."

For months after Richard went to work at Rutherford, Mina had flirted with him shamelessly and hinted that she was interested in having a little fling with him. That was all that happened in the end—flirting. In actual fact, he'd hardly ever gotten to first base with any real women. They scared the hell out of him. Richard talked a good game, but when it was time to deliver the goods, he always came up short.

He had hoped things would be different with Mina, but the flirting had come to naught. Later, when he'd been given his pink slip, rather than facing up to his own shortcomings, Richard had convinced himself that was why he'd been let go—because Mark had somehow caught on to what Mina was thinking. That was the real reason Richard had dropped that little programming bomb into the Rutherford works. It was the best way for him to even the score. And now, months later, when they finally knew they had a problem, not only did they not know he was responsible for their difficulty, they had come to him to fix it. How wonderful was that?

Richard wanted to leap off the couch and dance a little jig. Instead, he sighed and shook his head as though he were allowing himself to be persuaded entirely against his will.

"All right," he said resignedly. "What do you need and when?"

"I need to fly a ten-kilo payload, one hundred or so miles, to predetermined coordinates."

Richard had been wondering about the end user. Mina's statement provided the answer. After all, this was California. Other businesses might be struggling to survive, but the illegal drug industry was still booming. Richard wanted Mina to verify it, though. He wanted her to understand he wasn't as dumb as she thought he was.

"I suppose that means we're dealing with one of the drug cartels," Richard said.

Mina looked him square in the eye and didn't deny it, and she didn't object to his use of the word *we* either. In fact, she used the same word herself.

"We'll make a lot of money," she said.

"Who's we?"

"All of us—you, me, Mark. How long do you think it'll take to troubleshoot the problem?"

The real answer was about two minutes, but he didn't tell her that. She wouldn't pay for two minutes.

"I don't know how you expect me to do that," he said. "I don't have any of the code, and even if I did, finding something like this won't be easy."

Mina reached into her purse and pulled out a thumb drive, which she handed over to him. "I brought the latest version of the programming with me. Here it is," she said. "Everything you need should be on that."

The fact that Mark and Mina still had drones and were getting ready to sell working models meant that the Blaylocks had gone over to the dark side. From Richard's point of view there was a definite upside to working the dark side—lots of money.

"It'll take me at least six months, but that's not a guarantee," he said. "Fifty thou total. All communications are to be done this way, in person and eyeball to eyeball. No e-mails back and forth; no telephone communications; all payments to be made in cash. Half down; half on delivery."

"Five months, not six," Mina countered. "I need to be able to do the test flight before the end of January. I'm offering twenty thousand down, and ten a month until the job is completed. Plus, I'll give you a twenty-five-thousand-dollar bonus in January after a successful test flight."

Once again Mina reached into her oversized purse. This time she plucked out a packet of cash and handed that to him as well. "Count it if you want."

Richard didn't have to count it. He knew it was all there. He couldn't help but be a little disappointed. He'd had no idea that she knew him so well. The fact that she was offering more than he'd asked was surprising.

"Oh," Mina added. "There is one more thing. We'll need the ability to remotely detonate this thing."

"As in blow it up?"

"Yes," she said. "Blow it to pieces."

"That's a little more complicated," Richard said with a laugh. "But I get it," he added. "It's like the beginning of one of those old *Mission: Impossible* stories on TV where they say, 'This tape will self-destruct in thirty seconds.'"

Mina frowned. "I don't think I ever saw that movie."

"It wasn't a movie," Richard said. "It was an old TV series. From the sixties."

"I never saw that either," Mina said.

But Richard had seen those shows, countless times. Ron Mills, Richard's stepfather, had loved *Mission: Impossible,* especially Cinnamon. He had owned DVD versions of all three seasons. Richard had found those DVDs in the same box in the basement where he had found his mother's prized boxed sets of *Murder, She Wrote* VCR tapes.

"Too bad," he said. "You're missing out on an essential piece of Americana."

Mina stood up and gathered her purse. Richard didn't bother getting up to show her out. He looked at the money—money he had never expected to see. Without having to pay taxes and at his current rate of expenditure, that much money and the rest Mina had promised him would last for a very long time.

Richard felt an immense sense of satisfaction. He had Mina Blaylock just where he wanted her. Richard knew that if there was that much money lying around just for the asking, then there was obviously far more where that came from.

Sacramento, California

Brenda's enforced jail-based sobriety didn't exactly take. It lasted long enough for Valerie to drive her home to Sacramento from Barstow. It lasted long enough for Brenda to be far too sober during the name-calling blowup between her sister and her mother, Camilla, when Valerie dropped Brenda off at their mother's P Street home.

"Here's your jailbird," Valerie had said, opening the door so Brenda could make her way inside. "I brought her home to roost."

Camilla heaved herself up out of the chair and hurried to meet them. "I'm so glad you're safe," she said, hugging Brenda close. "When I didn't hear from you, I was worried sick."

"She's a drunk, Mom," Valerie said. "She wrecked her car and she damned near killed herself. She probably would have done us all a favor if she had."

"Valerie," Camilla said, "you mustn't talk like that."

"Why not? You don't think she's learned her lesson, do you? Just wait. She'll be drinking again the minute your back is turned."

"Valerie . . ."

"Save your breath, Mom. I don't want to hear it, and the next time she gets in hot water, don't bother calling me. I did this once. I won't do it again."

Valerie had slammed out the door on that note and hadn't been heard from again. She hadn't phoned. Camilla called and left messages. Valerie didn't call back.

As for Brenda? Unfortunately, Valerie's assessment proved to be correct. Brenda was all right for a couple of days, but then she got around to opening the mail, including the background check on Richard—Lowensdale, it turned out, not Lattimer. Reading through the material and uncovering the fabric of lies behind everything he had told Brenda was enough to push her off the deep end once more.

That night, after her mother was asleep, she let herself out of the house, walked six blocks to the nearest liquor store, and bought a supply of booze that she smuggled back into the house and upstairs to her room. One of the pieces of furniture in the room was her mother's old hope chest. From Brenda's point of view, the best thing about it was the fact that it came with a lock and key. Brenda deposited her booze purchases in among mother's extra sheets and pillowcases, then she turned the old-fashioned key in the lock and hid the key in her purse, concealed in her hard plastic tampon holder.

She drank the rest of the night, reading and rereading the background check and fanning her anger to a fever pitch. She was furious to think that while she had been sick with worry about Richard's health, he had been fit as a fiddle and only an hour or so away. She thought about calling him, but then she realized that wouldn't work. He had stopped taking her calls, and once he recognized her new cell phone number, he wouldn't take calls from that device either. No, what was called for was a visit—a personal visit, one where Brenda would have the opportunity to let Richard have it. She wanted to talk to him face-to-face and tell him how contemptible he was.

She fell asleep around four a.m. and woke up at eleven. She had breakfast in the kitchen while her mother was having lunch. Camilla greeted her daughter with a smile. "Good morning, sleepyhead," she said. "You're keeping the same kind of hours you did in junior high."

"I couldn't sleep," Brenda said.

"Is there anything I can do to help?" Camilla asked.

Yes, Brenda thought. *Leave me alone.* "Can I borrow your car for a while this afternoon?"

"Well, of course," Camilla said. "When do you expect to get your own car back?"

The answer to that was never. Valerie would have spilled the truth about that in a minute. Fortunately for Brenda, Valerie hadn't hung around long enough to do a huge amount of damage.

"They're getting the parts in," Brenda lied. "It's going to be a while."

On that sunny afternoon in early October, Brenda stocked her purse with enough booze to tide her over, then she borrowed her mother's car keys and took off for Grass Valley in Camilla's twenty-year-old Taurus. All the way there, Brenda rehearsed exactly what she would say to Richard Lattimer Lowensdale. By the time she reached the house on Jan Road, she was only partially drunk, but she had worked herself into a seething rage.

Ready for war, she marched up to his door, stomped across the front porch, and gave the doorbell button a furious punch. But nothing happened. Richard didn't come to the door. The house was totally silent. Convinced he had recognized her and was simply hiding from her, she wandered around to the side of the house, where she found a second door. This one didn't have a doorbell, but it did have a series of glass panes.

Without giving any thought to the consequences, Brenda picked up a rock and smashed one of the lower panes. Then she unlocked the door and let herself inside. Entering through a utility room, she found herself choking on the terrible odor. It made her throat hurt and her eyes itch. The kitchen was fine, but the mess in the remainder of the house was appalling.

Richard had passed himself off as an urbane, witty, neat guy, yet here he lived in a squalid hovel. Brenda wandered through the filthy house, letting the scales fall from her eyes. Richard had lied about far more than his name and his place of employment. Everything about him was false.

With Richard not there, Brenda was ready to vandalize the place. Standing in the living room, surveying the mess, she caught sight of the most logical target. Richard's command central, his computer desk, stood at the far end of the room.

Brenda remembered Richard's telling her that he never turned off his computer. *Maybe I'll turn it off for him,* she thought. *Permanently.*

She looked around for a suitable weapon and settled on a sooty fireplace poker. She carried it over there and was ready to smash the CRT when she saw there was an open file showing on the screen. The file name was Martinson in a folder called Storyboards.

Scanning through the open file, Brenda learned far more than she wanted to about Lynn Martinson's sad life—her drug-addicted son, her difficult ex-husband, her complicated job, and her loving relationship with someone named Richard Lewis who had a troublesome ex-wife named Andrea and a teenaged daughter, Nicole, who was also involved with drugs. Lynn's social security number was there. Her preferred nicknames and suitable terms of endearment were duly noted. There was also a log of calls and e-mail conversations that included transcripts of what Richard had said to her and what Lynn had answered in return. Glancing at the contents of the storyboard was like eavesdropping on a two-way conversation.

Suddenly a light went on in Brenda's head. Making a mental note of Lynn Martinson's name, Brenda hit the open file command. When a list of fifty-seven items appeared, Brenda scrolled through it. She found her own name, Brenda Riley, three-quarters of the way down the list.

She could have opened her file just then, but she didn't dare take the time. She wanted the contents of this folder—all the contents. Fortunately Brenda was conversant with the Mac operating system. She went back to the Storyboards folder and hit command P to activate the printer. As pages spun out of the printer, one after another, Brenda scanned one or two, realizing as she did so that she was far from alone in being victimized by Richard Lowensdale and his various aliases.

It took precious minutes and more than a hundred pages to print the storyboard folder. At one point, the printer ran out of paper and Brenda had to look around to find paper to load into it. As soon as the printing job was finished, Brenda reopened the Lynn Martinson file, leaving the computer much as it had been when she found it.

Then she picked up the printed material and fled. Back at her mother's home on P Street in Sacramento, Brenda locked herself in her room and read through what she had printed, studying every single page and drinking as she read.

By the time she finished reading and passed out again—at five o'clock the next morning—Brenda Riley had given herself a new purpose in life: one way or another she would find a way to take Richard Lowensdale down if it was the last thing she ever did.

10

Sedona, Arizona
January

Four months after graduating from the Arizona Police Academy, Ali Reynolds was doing something she had never expected to do again—manning her mother's lunch counter in the Sugarloaf Café.

"Order."

Summoned to the serving window by the café's substitute short-order cook, Ali Reynolds picked up two platters of ham and eggs and delivered them to the two customers seated at her station.

This Friday morning in January the restaurant had been slammed from the moment Ali opened the doors at six a.m. until only a few minutes ago. Once the pace slowed slightly, Ali leaned her hip against the counter and gave herself permission to sip a cup of coffee.

Six days down, one to go, Ali told herself.

Ali's parents, Bob and Edie Larson, were on the next-to-last day of their seven-day Caribbean cruise. Ali was on the next-to-last day of filling in for them.

After nearly a week of working her mother's early morning shift, Ali had a renewed respect for the jobs her parents had done in running their Sedona area diner for all those years. She also had a renewed respect for her mother's killer schedule. Edie Larson came in to the restaurant at four a.m. every day to bake the restaurant's signature sweet rolls as well as that day's supply of biscuits.

Ali's one attempt at duplicating her mother's sweet roll recipe had been nothing short of disastrous. Fortunately, Leland Brooks had come to her rescue. For the remainder of the week Edie and Bob Larson were gone, Leland had agreed to come in each day to handle the baking. Leland went back home each morning about the time Ali and the substitute short-order cook turned up to take over.

When Ali had first broached the topic of a Caribbean cruise as that year's Christmas present to her parents, they had turned the idea down cold. Both of them had insisted that they couldn't possibly be away from the restaurant for that long. Ali, however, had refused to take no for an answer. She had found a substitute cook and had sorted out a passport renewal for her mother and a new passport for her father. But it was only when she agreed to come in to the restaurant herself every day to keep an eye on things that Bob and Edie finally acquiesced.

To Ali's knowledge, this was the first long vacation her parents had ever taken together. From the tenor of the short e-mail updates Edie sent home on a daily basis, it seemed they were having the time of their lives. Ali was not having the time of her life. She was tired. Her feet hurt. Her back hurt. She put on her smile every morning when she put on her uniform—a freshly laundered Sugarloaf Café sweatshirt and a pair of jeans. She did her best to be cheerful and pleasant as she served coffee and wiped up spills, but the truth was Ali Reynolds was still annoyed. She was also bored.

This wasn't the way her life was supposed to be right now. She loved her parents and was glad to help with giving them a break, but the truth was she shouldn't have been available to work for a week as a substitute server in the Sugarloaf Café. The way she had seen her future, she should have been working as the media relations officer for the Yavapai County Sheriff's Department. The problem was, she wasn't.

The previous September, Ali Reynolds had graduated third in her class at the Arizona Police Academy in Peoria. For someone who was the oldest member of her class and a female besides, that had been a big accomplishment. She had been tossed into a class filled with much younger recruits, and she had made the grade.

Her parents, her son and daughter-in-law, and B. Simpson, her significant other, all of them beaming with pride, had shown up for her graduation. They had congratulated her and told her what a great job she had done. And she had shaken hands with all her fellow graduates, who, like her, were going back to towns all over the state of Arizona to begin their law enforcement duties. The whole experience had been an incredible high.

As a result, nothing could have prepared her for what happened to her the following Monday morning. Dressed in a perfectly creased uniform, she drove to Prescott fully expecting to resume her media relations duties. Before the scheduled preshift roll call meeting at nine, however, Sheriff Gordon Maxwell called her into his office, sat her down opposite his desk, and gave her the bad news.

"I'm sorry to do this, Ali, but I'm going to have to furlough you."

At first Ali didn't think she'd heard him right. "Furlough?" she repeated. "As in let me go?"

He nodded.

"Are you kidding? I just busted my butt for six weeks getting through the academy."

"I understand," he said. "And no, I'm not kidding. Believe me, I'm very, very sorry. The county budget-cutting axe fell on every aspect of county government about three weeks ago. I knew then this was going to happen. I didn't tell you, because I didn't want you to drop out without finishing the course. And you did great, by the way."

"Right," Ali replied sarcastically. "I did so well that now I'm being fired."

"Furloughed, not fired," Maxwell insisted. "Once the fiscal situation straightens out, I fully expect to bring you back as a sworn officer, but right this minute my hands are tied. Last in, first out, and all that jazz. Hell, Ali, it was either you or Jimmy. He's got a couple of kids and really needs this job."

Deputy Jimmy Potter happened to be a recent hire as well. He and Ali shared office space in the Village of Oak Creek Substation. He was a nice guy with a wife and a pair of preschoolaged children. Ali could see that Sheriff Maxwell had a point. Ali had no dependents. Her financial situation made work an option for her rather than a necessity, but she really wanted this job. She loved it. She was good at it.

"So that makes me expendable?" Ali asked.

"Not expendable, not at all."

Despite what he said, it turned out Ali Reynolds was indeed expendable. Without ever attending that morning's roll call, she turned in her laptop, her cell phone, her weapons, and her badge and went home. She wasn't in disgrace, but it certainly felt like it.

In a way, losing the media relations job was somehow worse than losing her newscasting job in California years earlier. Her response to that had been to pack up and go home to Sedona. This time she was already *in* Sedona. That left her nowhere else to run. L.A. was big enough to allow for a certain amount of anonymity. Sedona was another proposition entirely. Everyone seemed to know she'd been laid off. Even though most of the comments came in the inoffensive guise of harmless well-wishing, the lack of privacy in both her love life and job situation bothered her.

She had been forced to sit on the sidelines licking her wounds and watching while the media storm over the "sweat lodge wars" once again catapulted the Yavapai County Sheriff's Department to national prominence. And who was doing the media relations work for the department in the midst of that maelstrom? The guy with his face on TV and voice on the radio was Mike Sawyer, a twenty-two-year-old college kid Ali had brought on board as an unpaid summer intern while she was down in Phoenix at the academy. Instead of returning to school to work on his master's degree in the fall, he had stayed on.

It irked Ali that Sheriff Maxwell couldn't scrape up enough money to pay her but had managed to find enough funds in the budget to pay Mike. It probably wasn't a living wage, because Mike was living with his parents, but still . . .

One of the customers at the counter held up his coffee mug and caught Ali's attention. "Can I have a refill?"

"Sure."

Ali poured coffee, dropped off a check, picked up some menus, and put them back in the holder over by the cash register.

So what had Ali done since that day of her surprising "furlough"? She'd read books, dozens of them. She was just now working her way through *The Count of Monte Cristo*. It was a book Mr. Gabrielson, her English teacher at Mingus Mountain High, had recommended to her years ago. With nothing else pressing, Ali had decided this forced hiatus was a perfect opportunity to read all those books she had said she would get around to reading someday when she had time. At the moment finding time for reading was not a problem.

Reading aside, Ali Reynolds was bored. She was beyond bored. When she'd been working for the department, she'd enjoyed everything about her job including the hour-and-a-half commute on those days when she'd drive from Sedona to the county seat in Prescott. Yes, she hadn't been well accepted by some of the old-timers there, but she'd been working on getting along with them and she was surprised to discover that, once she was sent packing, she missed everything about her work for the Yavapai County Sheriff's Department, including some of the prickly clerks in the front office.

Ali's mother had suggested that Ali give the garden club a try, but Ali's lack of anything resembling a green thumb precluded that. She had zero artistic skill, so taking up drawing or painting wasn't an option. She didn't play golf or tennis. She didn't ride horses. She wasn't into hot-air ballooning.

When B. was in town, the two of them had fun hiking in Sedona's red-rock wilderness, but these days B. was out of town as much or more than he was home. Most of the time her parents were bound up with the Sugarloaf Café and their own peculiar squabbles. Chris and Athena were building their own lives together and getting ready for the birth of their twins.

Ali had Leland Brooks to fall back on, of course. He kept her house running in tip-top shape. Theirs was a pleasant, untroubled relationship with each respecting the other's privacy, but Leland wasn't someone she could talk to, not really talk.

What Ali missed more than anything was having friends, close friends. Her best pal from high school, Reenie Bernard, had been dead for years. Dave Holman was still working for the sheriff's department as their lead homicide investigator. Dave and Ali were friends, but when Dave wasn't at work, he was preoccupied with raising his two teenaged daughters.

Ali had one new friend, a seventysomething nun named Sister

Anselm. They had met in the course of caring for a badly injured burn victim and had bonded after surviving a shootout with a suicidal ecoterrorist. Sister Anselm lived at Saint Bernadette's, a Sisters of Providence convent in Jerome that specialized in treating troubled nuns. Unlike Ali, Sister Anselm was fully employed, either at the convent itself or traveling all over Arizona as a patient advocate for severely injured and mostly indigent patients.

Had anyone asked Bob and Edie Larson about their religion, they would both have claimed to be Lutheran. Because Sunday mornings were big business at the Sugarloaf, other than attending occasional weddings and funerals, they'd barely stepped inside a church of any kind for years. Having grown up as a relatively unchurched child, Ali had remained so as an adult and had raised Chris without regular church attendance. In advance of the twins' birth, Athena and Chris had joined the congregation of Red Rock Lutheran.

All that background made the growing friendship between Ali and Sister Anselm seem unlikely, but the two women managed to get together once a week or so for a quick dinner or for one of Leland Brooks's sumptuous English teas. Sister Anselm was a trained psychologist, and it sometimes occurred to Ali that their visits turned into informal counseling sessions in which Ali ended up grumbling about being let out to pasture.

It was at Sister Anselm's gentle urging that Ali had broached the idea of sending Bob and Edie away on a January cruise. January, of course, was the best time for them to go since it was still far too chilly in Sedona for a full snowbird onslaught. That would come later in the spring.

The front door opened. Ali was pulled from her reverie by a group of eight people who piled into the room, bringing with them a gust of cold air and a buzz of conversation. Jan Howard, the Sugarloaf's longtime waitress, had been outside on a break, puffing on one of her unfiltered Camels. She hurried inside as well. She grabbed up a handful of menus and helped the new arrivals sort themselves into three groups. A four-top and a two-top went to booths in Jan Howard's station. The other two made for Ali's counter. As they sat down to study the menus, Ali went to make a new pot of coffee.

For the next two hours she worked nonstop. When they finally closed the Sugarloaf's front door on the last lunchtime customer at two thirty in the afternoon, Ali was beyond tired, and that was before they finished doing the cleanup work necessary to have the place ready to open the next morning.

When it was finally time to head home, she could hardly wait. She was ready to shower, take a nap, and sit with her feet up.

She had earned it.

11

Sacramento, California

In terms of getting sober, Brenda's breaking and entering arrest the previous October had proved to be pivotal. That humiliation was the last straw, the one that had finally convinced her to crack open the door to her very first AA meeting. Since then, she'd been fighting for sobriety on a daily basis and was halfway through those first critical ninety meetings in ninety days.

Just past noon on a Friday in late January, Brenda Riley's cell phone vibrated inside her pocket just as the AA meeting moderator was leading the Serenity Prayer. Her mother, Camilla Gastellum, hadn't been feeling well that morning as Brenda left for the meeting. Concerned about her, Brenda hurried out of the church basement and answered the phone without bothering to check caller ID.

"Hi, Mom," Brenda said. "Are you okay?"

"Someone just called here looking for you," Camilla said. "At first I thought she might be another bill collector, and I wasn't going to give her your number. It turns out, though, that she's calling about your book. She says you've contacted her before and wanted to interview her."

Of the fifty-seven names listed in Richard Lowensdale's Storyboards folder, Brenda had spoken or attempted to speak with all of them. Some of them had refused to speak to her outright or had accused Brenda of lying about their particular iteration of Richard. Others had been happy to have the mask ripped from the face of their present or former "cyber-lover" so they could begin to come to grips with the emotional damage he had done in their lives. Embarrassed by their own gullibility, some of those spoke to Brenda only on condition of anonymity.

Brenda was a trained journalist. She knew how to follow stories, and she had done so. Using the storyboard data as a starting point, she had tracked down one woman after another. What she found most disturbing in all this was that the details she discovered about the women's lives appeared to coincide with the information gleaned from Richard's files. Each of them had willingly revealed her innermost life to a man who had given her nothing but empty lies in return. From what Brenda's mother was saying, it appeared that one of the reluctant interviewees was now ready to come forward.

"Did she leave her name?" Brenda asked.

"No, but I did give her this number. I hope that's okay. She said she was going to call."

"Sure, Mom," Brenda said. "That's fine. Are you okay?"

"I'm still feeling a little puny. I think I'm going to go lie down for a while."

"Turn off the phone then so you can get some rest." Brenda's phone alerted a new incoming call from a number unavailable phone. "I'm sure that's her calling now. I have to go."

"Is this Brenda Riley?"

"Yes," Brenda said. "Who is this?"

"My name is Ermina Blaylock, but everyone calls me Mina," the woman said. Her English was precise, but there was more than a hint of an eastern European accent. "Your mother gave me your number. I believe you attempted to contact me a few months ago about a book you're writing about Richard Lowensdale. At the time I wasn't interested."

Ermina Blaylock's Storyboard file was the only one that had contained no information other than her name, date of birth, and social security number. There were none of the phone or e-mail exchanges that had been part of the other women's files, so there had been no details for Brenda to check on either. The lack of information had intrigued her. If there had been no correspondence between them, why was Ermina's name in Richard's list in the first place? Was she someone Richard had targeted who had been smart enough to turn him down?

Even Richard couldn't have had a one hundred percent success rate, and Brenda suspected that the names of the women who didn't make that initial cut never hit the Storyboard folder. Brenda had attempted to do some fact checking on her own, but as far as Ermina Blaylock was concerned, she could locate nothing about the woman prior to her marriage to widower Mark Blaylock in 2002.

"Are you interested now?" Brenda asked.

"Yes," Ermina said. "If you still want to speak to me, that is."

"You're aware that Richard was involved with any number of women?"

"Yes," Ermina said. "In your book, will you be naming names?"

"Only with permission," Brenda said. "Some of the women who spoke to me insisted on anonymity."

"Sounds good," Ermina said. "I'd probably want that too."

"When do you want to get together?" Brenda asked.

"It happens I'm in Sacramento today, and I believe you are

too. I know it's late, but what about lunch? We could meet some-where, or I could stop by and pick you up."

After receiving yet another ticket for driving with a revoked li-cense, Brenda had given up "borrowing" her mother's car. These days when she went someplace, she took a cab or a bus or she walked.

Brenda glanced at her watch. She had already missed most of the meeting. She was wearing a pair of sweats, which meant she wasn't dressed to go anywhere decent for lunch. It would take her half an hour to walk home and change clothes. If her mother was taking a nap, maybe she could get in and out of the house without waking her.

"If you wouldn't mind, how about picking me up in about an hour?" Brenda gave Ermina the exact address and then set off at a brisk walk. One of the things she had done was use other sources to verify what the women in Richard's life had told her about their lives. As far as Ermina was concerned, there was no information available. By the time Brenda reached the house on P Street she had come up with a plan.

She entered the quiet house and hurried to her upstairs bed-room. Brenda changed into more appropriate clothing, wishing she had footwear that weren't tennis shoes. She took another crack at fixing her hair and makeup and went downstairs. The dining room often doubled as Brenda's home office. She kept a printer and an elderly laptop on top of the wooden hope chest she had moved from her bedroom to her make-do headquarters.

With the printer and the computer out of the way, Brenda used the key from her purse to unlock the chest. The booze bottles she had once concealed inside it when it had been what she called her "hopeless chest" were long gone. Some of the liquor had been drunk, but when she finally got serious about getting sober, she had emptied the others down the drain in her bathroom. Now the locked chest held hope once more. It was where Brenda filed everything about her book project, including her copies of the contract she had signed. It was where she kept the passbook to her newly established bank account, printed accounts of her interviews with Richard's various victims, as well as the printouts she had made from Richard's Storyboard folder.

At very the bottom of the heap, she found the file that contained the original background check High Noon Enterprises had done on Richard, the one Ali Reynolds had ordered for her. There was a phone number at the top of the page. She dialed the number and then disconnected the call while the phone on the other end was ringing.

Instead, after returning all the paperwork to the chest, locking it, and then stowing the key in her purse, she opened her laptop, booted it up, and jotted off a quick e-mail.

> Dear Ali,
>
> You'll be glad to know that I'm finally getting my head screwed on straight, and yes, I am in treatment. Finally. I'm working on a book about Richard Lowensdale and all the women's lives he has adversely impacted through his cyberstalking.
>
> I'm having trouble locating information on one of the women on his list, Ermina Vlasic Cunningham Blaylock, who is either Richard's former employer or the wife of his former employer. I'm guessing the company was in her name in order to latch on to the women-owned business gravy train in government contracts.
>
> I started to call the company you had do the background check on Richard last summer. Then I decided that they might take the request more seriously if it came from you instead of from me. If there's any charge, you'll be relieved to know that I'm now in a position to pay for it myself even if I haven't earned back the right to have my own credit card.

I'm attaching everything I know about Ermina below. Thanks in advance for your help. I expect I'll be talking to her today and tomorrow, so the sooner I can have the info the better.

Brenda R.

After pressing send, Brenda closed the laptop and put it away. Then she hurried downstairs. Her mother's worsening vision problems made leaving Camilla a note impossible.

I'll call her later, Brenda thought.

She stepped out on the front porch just as an older-model silver Lincoln Town Car pulled to a stop in front of the house. As Brenda hurried forward, the passenger window rolled down. A well-dressed woman was at the wheel.

"Brenda?" she asked.

"Yes," Brenda answered.

"I'm Ermina," the woman said. "Get in."

Ermina Blaylock was lovely. Her auburn hair glowed in the cold winter sunlight that came in through the sunroof. She had a flawless complexion and fine features.

"Thank you for picking me up, Ermina," Brenda said. "I don't have a car right now, and that makes getting around tough."

"No problem," the woman said. "But call me Mina. Everybody does."

12

Grass Valley, California

Waiting to see if Mina would show that Friday, Richard had a tough time concentrating. He was distracted enough that he didn't dare do any of his usual Internet correspondence. It was important to keep all his stories straight, and he didn't want to end up saying the wrong thing to the wrong person.

He had delivered his completed programming fix to Mina the week before. He knew the test flight had been scheduled for Wednesday. He and Mina were still operating under his eyeball-to-eyeball protocol, so she didn't send him an e-mail. She didn't call.

She had told him that if the test flight was successful, she would bring him his bonus on Friday, so Richard waited on tenterhooks. Earlier in the morning he had briefly considered cleaning house in advance of her visit, but he had eventually decided against that. He was sitting at his desk watching for her through the living room window when she arrived, apparently on foot. She pushed open the lopsided gate and walked up the weed-littered sidewalk.

When Richard had first returned to Grass Valley, his neighbors had been incredibly curious about him. He wasn't a very personable guy, and he'd been firm in rejecting their overtures of friendship. Over time they had adjusted to the fact that he was reclusive. If they wondered about why he ordered anything and everything online, they didn't discuss any of that with him.

Because the neighbors were used to a steady stream of delivery folks who left their vehicles on the street below and trooped up and down the sidewalk leading to Richard's house, he and Mina had hit upon her masquerading as a delivery person whenever she came to see him.

Today, as usual, Mina arrived on his doorstep using a faux UPS driver uniform with brown khaki trousers and a brown jacket. And as she had done on previous occasions, she carried a stack of boxes to lend credence to the disguise.

Richard didn't want to appear overeager. Nonetheless, he hurried to the door to meet her. "It's about time you got here," he said. "How did it go?"

"How do you think it went?" Mina asked with a smile as she set down her boxes. "I'm here bearing gifts, aren't I?"

"Great." Richard could barely contain his relief. "Come on in."

He led the way into the living room. He was halfway back to his desk when a powerful blow hit him squarely on the back of the head. Down he went.

By the time Richard struggled back to woozy consciousness, she had secured him to one of the dining room chairs with packing tape—probably his own packing tape from the dining room—and there was tape over his mouth as well. He was in a sitting position, but the chair had tipped over onto its side.

The room was surprisingly dark, as though night had fallen while he was unconscious. Mina was seated at the desk in front of his computer, her face eerily aglow in the lamplight. She was dressed in clothing that was different than he remembered. The brown uniform was gone. Her shoes were covered with something that looked like surgical booties; she wore gloves.

Struggling to loosen the bonds, Richard tried to speak. He meant to say, "What are you doing?" but his words came out in an incomprehensible mumble.

"Quiet," she ordered. "Be still!"

She left the computer and came back over to where he lay on his side on the floor. Picking up the hammer, she waved it in front of his face. "Do not make a sound," she said.

Richard understood that the hammer was a very real threat. He fell silent.

"Where's the money I gave you?" Mina said. "I want it. I also want my thumb drive."

Richard tried to make sense of this. She was robbing him of the money she had paid him? Worried about the possibility of some drug-crazed addict breaking into his house, Richard had hidden the money, and he had hidden it well, but it had never occurred to him that Mina might be the one trying to take it away.

But it was *his* money. He had worked for it. She owed him for getting her damned UAVs back in the air, and he *would not* give her back that money, not in a thousand years. The same thing with the thumb drive. He looked at her and shook his head.

That seemed to throw Mina into a fit of rage. She ran back to the dining room and cleared his mother's curio shelves of Richard's entire model airplane collection, knocking them to the floor, where she stepped on them and ground them to pieces.

"Tell me," she said.

With his mouth taped shut, he couldn't have told her if he had wanted. But it was a grudge match now. He wouldn't tell her no matter what. He shook his head. Emphatically.

She disappeared from view for a time. When she returned,

she was carrying his mother's old kitchen shears. At first he thought she was going to cut through the tape and free him. Instead, she walked behind him. The pain when it came was astonishing. Even with the tape over his mouth, he howled in agony.

When he could breathe again, tears were streaming down his face. She came around and dangled the remains of one of his fingers in his face.

"Tell me," she said.

He knew then that he was going to die, and the only satisfaction he could have was to deny this woman what she wanted. Twice more she went behind him. Twice more Richard's world exploded in absolute agony. He passed out then. When he came to sometime later, he was aware of a peculiar racket, and the air around him was filled with the stale odor he always connected with his mother's old vacuum cleaner.

Why is that running now?

Then she appeared again, bringing with her another of the dining room chairs. She set the chair close to his head and then sat on it.

"Tell me," she said again.

"No," he managed. Even with the tape over his mouth, it sounded like what he meant to say, *"N-O!"*

Suddenly, out of nowhere a plastic bag appeared. With a single deft movement, she pulled the cloudy plastic down over his head.

"Tell me and I'll let you live."

Richard was an experienced liar. So was Mina Blaylock. He knew that, no matter what, she going to kill him anyway. So since it would make no difference, Richard would not give her his money. No matter what.

He heard her tear loose a swath of transparent packing tape. He felt it tighten around his neck. For a few moments—a minute or so—there was enough air to breathe inside the bag. As the plastic went in and out with each breath, he could see her sitting there, watching and waiting, hoping he would give in.

He didn't. Instead, he closed his eyes so he didn't have to see her. Soon he felt himself struggling for breath as the oxygen inside the bag became depleted.

"Tell me," he heard her say from very far away.

He shook his head once more, and had a fleeting moment of victory. He knew he was dying, but he also knew he had won and Mina Blaylock had lost.

13

Sedona, Arizona

Ali's phone rang as she pulled out of the Sugarloaf parking lot. "Hey, Ali," her very pregnant daughter-in-law said. "Are you busy?"

Knowing a little of Athena's background, Ali did her best to tread lightly in the mother-in-law department. There was enough bad blood between Athena and her own parents that Athena's folks hadn't been invited to Chris and Athena's wedding. The only family member who had broken ranks with everyone else and attended the wedding was Athena's paternal grandmother, Betsy Peterson.

The rift with Chris's in-laws was something Ali couldn't understand. As far as she could see, Athena was a remarkable young woman. She had served in the Iraq War with the Minnesota National Guard and had returned home as a wounded warrior. She was a double amputee, minus her right arm from above the elbow and her right leg from below the knee. When her first husband divorced her—while she was still recovering from her injuries in Walter Reed—Athena's parents for some unaccountable reason stuck with their former son-in-law and his new wife. The previous summer Chris and Athena had made the trek to Minnesota in hopes of normalizing relations, but nothing had changed. The ex-son-in-law was still more acceptable to Athena's parents than their own daughter.

Chris and Athena had met while they were both working at Sedona High School, where Chris taught American history and welding technology and Athena taught math. Athena was fiercely independent, and Ali admired both her spirit and her spunk. Athena had taught herself to do most things, including playing basketball, with her left hand, although she now had a realistic-looking prosthesis in place of her right arm. Getting pregnant, and especially getting pregnant with twins, had set her back some in the self-confidence department. And having two babies this early in their marriage wasn't something that had been in Chris and Athena's game plan either.

As far as Ali was concerned, the appearance of twins was no surprise. After all, Chris's grandmother was a twin, so the tendency was right there in his DNA. Athena's ob-gyn, Dr. Dixon, had allayed many of Athena's worries by telling her that people who can *get* pregnant usually can *be* pregnant. She had also said that studies with pregnant women who had been born missing whole or parts of limbs due to the drug thalidomide had been able to carry babies successfully. Their only major difficulty had been maintaining balance late in their term.

A counselor from the VA had put Athena in touch with another young woman who was also an amputee and a new mother—although she was only a single amputee with a single baby. It helped Athena to know that she wasn't alone, that there was someone else out there with similar problems and dilemmas.

"Just on my way home from the Sugarloaf. Why, is there something you need?"

Athena sighed. She sounded upset. "Yes. I could really use your help. I'd appreciate it if you could come by for a little while."

"Of course," Ali said. "I'll be right there."

"Just let yourself in when you get here," Athena said. "I'm supposed to be on full bed rest."

Ali glanced at her watch. At 2:45 Chris was probably still at school. Then instead of heading home, she drove up to her old place on Andante Drive, where Chris and Athena now lived. Ali had inherited the place from her aunt Evie, her mother's twin, and had sold it to Chris and Athena when she moved on to Manzanita Hills Drive.

The house was actually a "manufactured home," a nonmobile mobile that had been permanently attached to a set of footings and a concrete slab built into the steep hillside, an unusual set of construction circumstances that allowed for an actual basement, which Chris used as a studio for his metal artwork.

As soon as Ali opened the front door, she caught a whiff of fresh paint. With the twins, Colin and Colleen, due within the next three weeks, Ali knew that Chris had been intent on pulling the nursery together. Athena was lying on the living room couch with one of Edie Larson's colorful quilts pulled up over her baby mound.

"How's it going?" Ali asked, closing the door behind her.

"After I took that little tumble last week, Chris made me promise that I'd stay put while he was gone."

Some of Athena's fellow teachers had thrown a shower on Athena's behalf. On the way back to the house, loaded down with gifts and determined to carry them herself, Athena had tripped and fallen. She had scraped both knees and her one elbow but had suffered no major damage. Chris, however, had been beyond upset.

"So what's going on?" Ali asked. "Are you okay?"

"The twins obviously aren't on the same schedule," Athena said with a wan smile. "When one of them is asleep, the other one is wide awake and kicking like crazy. So I'm not getting much sleep, and neither is Chris."

Ali smiled. "That's going to get a lot worse for both of you before it gets better. Is there something I can do to help?"

"It's about the nursery," Athena said.

"What about it?"

"We had a big fight about it before he left for school this morning."

"What about?" Ali asked.

To Ali's amazement, Athena burst into tears. Since Athena was one tough cookie, Ali figured it was either something terribly serious or else it was about nothing more than a storm of late-pregnancy rampaging hormones.

"Chris is determined to have the nursery completely finished before your parents come home tomorrow, so he's been working like crazy, painting until all hours. Last night he managed to get all the furniture put together too—the changing tables and the chests of drawers and the cribs."

"That doesn't sound so bad," Ali ventured.

Athena nodded and blew her nose. "We managed to get all the clothes washed and dried, but when he started to sort them, it turns out he's completely hopeless. I ended up dumping everything back out into one of the cribs. I could sort them myself, but I'm not supposed to be on my feet that long."

"I suspect you both have a bad case of impending parenthood nerves," Ali said. "And I'm happy to do it. Thrilled, even. Now let me at 'em."

Athena offered a thin smile and then allowed Ali to help her off the sofa. She led Ali to the nursery that had once been Chris's room. The room smelled of freshly applied paint. Two walls were pink; two were blue. The changing tables, dressers, and cribs were white. In one crib was a mountain of baby gear—some of it new and some of it secondhand. With Athena sitting in the rocker supervising the process, Ali commenced folding all the incredibly tiny outfits and separating them first by sort (blankets, shirts, nightgowns, and snuggle outfits) and second by colors (blues and greens, pinks and yellows). The blues and greens were destined for Colin's drawers while the pinks and yellows would go to Colleen's.

As Ali did the sorting and folding, she also listened. In the process she couldn't help but think about and be grateful for how different Chris and Athena's situation was from what hers had been when Chris was born. His father, Dean, had died of a glioblastoma weeks before Chris appeared on the scene. Ali had been a single mother from day one—from before day one, actually.

Chris and Athena were in this together. They expected that Athena would be going back to work as soon as possible after the babies were born. The school district had accepted Chris's request to stay home on parental leave. Ali knew he was hoping that he'd be able to look after the twins and still do some metal sculpture work in his basement studio. Ali had sincere doubts about his ability to carry that one off, but she was careful not to mention her motherly case of skepticism. Experience had taught her that looking after two babies would make welding metal art-work pieces an impossible pipe dream.

"You know," Ali said, casually, "I don't mind doing this, but even if he doesn't do it quite the way you want it done, shouldn't Chris be in on this? Once the babies get here, you'll be lucky to get the clothes out of the dryer and into the basket, to say nothing of drawers, but if he's going to be the one staying home, it seems to me he should be in charge of putting all this stuff away."

Athena shook her head. "You don't know, do you?"

"Know what?" Ali asked, although something in Athena's tone suggested that whatever it was, Ali might not want to know about it.

Athena sighed. "I hate to be the one to break this to you, but your son is color-blind. Not completely. Primary colors he can do. Reds and greens at stoplights he can do. Pastels? Not so much. According to him, all these clothes are gray." She waved her one good hand in the direction of the stacks of clothing, now properly sorted by color.

Ali was thunderstruck. "Are you kidding? You're telling me my own son is color-blind?"

The news came as a complete surprise. Eventually, though, Ali dissolved in a hopeless case of giggles. Before long Athena was laughing too.

"I never knew," Ali gasped at last. "I had no idea. From the time he was little he gravitated to blues and reds. I thought he just liked them."

"No," Athena said, sobering. "Those are the only colors he could see. So tell me, how long will it be before the twins can choose their own clothes?"

"They probably start doing that when they're three or four."

"I hope they hurry," Athena said. "Between now and then, with their father dressing them, it's not going to be pretty."

By the time Ali had the last of the clothing put away, Chris turned up with a bouquet of store-bought flowers and a sweet thinking-of-you card. The guy may have been color-blind, but he knew when it was time to turn up with a fistful of flowers.

Ali left Chris and Athena's house still feeling bemused. She and Chris had always been close, and she was incredibly proud of him, but as it turned out, Ali Reynolds didn't know her own son nearly as well as she thought she did.

FATAL ERROR

San Diego, California

Mark Blaylock set off for San Diego that Friday morning tired and hungover but elated. After months of watching their financial situation deteriorate and then more months of worrying about the programming, he had cause to feel happy. It seemed to him that they were about to see some light at the end of the tunnel.

Wednesday's flawless early morning test flight had put his programming worries to rest once and for all. Both reprogrammed UAVs had flown properly. Both had taken off as expected and had followed their prescribed flight plans. The first one had landed exactly as the flight plan dictated, while an operator-issued command had blown the second drone to smithereens.

That night he and Mina had driven into Palm Springs for a celebratory dinner. The next morning Mina had set off for Grass Valley in her older-model Lincoln. She had flown up to meet with Richard that first time, but since then, not wanting to deal with TSA scrutiny or to leave much of a paper trail, she had driven back and forth. The trip usually took a couple of days. Knowing how much Mina despised living in the cramped cabin in Salton City, Mark tried not to begrudge her her periodic absences.

Mark had especially made it a point not to think about her monthly trips to see Richard Lowensdale, give him his partial payment, and check on his progress. If sex with Mina was part of what was keeping Richard on the job, Mark was prepared to overlook it. After all, he had his own occasional dalliances, and he wasn't enough of a hypocrite to begrudge Mina hers. Besides, this was the end of it. Once the program fixes had been installed in the rest of the UAVs, they wouldn't need Richard Lowensdale anymore.

"See you on Sunday," she said, when he kissed her goodbye.

"Stay safe," he told her.

Knowing he'd need to spend a couple of days in San Diego, Mina had left him a fistful of welcome cash to cover food and lodging. Much as he tried not to, Mark couldn't help regarding it as being given an allowance. To regain a little self-respect, he spent most of the day on Thursday drinking and gambling at his favorite hangout, the Red Earth Casino. With some luck and what he liked to regard as skill, he managed to add to that initial sum. On Friday morning, with a smile on his face and money in his pocket, he finally set off for San Diego to fulfill his part of the bargain and install Richard's programming fix in each of their remaining UAVs.

He didn't rush. He stopped off for a beer here and there along the way. One thing he really missed on the drive was the Sirius radio he used to have in his Mercedes. That was one of the problems with being kicked downstairs. Now, tooling along in a secondhand Honda, instead of being able to hum along with the country-western tunes he preferred on the Roadhouse or Willie's Place, he had to search through what was available—mostly Spanish-speaking stations or blabbing news.

So losing the Mercedes was a noticeable blow that was both economic and emotional. When he reached the industrial park complex that had once been home to Rutherford International, he took another hit as he drove past what had once been their official headquarters. There was a new name on the sign above the door, and Mark couldn't help but take the change personally. Rutherford's failure was Mark's failure, and he was grateful that Mina had found a way to breathe some life into the smoldering ashes of their financial catastrophe.

He drove through the familiar maze of light industrial and warehouse streets. When they had been looking for a location, having their office address on Opportunity Road had seemed exactly right. And having their warehouse/manufacturing facility on Engineer Road had seemed perfect as well, especially considering the proximity of Montgomery Field, where they had expected to do their test flights.

Whether based on hubris or unbounded optimism, their assumption that they would actually win the much sought-after drone contract had been naive. Mark's contacts had led them to believe that they had an "inside track" and that it was a "done deal." They had leveraged everything they owned to grab the opportunity, and when the contract went elsewhere, they lost big and were still left holding leases they could no longer afford.

Unfortunately their misfortunes coincided with what was going on in the general economy. As they were taking their financial hits, so was everyone else. California commercial real estate went into a downward spiral right along with the residential market, and that was as true for this office park as it was for similar projects throughout the country. Buildings that had once been fully occupied and busy now stood empty and forlorn, their entrances weedy, their walls covered with gang-related tags. Mark was relieved when he saw that no new tags were in evidence on the part of the one building that still had Rutherford International stenciled on the doors.

For a time their company had occupied office space in a building on one street and in two adjacent sections in one of the nearby buildings that had been designated for light industry. One space, equipped with rolling garage-type doors, had been used primarily for shipping and receiving. In the other, and at great expense in tenant improvements, Rutherford had constructed a clean room, which they planned on using as an assembly facility.

When it was clear Rutherford was going down the drain, the

landlord had been lucky enough to find someone who was willing to take over the office part of their lease. Because the property manager wanted to maintain a minimum level of occupancy, he had offered Mark and Mina a huge break on the lease for warehouse space. In other words, Mark was glad they still had a place to store their stock of illegal UAVs, even though he sometimes worried about how Mina was managing to pay the rent, even with the steep discount.

Mark used a clicker to let himself into the shipping/receiving bay, then he used a connecting door between the two to gain access to the assembly area. After turning off the alarm and switching on the lights, he set to work.

The UAVs were stored in the cage—a locked interior chain-link structure that had been been constructed in the assembly area. Originally it had been intended to hold their inventory of needed parts. Now there was no assembly operation and no need for parts either.

One by one he removed the UAVs from the cage and deposited them on the remaining assembly tables. Installation of the programming upgrade took approximately fifteen minutes per drone. Once each one was finished, Mark loaded it into a specially designed cardboard shipping box. After cushioning the UAV with a collection of air-filled plastic bags, he then closed the box, taped it shut, and slapped on a suitable collection of labels. If anyone asked, these were model airplanes. Large model airplanes. Specially ordered model airplanes, manufactured in China and shipped to dealers in the United States.

As each box was loaded, closed, taped, and labeled, Mark carried them back to the cage and stacked them one on top of another. There was no particular hurry. The timetable Mina had given him said that she would return to the cabin sometime on Sunday and that they would deliver the finished UAVs to

Enrique on Tuesday. By Wednesday morning, Mark and Mina would be new people. Armed with new names and matching IDs, they would head off into their new lives.

Mark was excited by the prospect. He was ready for new faces and new places. He was still hurt and disappointed by the number of people he had thought of as friends who had simply turned their backs on Mark and Mina once they fell on hard times. Mark was ready to be someone else entirely. He wanted to go live on a tropical island somewhere with no worries except maybe what kind of fish to catch for dinner. He had tried running the show with Rutherford, and that hadn't worked out very well for either of them. Now Mark was content to step back and let Mina do the running.

That wasn't to say he wasn't grateful, because he was. It was Mina's wheeling and dealing that had made this deal possible. Mark's part of the bargain was to be the on-site tech guy and have the UAVs properly reprogrammed, packed up, and ready for delivery. Ten hours later, right around midnight, Mark stacked the last box in the cage. After locking the door behind him, he put his tools away, turned off the lights, and set the alarm.

Leaving the warehouse, Mark decided he would reward a job well done by having some fun before leaving for home. Retracing his route back through the office park and back out onto Clairemont Mesa Boulevard, he pulled into the familiar parking lot of the Demon Sports Bar. When he had worked in the neighborhood, Mark had been a regular here. When he walked into the place just prior to last call, he was shocked by how much it had changed.

In the time Mark had been away, the Demon had apparently undergone a remarkable transformation. There was a redesigned menu. Flat-screen TVs had replaced the old rear-projection models. Settling onto a barstool, Mark looked around in search of a familiar face, but a whole new crop of female bartenders and cock-tail waitresses had replaced the ones he had known previously.

"What'll you have?" the bartender asked. She was red-haired, good-looking, and maybe five years younger than Mina, which made her much younger than Mark.

"A draft beer and a burger," he said with a wink, "with maybe a little salsa on the side."

She gave him a look that said she got the message. "Coming right up," she said.

So there's been some turnover since I was here last, Mark thought as he sipped that first beer. *No problem. If you're a good enough tipper, it's easy to win friends and influence people.*

14

Sedona, Arizona

When Ali let herself into the house well after four on Friday afternoon, the aroma of baking scones reminded her that this was Friday, and Sister Anselm was expected around five for what Leland liked to call his Cornish cream tea.

"I forgot," she said.

"No worries," Leland said. "Sister Anselm called a little while ago and said she was running late too."

Realizing that a nap was out of the question, Ali hustled out of her Sugarloaf Café duds and took a quick shower. Then she settled down on the love seat to let her hair air dry for a few minutes. Within seconds, Samantha appeared at Ali's feet and then scrambled up on the love seat next to her.

Sam had arrived in Ali's life in what was supposedly a temporary fostering situation with no official papers of origin. Ali hadn't particularly liked cats in the beginning, but Sam had grown on her. Their temporary situation had now stretched into years. Sam's vet estimated her to be somewhere in her early teens, which meant she was verging on feline elderly. Her sixteen-pound body could no longer deliver the graceful leaps that had once carried her to the top of the running clothes dryer, her favorite snoozing perch during the day.

Leland Brooks's concession to Sam's diminished mobility was a kitchen step stool he placed next to the dryer, an aid which she deigned to use on occasion, but only when no one was looking. Ali had done her bit to solve Sam's mobility difficulties by placing a set of pet steps next to the bed in her bedroom. That way Sam could make it on and off her favorite spot on the bed without having to suffer the indignity of being lifted up and down.

With Sam purring contentedly at her side, Ali checked her e-mail. There were more than a dozen lined up and waiting, but she chose to open only four.

The first one came from her mother:

> Your father is acting like a kid. He bounces out of bed at the crack of dawn and doesn't go to sleep until all hours. I can't believe he's the same man I've been married to for all these years.
>
> I think he's sad that today is our last full day on the ship. So am I, but I'm like an old dray horse, and I'm ready to get back in harness. See you tomorrow. There's a chance we may be able to switch our reservation to an earlier flight.

Next up was an e-mail from someone named Robert Dahl-good with a subject line that said, "Velma Trimble."

Years earlier when Ali had retreated to Sedona in the aftermath of the end of her marriage and the loss of her job, she had started a blog called cutlooseblog.com. Velma Trimble had been one of her blog's most ardent fans. During the dark time Ali had been dealing with Paul Grayson's death, Velma had taken a cab from her home in Laguna Beach and had come all the way across Los Angeles to Ali's hotel in Westwood in hopes of offering her assistance.

As a result of that selfless action despite the age difference between them, Ali and Velma had become good friends in a way that was not unlike Ali's friendship with Sister Anselm. When Velma had been diagnosed with breast cancer at age eighty-eight, her son had opposed her seeking treatment. Ali had encouraged it, and the treatment had worked. In the intervening years, Velma had managed to take a round-the-world first-class private jet tour with another new friend, Maddy Watkins.

Now, though, Velma's cancer had returned. Expecting bad news, Ali opened the e-mail from Velma's nephew with a sense of dread.

> Dear Ms. Reynolds,
> Robert Dahlgood here. I'm not sure if you remember me, but my aunt, Velma Trimble, asked me to be in touch with you.
> I regret to inform you that her situation is deteriorating rapidly and she is now receiving hospice care at her home in Laguna Beach. The nurses are able to manage her pain, which is a real blessing.
> I'm helping her put her affairs in order, and she is most interested in meeting with you and would like very much to do so in person. I know that a request of this kind is a major inconvenience, but as you know, once Velma sets her mind to something, she is not easily dissuaded.
> If you could see your way clear to come see her any time in the next few days—time is of the essence—I would be eternally grateful. If it's not possible, I certainly understand

and will be glad to pass along that information in hopes I can
convince her to settle for some other arrangement.
Sincerely,

Robert Dahlgood

Considering what Velma had done on Ali's behalf years earlier,
Ali could hardly ignore this very real plea for help. She wrote
back immediately:

Dear Robert,
I'm so sorry to hear this. I have a prior commitment that
will keep me stuck here in Sedona until tomorrow at the earli-
est. I may be able to fly over tomorrow evening or Sunday morning. I'll let you know.
Please tell Velma that I'm thinking about her and that I'll
be there as soon as I can.

Ali

Next Ali opened the e-mail from Brenda Riley. What she
read there left her feeling both relieved and anxious. On the
one hand she was delighted that Brenda was evidently working
at putting her life back together. That was a good thing, but
the idea that she was writing a book about Richard Lowensdale
was worrisome.

Ali was well aware that without the information contained in
the High Noon background check, Brenda wouldn't have known
the man's real name, to say nothing of the names of his former
employers. If Brenda was writing a book about her experience
with him as well as that of "other women" in his life, there was
a chance that B.'s company might well be pulled into some kind

of unsavory drama. On the other hand, doing background checks was part of High Noon's bread-and-butter business.

In the end, Ali simply forwarded Brenda's request to B. with a subject line that said, "What do you think?"

The last e-mail she opened was one from B., written to her during a lunch break at his conference in D.C. Ali scanned it quickly and then marked it unread because by then it was past time to be dressed and ready for tea.

Sister Anselm was already seated by the gas log fireplace when Ali entered the library a few minutes later. A driver from the Phoenix archdiocese had dropped her off for tea on the condition that Leland Brooks agree to take her the rest of the way back to Jerome once the visit was over.

They passed a pleasant hour together in front of the fire, sipping English breakfast tea, nibbling on Leland Brook's tiny egg salad and cucumber sandwiches, and downing still-warm scones slathered with clotted cream.

In the course of their conversation, Ali mentioned her dying friend's request that Ali come visit her. "You're the one with the Angel of Death moniker," Ali said to Sister Anselm. "I know you deal with ill and dying people all the time, but how do you handle it? How do you know what to do or say? I know Velma has a son. Why is she asking for me to be there instead of him?"

Sister Anselm's blue eyes sparkled cheerfully behind her gold-framed glasses as she answered Ali's question.

"You don't know that," Sister Anselm said. "The son may very well be at her side when the time comes. When someone in a family is dead or dying, it's been my experience that one of two things may happen. Occasionally, long-standing quarrels and fissures in families are suddenly and inexplicably healed. In other families, relationships that may have seemed untroubled in the past sometimes splinter completely due to some invisible fracture that has long lain hidden beneath an otherwise placid surface. When I'm summoned in this fashion, I always set off on the journey trusting that I've been called there for a reason and that I'll be able to offer comfort to those in need."

"But going there at a time like this feels like an intrusion somehow," Ali objected.

"The nephew indicated that your friend wants you there, right?"

Ali nodded. "She specifically requested that I come. I told the nephew that I'd fly over to California either tomorrow or the next day."

"Go as soon as you can," Sister Anselm advised. "A lot of the time, loved ones are in denial and think they have more time than they actually have. Whenever you go, Ali, do so in the knowledge that what you're doing places you in your perfect place to do the perfect thing, whatever that may be."

Ali smiled at her friend. "You really believe that, don't you?"

"Yes," Sister Anselm said forcefully. "I certainly do."

When Leland left to take Sister Anselm home, Ali retreated to her bedroom once more.

An instant message from B. told her he was off to a conference banquet and wouldn't be available until much later. He also told her he had alerted Stuart Ramey about Brenda's request for a background check and that Stuart would be working on the problem.

Ali knew that her parents were due to be back home on Saturday afternoon and that they would be on duty at the Sugarloaf bright and early on Sunday morning. With that in mind, Ali made arrangements to fly out of Phoenix to LAX Saturday night. After her conversation with Sister Anselm, leaving sooner rather than later seemed like the right thing to do.

Once all the travel arrangements were in hand, Ali tried calling B. His phone was still off, so she sent him an e-mail bringing him up to date on Velma Trimble's situation as well as her travel plans. After that, Ali took to her bed in the company of the Count of Monte Cristo. Within minutes, the book was facedown on Ali's bed covers, and she was sound asleep.

15

Scotts Flat Reservoir, California

Brenda Riley awakened confused and frightened in a terrible moving darkness. Somewhere nearby her cell phone was ringing, but she couldn't reach it, couldn't answer. Her hands were bound behind her. Her feet were bound too. There was a strip of something fastened to her face, and she was desperately cold.

She realized she had to be in the trunk—the large trunk—of a moving vehicle. She could hear the rush and scrape of pavement under the tires, but she had no idea where she was, where she was going, or how she came to be there.

Her memory was fuzzy. Foggy. She vaguely remembered being at home in the morning. After that she had gone to her meeting, her usual Friday noon meeting. And then she was supposed to meet someone for lunch, but right that minute, Brenda couldn't recall the woman's name. She had no idea of what had happened to her or how much time had elapsed. What she did know for sure was that she needed to pee desperately.

Brenda tried moving her legs and managed to make a few

feeble thumps with her feet. It didn't do any good. The car kept on moving and her sudden movement, compounded by the cold, made her need to urinate that much more critical. If the person driving the vehicle heard the racket from the trunk, it made no difference, at least not at first, but then the car seemed to hesitate. It turned off the pavement onto a rough gravel track of some kind.

As the vehicle came to a stop, Brenda's heart filled with dread. Moments later, the engine died. With a thump, the trunk release was engaged and the lid opened automatically. For a moment she was astonished by how bright the night sky was overhead. After the impenetrable darkness, the stars above were more brilliant than she had ever seen.

She heard the crunch of footsteps on gravel. A moment later a woman's face appeared in the starlit night. In that moment of clarity, Brenda recognized her. Mina Blaylock, the mystery woman on Richard's list.

Brenda struggled against her bonds, tried to say something. "Please, let me out. I need to use the bathroom."

For an answer, Mina reached inside. Brenda saw the hypodermic in her hand. She tried to dodge out of the way, but she couldn't. The needle plunged deep into the muscle of her upper arm. That was one of the reasons Brenda was so cold. Her arms were bare. Where was her coat? Where was her blouse? Brenda tried to struggle, but she couldn't escape the woman's fierce gloved grip. At last Brenda lay still.

"Good," Mina said. "That's better."

She reached inside the trunk again. As Brenda watched, Mina took Brenda's purse out of the trunk. With the purse gone, so was Brenda's cell phone and so was any hope of summoning help. Next Mina wrenched off Brenda's shoes.

"Where you're going, you won't be needing your purse anymore, and you won't need shoes either."

Dimly, Brenda heard a sound from somewhere nearby. Mina heard it too. She looked over her shoulder, then slammed the trunk lid shut. There were more footsteps, hurried ones this time, then the engine turned over, and the car moved. As darkness enveloped her again, Brenda realized that her prison was now lit with an eerie reddish glow leaking into the trunk from the taillights outside the car. She wondered how much time had passed, enough to turn day into night.

Brenda considered briefly about the kind of substance that had been in the hypodermic. Moments later, however, she felt her heartbeat speed up. For a time she had difficulty catching her breath. Then, gradually, the drug overwhelmed her and she drifted into unconsciousness once again, unaware and unembarrassed that when she lost control of her mind, she also lost control of her bladder.

16

San Diego, California

The trip from the Scotts Flat Reservoir to San Diego took
more than ten hours. Mina stopped for gas only once,
in Bakersfield. She worried that Brenda might awaken
when the vehicle came to a stop and start bumping and thumping around in the trunk. Fortunately that didn't happen.

Maybe she's dead, Mina thought. Considering how much
Versed Mina had plugged into Brenda's system, death by over-
dose would have been a likely outcome. Parking at the pumps,
Mina stood for a moment listening. When there was no sound
from the trunk, she hurried into the gas station, where she used
the restroom and paid cash for her fuel as well as for bottled
water and a collection of energy bars.

Back outside, there was still no sound from the trunk as Mina
filled the gas tank and drove away. Once she was on I-5 heading
south, Mina kept herself awake by thinking about Richard Lowensdale.

When Mina waved the hammer in front of Richard's face, he
must have known that it wasn't an empty threat. He had fallen

still and silent just as Mina had known he would. That was what most people did when they were faced with an unanticipated threat: they complied.

That was exactly what Mina's family had done all those years earlier when a gang of marauding Serbs had invaded their home in Bosnia. In hopes of surviving, they too had done exactly what they'd been told. Not imagining that people who had once been their neighbors would turn against them, Ermina's family had allowed themselves to be herded into the living room, where a gang of armed thugs had opened fire and gunned them down.

That was the first defining moment of thirteen-year-old Ermina Vlasic's life. Hidden in the stone cellar under the barn with her flickering candle and her precious books, she had heard the arriving vehicles first and then the shouting and finally the gunfire. Staying hidden was the only thing that saved her life that day. And only later, long after silence returned and as the sun set, she finally crept out of the cellar and went in search of her family.

She had found them, slaughtered in a bloody heap in the darkened living room, all of them riddled with bullets. Crumpled and dead, they had been left where they'd fallen to send a message to other Croats in the neighborhood—leave or die. It was a scene that was forever indelibly inked in her consciousness, and standing there in the carnage she had made the first decision of her new life: she decided to leave.

Leaving her loved ones where they lay, Mina went to her room, packed a bag with a few clothes and as many books as she could carry, and went in search of help. It was a group of Bosnian Serbs who had murdered her family. Ironically, it was another group of Serbs, a family whose farm was just down the country road, who took her in, cared for her, and who finally took her to the orphanage that had eventually led her to her adoptive home in Jefferson City, Missouri.

Mina had always supposed that was the difference between her and people like Richard Lowensdale and Mark Blaylock. She was tough. But for the first time in as long as Mina had known Richard, he had surprised her. He had stood up to her. She had thought he would cave, but he hadn't. In the grand scheme of things, the fifty thousand dollars she had paid Richard was chump change, but it was Mina's chump change.

Had she been able to keep on looking, Mina probably could have found Richard's stash, but by then Mina's other guest, treated with a hefty dose of Versed and bound with the same transparent packing tape she had used on Richard, had been left alone in the trunk of her parked Lincoln on a city street for far longer than she should have been. Still Mina waited until it was over, until Richard's pitiful struggles ceased completely, before she rose from the chair and walked away.

And even though she walked away without her money, Ermina Blaylock had left Grass Valley with something unexpected—a grudging respect for Richard Lowensdale.

There was very little traffic as she made her way up and over the Grapevine, but by the time she hit L.A., rush hour was starting. Just past eight o'clock in the morning, Mina pulled into the shipping/receiving bay of Rutherford International in Clairemont Mesa Business Park and closed the rolling garage door behind her.

She had given Mark a strict set of instructions. Once he finished installing the programming fix, she had told him to pack the UAVs in shipping containers and put them in the shipping/receiving bay. When they weren't there, Mina's heart went to her throat.

What if Mark had betrayed her? What if he had unloaded the UAVs to someone else?

Then she turned on the lights in the assembly area. Much

to Mina's relief, the UAVs were there, locked in the parts cage. They appeared to be properly boxed and labeled, so maybe moving them to the shipping bay was the only part of Mark's to-do list that he had ignored.

Luckily Mina had her own cage key on her key ring. It was inconvenient for her to have to do all the moving and lifting herself, but she finally managed to lug all the boxed UAVs into the shipping bay. When she popped open the trunk of the Lincoln, a cloud of urine-permeated air rose up out of the trunk. It struck her as funny that she had cut off Richard's fingers without a qualm but the smell of Brenda's having wet herself made Mina want to gag.

Brenda was still asleep. After donning her gloves, Mina used a box cutter to slice through the tape imprisoning Brenda's ankles, although she left her wrists firmly bound. Then, after removing the tape from Brenda's mouth, Mina shook the unconscious woman's shoulder.

"Wake up!" Mina ordered. "We need to get you out of there."

Brenda's eyes popped open. She looked around fearfully. "Where am I?" she rasped. "What's happening?"

"I need you to walk with me," Mina said. "It's not far. Let me help you."

She reached into the trunk, grabbed Brenda's shoulder and wrestled her into a semi-sitting position.

"Please," Brenda begged. "Not so fast. I'm dizzy."

The slight pause seemed to bring more clarity to her thought processes. "Wait. I remember now. We went to lunch. That's the last thing I remember. What are you doing?"

"Tying up a loose end is all," Mina said. "Now come on."

Eventually she was able to lever Brenda up and onto the edge of the trunk. Leaving Brenda's arms taped behind her, Mina walked her prisoner from shipping/receiving into the assembly room, where she shoved her into an old desk chair they hadn't managed to unload with the rest of the furniture. Mina used that to wheel Brenda the rest of the way into the cage.

"Let me go," Brenda said.

"No. That's not possible."

"I'll scream."

"Go right ahead," Mina said. "Be my guest. No one will hear you."

She turned and walked away. Brenda was screaming after her as she left, but Mina paid no attention. After locking the cage, she set the alarm, turned off the lights, and let herself out. She was weary, almost to the point of exhaustion, but she didn't linger. Instead, she headed for the cabin in Salton City with every intention of giving Mark Blaylock a piece of her mind.

17

Sedona, Arizona

On Saturday morning, the Sugarloaf Café was an absolute zoo. By eight a.m. there were people standing outside in the cold because there was no room to wait for a table inside. By ten o'clock they were on the last tray of that morning's sweet rolls, and Ali's feet were killing her. Things had lightened up a little and she was finally grabbing a cup of coffee when her cell phone rang.

Hoping it might be B. cut loose from his morning conference sessions, she answered without glancing at the caller ID.

"Is this Ali Reynolds?"

She didn't recognize the man's voice and she wondered how he'd gained access to her cell phone number. "Yes, it is," Ali said. "Who's calling, please, and who gave you this number?"

"My name is Camilla Gastellum. I'm Brenda Riley's mother. Have you seen her or heard from her?"

Obviously the gravelly voice that sounded like a man's wasn't.

"No," Ali said. "The last time I saw Brenda in person or spoke to her was months ago, right at the end of August."

"Yes," Camilla said. "She was on her way home from seeing you when she wrecked her car. She landed in jail in Barstow charged with driving under the influence."

"I'm sorry," Ali said. "I had no idea."

"She's taken off again," Camilla said. "She left home Friday morning and hasn't been back."

"I had an e-mail from her on Friday," Ali said. "She said she was doing well and that she was working on a book about her former fiancé."

"She may have been doing well then, but she probably isn't now," Camilla said disparagingly. "This is what always used to happen to her. She'd do all right for a while, then she'd fall off the wagon, go off on a binge, and disappear for weeks at a time."

"But I still don't understand why you're calling me," Ali said. "And how did you get my number?"

"I have macular degeneration," Camilla explained. "I had a neighbor come over today to help go through my phone records, which are also Brenda's since I pay the bill for her cell phone. She read off the numbers from last summer's bill. I guessed that this one might be yours and here I am. And the reason I called you is you're where she went for help the last time this happened. I was hoping lightning might strike twice in the same place."

"She sent me an e-mail," Ali said. "But she didn't hint that anything was amiss."

"When?"

"I'm not sure exactly what time. Sometime in the late morning or early afternoon. I could check my e-mail account and call you back with the time it was sent."

"And what did she want?"

"From me? She wanted one of my friends to do a background check on Richard Lowensdale's former employers, Mark and Ermina Blaylock."

"Did she say why?"

"Something about meeting with Ermina sometime soon, but she didn't give me a lot of detail about why she needed the information. Tell me about this book. What's it about?"

"I tried to tell Brenda that Lowensdale was trouble, but she wasn't interested. It seems he had any number of women hanging around and I suppose Ermina was one of them. When Brenda finally wised up about him, she decided to track down all his women friends. I believe what she said he was doing was cyberstalking."

"And now she's missing," Ali said. "Since when?"

"Since she left to go to an AA meeting yesterday morning. I tried talking to our local police department. At first the guy was really sympathetic, but then he was off the line for a while. I suppose he was checking her record. When he came back on the line, he pretty much told me to go jump in the lake."

Ali waited while Camilla took a ragged breath. "You see, I don't care if Brenda's drinking again. I just need to know that she's okay. That she isn't lying dead in a ditch somewhere."

"Was she driving?" Ali asked.

"No. She lost her license. I used to let her drive my car, but not anymore. If she had an accident, my insurance wouldn't cover it."

"So she left your house on foot?"

"Yes. She walked from here to her meeting. At least I assume she went to her meeting. That's where she told me she was going."

"Couldn't you ask some of the people who were at the meeting?"

"I don't know their names," Camilla said. "They're anonymous. That's the whole point, you see. I was hoping I could talk you into coming here to help me with this situation. You've been a police officer. That guy at Missing Persons would probably listen to you, even if he won't listen to me."

"Don't count on it," Ali said with a self-deprecating laugh. "Professional courtesy isn't always offered to visiting cops. I suggest you keep right on calling until you get someone who's willing to take a report."

"What if she doesn't come back?" Camilla asked. "What if we never find her?"

"Don't think like that," Ali said. "You're probably one hundred percent right. She's off on a toot somewhere. Eventually she'll sober up and come home."

"But would it be possible for you to be here?" Camilla insisted. "Just in case?"

Ali seemed to remember there was another daughter. "What about Brenda's sister?" Ali asked. "Can't she help out?"

There was a pause before Camilla said, "I'm afraid Valerie and I are estranged at the moment. She's made it perfectly clear that if it's something involving Brenda, she won't lift a finger to help. If she were here, all she'd do is say she told me so."

"I'm sorry to hear that," Ali said sincerely. "And I'm also sorry that I can't come help out right now. I have another obligation that's taking me to L.A. for the next day or two. If I can clear that up in a timely fashion, I might be able to come by Sacramento while I'm still in California, but I can't promise."

Two of Ali's counter customers had walked over to the cash wrap, where they were waiting patiently for her to deliver their check and take their money as two more customers settled onto the recently vacated stools.

"I'm so sorry, Mrs. Gastellum," Ali said. "I'm really busy right now. I'll have to get off the line. Keep this number handy so you can give me a call the moment Brenda shows up."

"I will," Camilla said. "I surely will."

Ali closed her phone, grabbed her order tablet out of her pocket, and added up the checks for the two waiting customers.

By the time she did that, several more people had filtered into the restaurant and the rush was back on in earnest.

Ali glanced up at the clock. Eleven thirty. Three more hours to go, then Edie and Bob would resume command.

If I live that long, Ali thought. *And if my feet don't give out completely.*

18

San Diego, California

Brenda's prison was completely dark and silent. Not so much as a crack of light appeared under either of the doorways she knew to be off toward her right, across the part of the room that wasn't enclosed in the chain-link fence. Occasionally overhead she heard the sound of what seemed like military aircraft. They were certainly noisy enough to be military aircraft, but that was the only sound she heard. There were no traffic sounds, no sirens, no trucks.

After Mina went away and left Brenda alone, she had tried screaming, but no one responded. Finally, falling silent, she had drifted into despair. For a long time, she simply sat and sobbed until she realized that at least she was sitting in a chair. It could have been worse. She could have been thrown down and left on the cold hard floor. With her hands taped—she assumed they were taped—behind her, they soon fell asleep. She finally managed to shift to a partially sideways position in the chair. That at least allowed circulation to return to her hands.

For the first time she was aware of how thirsty she was and

how hungry. How long had it been since that last meal and her last drink? That had to have been sometime on Friday, but she had no idea what day it was now or what time of day. And she had no idea if anyone would ever come here again. What if Mina Blaylock had simply walked away and left her? Would the next person who walked through one of the doors find only her dead and stinking corpse?

How long did it take to die of thirst and starvation? It had taken a surprisingly long time—several days—for her grandmother to die, even after the hospital disengaged her feeding tube and stopped giving her IV fluids. But Grammy had been old and ready to die. Brenda wasn't ready to give up. She still wanted to live.

Finally, she drifted into an uneasy sleep.

Salton City, California

Mark Blaylock was astonished when he pulled into the driveway late on Saturday afternoon and found Mina's Lincoln parked in the carport. She wasn't supposed to be home until Sunday. Obviously there had been a change of plans. It was possible she had tried to call and let him know, but he had left his phone turned off. He was having fun with Denise, the bartender, and he hadn't wanted anything or anyone—including his wife—to infringe on that.

He let himself into the house. The AC was on. That was the funny thing about this part of the desert. Overnight you'd need to turn on the heat. During the late afternoon, you'd have to turn on the AC.

But if Mina was behind that closed bedroom door, Mark didn't want to disturb her. There would be questions—a real grilling—

about where he'd been, who he had been with, and what he had been doing. No, better to let sleeping dogs lie.

Mark was still about half drunk. He grabbed one more bottle of beer out of the fridge, kicked off his shoes, and then lay down on the couch. Fortunately it was long enough for him to stretch out full length. In no time at all, he was fast asleep.

19

Sedona, Arizona

We did it, Ali told herself when two thirty finally rolled around that Saturday afternoon and she was able to lock the restaurant's front door.

She and Jan Howard met in the middle of the dining room to give one another high-fives, then they both turned their attention to the cleaning, sweeping, and mopping necessary for the Sugarloaf to be ready to open the next morning when Bob and Edie Larson returned. There had been some question about their possibly returning on an earlier flight. That wasn't Ali's concern. All she wanted to know was that they would be in charge come Sunday morning and that she wouldn't.

The substitute cook finished cleaning up the kitchen and left for the day. Jan and Ali were within minutes of leaving themselves when the door opened and in walked Bob and Edie.

"We're home!" Bob announced, beaming proudly. He was as tanned as Ali remembered ever seeing him. "That cruise was just what the doctor ordered and it doesn't look like you managed to burn the place down while we were gone."

Ali put down her broom and let herself be engulfed in one of her father's bear hugs, then she went on to hug her mother.

"I take it you caught the earlier flight," Ali observed.

"You know your father. Once we got off the boat, he was hot to trot to get home. He wanted to get here in time to make sure everything was shipshape for tomorrow."

As Bob drifted away to inspect the status of his kitchen, Edie sank into one of the booths.

"How was it?" Ali asked.

"Glorious," Edie replied. "I've never had so much fun in my life, not even when you and your aunt Evie and I went to England. Your father was like a kid again. You should have seen him on the dance floor."

Ali was taken aback at her mother's effusiveness, and the idea of her father on a dance floor was beyond belief. "Dad can dance?"

"Yes, he can," Edie said. "We have the photos to prove it. The fridge at home is empty, of course. I was going to run to the store before dinner, but we called Athena and Chris while we were riding up from Phoenix in the shuttle. They invited us to come to dinner—all of us, you included. Athena said they have the nursery pulled together. They want to show it to us."

Suddenly Athena's urgency to have the nursery completely finished on Friday made a lot more sense. If the sorting and folding was all done before Bob and Edie got home, there would be no need for Edie Larson to do it.

"You're sure they won't mind if I tag along?" Ali asked.

"Scout's honor," Edie said with a smile. "What about B.?"

"He's in D.C. this week," Ali said. "A conference this weekend and meetings next week."

"Too bad," Edie said. "We'll miss him."

I do too, Ali thought.

Once Ali was in the car, she dialed Chris's number. "Mom and

Dad told me I was invited to dinner," Ali said. "But I'm checking with you all the same."

"It's fine. Athena wants to show off the nursery," Chris said. "I'm barbecuing."

The thermometer on the Cayenne's dashboard indicated the outside temperature was in the low forties.

"Isn't it a little cold for barbecuing?" Ali asked.

"Believe me, Mom," Chris said, "right this minute, freezing my butt off over an outdoor grill is preferable to making any kind of a mess in the kitchen. Athena would have a fit."

"She's into nesting?" Ali asked.

"I'll say," Chris replied. "In a big way."

"It's a good thing you got that nursery situation handled," Ali said. "I don't care what Dr. Dixon says about the official due date. If the nesting instinct has come into play, the twins are liable to turn up any day now. What time is dinner?"

"Grandpa and Grandma are operating on East Coast time. They asked to eat early. I told them to come around five or so."

"Great," Ali said. "I'm catching a plane for L.A. at ten o'clock tonight, but if I leave Sedona by six, that should give me plenty of time to eat and run."

"You're going to California?" Chris asked. "Now? How come?"

Ali explained about what was going on with Velma, who had actually been among the out-of-town guests at Athena and Chris's wedding.

"Don't worry, though," Ali said. "If those babies of yours decide to make an early appearance, I'll be able to get myself home in a hurry."

Back at the house, Ali retreated to her room, where she showered and dressed. Then, after packing a single suitcase, she was on her way out the door for dinner when B. called. He was back in his hotel room for a few minutes before a dinner meeting.

"Your week at the Sugarloaf is over," he said. "Did you live?"

"I'm not sure my feet did," Ali answered with a laugh. "And I'm not sure how my parents do this day after day, week after week, and year after year, but they do. They're back, though. Had a great time. We're all meeting up at Chris and Athena's for dinner. The nursery is twin-ready, and they want to show it off. After that I have a plane to catch."

"A plane? Where are you going?"

Over the next few minutes, she brought B. up to date about her e-mail from Velma and the troubling phone call from Camilla Gastellum. She explained that after seeing Velma, if Brenda still hadn't turned up, Ali planned to make a quick dash up to Sacramento to see if she could be of help to Camilla.

"Let me get this straight," B. said thoughtfully. "Brenda went missing right after she asked you for that background check?"

"That's how it seems," Ali said.

"So the two things could be connected."

"Brenda's mother seems to think she just fell off the wagon, but it's possible," Ali agreed.

"What time are you heading for the airport?"

"My L.A.-bound flight leaves Sky Harbor ten p.m. I'll come back home right after dinner, then Leland will drive me down to Phoenix and drop me off."

"I'll give Stuart a call and see what, if anything, he's come up with on the background check. I'll ask him to swing by with whatever he has before then so you'll be able to take it with you."

When Ali reached Chris and Athena's place, her parents were already there. Chris, wearing a jacket, was out on the deck overseeing the grill. Bob and Edie had come equipped with a stack of cruise photos and were inflicting on their granddaughter-in-law their tandem cruise travelogue.

"And here's the girl who made it happen," Bob said heartily

when Ali joined them. "Cruises are great. I can hardly wait to go on another one, maybe an Alaskan cruise next summer, if we can talk you into looking after the Sugarloaf again. Everything is clean as a whistle. You did a great job."

"Now look what you've done," Edie said, smiling at Ali. "You've turned your father into a cruise-loving monster. Who would have thought it?"

Certainly not Ali.

"Now sit," her father ordered. "Let me show you the pictures. Edie already managed to download and print most of them."

There were candid shots as well as a collection of standard cruise ship photos. One showed Bob and Edie coming on board and standing at the top of the gangplank. Another showed them dressed in formal attire. It was only the second time in her life that Ali had seen her father in a tux. A third showed them standing together on a sandy beach.

From the wide grins on their faces in the various photos, it was clear that Bob and Edie had been having a great time. They had some videos as well. Chris came in long enough to download those onto his iMac for all to see. Ali deemed the one of Bob attempting to dance the limbo and coming to grief in the sand as worthy of either YouTube or America's Funniest Videos.

By the time Ali finally left Chris and Athena's, it was later than it should have been. There was enough time to make the plane, but just barely.

Back at the house she found Leland pacing in the kitchen and checking his watch. Ali's packed suitcase sat on the floor next to the door into the garage. "We don't have much time," he said, "but don't forget. Both your Taser and your Glock need to be in your checked luggage."

"Thanks," Ali said. Without his timely reminder, she might well have forgotten.

When she had finished stowing both of those, Leland handed her a thick manila envelope. "Stuart Ramey from High Noon dropped this off a little while ago. I'm assuming you want to take it along as well."

"Thanks," Ali said, stuffing it in her purse. "Something to read along the way."

But reading it along the way didn't happen. She was beyond tired. The week's hard work had taken a physical and mental toll. With Leland behind the wheel, she fell asleep almost as soon as she got in the car. She made it to Sky Harbor with just enough time to clear security before boarding her plane. Once the flight was airborne, she fell asleep again.

What Ali really wanted to do was collapse into her very own bed and sleep for twenty-four hours straight, but that wasn't in the cards. She had told Velma Trimble and Camilla Gastellum that she was coming to see them, and she was. What kind of condition she'd be in by the time she got there was anybody's guess.

Ali had made arrangements for a rental car to be waiting at LAX. Knowing she'd be arriving in the middle of the night, she had made a hotel reservation at the airport Hilton. By the time she collected her luggage and her car and staggered up to the hotel registration desk, she was just barely upright.

Ali fell into her unfamiliar hotel bed. Lying awake for a few short minutes, she was grateful that it was her mother who would be in charge of the Sugarloaf Café in a few short hours. Walking in Edie's very capable shoes for just one week had left Ali exhausted.

She fell into a deep sleep. There may have been countless airplanes passing overhead and traffic streaming by outside, but Ali didn't hear any of it. She was far too tired.

20

Salton City, California

At precisely 3:28 a.m. on Sunday morning, Florence Haywood smelled smoke. Flossie's maternal grandmother had been a smoker, and she had died a gruesome death when she fell asleep while smoking in bed. Florence had been only six at the time, but that event had a lasting influence on her life. She was scared to death of house fires. Her husband, Jimmy, assured her that their motor home was completely safe, but Flossie remained unconvinced. She insisted that he replace the batteries in their smoke alarm every six months rather than once a year, just to be on the safe side.

For the past ten years, starting in November, she and Jim had driven their aging Pontiac down from Bismarck, North Dakota, so they could spend the worst five months of winter in their motor home near the Salton Sea. Their "affordable" RV lot was part of a mostly failed residential subdivision called Heron Ridge, where they had an electrical hookup, a concrete slab, and nothing else. Once a week they had to drive into town to empty the RV's holding tanks.

The beach cabin closest to them belonged to Mark Blaylock. For several years, Mark had been the cabin's sole sometime occupant. Up until a few months ago, Flossie and Jimmy had assumed he was single. In the past two months, however, his witch of a wife, a woman named Mina, had shown up. She had been living at the cabin more or less on a full-time basis ever since.

Flossie believed in being neighborly, and she had done her best, but Mina had rebuffed all of Flossie's best efforts. She had taken over a plateful of freshly baked cookies. She had given cookies to Mark Blaylock on occasion, and she knew chocolate chip cookies were his particular favorite. Mina had accepted the plate but hadn't bothered to invite Flossie inside.

Fine, Flossie told herself. *Be that way.*

She continued to be on good terms with Mark, but she had nothing further to do with his standoffish wife.

That Sunday morning, after pulling on her robe and ascertaining that there was no sign of fire inside their RV, Flossie went from window to window. Flossie's recent cataract surgery had left her with something she had never had before—perfect 20/20 vision. Once she located the source of the flames, she could see quite clearly that Mina Blaylock was standing outside, wrapped in a coat, and tossing items into the already roaring fire burning in her husband's trusty Weber grill.

Yes, there was definitely some wood smoke thrown into the mix. Mark Blaylock usually ordered a cord of mesquite each fall that was delivered to the far end of his lot. This year he hadn't ordered new wood. Last year's load was dwindling, but there was definitely a hint of mesquite in the smoke Flossie smelled.

But there was something else too. Flossie was old enough to remember how back in the old days before there were plastic trash containers at the end of every dirt road in America, people had been responsible for their own garbage. Many people, especially people living out of town, had maintained their own personal burning barrels. That's exactly what this smoke smelled like—burning garbage.

The whole thing seemed odd. Flossie was tempted to go outside and ask Mina if everything was all right, just to see what she'd say, but then Jimmy woke up.

"Floss," he called from the bedroom. "Are you coming back to bed or not?"

"Coming," Flossie said. "I'll be right there."

21

Grass Valley, California

The call came into the Nevada County Emergency Communications Center at ten past eight on a cold but quiet Sunday morning. It was January in the foothills of the Sierras, but it was also unseasonably warm. It wasn't snowing or raining, and the roads were relatively clear. The Saturday night drunks had all managed to make it home without killing themselves or anyone else.

Phyllis Williams was one of only three emergency operators working that shift, and she was the one who took the call. The enhanced caller ID system listed an out-of-state telephone number. There was no way for Phyllis to tell if the call was coming from a cell phone or a landline.

"Nine-one-one," she said. "What are you reporting?"

The caller paused for a moment, as if uncertain what she should say. "It's about my fiancé," she said finally. "He lives there in Grass Valley. I'm worried about him. I'm afraid something may have happened to him. He always calls me on Saturday night, but last night he didn't. I've been calling and calling ever since last night. He doesn't answer. He may be sick or hurt."

This was going to end up being a judgment call on Phyllis's part. If the woman was talking about somebody who was elderly and frail or if it was a kid, it was a different story, but at first blush this sounded like this guy had missed making a phone call by a little over twelve hours. Something that trivial was hardly the end of the world. Twelve hours wasn't nearly long enough for most police departments to be willing to take a missing persons report, but maybe a routine "welfare check" was in order.

"What's his name?" Phyllis asked. "Where does your fiancé live?"

The woman blurted out the name Richard Lydecker and a street address on Jan Road in Grass Valley.

"Your name?" Phyllis asked.

"My name is Janet," the woman said. "Janet Silvie."

"And where are you located?"

"I'm at home," Janet said. "In Buffalo. Buffalo, New York. I don't know what I'll do if something has happened to him. What if Richard's dead? I know he has an ex-girlfriend who's been stalking him. She's evidently dangerous and very unstable. What if she did something to him?"

Janet Silvie's voice was rising in volume. Phyllis could tell the woman was close to losing it. A lot of callers did that. They worked themselves into such a frenzy before making the first call that they fell apart on the phone. Often it was virtually impossible to retrieve any usable information from someone who was hysterical. Still, the idea that a threat had been made upped the ante and Phyllis needed to learn what she could.

"Please calm down," Phyllis said. "You'll be better able to help us help Mr. Lydecker if you stay calm. Does this woman who threatened him have a name?"

"Brenda something," Janet said. "Something Irish, maybe. O'Reilly or maybe just plain Riley. I don't remember her name.

She even called me once, trying to feed me some line about Richard cheating on me. When I told Richard about it, that's when he warned me that she's some kind of nut, like on drugs or something. I don't blame him for being scared of her."

"You actually spoke to this woman?"

"There was no speaking. It was more like she was talking—yelling really—and all I could do was listen."

"Does she live at the address you gave me?"

"No. They're not married. I already told you Richard is *my* fiancé. We're going to get married next summer. Sometime in June. We haven't set an exact date."

Phyllis tried not to roll her eyes. TMI—too much information—and none of it was the information she actually needed. In the meantime, Phyllis did a quick check of the records available to her. According to the county assessor's office, the property on Jan Road belonged to Richard Stephen Lowensdale. There was no Grass Valley listing of any kind for someone named Richard Lydecker.

"Tell me about Brenda. Do you know if she's armed?" Phyllis asked her questions calmly. That was the secret to working as a 911 operator. You had to remain calm no matter what. "Is she dangerous?"

"Maybe she is or maybe she isn't," Janet replied. "How would I know? I've never met the woman. I've never even seen her. After all, I'm a whole continent away. You're right there in Grass Valley. Isn't there something you can do?"

Phyllis's desk in the Nevada County Communications Center was actually located in Nevada City rather than Grass Valley, but she didn't quibble.

"Yes, ma'am," Phyllis told her caller. "I'm dispatching officers right now to do a welfare check."

"And you'll get back to me if you find out that something's wrong?" Janet Silvie asked.

"I'm only an emergency operator," Phyllis told her. "I won't be the one getting back to you. The address you gave me is inside the Grass Valley city limits. Once I pass this information on to them, the Grass Valley Police Department will be handling the response. Maybe one of their uniformed officers will call you back. Or else Mr. Lydecker himself. I'm sure the officers on the scene will let him know that you're concerned."

"Thank you," Janet Silvie said gratefully, then she blew her nose loudly into the mouthpiece.

Phyllis Williams wasn't offended. She was used to it. In her line of work, nose blowing was actually a good sign. It beat hyperventilating. Or screaming. Or the devastating sound of gunshots when a simple domestic violence call suddenly spiraled out of control and into a homicide situation.

That had happened to Phyllis on more than one occasion. Once she heard the sound of gunfire, she knew there was nothing to be done. Nothing at all. It was over. People were already dead or dying. All Phyllis could do then was send officers to the scene even though she knew their arrival would be too little, too late.

Nose blowing, on the other hand, meant that the people on the other side of the telephone conversation were still alive. They were trying to pull themselves together and regain control. Their grip on self-control might be tenuous but it counted big in Phyllis's book.

"Try not to worry," Phyllis said reassuringly. "As I said, officers are currently on their way to that address."

That was a small white lie because the officers weren't on their way right that very minute. They wouldn't get word until Phyllis notified Dispatch at the Grass Valley Police Department. Phyllis did that immediately, but she still felt that there was no real urgency to the matter. After all, it was a simple welfare check. No big hurry. No need for lights or sirens. The officers would get there when they got there, probably after taking their morning coffee break rather than before.

Phyllis then glanced at the clock on the wall across the room. It was almost time for her coffee break. Wanda Harkness, the operator at the next desk, had just come back from her break, and she was now involved in taking a call that sounded no more critical than the one Phyllis had just handled.

For the remainder of that Sunday morning, Phyllis and Wanda handled calls most of which shouldn't have been 911 calls in the first place. One woman was frantic because her declawed house cat had escaped through an open door and taken off for parts unknown. What if a coyote caught it and ate it? Couldn't they please do something to help? Someone else had crashed into an empty plastic garbage can hard enough to split it wide open. The car was most likely damaged, but apparently no people were. And one woman, an almost weekly caller, begged them to do something about the noise of those church bells: did they have to ring that loud every single Sunday morning?

Time dragged. Between calls, Phyllis sipped her coffee, worked the *New York Times* Sunday crossword, and kept an eye on the clock.

At eleven thirty-eight, Phyllis's phone lit up. "Nine-one-one," she said. "What are you reporting?"

"I want to report a missing person," a woman said, sounding reasonably controlled. This one wasn't panicky. She wasn't yelling.

Caller ID said that the call had originated in area code 541. Phyllis recognized that as being somewhere in Oregon. Phyllis's sister and brother-in-law lived in Roseburg.

"Is the missing person a child or an adult?" Phyllis asked.

"An adult. He's fifty-three."

"He's a relative of yours?"

"Well, sort of. We're engaged. At least we're going to be. We had this little disagreement on Thursday. He sent me a link to an engagement ring he was thinking about getting me for Valentine's Day. The problem is, I didn't like the one he picked out, and I told him so, but I can't imagine he's still mad about that. We talked briefly on Friday morning. He was still upset, but he thought we'd be alright."

"All right, then," Phyllis said. "Let me get some information. What's your name?"

"Dawn," the woman said. "Dawn Carras from Eugene, Oregon."

"And your missing fiancé's name?"

"Richard," Dawn said. "Richard Loomis."

"Do you have an address?"

"Yes. It's nine sixteen Jan Road."

Whoa! Phyllis thought. *Another man named Richard AWOL from the same address? How interesting.*

Phyllis managed to keep her voice even and businesslike as she checked Grass Valley records for any listing for Richard Loomis. She found nothing, just as earlier she had found no listing for Janet Silvie's Richard Lydecker.

This seemed like more than a mere coincidence. Two women had called from opposite ends of the country on the same morning to report two missing fiancés both of whom were named Richard and who evidently shared a residence with yet a third person, also named Richard. Once you added a psychotic ex-girlfriend into the mix, Phyllis's Sunday morning shift at the com center was suddenly a whole lot more interesting than it had been earlier.

Dutifully she took down all of Dawn Carras's information, but the moment Phyllis was off the phone, she called Grass Valley PD and spoke to Sandy in Dispatch.

"About that welfare check I called in earlier—"

"I forgot to get back to you," Sandy said. "It's turned out to be

a whole lot more serious than a welfare check. Responding officers found a body. If this is Mr. Lydecker, the guy's dead and has
been for some time—a couple of days at least. The ME is on his
way there right now. The cops on the scene said someone trussed
him up with packing tape, put a plastic bag over his head, and
taped that shut as well. Can you give me any additional details?"

"No," Phyllis said. "I already gave you everything I had on
that one, but it turns out I do have one more piece of the puzzle.
I just had some other woman, one from Oregon this time, who
called in a missing person report on her fiancé. This guy is named
Richard Loomis. He happens to live at the same address on Jan
Road that Janet Silvie gave me for Richard Lydecker.

"The second caller is a woman named Dawn Carras who lives
in Eugene, Oregon. According to her, she and Richard Loomis
had a lover's spat the other night because she wasn't wild about
the engagement ring he had chosen for her. They had words
over it on Thursday evening. He was still upset when she spoke
to him on Friday morning, but she expected that all would have
blown over in time for their regular Saturday date-night phone
call, but he never called."

"So we've got three guys named Richard, one dead guy, and two
missing fiancés," Sandy said. "What does it sound like to you?"

"Sounds like our little Richard was playing with fire and got
burned. He must be one good-looking dude. Or else he's loaded.
Think about how ugly Aristotle Onassis was."

"Who?" Sandy asked.

Phyllis Williams, Phyllis James back then, had been a fresh-
man in high school on that day in November when President
Kennedy was gunned down by Lee Harvey Oswald. Years later,
she had been appalled when his widow and Phyllis's own personal idol, Jackie Kennedy, had taken up with billionaire Aristotle
Onassis. It seemed impossible to Phyllis that Sandy had no idea

who Aristotle Onassis was, but then again, Sandy might be so young that she didn't know who Jackie Kennedy was either.

This wasn't the first time in Phyllis's many years at the Nevada County Com Center that she had run headlong into a generation gap with her younger counterparts, and it wouldn't be the last.

"Never mind," she said. "It doesn't matter."

But if Richard Lowensdale, Richard Lydecker, and Richard Loomis were all one and the same, Phyllis wondered what exactly the guy had going for him. Whatever it was, it had obviously been good enough to attract women like flies to honey.

Too bad it wasn't enough to save his life.

22

Los Angeles, California

Ali Reynolds didn't awaken in her Los Angeles hotel room until after ten the next morning. As soon as she heard the rumble of planes overhead, she was surprised that she had been able to sleep through the racket. She ordered coffee and breakfast from room service. Knowing she needed to check on Velma before showing up at her home, Ali dialed Velma's phone number in Laguna Beach and then waited for someone—a hospice worker, most likely—to answer.

What if I waited too long? Ali wondered.

"Velma Trimble's residence."

The voice on the other end of the line was brisk and business-like.

"My name is Ali Reynolds," she began. "I was told Velma wanted to see me—"

"Ali? It's Maddy—Velma's friend, Maddy Watkins. I'm so glad you called."

When Velma had defied her cancer diagnosis by signing up for that round-the-world private jet cruise, she had been assigned a stranger, Maddy Watkins, as roommate by the travel agency. By the end of the trip, Maddy and Velma had become fast friends. Maddy, a wealthy widow from Washington State, was an aging dynamo who traveled everywhere by car in the company of her two golden retrievers, Aggie and Daphne. When she and Velma had been invited to attend Chris and Athena's wedding, the two dogs had come along to Sedona.

"How are your kids?" Maddy asked. "Aren't those twins due most any day now?"

"Soon," Ali said. "But how's Velma?"

"The dogs and I drove down and have been here for the past three days. Aggie and Daphne weren't trained to be service dogs, but try to tell them that. Aggie has barely left Velma's bedside. By rights her son should be the one who's here supervising the hospice workers, but he's not. If you don't mind my saying so, Carson is a real piece of work. If I didn't know better, I'd think he and my own son were twins. Anyway, I believe Carson is a little afraid of me, and rightly so. He was ready to pull the plug on his mother four years ago when she first got her cancer diagnosis. And I don't blame her at all for wanting people with her right now who don't have a big vested interest in what's going on."

"What is going on?" Ali asked.

"She's dying, of course," Maddy said brusquely. "But she's interested in tying up a few loose ends before that happens, you being a case in point."

"I flew into L.A. last night," Ali said. "If it's convenient, I could come by later this morning. It'll take an hour or so for me to drive there, depending on traffic."

"Midafternoon is a good time," Maddy said. "She takes a nap after lunch. If you could be here about three, it would be great."

"Three it is," Ali said. There was a knock on the door.

"Room service."

"My breakfast is here, Maddy. See you in a few hours."

Ali let the server into the room. Over coffee, orange juice, and a basket of breakfast breads, Ali opened the High Noon envelope, pulled out a wad of papers, and began to read.

23

Grass Valley, California

Detective Gilbert Morris of the Grass Valley Police Department wasn't having an especially good weekend. Once upon a time, when Gil first hired on with the department, being promoted to the Investigations Unit was more of an honor than anything else. Sure you had a few car thefts and break-ins to investigate from time to time, but not many murders. Maybe one every two to three years. At that point, the Investigations Unit would get called out to do their homicide investigation dance. That, of course, was back before the meth industry came to town and set up shop.

People had started killing one another with wild abandon about the time Gil got promoted to the I.U., and there didn't seem to be any sign of the homicide count letting up. That didn't mean, however, that the city fathers had seen fit to adjust the budget enough to allow for any more than four detectives. In the short term that had been good for Gil's overtime pay, but long-term it had been bad for his marriage. This week had been especially tough. Dan Cassidy, the lieutenant in charge, was out for knee surgery, Joe Moreno was off on his honeymoon, and Kenny Mosier's father was taking his own sweet time dying in a hospital somewhere in Ohio. That meant Gil was the only Investigations guy in town, and this was fast turning into a very crowded week.

Friday was a good case in point. That night, two brothers, some of Grass Valley's less exemplary citizens, had gone to war with each other and had both ended up dead. George and Bobby Herrera were a pair of homegrown thugs who had graduated from small-town thievery to running a meth lab out of their rundown apartment on the outskirts of town. Both had been pumped up on a combination of booze and meth. What started out as a verbal confrontation had escalated to physical violence when they took their furious sibling rivalry into the unpaved parking lot outside their apartment.

When weapons appeared, fellow residents ducked for cover and called the cops. By the time officers arrived on the scene, both brothers were on the ground. Bobby had died instantly. George died while en route to the hospital. Gil arrived at the crime scene to find both brothers were deceased, leaving in their wake a mountain of evidence and a daunting amount of paperwork.

Gil had spent all day Saturday working the crime scene. It wasn't a matter of solving the crime, because the double homicide pretty well solved itself. Several witnesses came forward to claim that they had seen everything that had happened in the weed-strewn parking lot. A hazmat team came by to dismantle the meth lab George and Bobby had been running in their cockroach-infested one-bedroom apartment.

"It's a good thing they're both dead," the hazmat guy told Gil. "If they had started a fire in their meth lab kitchen, the place would have gone up like so much dried tinder and the other people who lived here might not have been able to get out."

Gil took one statement after another. The witnesses' stories were all slightly different, but the general outlines were all the same. When the brothers were sober, they were fine. When they were drunk or high, look out. Bobby and George had been pleasant enough earlier that Friday morning, but by the middle of the afternoon they were screaming at one another and, as one young mother of a three-year-old reported, using some very inappropriate language.

Bobby, the younger of the two, had come running out of their downstairs apartment carrying a rifle of some kind and wearing nothing but a pair of boxers. Gil Morris had to admit, going barefoot in Grass Valley in January was something of a feat. Friday had been clear but very cold. Obviously Bobby was feeling no pain.

Bobby stood there holding the gun pointed at the door and yelling at his brother to man up and come outside. Otherwise he was a lily-livered something or other—several expletives deleted. At that point several of the neighbors, crouched behind furniture, saw the weapon, picked up their phones, and dialed 911. Unfortunately, before officers could get there, George emerged from the apartment. He was fully dressed and carrying a firearm of his own.

According to witnesses, both men stopped screaming for a moment. They seemed to be listening to the sound of approaching sirens before Bobby resumed his rant.

"You stupid son of a bitch!" he screamed. "You had to go call the cops, didn't you."

Just like that, as though they were on the same wavelength, they both pulled their respective triggers. George was evidently the better shot of the two. His bullet removed most of his brother's head. Bobby was dead the instant he was hit. Bobby's shot went low and tore through George's femoral artery. By the time the EMTs were able to get to him, he had lost too much blood and couldn't be stabilized.

As a police officer, Gil found himself being grateful that those two dodos had killed each other without damaging someone else. Then, late Saturday evening as he was about to call it a day, he found himself face-to-face with Sylvia Herrera, Bobby and George's grieving but furious mother.

"Why?" she wailed at him. "Why are my boys dead, my poor innocent babies?"

Bobby and George had been twenty-six and twenty-nine respectively. As far as Gil was concerned, they were a long way from babies. And they were a long way from innocent too. They were a pair of drug-stupefied losers, but Gil couldn't say that to their mother, and Sylvia Herrera was inconsolable.

Finally, when she quieted enough for him to get a word in edgewise, Gil said, "I'm so sorry for your loss, Mrs. Herrera. It's the drugs, you know."

"Drugs?" she screeched back at him. "You say it's the drugs?"

He nodded. She reached out a hand and waggled a finger at him, thumping him on the chest as she spoke, like a mother remonstrating with a difficult child.

"Don't you know drugs are illegal?" she demanded. "You're the police. You should stop them."

"Yes, ma'am," he agreed. "We certainly should."

On Saturday night it wasn't necessary for him to call Linda in advance and tell her he was going to be late. Months earlier his wife of twenty some years had given up on being married to a policeman. She had taken the kids and the dog and the cat and had gone home to live with her folks in Mt. Shasta City. It was too bad, "a crying shame," as some of the guys at work had put it. The truth is Gil had done his share of crying about it, although he'd never tell his buddies at the department a word about that. Instead, he kept a stiff upper lip and motored along from case to case.

He was sorry about losing his family, but there didn't seem to be a damned thing he could do to fix it any more than he could stop the overwhelming flood of drugs that had taken the lives of Sylvia Herrera's sons.

So Detective Morris dragged his weary body home to his empty house that was furnished with whatever leavings Linda's father hadn't been able to cram in the U-Haul. Linda had left him one plate, one bowl, one glass, one coffee cup, and one set of silverware. That simplified Gil's meal planning, and it simplified clean up too. He washed every dish he owned after every meal. He thought about microwaving one of those Healthy Choice dinners, but he didn't bother. They tasted like crap, and anyway he was too tired to eat. Or even drink. He stripped off his clothes, fell crosswise on the bed, and fell asleep.

The next morning Gil was still in his shorts, eating the crummy dregs from the bottom of a nearly empty box of Honey Nut Cheerios, drinking instant coffee, and wishing he had a toaster so he could have an English muffin, when the phone rang.

"Uniformed officers are reporting what appears to be a homicide at the top of Jan Road," the dispatch officer for Grass Valley PD told him. And so, at eleven forty-five on a chill Sunday morning in January, Gil Morris found himself summoned to his third homicide case in as many days.

Yes, it's a good thing Linda is gone, Gil told himself as he hurried into the bedroom to get dressed. *Otherwise she'd be pitching a royal fit.*

24

Grass Valley, California

Gil got dressed and drove straight to 916 Jan Road. The front yard was unkempt and weedy. There were dilapidated remnants of what might have been flower beds long ago, but no one had planted anything in them for a very long time. The front gate on the ornamental iron fence hung ajar on a single bent hinge. Two uniformed officers, Dodd and Masters, waited for Gil on the front porch.

"What have we got?" Gil asked.

"It's pretty ugly in there," Dodd said. "One victim, but he's been dead for a while and the thermostat is set somewhere in the upper eighties."

With no explanation needed, Dodd handed Gil an open jar of Vicks VapoRub. Nodding his thanks, he slathered some of the reeking salve just under his nostrils. It stank to high heaven, but it would help beat back the pungent odors that were no doubt waiting for him inside the house.

"Cigar?" Dale Masters asked, offering one of those as well.

Linda had put a permanent embargo on Gil's having the occasional cigar. With her gone, it was time that prohibition was lifted.

"Thanks," Gil said. He took the proffered smoke and stuck it in his jacket pocket. "If you don't mind, I'll save it for later."

"Be my guest," Masters told him. "You're going to need it."

"What happened here, forced entry?"

"Not that we can see," Masters replied. "There's a deadbolt on the front door, but it wasn't engaged."

That means the victim probably knew his killer, Gil thought. *At least he let the bad guy into the house.*

"But we might get lucky," Officer Dodd said.

"How so?" Gil asked.

Dodd gestured to the upper corner of the front porch to where a CCTV security camera had been mounted on the wooden siding.

"The only way that'll help us is if it's turned on," Gil said. "Now what about the coroner?"

"Fred's on his way," Dodd said. "He should be here any minute."

Without waiting for the arrival of the coroner, Fred Millhouse, Gil slipped on a pair of crime scene booties and a pair of latex gloves. "Do we have a name?"

"Several actually," Officer Dodd said. "We were originally sent here to do a welfare check on a guy named Richard Lydecker whose fiancée called nine-one-one to report him missing. Later another woman called looking for her missing fiancé. She gave the nine-one-one operator the same address, only she says her guy's name is Richard Loomis."

"Curiouser and curiouser," Gil said.

Dodd nodded. "County tax records say the residence is owned by someone else named Richard, only his last name is Lowensdale. So I'm guessing the dead guy is one of those three or maybe he's all of them. According to them, Lowensdale is age fifty-three. Looks like he lives alone."

My age, Gil thought.

"Were the lights on or off when you got here?" he asked.

"The overhead fixture in the living room was off. The desk lamp is on in the corner, but the blinds were closed in both the living room and dining room. The only way to see inside was through the window in the front door. That allows a view of the entryway only, not the actual crime scene, which is in the living room."

"So no one could see what was happening from the outside."

"I don't think so. I suspect this all went down sometime in the course of the afternoon on Friday or maybe even Thursday. The porch light was off, and we found a UPS package here by the front door, so it was probably delivered on Friday afternoon at the latest. UPS doesn't deliver on weekends."

Gil paused long enough to look down at the label. Zappos. From information on the label and from the shape of the box, Gil figured the package probably contained a pair of shoes. The victim may have needed new shoes and he may have ordered new shoes, but he was never going to wear them.

"So the UPS guy may have some information for us," Gil said. "Any idea who he is?"

"The local driver is named Ted Frost," Dodd said. "I went to high school with him. He's a good guy."

Gil nodded. "See if you can get him on the horn."

While Officer Dodd set off to do Gil's bidding, the detective geared himself up for the task at hand. As he stepped on the grimy hardwood-floored entryway, Gil Morris encountered the appalling stench that immediately overpowered the puny efforts of his Vick's Vaporub.

That one sickening whiff was enough to tell him that he was also stepping into a nightmare.

For a moment, after he crossed the threshold, Gil stood still, trying to get the lay of the land and assimilate what he was seeing and feeling. As expected, the house was unbearably hot. If he had been able to see a thermostat, he would have turned it down. The overheated air reeked with an ugly combination of odors. Fighting his own gag reflex, Gil catalogued the unwelcome but familiar smells—both the putrid odor of decaying flesh and the lingering coppery scent of dried and rotting blood. Beyond those two, however, was something else besides, something obnoxious that Gil couldn't quite place.

As he stepped into the room, a small coat closet was to his immediate left. The door had been left ajar and the coats, jackets, and sweaters on the pole inside had all been pushed to one side in order to leave enough room for an old-fashioned Kirby vacuum cleaner that had been stowed in one corner of the closet.

For some strange reason that tickled Gil's funny bone. Where was it written that vacuum cleaners always had to be stored in entryway closets? That was where Linda had kept her Bissell and where his mother had kept her Hoover. At that moment, Gil was without a vacuum cleaner and without much hope of ever having one either.

But if I get one, he told himself, *I'm not keeping it in the entryway closet.*

The overhang of the porch and the closed blinds along the front of the house left the entryway shrouded in shadow. Making a note of how he had found the light switch, Gil used a pencil to turn on the overhead lights. Immediately he saw evidence of tracked blood, coming and going through the entryway, but the patterns were smeared and indistinct. Gil knew what that meant. Whoever had tramped through the blood had been wearing booties.

Gil turned back to the door. "Hey, Officer Masters," he called. "Did you or Dodd leave these tracks in here?"

"No, sir," Masters returned. "We saw the tracks. We walked around them."

Nodding, Gil dropped a numbered marker onto the floor next to each of three prints. Then, using a small digital camera, he took several photographs of the area indicated by the marker. Each time he snapped a photo, he paused long enough to make a corresponding note on three-by-five cards that he carried in a leather-bound wallet. That way, later, he'd be able to use the notes to explain what was in the photos and he'd use the photos to help decipher his sometimes illegible notes.

Gil knew that the corpse was in the living room. Instead of going directly there, he turned instead toward a room that had originally been intended as a dining room. Shelves that had probably once held knickknacks of some kind had been installed high on the dining room walls, but they were empty. An oak pedestal table stood in the middle of the room. There was only one chair at the table. Two others sat off to the side, just under the window. A buffet that matched the table was the only other piece of furniture. The top of the buffet was covered with packing boxes, tape dispensers, and blank shipping labels, while the top of the table was littered with tubes of epoxy and paint and brushes.

On the floor, scattered in among a snowdrift of foam packing peanuts, lay the smashed remains of what must have once been on the now-denuded bookshelves—dozens and dozens of model airplanes, all of them wrecked, ground to pieces on the floor. They had been stepped on . . . no, stomped on, in what Gil read as deliberate, thorough, and wanton destruction.

Okay, Gil told himself. *Kirby vacuum or not, if this is where the victim built his models, that means the guy definitely isn't married. And he isn't living with his mother either. No woman in her right mind lets a guy build model airplanes in the middle of her dining room table or spill packing peanuts all over the house.*

Gil stayed where he was, in the dining room doorway. If he tried stepping into the dining room, he knew that no matter how carefully he walked, he wouldn't be able to keep from crunching larger pieces of wings and propellers and fuselages into smaller bits of plastic, balsa wood, and dust.

At last, turning toward the living room, Gil was appalled by the mess. Except for the wrecked model planes on the floor, the dining room had been relatively neat and orderly. The living room looked like a trash heap, a lived-in trash heap that consisted of discarded magazines, packets of coupons, grocery bags, empty cans of chili, shipping boxes, and dead pizza containers, with little cleared paths like game trails leading through the mess from one place to another. It was possible someone could find out how long the debris had been there by shoveling through it like an archeological dig, but that wasn't Gil's job.

The small desk lamp on the far table did little to illuminate the rest of the room. Once again Gil tracked down a wall switch. Turning on the overhead fixture in the living room immediately revealed the same kind of fuzzy footprints he had seen in the entryway. They meandered in and out of the mess, sometimes following the trails sometimes stepping on or over the trash.

In the lamplight, the victim's body hadn't been immediately visible. Now it was. Just beyond the far end of the couch, a single sock-clad foot hung at an ungainly angle in midair. Only when Gil rounded the couch did he see that a large male was strapped to a fallen dining room chair by layers and layers of clear packing tape. His legs were fastened to the front legs of the chair while his arms and wrists, out of sight, were most likely similarly bound behind his back.

At first glance there was no evidence of any kind of bullet or stab wound that would account for the presence of all the blood that had been trod through the house. Instead, the man's head was encased in a clear plastic bag, the kind that customers in grocery stores peel off conveniently located rolls to carry home their freshly chosen vegetables—heads of broccoli, lettuce, or cauliflower—but the plastic was heavy, not likely to be easily chewed through. Underneath the bag, Gil caught sight of another piece of packing tape that had been plastered to the man's mouth to function as a gag. More tape had been used to fasten the open end of the bag tightly around the victim's bulging neck.

Asphyxiation then, Gil thought. *So why do I see so much blood?*

Stepping to the far side of the corpse, Gil found the answer to that question. The tips of several of the dead man's fingers—four in all—had been hacked off by poultry scissors that still lay where it had been dropped. Beside the shears were the blackened hunks of fingertips, although Gil counted only three, not four. It was likely the missing one had been covered by the man's falling body when the chair had tipped onto its side. And the amount of blood on the floor told Gil what he didn't want to know—that the victim had been alive when the fingers were hacked off one by one.

The gruesome savagery of that was enough to make even an experienced homicide cop want to toss his morning's batch of Honey Nut Cheerios. The other thing contributing to his gag reflex had to do with teeming hordes of insect vermin that were visible both inside and on the body. Since the house itself was a gigantic trash heap, that came as no surprise. The good news about that was that flesh-eating maggots would provide a foolproof way for the coroner to establish the victim's time of death with a good deal of accuracy.

Needing to step away for a moment, Gil turned toward the wooden desk. It was stacked high with a complicated collection of electronics—several printers as well as a single computer. A single glance was enough to tell Gil that this was high-end, top-of-the-line Mac equipment, and that struck him as odd. In the course of a normal home invasion, the electronics wouldn't have been there. They'd have been among the first items stolen or else they would have been smashed to pieces like the model airplanes in the other room.

Gil made his way around the living room, laying down more evidence markers and taking photos as he went. Finally, returning to the corpse, Gil stepped closer to the body and squatted down next to it. Only then did Gil catch sight of a tiny set of white wires. They came from what Gil assumed to be an iPod in the pocket of the dead man's sweatshirt. They threaded their way under the tape that was attached to his throat. With the victim lying on his side, Gil could only see the left side of the man's head, but he could also see that one of the earbuds was still stuck in the dead man's ear.

"So what went on here, big fella?" Gilbert asked aloud.

He often addressed questions to the corpses at crime scenes during those intimate moments when he was alone with murder victims. They never answered, but Gil's one-sided conversations usually helped him make sense of what he was seeing.

"You were listening to your tunes, and then something happened. What was it?"

It was as Gil rose from his crouch and readied his camera once more that he noticed the presence of an extra dining room chair. He had seen it before, but this was the first time it actually registered. Before that Gil had been too focused on the body itself to realize that a second chair had been brought into the living room and positioned in a spot that was close to the dead man's head.

It took a moment for Gil to grasp what he was seeing. Two dining room chairs had been brought into the living room, one to confine the victim and one to be used as an observation post. Murder was murder, and the bloody mutilations were nothing short of appalling, but the idea of sitting and watching while your victim struggled to take his last breaths moved what had happened in this room to a whole new level.

25

Grass Valley, California

Gil was still struggling with that reality when the Nevada County coroner, Fred Millhouse, arrived on the scene.

"Hey, Detective Morris," Fred said. "We've gotta stop meeting like this. Three in one week is more than I bargained for. Is it all right if I move this chair out of the way?"

"Just a moment," Gil said, laying down another marker. "Let me get a photo first."

While Fred went to work doing what he needed to do, Gil walked through the house. He was looking for evidence, yes, but he was also trying to get the feel of what he was seeing.

A good deal of the mess in the room was trash that had been there for a long time, but the wanton destruction of the model planes was recent. It had taken time to smash them one by one. If the plane smasher and the killer were one and the same, that meant that the culprit had been in the victim's house for an extended period of time. This wasn't a quick in and out. The killer had come here looking for something. The question was, had he found it and taken it?

Gil glanced again at the collection of electronics on the desk in the corner. Gil Morris was no geek, but he knew enough about computers to realize that the computer was a potential source of all kinds of useful information, including the names and e-mail addresses of the people the victim had corresponded with in the last days of his life. It would also tell investigators what, if anything, Richard Lowensdale had been working on at the time of his death. Gil looked around for a cell phone or a landline. At first glance, neither was visible. And if there were some way to view any of the footage from the security camera over the front door, that wasn't readily apparent either.

Not wanting to observe Millhouse at his grim work and not wanting to be in the way, Gil let himself out of the overheated, dimly lit house into bright sunlight and a welcome January chill. He paused on the front porch long enough to search for evidence that the bloodied footsteps had exited this way. There was nothing visible to the naked eye, but luminol might reveal the microscopic presence of blood evidence. A more likely scenario told him that the perpetrator had walked around in the house long enough for the blood on the bottom of his feet to dry.

Gil stood on the porch's top step and breathed in a lungful of fresh air. Even with the Vicks right there beneath his nostrils, some of the terrible odors of death still lingered. Gil walked down the cracked sidewalk and let himself out through the crooked gate. A patrol car was parked on the far side of the street. Officer Masters was inside and appeared to be talking on the radio.

Gil pulled the cigar out of his shirt pocket and mimed his need of a light to Masters.

When Dale Masters joined him at the rear of the black-and-white, he brought a second cigar for himself and a lighter, as well as a small metal container which, with the lid removed, served admirably as a makeshift ashtray. Leaving ashes of any kind near a crime scene was a bad idea. The black-and-white had a perfectly functioning ashtray in the front seat, but smoking in city-owned vehicles was not entirely verboten.

Once they both lit up, Gil was pleased to discover that the cigars were impressively obnoxious—the kind Linda had always regarded as "pure evil"—but the smoke helped displace the last of the noxious odors.

"Thanks," Gil said, holding up his cigar.

"You're welcome," Dale said. "You lasted a whole lot longer inside there than I did. By the way, I just got off the phone with Irene in Records. She said there was a B and E at this address on the twentieth of September of this past year. According to the report, an ex-girlfriend allegedly broke into the house in broad daylight while Lowensdale was off getting his Cadillac serviced."

"New Cadillac?"

"Old," Masters said. "The way I understand it, it used to belong to Lowensdale's mother."

Gil pulled out a new three-by-five card. "Name?"

"Mother's name?"

"No. The B and E suspect."

"Her name's Brenda Riley. She used to be Lowensdale's girlfriend."

"They caught her in the act?"

"Not exactly. Lowensdale came home, saw a broken window, and realized someone had been inside his place. Even though nothing of value had been stolen, he raised enough of a stink that the chief finally agreed to have our guys come by to do a crime scene investigation. Her prints were found everywhere. No effort to cover them up whatsoever."

"She's in the system?" Gil asked.

Masters nodded. "She's been booked for a number of moving violations, DUIs as well as driving without a license, and so forth. Once we told him who the perp was, Lowensdale declined to press charges. Said it was the aftermath of a bad breakup and since nothing was taken, he was prepared to let it go."

"Brenda Riley?" Gil asked with his pen poised to write.

"Brenda Arlene Riley," Masters confirmed. "She lives in Sacramento. Irene in Records can give you the exact address, but you may want to check. I believe there was something in that original nine-one-one call this morning about an ex being involved in all this one way or the other."

"Thanks," Gil said. "I'll look into it."

When Masters was called back to the radio, Gil stood there with a cloud of smoke circling his head while he studied his surroundings and the cracked and peeling exterior of Richard Lowensdale's house.

Jan Road was steep. The house was built into the flank of the hill, but the sidewalk leading up to the house was level. A cracked concrete walkway went from the front porch to a small detached garage and from the garage to a side door near the back of the house. Looking at the elevations, Gil realized that meant there was probably a basement under the house and maybe under the garage as well.

Ready to resume his examination of the house, Gil followed the walkway door to door to door. There were no visible footprints anywhere.

He went back to the small garage and opened the side door wide enough so he could peek inside. There was definitely no basement in the garage. The hard-packed dirt floor reeked of decades of old grease and oil. Above the workbench, the wall was lined with a collection of antique tools. The smell and tools hinted that the garage had long been used by a homegrown, do-it-yourself mechanic. What looked like most of a case of motor oil stood inside the remains of a cut-down cardboard box on a shelf above the work bench.

Clearly the garage had been built at a time when vehicles were smaller. Lowensdale's ten-year-old black Cadillac Catera barely fit inside the four walls. If this had been a standard robbery, most likely the car would have been taken along with the electronics. No, this was definitely something else.

Leaving the garage, Gil went to what he assumed to be the back door of the house. The first room inside was a small utility room that held a washer and dryer, an older model top-loading set. The utility room opened into an old-fashioned kitchen complete with a single-bowl porcelain sink and knotty pine cabinets, as well as an avocado-colored fridge and matching stove that had to date from sometime in the seventies. There was no dishwasher. There was a small white microwave on the counter and the freezer was packed full of Nutrisystem food. Obviously Richard wasn't much of a cook.

Considering the condition of the rest of the house, Gil fully expected the kitchen to be filthy. It was not. There was no junk on the floor and no dirty dishes in the sink. The counter was clean and the microwave wasn't greasy. There was a dish drainer with a few clean dishes sitting in it—a single plate, a single glass, a single set of eating utensils. It reminded Gil of his own kitchen. Yes, this guy definitely lived alone.

The kitchen was far enough from the living room that the odor of putrid flesh didn't penetrate. But the other smell, the one Gil had noticed earlier, was much stronger in this part of the house than it had been in the living room. Just outside the kitchen door in a hallway that evidently led to the bedrooms, he found a closed door that he assumed to be a possible broom closet.

When he opened the door, the stench was almost overpowering. Covering his mouth and nose, Gil groped for the light switch using his pen. When the light came on, he found he was standing at the top of a set of planked wooden stairs that led down into a true garbage dump. In the living room, the trash made a layer on the floor that was walkable. Here the heap was tall enough to come halfway up the steps, tall enough to reach Gil's shoulders if not his head. And on the steps were the faint fuzzy footprints he had seen before. The blood must have been nearly dry when the transfer was made. The prints ventured down only three steps then they turned and returned the way they had come. Whoever it was had considered wading into the garbage in search of whatever it was they wanted. But they hadn't wanted it badly enough to go digging through the garbage. No doubt the stench had proved to be too much for the killer just as it did for Gil.

Stepping back, he switched the light back off and then slammed the door shut behind him. Shutting the door didn't fix the problem. Even with it closed, the smell was still overpowering. It was almost as though the smell had leached into the wallboard and wooden trim. Gil wished fervently that Masters had offered him more than just that one cigar.

Unfortunately, at this particular crime scene, cigars were limited, only one to a customer.

26

Los Angeles, California

Ali left the hotel to drive to Laguna Beach as mad at B. Simpson as she had ever been.

When she started reading the High Noon material, the item on top had been a copy of the e-mail Brenda had sent to her on Friday that she had in turn passed along to B. She read through that. There was nothing at all that indicated anything out of the ordinary. It was lucid. There were none of the self-justifying excuses that are often employed by someone intent on doing something stupid. In fact, the message was exactly the opposite of that—purposeful, organized, and with no senseless meanderings that would indicate a drunken rant. Yes, Camilla Gastellum believed her daughter had gone off on a bender. If so, the decision to do that had come after she sent the e-mail rather than before.

Next up was the Richard Lowensdale background check—the same material that had been sent to Brenda almost five months previously. A copy of that had been sent to Ali as well. It contained nothing new, nothing unforeseen.

Ermina's background check came next, and it contained only

the bare bones of the story. She had been born in Croatia. There was nothing that explained how she had been orphaned. The story picked up again once she was adopted by a family in Missouri as a teenager. The adoptive mother died of heart disease a couple of years later, and the father committed suicide. Ermina moved to California and was doing minimum wage catering jobs when she hooked up with a widower named Mark Blaylock.

So far so good, Ali thought. *Sounds like it was time for her to have some good luck.*

But clearly the luck had recently turned bad once more. Their business, Rutherford International, had gone bust. In the documents section of the report, Ali found information about the Blaylocks' bankruptcy proceedings, foreclosure proceedings on their home in La Jolla, property tax information on a home in Salton City, California, as well as a puzzling document certifying Rutherford's contractual dismantling of forty-six UAVs, which was evidently shorthand for *unmanned aerial vehicles,* otherwise known as drones, as the form helpfully explained for the uninitiated.

Since Richard Lowensdale had previously worked for Rutherford and, as a consequence, the Blaylocks, there was nothing at all in Ermina's background report that gave any hint about why Brenda had been seeking the information or if her inquiry about Ermina Blaylock had in any way contributed to Brenda's sudden disappearance. There was a puzzling notation at the end of the report that said Stuart Ramey was awaiting more information from Missouri and would be sending that along as soon as it was available. Did Ali want him to fax it to her, or would it be all right for him to forward it to her cell?

She sent him an e-mail saying to send the information to her iPhone.

But then she hit the bottom set of papers, and that's when it all went bad. Those sheets were evidently additions to the original background check—they carried the same date stamp—but the material recounted there contained information Ali had never seen before. Apparently Richard had been "cyberdating" any number of women at the time he was involved with Brenda. Stuart Ramey was a skilled hacker who had managed to gain access to both Richard's numerous e-mail accounts as well as his computer.

The Storyboard material Ali read there was nothing short of stunning. It included transcripts of supposedly private e-mails and instant messages that Richard had added to the files as they came in. In each case Richard was Richard, but the last names varied. All of the last names started with an *L*, and Ali was certain those were simply convenient aliases.

Ali remembered clearly how dismayed she had been when she learned Brenda Riley had been engaged to a man she had never met, but Brenda was certainly not alone. By Ali's count there were over fifty women listed in the Storyboard file. A quick survey through the collected correspondence showed that most of the women involved were under the impression that Richard Whatever was their heaven-sent soul mate. More than once Ali saw discussions of possible ring purchases with Internet links leading to possible candidates.

Not surprisingly, Ali found Ermina Blaylock's name listed in the Storyboard index, but when she checked the file, it contained little information other than Ermina's name, her date of birth, and social security number, which Richard Lowensdale probably shouldn't have had.

On the one hand it was infuriating that Richard Lowensdale had preyed on needy women by exploiting them through their various weaknesses. No wonder Brenda had wanted to expose him. No wonder she was writing a book on cyberstalking. Why wouldn't she? But that still didn't explain why she had gone missing. Maybe Richard had learned what she was doing. If he had threatened her somehow, maybe Brenda wasn't out drinking. Maybe she was in hiding.

But what really got to Ali and what sent her temper boiling was the fact that this extra material had been available for months. Ali hadn't seen it, and most likely Brenda hadn't seen it either. Ali had requested that original background check, but what she and Brenda had been given was a severely edited version, a redacted version.

Seeing red, Ali picked up her phone and dialed B.'s cell phone. She was prepared to leave him an irate message. She wasn't prepared for him to answer the phone.

"Hey," he said. "I'm on a break. I was just getting ready to call you."

"You'll be sorry," Ali said. "You're in deep doo-doo at the moment."

"Me? What have I done?"

"It's not what you did; it's what you didn't do. I believe this is called a sin of omission."

"What are we talking about?"

"Richard Lowensdale's background check, both of them. There's the part you gave me and passed along to Brenda, and there's the part you left out. Why?"

There was a pause and a sigh. "It was a judgment call," B. said at last. "My judgment call."

"Why?"

"The material in the background check Brenda got was from readily available sources—sources that are open to most anyone with access to a computer. The other stuff Stuart dug up was a little dicier."

"You mean the stuff Stuart hacked."

"Yes," B. said. "The stuff he hacked. As I remember, he found evidence of a number of girlfriends Brenda probably didn't know about. From what you had told me about her mental state right then, I didn't think she could handle it. I was afraid learning about all that would push her over the edge. I'm the one who told Stuart to send out the ordinary background check material and leave out the rest."

"Why didn't you tell me any of this at the time?" Ali asked.

"Because right then it looked as though you were on your way to becoming a sworn police officer—an officer of the court. If you were in possession of possibly ill-gotten material, that would have been bad for you, bad for Stuart, and most likely bad for me too."

"In other words, CYA."

"Pretty much," B. said. He sounded genuinely contrite, but Ali wasn't buying it.

There must have been something in her voice that told B. the conversation was headed in a bad direction. When the call waiting sound clicked, he sounded downright relieved.

"Sorry," he said. "I've got another call. Do you mind if I take it?"

"Under the circumstances," she said, "that's probably an excellent idea."

Ali was still mad as hell as she showered, dressed, checked out of the hotel, and headed for Laguna Beach. She had no idea where she would spend the night, but she could probably find a decent spot somewhere near Velma.

That, however, wasn't what was on her mind as she drove south. It seemed to her that any decision about how to proceed with Richard Lowensdale's background check should have been hers to make and not B. Simpson's.

27

Grass Valley, California

Trying to put some distance between his nose and the smelly basement, Gil hurried down the hall. Halfway to the end he found a small bedroom stacked floor to ceiling with what appeared to be unopened moving boxes, as though the guy had recently moved in and hadn't quite gotten around to unpacking. The killer had clearly been searching for something, but Gil could imagine the perp looking at that massive wall of boxes and deciding not to bother searching there. Trying to hide something in among all those boxes would have been too much trouble.

There was a powder room off the hallway next to that first bedroom. The surprising cleanliness Gil had found in the kitchen didn't extend all the way to the bathrooms. This one was filthy. Both the sink and toilet bowl were permanently stained black with grime.

What was apparently the master bedroom was situated at the end of the hall. Next to it was a built-in linen closet. The contents of that—sheets, pillowcases, extra blankets, a quilt or two, towels, washcloths, bars of soap, and spare rolls of toilet paper—had been spilled onto the hallway floor.

Stepping around that, Gil went into the master bedroom, which was small in comparison to its counterparts in new construction. An unmade king-sized bed with a tangled mound of covers and grimy sheets occupied most of the floor space. The dresser at the foot of the bed sat against the wall with a small television set and DVD player perched on top of it.

Once again, Gil found the presence of the electronic equipment surprising. Like that in the living room, these devices—valuable electronic devices—had been left untouched. They hadn't been stolen or broken. Next to the bed was a solo bedside table. If there had been two of them at one time, its mate was missing, but every drawer in the room had been upturned and emptied, with its contents spilled out onto the floor or bed. On the table, however, along with an old-fashioned reading lamp, Gil saw a television remote, a set of car keys, and a worn leather wallet.

Picking up the wallet, Gil opened it and counted through a dozen hundred-dollar bills. He slipped the wallet into an evidence bag. Once again, this was no ordinary robbery. The wallet and car keys had been right there in plain sight.

Why not take them? Gil wondered.

The bathroom off the master bedroom was in slightly better shape than the one down the hall, but the presence of one towel bar and only one disgustingly dirty towel testified to Richard Lowensdale's solitary and unwashed existence.

The sound of voices from the front of the house told Gil that the crime scene team had arrived. By the time he returned to the living room, both the plastic bag from the victim's head and the tape gag had been removed and placed in separate evidence bags.

"Some sign of blunt force trauma here on the head," Fred Millhouse said as he dictated his initial findings while, at the same time, wielding a small handheld video recorder. "Enough to knock him out, but most likely not enough to be fatal."

While the coroner continued taping, Gil removed the wallet from the evidence bag and looked through it until he located a driver's license in a clear plastic sleeve. From the photo it looked to Gil as through the victim was definitely Richard Lowensdale, although that comparison wouldn't be enough to constitute a positive ID.

Gil closed the wallet, returned it to his evidence bag, and then added it to the growing collection of evidence being placed in a Bankers Box. He had just made a notation on the inventory sheet when he noticed that one of the CSI techs, Cindra Halliday, was about to remove the victim's iPod.

To Gil's way of thinking, Cindra looked far too young for the job, like she should have been enrolled in a high school biology class rather than being out in the field doing crime scene investigation.

"Is there any way to tell what he was listening to?" Gil asked.

The young woman shrugged. Instead of putting the device into its designated evidence bag, Cindra took it over to the table, examined a collection of power cords, chose one, and plugged in the device. A moment later, the tiny screen lit up. She shook her head. "It's called 'To All the Girls I've Loved Before' by some guy named Willie Nelson. Never heard of him. What do you think that means?"

What Cindra's question really meant was that Detective Gilbert Morris was old. Ancient, really, and out of touch. How could she *not* know Willie Nelson? How young was she?

"Beats me," Gil said wearily. "You guys do your stuff. I'm going to go talk to some of the neighbors and see if any of them noticed something out of the ordinary."

Once again grateful to leave the stink of the living room behind him, Gil had walked only as far as the front porch when Officer Dodd came through the crooked gate and started up the walkway.

"I've got the info you needed," he said, handing Gil a Post-it note. "The stuff about Ted Frost—his phone number and address."

At that point most cops would have reached for a notebook. Not Gil Morris. He took the Post-it note and stuck it to one of the cards in a leather wallet that carried not only his supply of extra three-by-five cards but a fountain pen too. Gil had inherited the pen, a Cross, from his father. The wallet had been a Father's Day present from Linda and the kids before it all went bad. Fortunately for Gil, the wallet and pen had both been in his shirt pocket the day Linda's father had shown up—unannounced as far as Gil was concerned—to move them out.

Gil liked starting his day by sitting at the kitchen counter—both the kitchen table and his rolltop desk had gone north in Linda's U-haul—and going through the ritual of filling his gold pen with that day's worth of ink. He liked taking careful notes on the blank cards. He felt that set him apart from the beat cops. Unlike Allen Dodd, Gil wouldn't have been caught dead passing out Post-it notes.

"Thanks, Allen," Gil said. "I'll give him a call."

But not right away. Gil had studied the street while he'd been standing smoking the cigar. Now he did so again, going inch by inch over the street that bordered Richard Lowensdale's fenced yard. Brittle dry grass took root at the edge of the pavement, so there was no dirt that held the possibility of finding either tire tracks from a vehicle parked in front of the house or of footprints going to or from it. There was no way to tell if the killer had parked there, coming and going in plain view of the neighbors, or if the perpetrator had parked some distance away and arrived at the victim's doorstep on foot.

Gil had directed Cindra and the rest of the CSI team to dust the gate and the doorbell as well as the front door assembly for prints, but he wasn't especially hopeful. This was a killer who had gone to a good deal of trouble to make sure there were no identifiable footprints left behind. Gil had a feeling that he would have exercised just as much care about leaving behind any latent fingerprints.

The killer had clearly spent a considerable period of time inside Richard Lowensdale's home. Either he had known his presence there was unlikely to be challenged, or he had an entirely believable reason for being there.

Gil didn't have much in common with Monk, the neurotic detective in the TV series. For one thing, as far as Gil knew, he didn't suffer from any obsessive compulsive disorders, but when it came to crime scenes, he trusted his instincts. This one struck him as exceptionally cold-blooded.

It was one thing for the Herrera brothers to get all drunked up together, shoot the shit out of one another, and, as a consequence, break their poor mother's heart. Had either of them lived long enough to be put on trial, it seemed to Gil that the charges against them would have tended more to voluntary homicide than to murder.

Richard Lowensdale's murder was on another scale entirely. What Fred Millhouse had referred to as blunt force trauma probably had been delivered for one purpose only—to disable the victim long enough for the killer to use the tape to bind him to the chair. Then, after disabling the guy, the killer had set the iPod ear buds in the guy's ears and had queued up Willie Nelson to sing the same song over and over until the device finally ran out of juice. "To All the Girls I've Loved Before."

You didn't need to be a rocket scientist (which Gil Morris wasn't) or an experienced homicide cop (which he actually was) to figure out that the killer was broadcasting a message with the choice of that particular piece of music, but what message was it? Was it from a rival or maybe a disgruntled lover?

The most chilling aspect of the whole scene had been the presence of that single out-of-place dining room chair in Richard Lowensdale's living room. Gil knew as sure as he was born that the killer had sat on that chair, waiting and watching, while Richard Lowensdale struggled for air inside the taped plastic bag. It seemed likely that he or she had stayed there until Richard gave up trying for a last gasping breath.

Murder as a spectator sport, Gil thought once more. The idea of someone doing that seemed astonishingly heartless. The house had been thoroughly searched for something, but nothing had been taken—at least not as far as Gil could tell. The model airplanes had been smashed to pieces, but the wallet and car keys were there. The electronic equipment was there.

In Richard Lowensdale's case, killing him was the main point, maybe even the only point. And the killer had gone to great lengths to make sure that the victim was helpless, that he couldn't fight back.

For the first time Gilbert Morris was forced to confront the idea that the killer might be female. Unless Richard turned out to be gay or a switch-hitter, it was likely he had been taken out by a woman, one with a very serious grudge.

Richard Lowensdale's house was the last one on the street. Just above the house was a small paved turnaround. Beyond that stood a piece of property covered with second-growth forest. Determined to learn something, Gil set off down the hill. The neighbors would have noticed the police activity around the house and he expected they would be eager to speak to him. That's how things usually worked in small towns. Most of the time witnesses were glad to come forward and help out.

Unfortunately most of the residents of Jan Road had been at work or at school on Friday afternoon. The only exception was Lowensdale's next-door neighbor, a gray-haired retiree named Harry Fulbright, who had spent part of the day out in his yard trimming an overgrown laurel hedge.

"Sure," he said. "I remember seeing the UPS driver go past here right around two thirty. Not the regular UPS guy," he added. "Ted must have been sick that day, 'cause it was earlier in the day than he usually shows up. But it was definitely UPS. Woman in a brown uniform and a brown leather jacket."

"A woman," Gil repeated. "Walking or riding?"

"Walking. The turnaround at the top of this here street is too damned small for them big trucks. Ted never drives up there, and he probably warned his substitute not to try it either."

"Can you tell me anything at all about her?"

"Not really. She was about average. Not fat, not skinny. Fairly long hair."

"What color?"

"Reddish maybe?"

"Did you see anyone else around that day?"

"Actually, now that you mention it, I think there was a second delivery later on. So maybe they made two drops at Richard's house that day."

As far as Gil was concerned, this information was all a step in the right direction.

Excusing himself to Harry, Gil went back out to the street and dialed Ted Frost's number.

"Allen Dodd told me what happened to Richard and that you might be calling," Ted said as soon as Gil introduced himself. "I'm sorry to hear it. Richard was a nice enough guy and he ordered lots of stuff. I stopped off at his house almost every day, and he's one that always gave out little presents when Christmas came around. Do you need me to come down to the station and give a statement?"

"I'll probably need you to do that eventually," Gil said. "Right now I'm just looking for a time line. What time was it when you dropped off that box from Zappos?"

"Right at the end of my shift. Around four thirty or so."

"Is there another driver who might have dropped something off earlier?"

"Not with UPS. This is my territory. As for what time I delivered it? I have a computerized log. I have to enter where and when I drop off anything. I'm definitely sure of when I made Richard's delivery."

"Why did you leave the package on the porch? Was there anyone home?"

"There was somebody inside the house. I heard a vacuum cleaner running. It was noisy. She probably didn't hear the bell."

"She?" Gil asked eagerly. "A woman? Did you see her?"

"The blinds were closed. All I could see was the entryway. I just assumed that Richard had finally gotten around to hiring himself a cleaning lady. I guess it didn't have to be a woman, though, huh? Anyway, I figured he'd got some kind of help. He sure needed it. He wasn't the best housekeeper in the world."

That, Gil thought, *is an outrageous understatement!*

"Thanks, Mr. Frost," he said aloud. "You've been most helpful."

Gil closed his phone, marched back into the house. He stopped by the entryway closet and opened the door. Inside was the old Kirby vacuum cleaner. He left the door open and walked into the living room. By then the body had been zipped into a body bag. Once the body was gone, Gil stopped to chat with the CSI techs who were busily collecting and cataloging computer equipment.

"Found several fingerprints for you," Cindra said. "Including a real clear one on the tape on the victim's mouth. Could be the victim's, could be the killer's. We'll run them through AFIS as soon as we can."

"Good," Gil said. "The sooner the better. While you're at it, be sure to pick up the vacuum cleaner in the entryway closet. Maybe we'll get lucky and find something useful inside the bag, like a missing finger, for instance. Oh, and dust it for fingerprints as well."

28

Salton City, California

Lola Cunningham had been a good cook, an excellent cook, actually, and she had been thrilled to pass those skills along to her adopted daughter. And in an effort to make Mina feel at home, Lola had tracked down a traditional Croatian recipe for *punjene paprike*, stuffed green peppers, and made it her own.

There was a lot about her adopted family and being in the Cunningham house that was repugnant for Mina, but she had loved being in the kitchen with Mama Lola, as her mother liked to be called. They would stand in the kitchen together, side by side, talking and laughing as they diced and sliced, chopped and cooked. Had Lola not died of an undiagnosed heart attack the year Mina turned sixteen, everything might have been different. Mina might have been different, but Lola's unexpected death had changed everything.

Today though, once Mark finished burying the ashes from the Weber grill, he'd probably return to the couch. Morosely silent, he'd sit there, drinking and watching some inconsequential golf tournament while Mina bustled around the kitchen. She prepared the stuffed peppers the same way Mama Lola had done—well, almost the same way—making two separate batches, one for Mark and one for Mina.

Working in the kitchen always made Mina happy. She hummed a little tune as she ground up the necessary ingredients—the beef and the pork and the onions—that would go into the green peppers she had brought home with her from San Diego for this very purpose. Finding decent green peppers or decent anything else in the godforsaken little grocery store in Salton City was pretty much impossible. She estimated that the extra doses of seasonings she added to the mix should be enough to conceal a few other things.

As she hacked the tops off peppers, Mina found herself thinking fondly of Richard. He had surprised her and proved to be far more of a man than she ever would have expected. She was sorry not to have the money back, but even so, Richard had won a measure of respect from his killer that he probably would have appreciated if he had lived long enough to know about it.

As for Mark? He was useless, spineless, and boring. His money had been a major part of his appeal. Now that the money was gone, so was the attraction. She enjoyed the prospect of torturing him with the idea that she expected him to take care of Brenda single-handedly and that she wanted him to do it tonight. It would be immensely entertaining to see him sitting there stone-faced while he struggled to come to terms with the very idea. She didn't doubt that he'd need to fill himself with some kind of liquid courage—gin most likely, gin on the rocks with a twist of lime.

Just to keep him off balance, she would pretend that everything was fine and that she believed that he'd do what she wanted. Wasn't that why she was hustling around in this grim little kitchen fixing him a sumptuous dinner?

Whenever Mina noticed that Mark's drink needed refilling, she would pick up his glass without being asked. And later, along with the brimming glasses, she would hand him one of his little blue pills. After all, Mark was an older man with a drinking problem and a much younger wife. In the shorthand of their marriage, the proffered drink was a peace offering. The little blue pill would be a bribe.

San Diego, California

Brenda awakened in the dark. She was stiff, hungry, and agonizingly thirsty. While she had been asleep, she had evidently shifted positions. The weight of her body had been resting on her imprisoned hands. As circulation returned to her hands and fingers, so did a storm of needles and pins.

"I'm going to die," she said aloud. Her voice was an unnatural croak. "I'm going to die here and alone and in the dark."

She would have wept then, but she didn't want to risk losing whatever moisture might be in her tears.

Her aching shoulder reminded her of her uncle Joe. She hadn't thought about her father's brother in years. Uncle Joe had come home after five years of being a POW of the Vietcong. His teeth were gone—broken out—and his broken limbs never healed properly. He had ended up in a wheelchair, but he had never complained. Brenda had asked him about his experiences once when she'd been putting together a Veteran's Day piece for the news.

"Yes, it was hard," he said, "but all I had to do each day was choose to live."

Returning to the States, he had refused to accept the idea that his life was over. He had gone back to school and married his high school sweetheart. He had gone on to become a teacher and a winning football coach who had taken his team to championship games year after year. He had also been the kindest and most amazingly positive man Brenda had ever met. Could she be like him?

Lying there alone, Brenda couldn't help thinking about how far she had fallen short in that regard, and she had no one to blame but herself. Losing her job and her marriage and being betrayed by Richard Lowensdale were nothing when compared to what Uncle Joe and his fellow wartime captives had endured. Unlike Uncle Joe, Brenda had capitulated. And now, when she was finally sober and getting back on her feet, this happened.

But what is this? she wondered.

Did it have something to do with Richard or with the book she was writing about him? The days before waking up in this place seemed shrouded in fog. Maybe one of the women she had interviewed had gone back to Richard and told him about *Too Good to Be True*, the book Brenda was writing. But this wasn't Richard's house. It couldn't be. This cold, hard floor was too clean.

Thinking about the unfinished book brought Brenda back to her mother. Even if she didn't let on to her sister, Brenda knew that she should have told her mother about the sale. It had been easier to keep quiet. She had kept everything about the book—her research materials, the signed contract for *Too Good to Be True*, and her laptop under lock and key in what had once been her mother's hope chest. She had carried the key with her, in her purse, because she had worried that someone—one of her mother's caregivers or even her sister—might go prying. But now her purse was gone and the key was gone. The only way anyone would be able to gain access to the chest would be to break the lock.

Brenda understood the huge debt she owed to her mother—financially and emotionally—and she fully intended to pay it all back. But not just yet. Brenda had known instinctively that with her still very fragile hold on sobriety, living on her own might well have been too much.

And so for whatever reason—whatever excuse—Brenda had kept a lid on news about the sale. Now, though, since she was probably going to sit in this chair until she died, that didn't seem like such a bad idea.

After all, Brenda had disappointed her mother more times than she could count. If Camilla didn't know about the book, she wouldn't have any unreasonable expectations. It was a blessing for Brenda to know that her mother wouldn't be disappointed.

Again.

In the darkness, Brenda drifted into something that wasn't exactly sleeping or waking. She was a girl again, maybe ten or eleven. It was a Sunday afternoon. She and her older sister were out in the driveway of her parents' house on P Street, shooting hoops at the basket that hung over the garage door.

Aunt Amy and Uncle Joe had come for dinner. As they were getting ready to go home, Uncle Joe had challenged Brenda's father to a two-on-two scrimmage, Uncle Joe in his wheelchair and Brenda against Dad and Valerie.

As Brenda fell back asleep—or into something that resembled sleep—she and Uncle Joe were winning.

29

Laguna Beach, California

By the time Ali fought her way through Sunday afternoon traffic from LAX to Laguna Beach, she'd had almost two hours to give further consideration to her conversation with B. She wasn't over it enough to call him back, but she'd come to realize that he might have had a point. Being found to be in possession of illegally hacked material probably wouldn't have been a good idea for someone who was a newly appointed officer in Sheriff Gordon Maxwell's Yavapai County Sheriff's Department. And it probably would have been a black mark against High Noon's reputation as a high-profile Internet security entity.

But still . . .

Ali's appreciated having a working GPS in her rental car. As she followed the turn-by-turn directions through very upscale neighborhoods, then onto Cliff Drive, and finally onto Lower Cliff Drive, Ali had to laugh at herself. When Velma Trimble had first appeared in the lobby of Ali's hotel years earlier, she had come in a cab and had sported a patriotic walker. The tennis balls on the legs of her walker were red, white, and blue, and a tiny American flag had been affixed to the handlebar.

Since she had arrived by cab, Ali had assumed she didn't have a car and was probably too old to drive. Looking up at Velma's multistoried, controlled-access condo with designated guest parking and spectacular ocean views, Ali could tell right off that Velma T. was anything but impoverished. Even in a down market, a condo that was within walking distance of the beach meant money—plenty of money.

Ali arrived at the gate a few minutes before three, the appointed hour. Once she punched the apartment number and the open code into a keypad, the gate swung open. Off to her left was a path that led to what looked like a covered picnic shelter on the curve of a steep bluff above the cliffs that gave the street its name. In front of her was a lobby complete with a uniformed doorman who called upstairs to announce that "Ms. Reynolds has arrived."

No, Velma T. might be dying, but she sure as hell wasn't poor.

Once on the penthouse level on the sixth floor, Ali found there were only two doors—600 and 602. Those two apartments, each with a panoramic ocean view, evidently accounted for the total number of penthouse units. Ali rang the bell on the one marked 602. The ringing bell set off an answering bark from what sounded like at least three canine residents—two large ones and at least one small noisy one.

"Quiet, everyone," Maddy Watkins ordered sternly. "Get on your rug."

Silence descended at once. Through the closed door Ali could hear the scrabbling of several sets of doggy paws on parquet floors as the dogs hurried to obey. Moments later, Maddy opened the door.

"Why, hello there," she said. "If you aren't a sight for sore eyes." Then, turning back toward the room, she said, "Velma, you're not going to believe it. Ali Reynolds has arrived in the flesh."

Maddy took Ali's arm and led her into what had once been a gracious living room but was now a hospice ward. There was a hospital bed with a rolling hydraulic lifter to aid in getting in and out of bed. There was a hospital-style IV tree and an assortment of other equipment including an oxygen concentrator and a PCA for pain relief. Next to the bed was Velma's walker with its signature patriotic decor.

The whole west-facing wall was nothing but windows that overlooked a panorama of limitless blue water, and the hospital bed had been placed in a position so that when Velma was in the bed, she could gaze out at that million-dollar view. One of the sliders had been left slightly open, allowing an ocean-scented breeze to blow into the room. Velma sat in a wheelchair that had been parked directly in front of the window. A red, white, and blue afghan covered her legs and helped fend off the draft. She looked gaunt—little more than skin on bones—and the skin that was visible was an alarming shade of yellow that Ali knew indicated the beginnings of kidney and liver failure.

"Oh, good," Velma said. Her face brightened as she turned from the window to greet Ali. "I'm so glad you're here. We were about to have our midafternoon round of Maddiccinos."

"Of what?" Ali asked.

"Frappuccinos made with lots of Bailey's," Velma said with a tired smile. "Maddy downloaded the recipe from the Internet, but we can only have those when the nurses are between shifts. They disapprove of my having liquor or coffee, although I can't see what difference it makes."

"Coming right up," Maddy said. She headed for what Ali assumed to be the kitchen. "Come," she added, speaking to the three dogs who were still on their rug command. They rose as one, Maddy's now somewhat white-faced, leggy goldens and some tiny ball of fuzz whose canine origins Ali could only guess.

"They do really well together," Velma said. "Candy is mine. She was a little upset when Maddy's interlopers first showed up, but now they're the best of friends."

Looking around the room, Ali had an instant understanding of why hospice home care was preferable to hospice care anywhere else. Velma was at home in her familiar surroundings. Her dog was here. Her stuff was here. Her view was here, and so was her good friend Maddy and her two dogs. What could be better?

From the kitchen, Ali heard the squawk of a blender as Maddy Watkins mixed the unauthorized treat. Ali moved aside a scatter of Sunday newspapers that littered half a nearby couch and took a seat.

"I'm so sorry . . . ," she began lamely, but Velma waved the comment aside.

"Nothing to be sorry about," she said. "I've had a good run. They're doing a good job of pain management. That was what scared me most—that I'd be in a lot of pain, but I'm not, and I'm reasonably lucid most of the time."

Maddy emerged from the kitchen carrying a tray filled with three rocks glasses filled with generous helpings of mocha-colored drinks. The dogs, having recovered from the arrival of a newcomer, followed docilely at her heels and arranged them-selves around the room. Candy scrambled up into Velma's lap, Aggie settled comfortably near the wheel of Velma's chair, while Daphne shadowed Maddy as she bustled around the room deliv-ering drinks.

"Make that lucid *some* of the time," Maddy corrected with a smile as she settled on the far end of the couch. "But when she sets her mind to it, she can still beat the socks off me at Scrab-ble." She held up her glass. "Cheers."

Ali raised her glass along with the others and tried not to notice the visible tremor in Velma's hand as she lifted her drink to her lips and took a tiny sip. Then she set the glass down on a nearby tray and smiled. Ali tried her drink. It tasted of coffee and chocolate and maybe a hint of whiskey, but not much more than that. Ali suspected that there was probably a thimbleful of booze in the whole blender pitcher.

"The nurses really do disapprove," Velma said. "They think Maddy is a bad influence."

Maddy raised her glass in another toast. "I am a bad influence," she agreed. "And the nurses are unanimous in their belief that a sickroom is no place for dogs, but isn't that what friends are for—to cause trouble whenever possible?"

Both women laughed at that, comfortably, the way only old friends can laugh, although Velma's laughter ended in a fit of coughing. When the spasm passed, she picked up an envelope from the same table where she had placed her glass.

"Here," Velma said, holding it in Ali's direction. "This is for you."

As Ali stood up to take the proffered envelope, her silenced iPhone vibrated in her pocket, but she ignored it. The envelope was made from thick linen-based paper and had Velma's name elegantly embossed on the flap. Ali's name was on the front, written in spidery, old-fashioned handwriting—Spencerian script.

"What's this?" Ali asked.

"Go ahead. Open it," Velma urged.

Inside Ali found a single piece of papers—a printed cashier's check in the amount of $250,000 made out to the Amelia Dougherty Askins Scholarship Fund. The scholarship program, established in honor of the mother of one of Sedona's movers and shakers, was designed to help young women from Arizona's Verde Valley go on to college. As a high school senior, Ali had gone to school on an Askins scholarship. Now, in adulthood, she administered the scholarship that had once benefited her.

Ali looked at Velma in surprise. "Thank you," she said, "but this is a lot of money. Are you sure you want to do this?"

"Absolutely," Velma confirmed with a nod. She took another sip of her drink, and it seemed as though she was somehow reenergized, more vital.

"I can say with a good deal of confidence that my son won't like it. As far as he's concerned, everything I have should come to him. Everything else will go to him, but I've noticed over the years that Carson is far more interested in accumulating than he is in doing—like a kid who collects marbles but never plays with them. Carson had the misfortune of being born with a silver spoon in his mouth, and I'm afraid he's never gotten over it. You, my dear Ali, come from humble stock. I know the kind of impact receiving that scholarship had on your life and on the lives of countless other deserving young people. I don't want that well to run dry."

The long speech seemed to have drained her. Closing her eyes, she leaned back in her chair to rest and gave the morphine pump button a discreet punch.

"That's one of the reasons Velma asked me to come down to help out," Maddy explained. "She was going to do this as an addendum to her will, but her nephew—I believe you may have met her nephew—was afraid that if she did that, Carson would hold things up in probate for as long as possible. I was able to do the legwork for her, and now she gets to have the pleasure of giving the check to you herself. But if I were you, I'd deposit that check immediately. Monday's a bank holiday, but I'd do it on Tuesday for sure."

Ali had to think for a minute before she realized that Monday was Martin Luther King Day.

"You think her son might try to make trouble?" Ali asked.

Maddy laughed. "Oh, yeah," she said with a knowing grin. "Carson is what my husband used to call a piece of work. He's going to have a conniption fit when he finds out about it, but he won't have a leg to stand on. He's a signer on all her other accounts, but she left him off one. Velma called that account her 'mad money.' It's empty now—empty and closed."

Next to the window, Velma's breathing slowed and steadied as she slipped into a morphine-induced doze. Maddy got up and shut the door. Without the breeze, Ali noticed for the first time the pervasive sickroom odors that the fragrant ocean air had kept at bay.

"How long does she have?" Ali asked.

Maddy shook her head. "No way to tell. It's already longer than Carson expected or wanted to pay for. He's the one who hired the nurses, and he's made it quite clear that they answer to him rather than her. Generally speaking, hospice is a pretty short ride, but Velma was determined to do this—to get you the money. Now she may be willing to let go."

Ali looked down at the check. The scholarship fund's investments had taken a big financial hit during the economic downturn. This unexpected infusion of cash from Velma was going to make a big difference in the program's long-term sustainability.

She slipped the envelope into her purse while, in her pocket, the silenced cell phone buzzed again. For the third time. Ali took another sip of her drink. It was delicious, if not powerful.

She set the glass down. "I should probably go," she said.

"Where are you staying?" Maddy asked.

"I'm not sure. I'm sure I'll be able to find a room somewhere."

"This is a beach town on a three-day weekend," Maddy said. "Velma was worried you wouldn't find a suitable place. There's a two-bedroom guest unit in the building. As soon as we knew you were coming, we took the liberty of reserving it for you just in case. You could stay here, of course. There's plenty of room, but with all the comings and goings overnight, I'm afraid it's not very restful."

Right that minute, the idea of not having to go look for a hotel room was appealing.

"Thank you," Ali said. "That's very generous."

Maddy got up and collected the glasses. Velma had taken only a few tiny sips from hers.

"I'll just wash up," Maddy said. "The night nurse comes on duty at four. We wouldn't want her to catch us with our Bailey's showing, although what Velma thinks is full-bore Bailey's is a very low-octane substitute. After all the excitement, she'll probably sleep for the next couple of hours. A little later, perhaps you'd like to join the dogs and me for a walk on the beach. I can manage two dogs by myself. Three is more problematic. After that you can join us for a late supper."

"A walk sounds good," Ali said, "and so does dinner."

"It won't be anything fancy," Maddy warned. "Cheese, toast, some fresh fruit. Just go downstairs and let the doorman know that you've decided to stay over. He'll give you a key and show you to the unit."

30

Grass Valley, California

It was late in the afternoon before Gil Morris finally headed back to the department. Sometime in the course of the evening, he would need to consult with the coroner's office to figure out who would be doing Richard Lowensdale's next-of-kin notifications. The problem with that was that Richard's driver's license still listed his mother, Doris Mills, as his next of kin, and Gil was pretty sure Doris was deceased.

Now that he had finally left the crime scene behind, Gil's first consideration was food. He hadn't eaten since breakfast, and he was starving, so he picked up a Subway sandwich, and on the way to his cubicle, he stopped off in the break room to grab a cup of coffee.

Rachel Hamilton from Dispatch was there ahead of him. "How's it going with lover-boy?" she asked.

He gave her a quizzical look. "Who?"

"You mean nobody's told you yet? I talked to Allen Dodd about it but then he got pulled off your case to answer another call. It turns out that dead guy of yours has two fiancées. Two! One lives somewhere in New York and the other one is from somewhere up in Oregon. What happens if they both turn up at the same time? That could turn into some kind of catfight. If you want somebody to sell tickets, here I am!"

Gil stared at Rachel in amazement. From Richard Lowens-dale's driver's license photo, he had appeared to be a pretty average-looking guy, but an average-looking guy with at least two different aliases. He also lived like a hermit in a filthy garbage dump masquerading as a house. How was it possible for someone like that to have not just one but two women on the string?

Obviously I'm missing something, Gil told himself. *I've been out of the dating game way too long.*

Since Rachel seemed to have no intention of leaving the break room, Gil didn't leave either. He poured his coffee. He could tell from the acrid smell that it was old coffee—this morning's coffee. On Sundays there weren't nearly enough coffee drinkers around the department to keep the pot fresh, but Gil was desperate.

Taking a seat across from Rachel, Gil unwrapped his sandwich.

"Where'd you hear all that?" he asked. "About Richard having two fiancées?"

"From Phyllis," Rachel said. "Phyllis Williams at the Nevada County Com Center. She took both missing persons calls. The first one was earlier this morning. That's when Phyllis asked Sandy to have officers do a welfare check. The second one came in closer to noon. Phyllis says that as far as she knows, two fiancées is some kind of record."

Rachel was eating a Twinkie. Gil wished they had Twinkies in the vending machine, but they didn't.

"It's a record all right," Gil said. "Is Phyllis still on duty?"

"Nope. Her shift ended at two."

Gil munched his sandwich and made a mental note to track Phyllis down as soon as he got back to his desk. If a pair of feuding fiancées showed up when he and the coroner had yet to have an official next-of-kin positive ID, Gil's life would be infinitely more complicated and so would Fred Millhouse's.

Not only that, the Willie Nelson component in the homicide told Gil that Lowensdale's murder might well be a love affair gone awry. The fact that the two fiancées claimed they were elsewhere at the time of Richard's death didn't count for much. Gil would need to look into both women's backgrounds to see if one or the other of them had the kind of connections that might make it plausible for a pissed-off fiancée to hire a hit man. As far as he knew, that hadn't ever happened in Grass Valley, but there was always a first time.

Once his sandwich was gone, Gil dumped out the dregs of his coffee in the kitchen sink and headed for his cubicle, where he turned on his computer. While he waited through the interminable boot-up function, Gil picked up a well-thumbed hard copy of the Nevada County Employee's directory, where he located Phyllis Williams's home phone number.

When Gil dialed, a male answered the phone. "Hey, Phyl," he called. "It's for you."

"Who is it?" Her voice came from somewhere in the noisy distance, as if the house was full of noisy kids and probably grandkids.

"Work," Gil told him. "Tell her I'm calling from work."

Phyllis came on the line soon after that. She was glad to give Gil the details she could remember from the 911 calls. He'd be listening to the tapes himself in a matter of minutes, but he knew that Phyllis was a longtime emergency operator. He wanted to hear her impressions in case she had picked up vibes from either of the women that someone less experienced might have missed.

"They both sounded like nice women," Phyllis told him. "Worried. Upset. Concerned. Too bad they were both hooked up with a lying, two-timing bastard."

Phyllis Williams also had no strong opinions.

While Gil was talking to her, the department's ponderous computer system finally managed to finish the prolonged boot-up cycle. He typed in the name Richard Stephen Lowensdale and the birth date he had jotted down after looking at the victim's driver's license. There were no citations on his record—not even so much as a parking enforcement listing.

Typing in the address on Jan Road came back with the same information he had heard from Dale Masters concerning the B & E case from early October. Once the investigation had zeroed in on a named suspect, Richard Lowensdale had declined to press charges against the woman he referred to as his troubled former fiancée. He had been advised to swear out a restraining order, but he had declined to do that.

Looks to me like you should have, Gil thought.

The next name Gil typed into the computer was Brenda Arlene Riley, and he hit a gold mine. In addition to the arrest on suspicion of breaking and entering, there were multiple moving violations, including DUIs and driving on a suspended license. Court documents listed her address as an apartment in one of the scuzzier neighborhoods in Sacramento.

"Bingo. Not two fiancées," he muttered to himself. "The count just went up to three."

Gil spent the next hour or so doing a detailed study of Brenda Riley and her arrest record. He spent a long time studying the cavalcade of mug shots. For some reason Gil couldn't quite fathom, the woman looked familiar, as though she were someone he should know. It was only when he made it back to the very first DUI arrest that he made the connection and put the name and features together. That Brenda Riley! The news babe Brenda Riley. How could someone like her be hooked up with someone like Richard Lowensdale?

Scrolling back through the mug shots in reverse order was like looking at time-lapse photographs of meth users. Each photo showed her a little more bedraggled, a little more ill-used. She had put on weight. When she had been queen of the news desk in Sacramento, Brenda Riley had been known for her perfectly blunt-cut blond hair. Now, though, the chic haircuts were clearly a thing of the past as were the blonde dye job touchups and the careful application of flaw-concealing makeup. The last piece of information Gil gleaned in his cursory overview of Brenda Riley's unhappy and swift decline was an eviction order from that scuzzy apartment.

As far as Brenda Riley was concerned, this was all very bad news, but from Gil Morris's point of view, it was terrific. He had a suspect—a real suspect, a suspect with a name. A few hours into his third homicide investigation in three days, Detective Morris felt he was on the way to solving it. All he had to do to clear his case was to track down Brenda Riley and talk to her.

Gil had a feeling that, once the guys in the lab made their way into Richard Lowensdale's computer, he'd have a way to find her. In the meantime, her old driver's license information listed her mother's address on P Street in Sacramento. That was the place to start.

Before leaving, though, he did one more pass through the computer. This time he was looking for information on Richard Lydecker, Janet Silvie's missing fiancé, and the man in Dawn Carras's life, Richard Loomis. As far as Gil could find, there was no record of either one of them, not in Grass Valley and not anywhere in California either. Both men seemed to be figments of their respective fiancées' vivid imaginings.

Finally, shutting off his computer, Gil picked up his car keys and hurried out to the parking lot. When the motor of his Crown Vic turned over, Gil checked the gas gauge. It wasn't quite on empty, but the needle showed there wasn't enough gas for him to go to Sacramento and back. Rather than leaving right away, he stopped by the motor pool long enough to fill up. He'd be better off doing that than trying to be reimbursed for a credit card charge later on.

In Randy Jackman's nickel-diming department, credit card charges—even justifiable credit card charges—had a way of being disallowed.

Same way with overtime, Gil thought grimly.

By the time this long weekend was over, he was sure to have a coming-to-God session with Chief Jackman. With any kind of luck, he'd be able to mark Richard Lowensdale's murder closed before that happened.

San Diego, California

A distant rumble awakened Brenda from a restless, dream-ridden slumber. She had been caught in a nightmare, buried alive in horrible darkness, trapped under the rubble of some catastrophic earthquake. The waking darkness was even more complete than that in her dream. The rumble, she realized, wasn't the arrival of another aftershock but the distant roar of an airplane.

Once she was fully awake, she realized that she needed to relieve herself. Desperately. Even though she'd had nothing to drink—even though she was thirsty beyond any hope of quenching—her kidneys were still trying to function. But there was no way to stand up. Her feet were still bound together. If she once left the rolling desk chair, she might never get back into it. Sitting in the chair was preferable to lying on the cold, hard floor.

Shameful as it was, she had no choice but to relieve herself. Right there. In the chair. As the pungent odor of urine filled the air, Brenda let out a strangled sob. But she didn't let herself cry for long. She couldn't afford to squander the tears.

31

Laguna Beach, California

The doorman from the lobby let Ali into a unit on the second floor. It was neat and clean, modestly furnished, and about a quarter of the size of Velma's penthouse suite. The kitchen contained a coffeepot, toaster, and microwave. There were dishes, glassware, and silverware in the kitchen cupboards as well as clean linens on the bed and in the linen closet. Ali was standing by the westward-looking windows enjoying the view when a doorbell rang, startling her.

It was the doorman again, bearing a paper grocery bag. "Mrs. Trimble's friend asked me to bring this down to you."

Taking possession of the bag, Ali looked inside it, where she found a bag of English muffins, a stick of butter, a collection of nondairy coffee creamers, and some ground coffee.

"And if you want to go for a walk on the beach," the doorman added, "Mrs. Watkins says that she and the dogs will be heading out about an hour from now. You can meet up with her down in the lobby."

"Thanks," Ali said. "I will."

Once she had stowed her groceries, Ali went out onto the deck. The setting sun warmed it enough that it was pleasant to sit there to listen to messages and answer phone calls. The first message was from her mother. Everything at home was fine. No need to call back. No news in the baby department.

Ali erased that one. Second was a contrite call from B. saying he hoped he had been forgiven. Things were better on that score. She called him back. They were evidently doomed to playing phone tag for the duration, because B. didn't answer. She left him a message telling him about Velma's situation and the amazing donation the dying woman had made to the Askins Scholarship Fund.

The third message was from Stuart Ramey. "Call me," he said.

Ali did so, immediately. "What's up?" she asked when Stu came on the line.

"Have you had a chance to look at the material I dropped off?"

Evidently B. hadn't mentioned to his second in command that there had been a big blowup between Ali and B. as a result of that so-called material.

"I skimmed through most of it," Ali said. "Why?"

"I just got off the phone with a retired homicide detective named Jim Laughlin in Jefferson City, Missouri," Stuart said. "I don't know if this has anything to do with what your friend was looking for, but I thought it was intriguing. I mentioned in the background check that Ermina's adopted parents, Sam and Lola Cunningham, died about three years after the adoption was finalized. Lola died of a heart attack. The father's death is a lot more problematic."

"What do you mean?" Ali asked.

"His cause of death was officially listed as suicide. Detective Laughlin doesn't buy that. He thinks Ermina was responsible for the father's death, but there was never enough evidence to charge her."

"What else did he say?"

"When he found out I was just looking for background information, he clammed up. I told him you were an independent investigator who was looking into the matter. He said you should give him a call."

Ali laughed aloud at that. "I'm independent, all right," she said. "Give me his number."

A few minutes later, she was talking on the phone with Detective Laughlin.

"Oh," he said, when she said her name. "You're the private investigator Mr. Ramey was telling me about."

"Yes," she said, letting his misconceptions rule the day. "I'm the one looking into Ermina Cunningham Blaylock's background."

"Some teenagers are gawky," Detective Laughlin said. "Not Ermina. She was a looker and cool as can be—cool and calculating. When people hear about someone's death, there's a right way to react and a wrong way. She got it wrong, but I could never prove it."

"The father's death was ruled a suicide. Did he leave a note?" Ali asked.

"No note. According to his friends, he was despondent after his wife's death."

"How did he die?"

"Got himself good and drunk, then he put a plastic bag over his head. It happened on a Sunday night. Ermina was evidently home at the time. She got up the next morning and went to school. When Sam didn't show up for work at his office that day and when he didn't answer the phone, his secretary stopped by to check. She's the one who found him.

"I personally went to the high school to let Ermina know what had happened. Called her out of her English class and took her to the guidance counselor's office to give her the bad news. 'Oh,' she says just as calm as can be when I told her. 'If he's dead, what's going to happen to me?' Her reaction was totally out of kilter—as though I'd just given her a weather report for the next week."

"What did happen to her?" Ali asked.

"Social services put her in a foster home for a while, but she ran away. As far as I know, she was her parents' only heir. I know she received some money from their estates when she reached her majority, but I don't know how much it was. Sam Cunningham was a well-respected attorney in town here. I suspect she picked up a fair piece of change."

"I take it Stuart Ramey had to do some digging to come up with this," Ali said.

"Ermina was never officially charged in relation to Cunningham's death," Laughlin said. "It happened a long time ago, but there are still enough people in town who are upset about what happened to him. One of them called to let me know that High Noon was making inquiries about Ermina Cunningham. I took it upon myself to call him back. Can you tell me what this is all about?"

"On Friday a friend named Brenda Riley sent me an e-mail asking me for help doing a background check on Ermina Cunningham Blaylock. Brenda disappeared shortly after sending that e-mail and she hasn't been heard from since."

"If your friend got crosswise with Ermina Cunningham," Jim Laughlin said, "you have good reason to be worried. And if there's anything I can do to help, let me know. I still have a score to settle with that girl."

Ali was still thinking about that disturbing phone call a few minutes later when her phone rang again.

"The dogs and I are downstairs waiting," Maddy Watkins said. "Care to join us?"

"Yes," Ali said. "A brisk walk on the beach is just what the doctor ordered."

32

Sacramento, California

When Gil parked in front of Camilla Gastellum's house on P Street in the early evening, it looked as though he had made the trip for nothing. The house was dark. There was no flickering glow from a television set. Having come this far, however, he refused to give up without at least ringing the doorbell.

Once on the porch, though, he thought he heard the sound of classical music coming from somewhere inside the house. He found the doorbell and rang it. Moments later he heard a faint shuffle of footsteps approaching the front door. Two lights snapped on—one in the entryway and one on the porch. The door cracked open as far as the end of a brass security chain.

As far as Gil was concerned, those security chains were worse than useless. They gave the homeowner a false sense of security. If a bad guy wanted to get inside, he would.

"Who's there?" a woman asked.

"My name is Detective Gilbert Morris," he said, holding his

ID wallet up to what he assumed was eye level. "I'm looking for Camilla Gastellum. It's about her daughter."

The security chain was disengaged with a snap, the door thrown open. A gray-haired woman, dressed in a robe and night-gown, stood exposed in the doorway. The way Camilla Gastellum squinted as she looked up at him made him think she couldn't see very well.

"Don't tell me!" she exclaimed. "Have you found Brenda? Is she all right? Come in. Please."

She stepped back and motioned Gil into the house. "Are you saying your daughter is missing?"

"Well, of course she's missing. She left on Friday morning and never came back. I've been trying since Friday night to get some-one to take a missing persons report. The last person I talked to told me that since Brenda's an adult, she doesn't have to tell me where she's going. I thought that was why you were here—that you had found her. Where did you say you're from again?"

The fact that Brenda had disappeared the morning of Rich-ard Lowensdale's murder caused a rush of excitement to course through Gil's veins, but he didn't let on.

"Grass Valley," Gil said noncommittally. "I'm with the Investi-gations Unit of the Grass Valley Police Department."

"Oh, no," Camilla said with a sigh. "Not again."

Using both hands, she reattached the security chain, then she led the way into the house, turning on lights as she went. In a room that seemed more like a parlor than a real living room, she motioned him onto an old-fashioned and exceedingly uncom-fortable horsehair couch while she settled in an wooden-armed easy chair. The source of the music was a CD player, which she muted by clicking a remote.

"When I'm here by myself, I generally sit in the dark and lis-ten to music," she explained. "I have macular degeneration. Sitting in the dark helps keep me from thinking about how much I can't see. So tell me," she added, sounding resigned, "what kind of trouble is Brenda in this time?"

"What can you tell me about Richard Lowensdale, Mrs. Gastellum?" Gil asked.

"Please," she said, "call me Camilla. Richard and Brenda were supposedly engaged for a time, but he never actually gave her a ring. It turned out that he had other girlfriends—several other girlfriends. She found that out this past October."

"That would be when she allegedly broke into his house?" Gil asked.

"She didn't 'allegedly' break into his house," Camilla said. "She really broke into his house. She started working on her book right after that—a book about something called cyberstalking. I don't know much about it, but she claims that's what Richard has been doing. And what he did to her personally really hurt her," Camilla added. "She sort of went off the deep end for a while, but I thought she was finally pulling out of it. You know, that she was starting to recover. At least that's what I was hoping. But you still haven't told me what this is all about, Mr. . . ."

"Morris," he supplied. "Detective Gilbert Morris." He removed a business card from his wallet, placed it in her hand, and closed her fingers around it. "That has all my contact information on it."

"But why are you here?"

He didn't want to lower this boom on Camilla Gastellum. She was truly an innocent bystander. Still, he had no choice.

"I need to speak to your daughter," he said. "I need to speak to Brenda."

"Why?"

"A man was murdered in Grass Valley sometime over the weekend, possibly on Friday afternoon. When I left to come here, we still hadn't established a positive ID, but indications are that our victim is Richard Lowensdale. Someone put a plastic bag over his head and taped it shut. He died of asphyxiation."

"Oh," she said. And then a moment later she added, "No, that's not possible. My daughter could never do something like that. Ever."

"Even so," Gil began, "you can see why we're interested in speaking to your daughter. She may know something."

Camilla Gastellum stood up abruptly. "You aren't here to talk to Brenda. You're here to arrest her. You think she did it."

"Mrs. Gastellum, please—"

"You need to go now," she insisted. "You're no longer welcome in this house. And the next time you come back, it had better be with a search warrant."

Camilla escorted him back to the front door. He heard the security chain lock into place as the door closed behind him. Gil headed back to Grass Valley feeling like he was making real progress. He had a suspect. True, Brenda Riley might be among the missing. He didn't for even a moment consider that Camilla Gastellum knew her daughter's whereabouts, but someone did, and Gil was determined to find that person.

In his experience, most people didn't disappear without a trace. Somewhere in Brenda's mother's house on P Street he would find a clue—an e-mail to a friend, a plane or hotel reservation—that would tell him what he needed to know. But in order to find that information and have it admissible in court, he would have to come back with a properly drawn search warrant. To get a warrant, Gil would need to have enough pieces of the puzzle in place to convince a judge that he had probable cause. Probable cause took work, sometimes a whole lot of work.

33

Grass Valley, California

On his way back to Grass Valley Gil called Fred Mill-house. "How are you doing on next of kin?" Gil asked.

"I'm getting nowhere fast," Fred said. "As far as I can tell, Lowensdale is an only child. Both of his parents are deceased, which leaves me at a bit of a loss about what to do about getting a positive ID."

"Maybe one of the neighbors will give us a hand." Stopped briefly at a stoplight, Gil shuffled through his stack of three-by-five cards. "Try getting ahold of Harry Fulbright. He's one of Lowensdale's neighbors. He's a grizzled old Vietnam War vet who clued us in on the presence of that second UPS delivery person. I'm about half an hour out," Gil added. "I'll meet you at the morgue."

Harry Fulbright and Fred Millhouse were waiting in Fred's office when Gil arrived. Once the formality of the positive ID was out of the way, Gil returned to his office and tackled the unpleasant duty of notifying both of Richard Lowensdale's fiancées that the man they knew by another last name had been murdered. Passing along that kind of news to grieving friends and relations was always difficult. In this case it was even more complicated since, in the process, he would also be revealing the fact that their supposed loved one was also a cheat.

Gil dialed the East Coast number first. It was already the middle of the night in New York, but it had to be done. He tried to be kind, but ultimately there was no way to soften the blow.

Janet Silvie listened to what he said with utter mystification. "I don't understand what you're saying," she said. "Is Richard dead or isn't he?"

"That's what I'm trying to explain," Gil said patiently. "Officers went to the address you gave the nine-one-one operator, the house on Jan Road, to do a welfare check. Once they, they discovered the body of a man who has since been positively identified as Richard Lowensdale. We can find no record of anyone named Lydecker living there. Our assumption is that Richard Lowensdale and Richard Lydecker are one and the same."

"You're wrong," Janet declared. "That's just not possible."

"If you happened to have a photo of Mr. Lydecker," Gil suggested, "perhaps you could fax it to me."

"I don't have any photos of him," Janet replied. "None at all. He's so self-conscious about the scar."

"What scar?" Gil asked.

"Richard was in a terrible car wreck when he was sixteen, just after he got his license. He was driving. His best friend was killed in the accident, and Richard was left with a terrible scar on his right cheek. He's spent his whole adult life looking at his face in the mirror every morning, seeing the scar, and remembering what he did to his friend."

"Then most likely the dead man isn't Mr. Lydecker," Gil said. "I was there at the morgue for the positive identification. There was definitely no scar visible."

"Thank God," Janet Silvie said. "I'm incredibly relieved, but if Richard—my Richard—isn't dead, where is he? If you thought you'd found him and you were wrong, does that mean no one is looking for him?"

The truth was, Gil had been looking for Richard Lydecker with all the tools at his disposal, and he had come up empty.

"You should probably call in an official missing persons report."

"But I already did that."

"No," Gil corrected. "The call you placed to the com center turned into a welfare check. I don't think it was ever passed along as a missing persons report."

"Can't you do that much at least?" Janet demanded. She sounded angry.

"Ms. Silvie," Gil explained patiently. "I'm a homicide investigator. That's what I'm doing—investigating a homicide that may or may not be related to your Mr. Lydecker. Since I know nothing about him, however, I can't do the missing persons report. I suggest you call this number tomorrow—"

"Like hell," Janet responded coldly. "Richard is my fiancé. You expect me to just sit here and do nothing? That is so not going to happen. I already called my boss and told him I'm taking a few days of personal leave. I'll be in California as soon as I can possibly make it. I'll be on the first plane out of Buffalo tomorrow morning. I'll call you back after I make the reservation and let you know what time I'll be there."

The idea that Janet Silvie was coming to Grass Valley complicated Gil's life, but it would make it far easier to interview her.

"Good," he said. "Will you want to be picked up at the airport?"

"No. I'll rent a car. If no one else is going to lift a hand looking for Richard, I need to have my own wheels so I can do it myself. My guess is that once you find that crazy woman, that Brenda, the one who was always making up terrible stories about Richard and threatening him, you'll find Richard too. They were engaged once. When Richard broke it off, she went crazy."

Gil didn't let on that Brenda Riley was among the missing, and he wasn't at all sure who was crazy and who wasn't, but he didn't argue the point. "Let me give you my phone numbers," he said. "That way you can get in touch as soon as you get to town."

After putting down the phone, he sat and stared at it for a while. He'd never had a next-of-kin notification go quite so haywire. He personally was convinced that, scar or no scar, Richard Lowensdale and Richard Lydecker were one and the same. Gil was convinced; Janet Silvie wasn't.

Shaking his head, he picked up the receiver and dialed the number for Dawn Carras in Eugene, Oregon. Once again he gave a recitation of who he was and what had happened—that the body of a murder victim, presumably Richard Lowensdale, had been found and that his investigation into the matter indicated that Lowensdale was in fact Richard Loomis, the man Dawn had reported missing earlier in the day.

Dawn heard him out in such aching silence that for a while Gil wondered if the connection had been broken.

"Did you say Lowensdale?" Dawn asked finally.

"Yes. Richard Lowensdale."

"That sounds like it could be the name she told me," Dawn said, her voice suddenly hollow and devoid of any inflection. "But if Richard had to go by another name, he probably had a very good reason."

Yes, Gil thought, *because he's a lying creep.*

"She who?" Gil asked. "Who was it who gave you that other name?"

"Brenda. Richard's ex-fiancée. Somehow she gained access to his computer, and she started calling all of Richard's friends and trying to tell us what a terrible person he was. That his name wasn't really Richard Loomis, that it was Richard Lowensdale, that he was a liar and a cheat."

Which seems to be absolutely true, Gil thought.

"How did she get inside his computer?" he asked.

"I have no idea, but I'm sure Brenda is behind whatever has happened."

Gil thought it interesting that both Janet and Dawn seemed to know about the alleged stalker, Brenda, who probably really was a stalker. It seemed unlikely, however, that Janet knew about Dawn and vice versa.

"Do you have a photo of Mr. Loomis?"

"No," she said. "Richard doesn't allow any photographs of himself."

Right, Gil thought. *The car wreck.*

"He was terribly disfigured by a campfire accident when he was younger," Dawn said. "You can imagine how painful it must be to live with that kind of disfigurement." She paused and then added, "Do you think there's a chance my Richard is still alive?"

Richard, Richard, Richard, Gil thought. *You lying turd!*

"No," Gil said. "I don't think so." It was a brutally honest answer.

"What should I do now?" Dawn said. "If I come down there, do you think I could help find him?"

With Janet Silvie already planning on flying in from Buffalo, the last thing Gil needed was for Dawn to show up as well. His investigation was already complicated enough without having two feuding fiancées land in the middle of it. He remembered what Rachel had said about selling tickets to the catfight.

"It might be best if you didn't do anything right now," he said. "If I find anything out, I'll be sure to be in touch with you."

"All right," she said quietly. Dawn sounded strangely subdued. "Thank you for calling me. I appreciate it."

Gil gave her his cell phone number in case something came

up, not that he thought anything would. He was dead tired. He was sitting there wondering if he should give up for the night and go home when Janet Silvie called back.

"Getting from here to Sacramento is going to take all day," she said. "Even if I leave here at seven-oh-five a.m., I won't be there until after six tomorrow night. That's the best I can do."

Gil was relieved to hear it. He wasn't thrilled that Janet was coming, but he hoped he had managed to deflect Dawn Carras. He stayed at the office for a while longer but not much. He was verging on putting in another twelve-hour overtime day. When Chief Jackman found out about that, he would not be thrilled.

Gil went back to his house. Opening the door, he stopped in the doorway and surveyed his desolate surroundings. There were only three pieces of furniture in the living room and that was it. Linda had left him the low-profile Ekornes recliner that she had always hated because it was so hard to get in and out of it. Truth be known, Gil loved it, but every time he settled into it and tried to relax, the phone rang. Still it was better than having no chair at all. Linda had also left Gil a single television set, his son's cast-off nineteen-inch. It was old-fashioned, definitely not high-def. It was also dying. On the right-hand side of the screen was a black border almost two inches wide. The television sat on top of the chipped brass and glass coffee table that had been deemed unworthy of moving.

That was the living room. In the kitchen he had no table, just a single stool parked by the kitchen counter. His cooking equipment included a coffeepot and his place-setting-for-one set of dishes. The only reason he still had a microwave was that it was a built-in. He had no pots and pans. No extra glasses. For bedroom furniture, he had the AeroBed that he and Linda had once used for out-of-town guests. Oh, and a pair of suitcases. When Linda removed the dresser and the chest of drawers in the bedroom, she had dumped Gil's clothes out of his drawers and into a pair of open suitcases on the bedroom floor. She had taken the washer and dryer too.

That was it. Linda had been gone for two months now. She had told him it was all about the job, but when he had driven up to Mt. Shasta to see the kids, they had told him about the new man in her life—someone she had hooked up with at last year's all-class reunion, one she had attended solo because, surprise, surprise, Gil had been working.

So here he was, living in an almost empty house on Rattlesnake Road. When he and Linda bought the house, they had gotten a great deal on it because the couple who lived there before were going through a nasty divorce. Gil probably should have thought about that and realized that a street address with the word *rattle-snake* in it was most likely a bad omen—that things probably wouldn't turn out well if they tried living there. And they hadn't.

Difficult as it was to fathom, he had fewer possessions now than he'd had in college. He had spent those two months going to work, doing his job, and feeling like a human train wreck. But today he had seen a real human train wreck, the bodily remains of Richard Lowensdale.

After spending so much time at the crime scene, Gil was appalled to see the resemblance between his place and Lowens-dale's house on Jan Road. His house didn't stink like that—he still took the garbage out to the street every week—and it wasn't overheated. All the same, it looked forlorn and empty and un-cared for, and there were several discarded newspapers on the floor next to his chair.

Someday soon he was going to have to do something about that. But right now he needed sleep, and having an AeroBed in the bedroom beat the hell out of sleeping on the floor.

34

San Diego, California

When Brenda awakened once more, enough time had passed that her clothing was no longer damp. She had no idea what time it was or if it was day or night. She wondered if she was still wearing her watch, but with her arms fastened behind her, there was no way to tell if it was on her wrist or if it had been taken from her somewhere along the way. And even if she had been able to hold it up to her face, she wouldn't have been able to see it. There was no light. Only the occasional rumble of an airplane passing overhead told her she wasn't marooned in outer space.

She tried not to think about how thirsty she was, but her mind tricked her into remembering all the words to an old country/western song that her father used to sing:

> *All day I've faced the barren waste*
> *Without a taste of water—cool, clear water.*

Even when she concentrated on something else, the unwelcome words continued to echo inside her head.

Keep a'movin', Dan.
Don't cha listen to him, Dan.
He's a devil not a man
And he spreads the burning sand with water.

How long will I last without food or water? Brenda wondered. *Six or seven days? Longer? And how long have I been here already?*

Then, just when she was ready to give up, when she was ready to pray to God and ask that in his mercy he take her, Brenda heard Uncle Joe's voice, speaking to her from across the years, his voice low and filled with quiet dignity. "All I had to do each day was choose to live."

Yes, Brenda thought as she drifted back into a feverish sleep. *That's what I choose too.*

35

Scotts Flat Reservoir, California

G rass Valley High School was generally thought to be divided into three separate but relatively equal groups—the jocks, the nerds, and the druggies. The jocks were somewhat smart and drank beer; the brainy nerds were incredibly smart. They were also geeky and drank whatever; the druggies were habitual underachievers who spent lots of time smoking grass, some of which they managed to grow themselves in out-of-the-way places.

John Connor, whose parents were big *Terminator* fans, didn't quite fit in any of the molds. He was a genuine jock—varsity football, basketball, and track. That should have put him firmly in the beer-drinking camp except for the fact that he was a born-again Christian who didn't drink anything, including coffee or tea or even soda. And although he was smart and could have been a nerd, the coffee, tea, and soda prohibitions counted against him.

John may have been "born again," but he wasn't a fanatic about it and didn't much believe in turning the other cheek, which meant that he had knocked the crap out of several guys on the JV football team before they gave up and decided they could just as well be friends. Now, as seniors with their final football season behind them and with basketball season in full swing, John and his best pals, Pete Bishop, Tony Alvarez, and Jack Whitney, were spending Sunday of their long MLK weekend celebrating Saturday night's basketball win and enjoying the fact that there was no school on Monday.

Tony's cousin worked in a liquor store. As usual, Tony had provided the single case of beer and, as usual, John was the designated driver. Pete's dad worked for Nevada County Irrigation, and Pete had grown up trailing his dad around the Scotts Flat Reservoir. On Sunday the boys followed Scotts Flat Dam Road across the dam and off into the woods to a secluded clearing where local teenagers did their illegal drinking.

Now, at eleven o'clock at night and with all the beer gone, they were heading back to town. Just east of the earthen dam, the drinkers started whining about needing a pee stop. John pulled off into a tiny parking area near the dam. While his friends went off into the woods to relieve themselves, John sauntered over to the edge of the lake. He and his father came here fishing sometimes in the summer, but now with a fringe of ice still clinging to the edge of the shoreline, fishing season seemed a long way off.

He stood there on the edge of the lake, watching a sliver of moon make a slender golden splash in the choppy water, and wondered what would happen to him; what did the future hold? John was still hoping for an appointment to West Point, but that was probably a pipe dream. Yes, John was smart and his GPA was outstanding, but his parents weren't well connected, and there were always political ramifications to consider.

So he looked at the cold water and wondered what would happen if he didn't get the appointment. Would he go on to college? He'd had a couple of scholarship offers but not enough to cover the full freight, and his folks couldn't really afford to pay his way. He could maybe try going the ROTC route or perhaps he would end up doing what his father had done and volunteer.

The water wasn't giving him much of an answer. The chill wind sliced through his letterman's jacket and made him shiver.

"Hey, John," Jack yelled at him. "We're done here. Are you coming or are you going to stand around gawking all night?"

Turning away from the water, John tripped over something soft. His eyes had adjusted to the dark enough that when he righted himself he could see the object that had tripped him was made out of leather and was most likely a purse. He looked around. There was no one in sight, no one to connect to this lost property, but then he caught a glimpse of something else—a pair of white tennis shoes, gleaming in the pale moonlight, parked at the edge of the frigid water.

For a moment John stood staring at the empty shoes. There was no other sign of life in this desolate place and no sign of a struggle either. John knew at once that if someone had gone into the water there, they had done so under their own power. They had gone in, and they hadn't come back out.

Of the four buddies in the car, John was the only one who understood the implications of suicide, from the inside out. His grandfather, his mother's father, had taken that road when he was diagnosed with terminal cancer. Gramps had left a note saying he wouldn't put his family through the pain of watching him die, so he had handled it himself. With pills. And the pain of all that—of Gramps's suicide and what had come after it—was one of the reasons the Connor tribe, previously a devout Catholic family, had abandoned Holy Mother Church and become devout Protestants.

Standing there in the moon-softened darkness, John saw the

purse and the shoes and made several calculations. If someone had committed suicide here, he should probably call the cops. With three not exactly sober eighteen-year-olds in his car—*his car*—John couldn't bring himself to do that. There would be questions: What were you doing out there in the woods in the middle of a cold January night? Who was with you? Why were you there? What did you see? All of which meant that if John did the right thing, it would be the wrong thing. He would be in trouble even though he hadn't been drinking and his friends would be in even more trouble because they had been.

But he couldn't just walk away either. That wasn't an option. Gramps had done the same thing this person had done: he had gone off into the forest by himself and taken his pills, washed down with plenty of Irish whiskey. It had taken a week to find the body—a week in the heat of summer.

John remembered vividly the terrible sense of unknowing that his whole family had lived through back then, between the time Gramps went missing and the time someone finally found him. And he remembered his grandmother sitting there in her living room, rocking back and forth and saying that she would never forgive him for going off and leaving her alone like that without even letting her say goodbye. And he remembered his mother's grief when the priest told them that since Gramps had taken his own life, there would be no mass.

John had been twelve at the time. He had been struck by the fact that the people who should have been there to help his grieving family—the cops and the priest—had made things that much worse.

John knew that somewhere nearby was a worried family waiting for answers. He also understood how much having those answers would hurt, but he knew from his own experience that knowing hurt less than not knowing. And so, without really thinking it through and without saying anything to the friends who were still waiting in the car, John reached down and grabbed up the purse and the shoes. On his way back to the driver's seat, he popped open the trunk and dropped the three items inside.

"What was that?" Jack asked.

"Nothing," John answered. "Just some trash someone left on the beach."

"That's John for you," Pete said. "Eagle Scout all the way."

Back in Grass Valley, John drove them to Pete's house, where they all went inside, watched some DVDs and hung out. The other guys finally crashed, but John didn't even try to sleep. A little past midnight he let himself out of the house. Instead of going home, he drove to the local Safeway. There, parked under one of the halogen lights at the far end of the lot, he got out the purse and brought it to the hood of his car.

It was large and made of some kind of soft leather. Intending to dump the contents out onto the hood, John was about to unzip the purse when a cell phone rang inside it. The noise startled him enough that he almost dropped the purse. Once he unzipped it, though, a foul odor spilled out of it, filling the air around him with an awful stench that was all too familiar. John had no choice but to step away from the vehicle. For the next few minutes he stood doubled over in the corner of the lot, retching onto the pavement.

He recognized the odor—the odor of death—because it was the same one that had lingered in his grandfather's old Suburban no matter what remedies his father used to get rid of it. Ultimately they'd had to total the SUV even though it ran perfectly and didn't have a scratch on it.

Finally the spasm of nausea ended. The odor was still there, slightly dissipated in the cold wind blowing down from the mountains. If there was something dead inside the purse, then maybe John was wrong about what had happened at the reservoir. Maybe the shoes by the lake didn't mean that someone had committed suicide. Yes, that was the point when John Connor definitely should have called the cops and reported what he had found, but he didn't do that. He couldn't.

There would be too many questions, ones that couldn't be answered without jeopardizing his future and his friends' futures too. But he couldn't just leave it alone either. Someone had been calling on the telephone inside the purse, looking for whoever owned the purse, and John Connor—this John Connor, not the teenager from the movies or the old TV series—was the only one who could answer that call.

Covering his mouth and nose with his shoulder, John returned to the purse and dug around inside it. Peering inside, he saw something that looked like a twig. When he pulled it out, he saw what it really was—a severed finger with a bloodied nail that gleamed in the yellowish light.

When John saw that, it was time for him to barf again.

This was far worse than he could have thought possible. With his eyes still watering, he forced himself back to searching the purse until he found the phone, an old flip Motorola. When he opened it, the message light lit up—fourteen missed calls, all of them listed as "Mom." A check of the battery life showed that it was down to a single bar.

With his hands shaking, John checked the details screen and copied the phone number into his own phone. Then, stowing the nearly dead Motorola in his shirt pocket, he zipped up the purse, locking in the odor, and returned it to the trunk. Then he punched send on his phone.

"Hello."

John breathed a sigh of relief when the man answered the phone after only one ring. He wanted to talk to a man, not a woman. It would be easier.

"Hello," the man said again. "Is anyone there?"

John cleared his throat. "I'm here," he said. "My name is John Connor. Who's this?"

"My name is Camilla Gastellum."

A woman, John thought. *A woman with a very deep voice.*

"I live up in Grass Valley," he said hurriedly. "I heard this phone ringing a little while ago. It was inside a purse I found."

"Inside a purse?" the woman asked. "A yellow leather purse?"

"Yes."

"The purse probably belongs to my daughter, Brenda. Where did you find it? And where is she?"

Those were questions John Connor didn't want to answer. "I found the purse by a lake, ma'am, a lake outside of town here. The purse was there along with a pair of tennis shoes."

There was a long pause before "They were all by themselves?"

"Yes," John said, "there was no one around at all."

"I'm down in Sacramento, and I don't drive. Could you maybe bring them to me?"

Remembering what was inside the purse, John knew he couldn't inflict that on anyone else.

"No," he said. "That won't work. I can't do that."

There was another long silence on the end of the phone. For a moment John was afraid the person had hung up, but then the silence was followed by a deep sigh.

"I'm sorry to hear that you're involved in all this, young man, but you need to do the right thing. I understand there's been a homicide in Grass Valley. The dead man's name is Richard Lowensdale. He and my daughter were involved at one time. A detective came to talk to me about this tonight. I believe his name is Morris—Detective Gilbert Morris. As much as I hate to say it, you'll need to take that purse to the police department there in Grass Valley. Talk to Detective Morris. Tell him exactly what you told me. Let him know what you found and where you found it."

John really wanted to say, "No. I can't possibly." Instead he mumbled, "Yes, ma'am. I will."

After Camilla Gastellum hung up, John stood there for a while longer, still holding his own phone and crying. He was crying because he wished he had never picked up the purse in the first place. Now, because he had made that stupid phone call on his own phone, the cops would be able to trace it back to him. Even though he hadn't done anything wrong, he'd be drawn into it. He and Pete and Tony and Jack would all end up being kicked off the basketball team. He would never go to West Point.

"Oh well," he told himself finally, "I can still enlist."

He knew where the Grass Valley Police Department was on Auburn Street, but he didn't want to go there by himself. Instead, he put the purse back in the trunk, then he went home and woke up his parents. He told them the truth, all of it.

"It's okay, son," Will Connor said, crawling out of bed and reaching for his clothes. "You did the right thing. Let me get dressed and we'll go see the cops."

36

Grass Valley, California

Detective Gil Morris had been asleep for just two hours when the phone rang at a little past one.

"What now?"

"You're needed," said Frieda Lawson, Grass Valley's night watch desk sergeant. Regardless of rank, nobody argued with Sergeant Lawson. It simply wasn't done.

"Great," Gil muttered. "Is somebody else dead?"

"That remains to be seen," Frieda said. "I've got somebody here who's asking to speak to the detective in charge of the Lowensdale case."

"That would be me, then," Gil said. "I'll be right there."

Despite the seeming urgency, he needed to clear his head. He took the time to grab a shower, wishing that he had more than just one ragged towel. He would have to do something about that very soon. He either had to buy more towels or go to the laundromat, one or the other.

He stopped off in the kitchen long enough to reload ink into his pen and to grab an additional supply of three-by-five cards.

Then he drove back to the department, watching for black ice as he went.

In the waiting room, Sergeant Lawson sat at her desk behind a glass partition. Two people rose from chairs as Gil walked into the room. Gil recognized the older man as Will Connor, the foreman at the local Discount Tire franchise. Beside him, looking miserable, stood a young man Gil also recognized. John Connor, Will's son, had been a tight end on the Grass Valley High football team and was currently a point guard on the varsity basketball team.

Will Connor stepped over to Gil and greeted him with a firm handshake. "Sorry to drag you out of bed like this," he said, "but I didn't think it should wait until morning. This is my son, John."

John stepped forward too. He held out his hand, but he averted his eyes. On the floor next to the boy's feet sat a purse, a big yellow leather purse. On the chair beside him was a paper bag.

"Do you want to come on back?" Gil asked, thinking he'd talk to them in one of the interview rooms and gesturing toward the security door that opened into the rest of the department.

"I think we'd better off doing this outside," Will Connor said.

"Why?" Gil asked. "What's going on?"

"My son found this purse earlier tonight up near the Scotts Flat Reservoir," Will said. "The purse and the shoes. I haven't looked inside the purse, but he tells me there's a finger inside there—a bloody finger. It's pretty rank."

"Crap," Gil said, reaching for his latex gloves. "Let's go outside and take a look."

Once outside, Gil offered Will and John Connor some Vicks VaporRub to put under their noses and gave himself a dose of it as well. Then he opened the purse and spilled the stinking contents into a Bankers Box he had brought outside for the purpose. He used a hemostat to gather up the bloodied finger and dropped it into an evidence bag, which he quickly closed, but isolating the finger did little to diminish the odor. It had bonded onto the leather itself, leaving the gagging stench to cloud the air. Gil zipped the purse closed. That helped some too.

At that point, John reached into his pocket and extracted a cell phone. "This was in the purse," he said. "I heard it ringing. When I tried to answer it, I found . . . that . . ." He nodded in the direction of the evidence bag.

"I called the number later on my own phone and talked to an old woman named Camilla Gastellum who lives in Sacramento. She said the purse probably belonged to her daughter and that I should bring it here and talk to you. She said her daughter's name was Brenda. Brenda Riley."

When it comes to solving homicides, Gil told himself, *I'm three for three.*

He put the lid on the Bankers Box. He would inventory all this later and then he would send it to the crime lab.

"There's a pair of shoes too," John said quickly, handing over a paper grocery bag. "Tennis shoes. I found them at the same time. They were with the purse."

"Where did you find all this treasure?" Gil asked.

Will Connor answered before his son had a chance to reply. "John and some friends were up by Scotts Flat Reservoir earlier tonight. That's where they found them. He and his buddies were just hanging out . . ."

Will was talking quickly, trying to gloss over the where, when, and why. And Gil got it. He understood. He recognized John Connor because he had seen his photo before in the sports section of the *Daily Dispatch*. The kid had a great record, and a whole lot of his future would be riding on what happened tonight.

Gil remembered how, as a kid, he had walked on the wild

side—gone to wild keggers and hung out with the wrong crowd. For a while during his senior year, it looked like he wasn't going to graduate with his class, but he managed to pull his GPA out of the fire at the last minute. Gil knew that no one would have been more surprised than his high school principal, Mr. Dortman, to learn that Gilbert Morris had grown up to be not only a cop but a well-respected homicide detective.

So Gil didn't need to ask what John Connor and his pals had been doing on a Sunday afternoon and evening at the Scotts Flat Reservoir in the middle of the winter. He already knew. They had definitely been up to no good, probably with booze or girls or both.

"Who else was there?" Gil asked.

John sighed. "Me and Tony Alvarez, Pete Bishop, and Jack Whitney."

Gil recognized those names as well. All four of the kids were starters on the Grass Valley varsity basketball team. If they got booted off the team, it was the end of what was starting to look like a championship season. Even so—even with all that at risk— John Connor had nonetheless done the right thing. He had picked up the purse and the shoes and had brought them to Gil.

"Tell me about the shoes," Gil said. He held them up to the outside light. They were Keds, white Keds. Considering what had gone on at Richard Lowensdale's house, they should have been speckled with blood. They weren't, and they weren't especially dirty either.

That struck Gil as odd. If someone had been out tramping around in the woods in them, they should have been a lot dirtier.

"They were right there on the edge of the lake," John Connor was saying. "Like somebody walked up to the water, kicked off their shoes, and went for a swim. I looked around. It's real sandy there. There could have been footprints coming and going, but I couldn't see them in the dark."

"Any sign of a struggle?"

John shook his head. "It was like she just took off her shoes and walked into the water on her own."

Gil nodded. "We'll need to check that out."

There was a problem with that. The Scotts Flat Reservoir was out in the country. That made for a whole other set of complications.

"Let's get your statement first," Gil said. "Then we'll need you to go back up to the lake so you can show us where all this went down."

Gil picked up the box and the bag. "I'll take these inside so we can maintain the chain of evidence," he said. "Then we need to go to an interview room so I can ask you some questions."

John nodded.

"I'll be recording the interview," he said. "It's important that you tell the truth. You know it's against the law to lie to a police officer."

John looked briefly at his father for guidance and then nodded again. The hopeless slump of his shoulders told Gil that the kid knew he was screwed, that he understood his hope of going to West Point was all over.

"All right," he said, sounding resigned. "Let's get this done and over with."

"Just to be clear," Gil added, "I have no particular interest in knowing what you and your friends were doing up at the reservoir tonight. You weren't drinking, were you?"

John Connor's eyes shot up and met Gil's questioning gaze. His shoulders straightened. "No, sir," he said. "I was not."

It was clearly an honest answer. John Connor had not been drinking, but that didn't mean the others hadn't been.

"Who else saw the shoes and the purse at the lake?" Gil asked.

"No one else. I was the only one."

"All right, then," Gil said, leading the way back inside. "We'll do the interview first. That shouldn't take long, and then we'll go back out to the lake so you can show me what you found where. Then we'll get you home to bed. Wouldn't want you to miss school tomorrow."

"No school tomorrow, sir," John Connor said. "Martin Luther King's birthday."

John didn't mean anything by that remark. It was informational only. Still it hit Gil like a blow to the gut. If his own kids were still here, he would have known that tomorrow was a school holiday.

"Come on," he said gruffly. "Let's get going."

During the interview, Gil asked only a few cursory questions about what John and his friends had been doing at the reservoir in the middle of the night. He let the answer "Hanging out" pass without demanding any more details. Gil focused instead on what had happened after John and his unnamed friends came back to town. How John had gone off on his own to open the purse, what he had found there, and his phone call to Camilla Gastellum.

When the interview was over, Gil picked up his phone and called one of the county detectives, Frank Escobar. He and Frank had worked together before on occasion, but they also went back a long way—back to some of those same wild high school keg parties. Gil wouldn't have to explain the situation with John Connor and his friends to Frank in any great detail.

"I've got a problem," Gil said, once Frank came on the phone. "A kid from Grass Valley was out at the Scotts Flat Reservoir tonight, hanging with a couple of his buddies. They found an abandoned purse and a pair of women's tennis shoes beside the lake. I'm thinking this could be a suicide, but according to the kid there's no sign of a body."

"Wait a minute," Frank said. "If I've got a possible suicide out in the country, what does it have to do with you?"

"It has to do with a homicide I'm working here in Grass Valley," Gil said. "The perp whacked off a few of the victim's fingers. Guess what the kid found inside the purse?"

"A finger?"

"Yes, and puked his guts out too."

"Okay," Frank said. "So my possible suicide turns out to be your possible prime suspect."

"That's it in a nutshell," Gil agreed. "So if you don't mind, once I inventory all this stuff, I'll turn it over to the crime lab for analysis. Later on, if your potential suicide turns into an actual suicide, we'll trade evidence as needed."

"Can you tell me where on the Scotts Flat Reservoir?" Frank asked.

"Somewhere close to the dam," Gil said. "I'm sure the kid can show us, but we're going to need to give him some cover on this."

"What kind of cover?"

"You tell me," Gil said. "Middle of winter, middle of the night, middle of basketball season."

"Gotcha," Frank Escobar said. "How about if you bring your confidential informant and I bring my crime scene tech and we all have a middle of the night powwow at the Scotts Flat Reservoir?"

"Sounds good to me," Gil said. "See you there."

Not wanting to have someone locked in the back seat of his unmarked vehicle, Gil let John Connor ride out to the lake in the front seat of Gil's Crown Vic with his father caravanning behind. On the way Gil couldn't help thinking both those guys were incredibly lucky: John had a great father and Will had a great son. For a change, this was a father and son duo who actually seemed to deserve one another.

At the lake, things were exactly the way John had described them. There was no sign of a struggle—and no sign of a body either. If Brenda Riley had walked into the lake and drowned herself, as cold as the water was this time of year, it could be weeks or even months before she floated back to the surface.

In the meantime, though, Gilbert Morris was hot on the trail of clearing his third case in three days. In the annals of homicide investigations, that had to be some kind of record.

37

Laguna Beach, California

While the three dogs—two big and one tiny—gamboled on the beach and darted in and out of the water, Ali walked beside Maddy Watkins.

"They make quite a pack, don't they?" Maddy observed. "I've never cared much for little dogs, but I promised Velma that I'll take Candy back to Washington with me when the time comes, which will probably be sooner than later."

"Her color's bad," Ali said.

"Yes," Maddy said. "I know."

As they walked, it had occurred to Ali that she had an odd collection of friends. Sister Anselm, Velma, and Maddy were all decades older than she was, yet she felt at ease with them in a way she couldn't understand. She remembered Aunt Evie telling her once that she, Ali, was "an old soul." Maybe being widowed in her early twenties had propelled her into a version of adulthood that usually came to people much later in life.

"Losing a friend is always hard," Ali said.

Maddy stopped walking abruptly and looked up at her.

"No," she said, shaking her head. "Not *having* a friend is what's hard. When Velma and I hooked up by accident on that round-the-world-cruise, it was a stroke of good fortune for both of us. We were by far the oldest people on the trip. There were some things we physically couldn't do, but we didn't do those things together. These past few years our friendship has been a huge blessing. I'll miss her terribly when she's gone, but I wouldn't have missed out on knowing her for the world."

Candy was the first to give up playing. She was small enough that she had to take three steps to each of the big dogs' one. She came back to Maddy and asked to be picked up and dried off. Ali did that while Maddy spent the next fifteen minutes expertly hurling a Frisbee for Aggie and Daphne to chase and fetch.

When the dogs finally tired of the game, the group walked sedately back to the condo building. Near the outdoor pool was a shower with a hose attachment. Maddy used that to remove lingering sand from the dogs' paws, then they made their way into the building through the basement garage.

By the time they got back to the apartment, the night nurse had helped move Velma from the chair to the hospital bed, but she was awake again. Maddy toweled off Candy's wet fur once more, then deposited the dog on Velma's bed.

"You keep her while I get the dog food dished up," Maddy said. "Once the dogs are fed, I'll see about rustling up some food for the humans."

Supper—a collection of cheeses, crackers, fresh grapes, and tangerines—was accompanied by glasses of chardonnay and eaten on trays in the living room. Velma barely touched her food or her wine, but at least it was offered. It was there if she wanted it. That was what Maddy offered her—the dignity of making her own choices.

They were still sitting over glasses of wine when there was a knock on the door and the dogs went into full-throated barking. Maddy gave Ali a wink.

"That will be Mr. Killjoy come to call. He doesn't like the dogs, and the feeling is entirely mutual. They don't like him either."

"Just a minute," she called. Maddy swiftly gathered glasses and trays and carried them into the kitchen. Then, before opening the door, she silenced the dogs and ordered them onto their rugs.

Ten minutes with Carson Trimble was enough to make Ali incredibly grateful for her son, Chris. Carson was arrogant and opinionated. To her misfortune, his hireling nurse had been outside smoking a cigarette when her boss arrived. He spoke mainly to her, asking the nurse pointed questions about Velma's condition rather than addressing his queries to the patient herself. He made it plain that he regarded both Maddy and Ali as unwelcome guests who should have had brains enough to go away and let his mother die in peace.

When Maddy announced that she was going to go clean up the kitchen, Ali followed.

"What a jerk!" Ali muttered.

Maddy smiled. "I told you so. He has a whole set of rules about how he expects his mother's death to play out, and it annoys him that she's doing things her way instead of his. As I said, you ever met my son, you'd think he and Carson Trimble were twins."

The mention of twins, real or not, reminded Ali that she needed to go down to her room and make some phone calls. By the time she returned to the guest suite, it was well after dark. Considering the time difference and her mother's early bedtime, she decided not to call her parents. Instead she called Chris and Athena.

"How are things?" Ali asked her son.

"Athena is already in bed but probably not asleep," he said.

"We went to Grandma and Grandpa's for dinner. That way I didn't make a mess in the kitchen. The laundry is done to the best of my ability. Athena's hospital suitcase is packed and waiting in the entryway closet."

Ali could have asked if "the best of my ability" meant that the colored clothing was improperly sorted, but she didn't. Chris had kept his color blindness a secret from her for a long time, and she decided to let that bit of family fiction go unchallenged.

"In other words, she's still a little grumpy."

"Do you think?"

"She's pregnant," Ali counseled. "If you were growing twins in your body, you'd probably be grumpy too."

"We see Dr. Dixon again on Wednesday," Chris said. "I'm hoping she'll say it's time to induce labor."

Ali heard the unreasonable assumption in what Chris said. He was hoping that once the babies were born, he'd be getting his wife back. Ali understood the reality of that particular pipe dream. Chris and Athena wouldn't be getting their previous lives back for the next eighteen or so years if ever.

"Get some sleep then," she told her son. "You're going to need it."

She spent half an hour IMing back and forth to B. He had moved from his conference hotel to a different one in downtown D.C. She brought him up to date on the day's happenings and about what she had learned from James Laughlin about Ermina Cunningham Blaylock.

She was in bed and sleeping soundly when her cell phone rang at one o'clock in the morning. Ali had left the cell plugged in and charging on the bathroom counter, so it took a few moments for her to stagger through the unfamiliar apartment to find it. She recognized the number. The call had originated at Camilla Gastellum's house, but it wasn't Camilla on the phone.

"Ali Reynolds?" the caller asked.

"Yes."

"I'm sorry to call in the middle of the night like this, but my mother insisted. I'm Valerie Sandoz, Brenda Riley's sister."

The estranged sister, Ali thought in relief. *Camilla must have called her after all.*

"Richard Lowensdale is dead," Valerie announced without further preamble.

"He's dead?" Ali asked. "When?"

"As far as I can tell, the detective didn't say when exactly. It must have happened sometime over the weekend."

"How did he die?" Ali asked.

"Somebody, Brenda most likely, put a plastic bag over his head. He suffocated."

There was a pause on the other end of the line. Ali heard Camilla's forceful objection to that conclusion rumble through the phone, but Ali was busy trying to sort out what she had just been told.

"Say again," she said.

Valerie sighed. "Somebody put a plastic bag over his head," she repeated impatiently. "The cops must think Brenda did it, since a homicide detective came here to the house looking for her. I don't think it was a social call. Naturally, Mom didn't get around to calling me until after the detective left. Brenda's been missing since Friday afternoon, and I didn't know a thing about it until Mom called me this evening.

"Then tonight, while Les and I were driving over from the Bay Area, some kid from Grass Valley called Mom too. It seems he spent this afternoon up in the mountains with some friends. According to him, he came across Brenda's shoes and purse abandoned by some lake or other. The kid found Brenda's cell phone in the purse and called Mom's number. She told him he should take it to the cops. I'm guessing Brenda knocked off Richard and then committed suicide."

Ali was trying to pay attention, but her ability to listen was hampered by what Valerie had said earlier about Richard Lowensdale's manner of death. A plastic bag over the head as a murder weapon? To Ali's way of thinking, it sounded a lot like Ermina Blaylock's dead father. In fact, it sounded *exactly* like Ermina's dead father. And if Ermina had gotten away with murder once, maybe she had decided to do so again.

Valerie was still talking when Ali started listening again.

"I tried to tell Mom we shouldn't bother you in the middle of the night this way, but she insisted. She said you were Brenda's friend—that you'd want to know."

"Your mother is right," Ali said. "I do want to know. Now about that detective who came to see your mother. Does he have a name?"

"Just a sec," Valerie said. She was off the phone for a moment, then she returned. "He left his business card. His name is Gilbert Morris. Detective Gilbert Morris. Do you want his numbers?"

Ali had gone out to the front room, where she hunted through her purse and found a pen. She jotted the name and phone number onto the back of Mina Blaylock's background check.

"All right," Ali said when she finished. "Please tell your mother thank you for having you call me. And tell her I'm sorry things are looking so bad for her, and for you too," she added.

Up to that moment, Valerie Sandoz had been all business—just the facts, ma'am, and nothing more. But those few words of sympathy from Ali were enough to crack the facade.

"Thank you," she muttered over what sounded like a sob. "Thank you very much."

Then the line went dead.

There was no question about what Ali needed to do. Checking the numbers Valerie had given her, she called the office number first and then the cell phone. In both cases she ended up reaching voice mail and left the same message. "My name is Ali Reynolds. I'm a friend of Brenda Riley. Her mother gave me this number. I understand you're investigating Richard Lowensdale's death. I may have some pertinent information. Please give me a call. Here's my number."

After leaving the messages, Ali sat on the sofa for a long time, watching a tiny sliver of moon appear in the section of midnight sky that was visible beneath the overhang of the balcony above her unit. The slender sickle of light gradually disappeared into an equally blackened sea.

I shouldn't have told Morris that I was Brenda's friend, she thought. *He probably won't even bother to call me back.*

Ali should have gone back to bed, but she didn't. She sat there for a very long time, thinking, turning over one mystifying question after another, and looking for answers. Her "gut instinct," as her friend Detective Dave Holman liked to call it, told Ali that Ermina Blaylock, not Brenda, had murdered Richard Lowensdale. But why? Had she too been duped by Richard and taken vengeance on him for playing her for a fool? And what about Brenda? Had she somehow put together the connection between Richard and Ermina? Was that what had prompted the background check request she had e-mailed to Ali shortly before her disappearance?

And what about Brenda? Ali wondered. *Did Ermina murder her too? Then again, is Brenda really dead, or is that what Ermina wants us to think?*

Ali switched on a table lamp and read through the background check one more time. There was nothing there in the written report that was the least bit damning. If it hadn't been for Stuart Ramey's going the extra mile, no one would have put two and two together. No one would have connected what happened years earlier in Missouri to what happened to Richard Lowensdale this weekend.

Which means Ermina probably has no idea anyone is on to her.

Ali studied the background check some more and found the address on Heron Ridge Drive in Salton City. That way, if and when Detective Morris called her back, she'd be able to tell him what she had learned and give him an exact physical location to search.

And then Ali remembered something else—a snippet of something Sister Anselm had told her that day when they'd had tea together. Ali couldn't remember the exact words, but it had something to do with stepping out with faith that you would be in the right place at the right time. Ali had come to California thinking she was being guided to do something for Velma Trimble, but maybe she was wrong. Maybe the real intended purpose was for her to do something about Ermina Blaylock.

If not me, Ali asked herself, *then who?*

By a quarter to five in the morning, she was dressed and ready to head out. It had been a pain in the neck, going through the process of putting her Glock in the lockbox and having a TSA agent supervise her locking it, just so she could bring it along in her checked luggage. And it had been a pain retrieving it from baggage claim at the end of the flight, but as Ali put on her small-of-back holster, she was glad to have it. Not that she intended to get into any kind of armed confrontation with Ermina Blaylock. Going after a suspect without backup was one of the dumbest things any cop could do. Still, she was glad to be prepared, just in case. As for her pal, the Count of Monte Cristo? He remained untouched in the suitcase and was likely to remain so.

After leaving the apartment, she rode up in the elevator and slid a note under the door of Velma's unit. In the note, Ali explained that she had been unexpectedly called away and would be returning later in the day. In the lobby she encountered a sleepy doorman who was able to check the schedule of the guest unit. No, it was not booked for tonight, and yes, she could stay in it for the remainder of the week if she wanted. It wasn't booked again until the following Friday.

Driving north to the ten, she remembered that she had never returned her mother's previous phone call. By now, Edie would have taken the first batches of sweet rolls out of the Sugarloaf's ovens and would be getting ready to open the doors.

With her Bluetooth in her ear, Ali speed-dialed her mother's cell phone.

"Is this about the babies?" Edie asked anxiously. "Is Athena in labor?"

"It's not about Athena," Ali said with a laugh. "I'm just now getting around to returning your call."

"Oh," Edie said. "It's about time. I thought you had fallen off the edge of the earth."

"Close to it," Ali said. "I'm on my way to Salton City. You'll never guess what happened. Do you remember Velma Trimble?"

"One of the two old ladies who came to the wedding? Was she the one with the dogs?"

"No," Ali said. "Velma's the other one. She's had a recurrence of cancer, and she's in hospice care at home. Mom, she gave me a two-hundred-fifty-thousand-dollar donation for the Askins Scholarship Fund."

"I'm sorry to hear she's so bad off, but bless her heart," Edie said. "What a wonderfully generous thing to do. But why are you going to Salton City? I was there once, years ago with your father. Back then it seemed like the end of the earth."

I'm pretty sure it still is, Ali thought.

"Do you remember last summer when my friend Brenda Riley showed up down in Phoenix?" she asked.

"The one with the boyfriend troubles and the drinking problem?"

"The very one," Ali replied. "Now her former boyfriend, Richard Lowensdale, has been murdered. Brenda is high on the list of suspects, but I may have come up with another possible suspect who lives in Salton City. I'm just going over to have a look."

"Do you have your Taser along?" Edie asked. "And have you done a spark check recently? You know what they say, 'No spark, no zap.'"

"Yes," Ali said, smiling. "I've got plenty of spark."

"Oops," Edie said. "Customers at the door. Gotta go. You take care."

38

Grass Valley, California

After coming back from the reservoir at five a.m., Gil managed to grab three hours of sleep. Once he was up, he found he was out of cereal and milk, so he made do with a bologna sandwich and a cup of coffee.

Sitting at the breakfast counter, he listened to a message that had come in to his cell phone overnight. He hadn't heard it because the phone had been in the other room on the charger. The caller, someone named Ali Reynolds, claimed to be a friend of Brenda Riley's.

Just what I need right now, Gil thought. *Somebody else telling me that poor, sweet Brenda would never do such a terrible thing.*

Yes, Gil would call Ali Reynolds back—eventually. When he was good and ready. Right now, though, it took all his flagging energy to drag himself to the Nevada County Crime Lab.

"So what's the deal with the amputated finger from Scotts Flat Reservoir?" he asked Mona Hendricks, the chief criminalist in charge of the lab.

"It's a thumb, not a finger," Mona corrected, studying Gil over the top of a chipped coffee cup.

"Well, excuse me all to hell," Gil said. "It looked like a finger to me."

Mona ignored his sarcasm and added some of her own. "Anybody ever mention that you look like crap this morning?"

Gibes from Mona went with the territory.

"Thank you so much for the update. Let's just say I'm overworked, underpaid, and missing a lot of sleep at the moment."

Mona grinned back at him. "I don't think the underpaid part is going to wash. If you've got as much overtime in as I think you do, Randy Jackman is going to have a cow."

Randolph Jackman was the Grass Valley chief of police and Gilbert Morris's boss. Jackman was nothing if not a political animal. He had moved up in the world of law enforcement not on the patrol side as a cop on the streets but on the administrative side. His view of the world was firmly aligned with the bean counters of the world; he was more a city manager type than a Sergeant Joe Friday. Gil already knew that the overtime he had logged that weekend was going to be a headache, but when you stacked the OT up against three solved homicides, he figured he was all to the good.

"Let me worry about Jackman," Gil said. "Tell me about the thumb. Does it belong to Richard Lowensdale?"

"I believe so," Mona told him. "I had my people dust the wall next to the toilet in Lowensdale's bathroom. That's always a good place to pick up usable prints. On the wall we found prints that match the two fingers that were found at the crime scene, and there are prints that match the thumb print too. So, yes, that would mean this thumb also belongs to Lowensdale unless there were two people using the facilities at that address who are both going around getting fingers whacked off."

"Let's hope not," Gil said sincerely.

Mona rolled her eyes. "That was a joke, Gilly! Get yourself

some coffee and get on the beam. Of course it's Lowensdale's thumb. There aren't any other damned prints in the whole house. Lowensdale was the only person living there, and whoever killed him was wearing gloves."

"I've got two women who claim their missing fiancées lived at that same address—Richard Lydecker and Richard Loomis."

"They're mistaken," Mona said decisively. "I'm telling you Richard Lowensdale was the only resident. We didn't find anyone else's prints anywhere in that house."

It annoyed Gil to think he was so tired that he'd totally misread Mona's black humor remark.

"But here's what I don't understand," Mona said. "Why would someone do that?"

"Do what?"

"Leave a bloody thumb to rot inside a perfectly good purse?"

"I don't know the answer to that either," Gil admitted. "But I'm going to find out. Having the thumb match my homicide victim gives me enough probable cause to ask for a search warrant. So that's my next step—getting a warrant to search Brenda Riley's residence."

"Today," Mona said, smiling.

"Of course today. First thing."

"Good luck with that," Mona said. "You do know it's a holiday, right? If it hadn't been for your damned thumb, I wouldn't be here either. I don't think you're going to find many judges at your beck and call at the moment. Do yourself a big favor, Gilly. Take the rest of the day off. Get your search warrant tomorrow; execute it tomorrow."

"No," Gil said. "I'll get it today." He started to leave, then turned back to her. "What about the computer? Did you find anything on that?"

Mona shook her head. "Nope. Not a thing. Someone reformatted the hard drive about four o'clock on Friday afternoon. There's nothing left on it at all. Since he was a Mac user, your victim might have used iDisk or some other kind of web-based backup system, but to gain access to that, you'll need his passwords."

Good luck with that, Gil told himself.

"That reformatting timetable is within an hour or two of what Millhouse estimates the time of death. That also means there probably was something on the computer," Gil said. "Something incriminating that the killer didn't want us to see. What about the vacuum cleaner?"

"No prints. We opened up the bag. Didn't find much in it. Looks like it hadn't been used in a very long time."

Remembering the mess inside Richard's house, that seemed more than likely.

"But the motor's burned up," Mona added. "Like somebody turned it on and left it standing in one place in the living room until it overheated. It's a wonder it didn't burn the place down."

"If they weren't cleaning, what were they doing?"

"Have you ever used a vacuum cleaner, Gilly?"

"Not that I remember."

"Kirbys are supposed to be excellent for cleaning but they're very high on the noise scale. I think maybe the killer was using the vacuum for noise cover."

Remembering what Ted Frost, the real UPS driver, had told him, Gil nodded. "I'll bet you're right," he said.

Gil left the lab and went straight back to the department to draw up his request for a search warrant. Yes, he knew it was a holiday, and no, he didn't care. That had always been one of Linda's major complaints about him. She claimed he was too stubborn, too bullheaded. That once he got an idea in his head, he wouldn't let it go. This was probably more of the same. Gil was determined to find a judge who would sign off on his request for a warrant, and he would, holiday or not.

At ten a.m. Gil had his warrant request in hand and was on his way to track down District Court Judge William Osborne when Sergeant Kathleen Andersson, the Sunday day shift desk sergeant, stopped him on his way out the door.

"Chief Jackman wants to see you," Kathleen said.

"But I'm on my way to pick up a search warrant," Gil argued.

"Take my advice," Kathleen told him. "This didn't sound like an invitation—more like an order. ASAP."

More like a summons to the principal's office, Gil thought. Reluctantly, he reversed course and headed for the chief's office.

"I hear you've been a very busy boy this weekend," Chief Jackman said when Gil entered his office. "From what I see on the time clock, you worked damned near around the clock for three days."

"Three homicides in three days means working round the clock, and since I'm the only guy on the Investigations Unit who's in right now—"

"Good work on the first two," Jackman interrupted, "but I've got to tell you, we can't handle this kind of expense. It's unfortunate that Investigations is so shorthanded at the moment, but while your team members are legitimately off work for one reason or another, they're still on my payroll. In the meantime, you're running up enough overtime that it's turning into a budget disaster."

It seemed to Gil that the chief would have been better off mentioning that to the killers who made the messes rather than to the cop charged with cleaning them up. That's what he thought, but he didn't mention it aloud, because Jackman didn't leave room in his rant for any kind of reply.

"And don't you go tracking Judge Osborne down at home

today either," Jackman continued. "He just called to tell me you were on your way. He read me the riot act about it. He and his wife are trying to have a relaxing day off. The last thing they need is you turning up on their front porch."

"I need a search warrant," Gil explained, "for a person of interest in the Richard Lowensdale homicide."

"Yes," Jackman said. "By all means, let's talk about that." He clicked a few buttons on his computer. "That would be for the residence of one Brenda Arlene Riley on P Street in Sacramento, correct?"

Gil nodded.

"And your person of interest would be the same person who apparently went for a one-way swim in the Scotts Flat Reservoir over the weekend."

"We don't know for sure that it's a case of suicide," Gil began. "Yes, Brenda Riley's personal effects—her purse and her shoes—were found next to the lake, but as far as her committing suicide—"

"Do you personally know of a single woman who would just walk away from her shoes and purse for no reason? Here's some news from the front, Detective Morris. Your prime suspect offed herself. She left her shoes and purse there as a message, and not a message for you either. It's just a fluke that the Connor kid brought the purse to you, but if she did commit suicide, that's the county's problem and not ours. Your pal, Detective Escobar, can be the guy who pisses off Judge Osborne. We don't have to. Let him be the one who goes to Sacramento to search her house. That way it's on the county's budget, not the city's."

In other words, this was a budgetary issue that had nothing to do with the real world of justice, crime, or punishment.

"So here's what I'm thinking," Jackman continued. "I want you to stand down, Detective Morris. Take the rest of the day off. Get some sleep. In other words, no more damned overtime! And before you start writing checks on all this accumulated OT, you might want to think twice. Once your unit members get their butts back on the job, you can take it out in comp time. Fair enough?"

It wasn't fair, but this was a rhetorical question that came with an obligatory answer. Right or wrong had nothing to do with it. "Yes, sir," Gil said.

"Very well then," Jackman said. "Do us all a favor and head home."

Still steaming, Detective Gilbert Morris did exactly that.

39

Salton City, California

In the old days, Ali had sped around on L.A. area freeways with wild abandon. Today, as she made her way north to the ten and then east toward Salton City, she was glad to have the rental's GPS giving her play-by-play directions. It was early enough on a holiday morning that people weren't yet creating their own day-off rush hour traffic jams. The only downside was that she did much of the three-hour-plus drive heading straight into the rising sun—a blinding rising sun.

Not sure what kind of food she would find available in Salton City, Ali stopped off in Palm Springs for close to an hour to have breakfast and take on a load of coffee. By the time she turned onto Heron Ridge Drive, it was verging on nine thirty. Heron Ridge Drive was far longer than she expected, winding north along the edge of the Salton Sea. The name had a grand sound to it. The reality was nothing short of grim. Yes, there were clusters of motor homes parked here and there, but most of the few permanent structures looked as though they weren't long for the world.

At least, that seemed to be the case until Ali caught sight

of the Blaylock place, which looked more like a fortress than a house. The windows and doors of the structure were covered with closed roll-down shutters—metal roll-down shutters. It occurred to Ali that although they weren't exactly aesthetically pleasing, they were probably downright impervious. A silver sedan of some kind was parked in the driveway. Other than that, the place looked deserted. Abandoned. It didn't seem likely that anyone would be inside the structure with all the shutters rolled down and buttoned up. Too dark. Too hot. Too claustrophobic.

Ali drove past once. Then she turned around in another driveway about half a mile farther on. As she drove past the Blaylock driveway a second time, she was startled to see a beefy woman standing in the middle of the street with her hands planted on her hips. When Ali started to drive past, the woman flagged her down.

Ali pulled up next to her, stopped, and rolled down her window.

"Can I help you?" the woman asked.

"I was looking for the Blaylocks," Ali lied. "Mark and Ermina."

"That's their place over there," the woman said, pointing toward the roll-down shutter marvel. "Nobody's home. I saw her leave first thing this morning. She was all alone in that big old Lincoln of hers. I don't know where Mark is. His car is here, which usually means that he's here too, but I can't imagine he'd be inside the house with all those shutters down all the way. One thing for sure, he wasn't in the Lincoln with that battle-axe of his when she left. Who are you?"

The woman went from volunteering information to demanding it in one easy segue.

Ali didn't want to make the mistake of impersonating a police officer. With all the Blaylocks' burgeoning financial difficulties, it wasn't too much of a stretch to pretend to be the minion of a circling creditor. And the way the woman referred to Ermina implied there was no love lost between this frowsy neighbor in her faded tracksuit and Ermina Blaylock.

"It's actually about her Lincoln," Ali said confidentially. "There's a lien on it. I'm doing some scouting for the repo company."

"You mean to tell me Miss High and Mighty is about to lose that fancy car of hers?" the woman said with a wide-faced grin. "Don't that just beat all! And it would serve her right too. Care for a cup of coffee? I just made a new pot."

Ali could hardly believe her luck. She held out her hand. "Coffee would be nice," she said. "My name is Ali Reynolds, by the way."

"Like that old baseball player from Oklahoma?"

"No," Ali said. "I'm Ali with one *L* not two. And you?"

"Florence Haywood," the woman said. "Most people call me Flossie. Just pull right in and park in the driveway. Jimmy went off to play keno at the casino. He won't be back for hours."

All her life Ali had marveled at her mother's ability to know everything that went on in town and outside it. From Edie Larson's station behind the lunch counter at the Sugarloaf Café, she managed to keep her finger on the pulse of everything that went on in and around the Verde Valley. At the police academy down in Peoria, Ali had sat through several classes on the ins and outs of conducting interrogations, but nothing she had been taught there could hold a candle to what she had learned at her mother's knee.

Ali knew at once that Flossie was golden. She was nosy, she was lonely, and she hated Ermina Blaylock's guts. From Ali's point of view, that was definitely a win-win-win situation.

40

Grass Valley, California

Chief Jackman had ordered Gil to go home for the day in no uncertain terms. When Gil did so, he left his city-owned Crown Vic in the departmental parking lot and headed home in his bedraggled five-year-old Camry, which had been sitting forlorn and abandoned in the city parking lot since Gil had been called out to the Herrera brothers crime scene on Friday afternoon.

On the way, Gil drove past Target. A few blocks beyond that, he made up his mind. Pulling a quick U-turn, he went back and parked in front of the store. He wasn't sure how much room was left on his Visa card, but he was about to find out.

Pushing a shopping cart, Gil marched through the homemaking aisles on the first genuine shopping spree of his entire life. He bought a set of dishes—four place settings of all blue dishes because blue was his favorite color and a set of silverware for four, stainless not silver of course. He picked up a set of twelve glasses—four each of three different sizes. He bought a toaster—$29.95—a dish drainer, a nonstick set of fry pans, a couple of spatulas, and a laundry basket. He bought two bath towels, two hand towels, and two washcloths as well as a new shower curtain to replace the moldy one with several missing rivets that currently hung in his bathroom.

Gil bought himself a new set of plain white sheets, a fitted sheet and a flat one that came with a pair of matching pillowcases. Then, just for good measure, he bought one of those bed-in-a-bag things that came with a blue plaid comforter and a couple of decorative pillows. At least from now on his damned AeroBed would look like a real bed. He also bought a four-drawer dresser that came in a box, some assembly required.

When he got to the checkout stand, he held back on the dresser just in case he ran out of room on his credit card. Fortunately, the charge went through without a hitch. Now, thank God and Visa, the time for Gil Morris to keep his clothing in one of Linda's discarded suitcases was finally a thing of the past.

He was alone now. It was high time he started living his own alone life.

Leaving Target, just for good measure and just because he could, Gil made two more stops on the way home. He went to the grocery store and replenished his supply of bread, cereal, milk, and cleaning supplies. Then he stopped by the liquor store and picked up a box of fifty Antonio y Cleopatra cigars. He was determined that the next time he had to show up at a crime scene, he would be the one handing out the smokes.

Before Linda took off, one of the things that had always mystified Gil about the woman was that whenever she was pissed at him, she turned into a housecleaning demon. In the past Gil had dreaded those cleaning marathons because he understood that the cleaner the house got, the more trouble he was usually in.

That Monday morning Gilbert Morris finally started to understand it. Huffing on one of the previously prohibited cigars and using his old cracked dinner plate as an ashtray, Gil went to work. He swept; he mopped; he dusted; he scrubbed. He decided that once he paid off his credit card purchases, he was going to buy himself a new television set, maybe even a baby flatscreen. He had seen some of those on sale at Target too and was surprised by how little they cost.

He unwrapped the dishes as well as the glasses and the silverware and ran them all through the dishwasher. He put his dirty clothes into the laundry basket along with his dirty sheets. He threw away his musty bath towel, the dead shower curtain, and his ragged, much-used sheets. He knew that Linda would never have considered putting new sheets and pillowcases on the bed without laundering them first, but Linda had taken the washer and dryer. Gil would be damned if he'd go to the laundromat and spend good money washing and drying brand-new sheets and pillowcases. He would sleep on them as is.

Linda had left the toilet bowl brush behind, but no toilet bowl cleaner. Fortunately he had picked up some of that at the grocery store. He didn't want his toilet bowel to resemble the ones he had seen in Richard Lowensdale's house. It took several tries and lots of scrubbing before, to his immense satisfaction, the stubborn stains finally disappeared.

He cleaned the bathroom sink until it gleamed and did the same thing to the porcelain sink in the kitchen. By then the dishwasher had run through its cycle. With the dishes still almost too hot to handle, Gil took them out and arranged them in the cupboard the way that suited him best, with the plates on the upper shelf and the glasses and cups on the lower one. This was his kitchen now; Gil would do things his way, not Linda's way.

The relatively mindless work of cleaning and scrubbing allowed plenty of time for thinking. Maybe that was what Linda had always known—the link between cleaning and thinking.

Gil let his mind wander back through the intricacies of those two somehow intertwined cases—Richard Lowensdale's murder and Brenda Riley's apparent suicide. Some of the puzzle pieces didn't make sense. For one thing, a luminol test of the shoes from the Scotts Flat Reservoir showed no sign of blood spatter of any kind. The booties might have accounted for that. Still, with as much blood as Gil had found on the scene, it surprised him that there were no traces at all. And for shoes that had evidently walked through the woods, the soles had been pristinely clean, with no dirt or gravel caught in the tread.

Since John Connor had handled the purse, Gil had been obliged to take a set of elimination fingerprints on the boy, but he was relatively sure that his manner of questioning John had left the kid—a good kid, evidently—plenty of wiggle room. There had been no questions about John's friends in the interview, and no mention of them in Gil's written report either. There was no reason to suspect that John and his friends were in any way responsible for what had happened to Brenda.

What mystified Gil most, however, were the contents of the purse, all of which he had carefully inventoried. It was the usual women's purse junk—a compact, several tubes of lipsticks, all the same color, two packages of new tissues as well as a loose collection of old ones, a change purse along with some loose change, a package of dental floss, some aspirin, several pens, a tampon container, and a wallet. The wallet contained four twenty-dollar bills, one credit card in Brenda's mother's name, and three crumbling photos—one of a man and a woman and a twenty-fifth wedding anniversary cake, and two high school senior photos of two women who looked very much alike. From the hairstyles Gil estimated that the photos were most likely of Brenda herself and maybe a female relative. A sister, maybe?

But what didn't fit in with all that was the bloodied thumb.

Why had Brenda taken it along to begin with? Without the thumb, it seemed likely that she would have gotten away with killing Richard Lowensdale. After all, as far as Gil had been able to discover, there was no physical evidence linking Brenda to the crime.

So what was the point of taking that one piece of incriminating evidence with her? Yes, killers often collected trophies, but collecting trophies and then committing suicide seemed illogical. After all, if Brenda was going to kill herself, why would she torture her poor mother by leaving behind the unmistakable message that her beloved daughter was also a murderer? That made no sense.

And then there was the purse itself. Gilbert was hardly a connoisseur of such things, but he knew that purses—even cheap ones—weren't free. Why would Brenda have decided to wreck hers? To Gil's unpracticed eye, the soft leather purse seemed expensive, but it was wrecked now. Because of the bloodied thumb, it now stank to the high heavens.

While returning all the separate inventoried items to the evidence box, Gil had picked up the tampon holder. On a whim, he pulled it open. Yes, there were two paper-wrapped tampons inside the plastic container, but there was also something else. A key of some kind, a key that could have been to a locker, perhaps, or maybe even a desk.

Gil had planned on taking the key to the crime lab later in the day to see if Mona and her crime techs could track down where it came from or what it opened. That, of course, was before Chief Jackman had sent Gil home, so chasing after the key was something that would have to wait for another day.

When it came time to tackle the dresser, Gil opened the box, fished out the directions, and determined what tools he would need—a Phillips screwdriver and an Allen wrench. With those in mind, Gil headed for the garage.

Had Linda made off with her husband's bright red rolling tool chest or if she had emptied it, there would have been all-out war. With two cars in the garage there had been barely enough room for both vehicles to park side by side. That had left the tool chest virtually inaccessible and had rendered the workbench under the window completely useless. Rather than a haven, the garage had become a passageway, good only for coming and going.

With Linda and the kids gone, Gil could have worked in the garage, but he hadn't. What had once been Linda's parking place was still stacked with a collection of stuff—items both loose and in boxes—that she had intended to take to Goodwill right up until she ran out of time. Other than that sad stack of discards, however, the garage was discouragingly neat—exhibiting the kind of cleanliness born of omission rather than effort, disuse rather than use.

As Gil opened the top drawer to retrieve his Phillips screwdriver, he had a sudden realization. Unlike Richard Lowensdale's house, the victim's garage had been clean—absolutely clean, utterly clean, with no trash on the floor and nothing out of place. For someone as messy as Richard, that could only mean that other than parking his car there, he never used it.

There had been no tools lying loose on his workbench, as in none at all—not a single one. Yes, there had been the smell of oil, but it was old oil, ancient oil. Still, Gil remembered clearly that there had been what appeared to be a whole case of motor oil—yellow plastic bottles of motor oil—on a shelf over that workbench. Why?

It seemed inconceivable that someone who left trash lying three inches deep on his living room floor and who dumped garbage down the stairs into his basement rather than hauling it out to the street would turn out to be a shade tree mechanic who did his own periodic automotive maintenance on the side. If Richard

Lowensdale couldn't be bothered with scrubbing out his filthy toilet, he sure as hell wasn't going to change his own oil.

With his heart beating hard in his chest, Gil left the Phillips screwdriver untouched in the drawer. On the surface this seemed like only the vaguest of hunches. It was hardly likely that Richard Lowensdale would have left anything of real value hiding in plain sight in his unlocked garage, but maybe he had. Gil was certain that the killer had searched for something all over the house without ever once venturing into that garage.

Chief Jackman's dressing down still echoed in Gil's consciousness. There was no way he was going to call in one of the uniformed officers to go check out his lead. If he was wrong and it came to nothing, then no one would be the wiser. If that happened, Gil would come straight home and finish assembling his dresser.

If he was right, though, and if there was something to be found in Richard Lowensdale's garage, Gil would see where that clue led him.

On the clock or off it, Detective Gilbert Morris was going back to work.

41

Salton City, California

On Sunday Mina sat at the kitchen table, drinking coffee, thinking about her life and listening to Mark's booze-fueled snores, which echoed from the bedroom and filled the whole cabin. She had no idea what time he had come home. She had awakened only when he finally came into the bedroom and crawled into bed beside her. That's when she had gotten up, gone outside, lit the fire in his precious barbecue grill, and burned up everything she had brought home from Grass Valley—the surgical booties, the blood-spattered clothing, and the Time Capsule. It was gone. By now the ashes should be almost cool enough to dump them out and bury in the beach's fine loose sand.

She sat at the remains of their once-grand dining room table. In the past the table had graced the immense dining room in their home in La Jolla. Polished to a high gloss and with all its leaves extended, the table with its inlaid mother-of-pearl trim had easily accommodated a dozen guests under a magnificent chandelier. Now, without the leaves, it was hardly larger than a card table. It sat in this grim excuse for a kitchen with its once-fine finish marred by scars left behind by the occasional cup of hot coffee or even a cigarette burn or two.

Mina had always hated the cabin. When she and Mark had lived in La Jolla, she'd never wanted to join him on his monthly outings to this desolate place. It was too rustic, too remote, too much like the childhood home she remembered from long ago. She had always been happy to let Mark go off on his weekends of "roughing it," because Mina knew too much about real roughing it. She didn't need to pretend. Besides, between having some time alone in the luxury of her water-view La Jolla home or making do in the gritty rusticity of the Salton City cabin, there had been no contest, not for her now and certainly not back then when there had been a choice in the matter.

At the moment, however, the choice part had been removed from the equation. In the face of forced bankruptcy, the cabin was all they had left—at least on paper, at least as far as Mark knew, as far as their creditors knew. The bank had taken the house back and most of the furnishings had been sold on consignment. They had been allowed to bring along a few pieces of decent furniture to replace the cabin's oddball collection of outdoor plastic.

Along with the humbled and shrunken table, they had brought with them a brown leather couch and matching easy chair that hadn't seemed all that large in their old living room but now seemed huge and occupied far too much of their diminished floor space. There was room enough for only two side tables, one at one end of the couch and one next to the chair. That one held Mina's precious laptop. The other served as Mark's drinks table as well as the spot for his collection of remote controls. He had installed a flat-screen TV on the living room wall. They had planned on keeping their king-sized bed, but it wouldn't fit inside the cabin's tiny bedroom. They'd had to settle for a queen-sized bed from one of their old guest rooms.

Mark was stuck in the past, grieving for everything they had lost. Mina was moving forward.

His snoring stopped abruptly, and she heard him stumble out of bed. Soon he appeared in the doorway of the bedroom, with his hair standing on end and his clothing rumpled. He had come to bed without bothering to undress.

He went over to the fridge, pulled out a beer, and opened it, spraying foam on the wall and floor, which he didn't feel obliged to clean up.

"Hair of the dog," he said unnecessarily.

"Where were you?" she asked.

"Busy," he said with a shrug. "You know how it is. Reprogramming the UAVs took longer than I expected."

"Right," she said. "I'll just bet it did."

Mark was hopeless when it came to lying. As he hurried over to the couch and reached for the television remote, Mina saw the deep flush that spread up his neck. She knew that she had nailed him, but she left him alone long enough for him to go surfing through the channels until he happened upon a golf tournament.

"Does that mean the UAVs are all reprogrammed?" she asked.

"Yes. All of them."

She was gratified that Mark didn't bother trying to explain what he'd been doing since then. Mina was convinced she already knew. He had been screwing his brains out with some bimbo or another. Besides, she had already seen the packaged UAVs with her own eyes, even though she'd had to move them herself. She hadn't dared leave them in the cage with Brenda there as well. Mina didn't believe Brenda would manage to get loose and damage them, but she didn't want to run the risk either.

"Good," she said. "About the UAVs, I mean. I figured you would have called me if there was a problem. And I already talked to Enrique. I told him we'd have them ready for pickup on Tuesday evening."

Mark nodded. "Good," he said. "It'll be good to finally have them out of our hair." Then, in a limp effort to keep Mina from questioning his absence, he tried changing the subject. "How did it go with Richard?" he asked.

Mina shrugged. "It could have gone better," she said.

"Why?" Mark asked, sounding worried. "What happened?"

"Richard Lowensdale is dead."

Mark sucked in his breath. "Dead? How can that be? Who killed him?"

"Who do you think killed him," Mina replied, "the Tooth Fairy? I asked him to give back the money we'd paid him. I asked him very nicely, but he wouldn't do it, so I killed him. I put a bag over his head, taped it shut, and waited until he stopped breathing."

Mina knew better than to tell Mark about the kitchen shears and the fingers. She hadn't a doubt in the world that hearing those ugly details would make the man puke.

As it was, Mark looked as though he was ready to cry. "Why did you do that? Are you crazy?"

"Hardly," Mina said. "You said yourself that you were worried we couldn't trust him, and I decided you were right. We couldn't. I also decided that once he was dead, he wouldn't have any use for our money. I looked all over his house, trying to find where he might have hidden it, but I couldn't find it." Mina shrugged. "No biggie, though. It's only fifty thou."

Mark was almost hyperventilating. His breath came in short, sharp gasps. She hoped he wouldn't have a heart attack and die. That would spoil Mina's fun.

"But what if the cops make the connection and come looking for us?" Mark objected. "What if Richard tried to double-cross us? What if he kept backups of the work he did for us that will lead investigators straight here? What then?"

"Do you think I'm stupid? Of course Richard kept backups," Mina replied. "He was that kind of guy, but I reformatted his hard drive. I also stole his Time Capsule. Had a big bonfire right here on the beach early this morning while you were sleeping the sleep of the dead. I burned up the capsule and I burned up the clothing I was wearing when I killed him. The ashes should be cool by now. I want you to go outside and bury them."

"Where?"

"Where do you think? Over on the beach. No one will pay any attention. People bury bonfire ashes there all the time."

Mark studied his wife. He seemed confused, as though he wasn't sure if she was telling him the truth.

"I don't believe any of this," he said at last. "You're kidding, right? Running me up the flagpole because I stayed out late?"

"I'm not kidding," she said. "Not kidding at all. But don't worry. They won't come after us. I've got the perfect fall guy for us—a fall woman, for that matter."

"Who?"

"Brenda Riley, Richard's old girlfriend."

"The one who came to the office looking for him a year or so after we let him go?"

"One and the same."

"You think you can pin this on her?"

"I don't just think we can pin it on her," Mina said. "I know we can. In fact, we already have."

She was careful to underscore the word "we." She wanted to let that one sink in. She wanted Mark to get the message. She wasn't going to let him get off easy simply by burying the ashes from her bonfire. She wanted to force Mark to accept the fact that he was an active player in all this, that he too was culpable.

"I don't understand," he said. "How do we frame her?"

"By providing blood evidence, which I've already done. There's only one tiny problem."

"What's that?"

"Right this minute, Brenda Riley is still alive. At least she's probably still alive. Somebody needs to kill her and ditch the body in some spot out here in the middle of the desert where no one will think to go looking."

"Who would do such a thing?" Mark asked. He sounded horrified.

Mina laughed outright. "Kill her and bury her? Oh, you poor baby," she said. "Who do you think? Do you think I'm going to do all the dirty work for you? I killed Richard Lowensdale. Now it's your turn. You kill Brenda Riley and get rid of her body, then we're even, fifty-fifty. And Tuesday night, once Enrique gives us our new IDs, we're gone. Out of here. Both of us together. Otherwise, somebody might be left holding the bag."

"I can't do that," Mark croaked. "I've never killed anyone in my life."

"It's not that difficult," Mina said. "I'm sure you can figure it out."

"Where is she?"

"In San Diego in the assembly room. I locked her inside the parts cage. She hasn't had food or water since Friday, so she's probably pretty thirsty right about now. And cold. I doubt she'll be in any condition to put up much of a fight."

Mark stared at Mina in apparent disbelief. "You can't be serious," Mark said. "You can't possibly mean this."

"Oh, but I do," Mina told him. "I mean every word."

He stared at her for the better part of a minute, then he raced for the bathroom. Mina listened while he puked his guts out. It did her heart good to hear it.

Richard Lowensdale hadn't had a clue about the dangers of messing around with Mina Blaylock. Neither did Mark. Sadly, Richard had already learned his very important lesson on that score, and Mark was about to do the same. Even if Richard had given up the money, Mina would have killed him anyway. The same thing was true for Mark as well, but he had yet to figure it out.

He had been a dead man walking long before he decided to screw around on her Friday night, but now there was more to it. Of course she would kill him, but before that happened she intended to toy with him a little.

He came back out of the bathroom still looking green—green and haunted. Mina knew he was a beaten man. So did he.

"Where are you going?" she asked as he headed for the outside door.

"To get my wheelbarrow," he said. "The wheelbarrow and a shovel."

42

Borrego Springs, California

Just after six on Monday morning, Mina closed the shutters on the Salton City cabin for the last time. She had every expectation that no one would go looking inside the place for a very long time. She left the house wearing a track suit and taking nothing but her purse and a single briefcase. Not that there was anything of value in the briefcase—only Lola Cunningham's cookbook. Mina had long since smuggled the contents of her safe out of the house. Everything that could be converted to cash had been, and all the cash, in turn, had been sent along to her numbered account.

She took Highway 78 west toward Julian and Escondido. Along the way, she looked for likely places to dump a body. Mina's original plan had been to fake Brenda's suicide by dumping the unconscious woman into the Scotts Flat Reservoir beyond Grass Valley on Friday evening. She had managed to unload both Brenda's purse and her shoes and was about to wrestle Brenda herself out of the trunk when everything had gone to hell. Some people—kids most likely—had turned up at a most inopportune time, leaving Mina no choice but to slam the trunk shut and drive off.

Mina prided herself on coping under pressure. With no other dumping places scoped out in advance, she'd felt she had no choice but to bring Brenda with her on the long drive back to San Diego. On the way Mina rationalized that things would probably work out for the best after all. It seemed likely that the abandoned shoes and purse would lead the local hick authorities to conclude that Brenda Riley, Richard Lowensdale's presumed murderer, had committed suicide. That assumption would hold regardless of whether her body ever surfaced.

Mina had gotten a kick out of tormenting Mark with the idea that she expected him to do the dirty work for her, but that had never been in the cards. She had known all along that he didn't have the stomach for it. She did.

It was a shame that Mina hadn't hooked up with someone like Enrique Gallegos to begin with. Compared to Mark, Enrique was a far more suitable partner, someone who did what he said he would do when he said he would do it. Mina had enjoyed doing business with him.

In exchange for the UAVs, Enrique had given her money. As a side deal, he had agreed to supply her with a specific set of illicit drugs without making any inquiries as to how she intended to use them. Finally, and for a steep price, he had delivered a set of impressively well-forged documents.

Mina's new passport, dog-eared and thoroughly worn, contained Mina's photograph, but the bearer of same was identified as one Sophia Stanhope, the divorced former wife of a British diplomat. Sophia herself hailed from Bosnia, with a home address in Sarajevo. Mina had no idea how Enrique had managed all those little details, and she didn't want to know, but according to the official-looking immigration stamps in the passport, Sophia had arrived in the United States via Cabo San Lucas two weeks earlier and was scheduled to depart for home on board an Air France transatlantic flight on Tuesday evening.

This evening she would have her final meeting with Enrique. He would give her receipts for the last transfers of money while she, in turn, would hand over a key to the warehouse and the alarm code. Tomorrow evening, about the time Mina was boarding her flight for Paris, Enrique would send a crew to Engineer Road to pick up the UAVs.

And sometime much later tonight, long after her meeting with Enrique ended, Mina would go to the warehouse, drag Brenda out of it dead or alive, and dump her somewhere in the Anza-Borrego wilderness where no one was likely to find the body.

Tomorrow, with all of Mina's hard work finished, Sophia Stanhope would go shopping and field-test her brand-new credit cards and ID. Mina had left the cabin in Salton City with nothing. Had she carried loads of luggage out of the house and into the car, she might have raised suspicion. On Tuesday she would do some serious shopping, probably at South Coast Plaza, where she would know no one. It pleased her to realize that she needed everything and she could afford everything: new underwear, new lingerie, new shoes, new makeup, new perfume, new clothes. And she'd also need some new luggage to transport all her purchases.

Mina was looking forward to that leisurely shopping spree. She'd be able to take her time, without Mark rolling his eyes at the expense or pointing at his watch to move her along. When Mina and Mark were first together, he had enjoyed spoiling her. He had given her carte blanche to buy whatever she had wanted. She, in turn, had loved every minute of it. Once money got scarce, though, and Mark started pinching pennies, it wasn't nearly as much fun. Too bad, Marky. Bye-bye.

Bottom line, most men were probably pretty much like Mark, she realized—fine to begin with, maybe even pleasant, but eventually troublesome, boring, and ultimately inconvenient. If you were lucky enough to be a woman with money of your own, why bother?

A few miles beyond the turnoff to Borrego Springs, Mina noticed a spot where the road had been straightened, leaving behind a generous pullout. She stopped there and walked over to the edge. Beyond the shoulder of the road was a steep drop-off that ended in a rock-strewn desert wash some fifty yards below. She was looking out at a stark landscape that remained largely unchanged since the days of a Spanish explorer, Juan Bautista de Anza.

Mina realized then that she would need something to contain the body. A bedroll might work, preferably a brown bedroll that would blend in with the desert surroundings. And she'd also need a way of making sure the body stayed inside the bedroll as it tumbled down the embankment.

Back in the Lincoln, Mina marked the location as a destination on her portable GPS. She'd be coming back here late tonight. This was the perfect spot, and she didn't want to miss it in the dark.

43

San Diego, California

When Brenda awakened again she was wet. Or at least slightly damp. And she had befouled herself as well. She could smell it, but there was nothing she could do. That was the thing about being in the dark. Sometimes she was awake, but mostly she slept or maybe it just seemed like she slept. It was hard to tell the difference.

She tried not to think about her kidneys shutting down, but they would. Eventually she would lapse into unconsciousness. At this point, that seemed like a welcome idea. At least she wouldn't feel the torture of hunger and thirst.

The temperature in the room hadn't changed, but she was hot now. Burning. So she was probably running a fever. Whenever she thought about it, she tried to flex her ankles. Wasn't that what people did on long plane trips so they didn't develop blood clots in their legs that could go to their hearts and lungs and kill them? But again, dying didn't seem like such a bad idea. At least it would be over.

Sometime long ago she had talked to . . . no, she had interviewed—there had been lights and cameras—a man who had spent days lost in the snowy Sierras. He had talked movingly about how hard it had been to resist the temptation to simply lie down in the snow and let the cold have its way with him.

This was the same thing even though it was just the opposite. She had loved Uncle Joe with all her heart, but she could never live up to the standard of courage he had set. She was no longer willing to choose to live that one more day. She was done. All she wanted was one thing—for it to be over.

Salton City, California

Once Flossie Haywood started talking, there was no stopping her.

"We've been coming here for years, and we've known Mark Blaylock all along since before his first wife died. His missus is Miss Johnny-come-lately around here. She couldn't be bothered slumming it, and we never saw hide nor hair of her until about three months ago, when she showed up with a U-Haul truck full of furniture from their other house."

"From the one they lost in La Jolla?" Ali asked.

It was important to put in bits and pieces of the story herself from time to time, so Flossie would feel like this was a conversation rather than a question-and-answer session.

Flossie nodded. "All kinds of fancy-schmancy stuff. And what did she do with the old stuff Mark had used for years? Tossed it out on the side of the street. Some Mexicans came by in pickup trucks and gathered it all up. Probably took it down to El Centro or Brawley and sold it at the swap meet. It was good enough to use, of course. Jimmy was going to go over and rescue some of the plastic chairs and the like. I told him if he did that, I wouldn't speak to him for a week. I wouldn't give a woman like that any more reason to look down her nose at us than she already had. I'll be damned if I'd be seen picking up her leavings. More coffee?"

Ali nodded and pushed her cup in Flossie's direction. "Please," she said. "Great coffee."

Flossie nodded. "Folgers," she said. "I can't stand all that Starbucks rigamarole. Five bucks for a cup of coffee? No way! So where was I?"

"She was moving her furniture into the house."

"Oh, yes. Her furniture. And that's it. Furniture, but no appliances. No washer or dryer. I'm good friends with Selma Thurgood, who runs the laundromat. It's one of those wash-it-and-fold-it kinds of places. I like to go there to save on water. That way we don't have to go into town to empty our tanks as often. And it's fun sitting around the laundromat jawing with people from all over the country while you wait for your clothes to finish up.

"Selma has a dry-cleaning service that comes over from Indio twice a week, to pick up and drop off. She told me she never did a lick of business with Mina Blaylock. She must take hers somewhere else. She sure as hell doesn't do her own washing and ironing at home."

"You call her Mina?" Ali asked.

"That's what Mark calls her. Short for Ermina. I mostly don't talk to her one way or the other. For one thing, she treats that poor husband of hers like he's so much crap. Jimmy Haywood may not be the brightest match in the box, but he married me and stuck by me, and he gets my respect, every day of the year. You don't see me taking off for days at a time a couple of times a month and leaving him out here batching it. That just ain't right.

"And if you ask me, Mark Blaylock is just a regular sort of guy. His first wife died, you know, and he married Mina on the rebound. Wouldn't be surprised if he's lived to regret it. He used to invite us over for a beer now and then, or a barbecue, but not since she rode in on her broom."

"What's the deal with the shutters?" Ali asked.

"There was a big fish die-off a few years back. This whole place stunk to the high heaven. People just had to walk away and leave their places for a while 'cause they couldn't stand to live in 'em. Of course, it wasn't enough to keep the damned looters out. They came through and stole everything that wasn't nailed down. After that a lot of people just gave up and didn't bother comin' back. Not Mark. He said he'd be damned if he was going to let the bad guys chase him away. That's when he installed the shutters. You ever seen things like that?"

"On shops in some places," Ali said. "Never on houses."

"It's the neatest thing. It works on something like a TV clicker, but it's even smaller. All you have to do is push the up and down buttons and them shutters just slide up and down as smooth as you please. I tried it once too," Flossie confided. "But don't tell Jimmy. He'd be mad enough to chew nails."

"You tried it?" Ali asked.

"Sure. Mark drinks some. He came home one night and had misplaced his clicker—not his television clicker, his shutter clicker. And there he was, stuck. Had to sleep the rest of the night in his car. He was pissed as hell about it. So he went out the next day and got himself a replacement—two replacements, actually. One to keep in his car and one to keep in a fake light fixture out in his carport. He told Jimmy about the extra, in case something went wrong with his house—like an electrical fire or something—so Jimmy and I could let the firemen inside to put it out.

"So one day, when Mark wasn't here and when Jimmy wasn't here either, I went over and tried it for myself. Works like a charm. They go up and down as smooth as glass with just the touch of a button. If I ever have another house that isn't a motor home, I'm going to get me a set of shutters just like 'em."

"My company is worried that Mina is trying to pull a fast one," Ali said.

"You mean like take the car and make a run for it?"

Ali nodded.

Flossie shook her head. "I saw her leave. She didn't have no luggage with her. Just her purse and a briefcase and what she was wearing. That was it."

Ali let her breath out. "That's good news then," she said. "And you haven't noticed anything unusual the past few days?"

"Well, let's see," Flossie said. "Mark was gone overnight this week. Friday night, I think it was. That's unusual for him. He's pretty much a stay-at-home. And then, there was the fire."

"Fire?"

"Middle of the night, Sunday morning, a little after three, I wake up smelling smoke. Believe me, you can't buy smoke detectors better than I am. Anyway, I look out the window, and there Little Miss Hissy Fit is tossing stuff into Mark's barbecue grill and it's burning like crazy."

"You could see all this from here?" Ali asked.

"Since I got my cataracts fixed, my eyesight is downright amazing. So I look out there, and she's got this roaring fire going in the grill. Like a bonfire. Only it stank to the high heavens. Mark only burns mesquite in his grill. He's like a purist or something. But she must have put some kind of plastic crap in there. That's what it smelled like. Burning plastic. I wanted to turn her in to somebody for burning garbage like that. We have waste management here. There's no excuse, but Jimmy told me to be a good neighbor and keep quiet, so I did.

"But then yesterday afternoon, what do I see? Poor Mark is out there in the yard wrestling with that Weber grill of his.

He loaded all the ashes in a wheelbarrow. Took 'em over to the beach, dug a hole, and buried 'em. We could go take a look if you want."

"What do you mean?"

"I was curious. So after Jimmy went off to the casino, I went over there with his metal detector. Screamed like a banshee, so there must be metal of some kind down there. I was going to wait for Jimmy to come home to check it out, but I know how to work the business end of a shovel. Want to go take a look?"

"Absolutely," Ali said. "Sounds like a great idea."

44

Grass Valley, California

There was yellow crime scene tape plastered across the front porch of Richard Lowensdale's house. There was crime scene tape strung across the broken front gate. There was no crime scene tape on the driveway or on the side entrance into the garage.

Donning yet another pair of latex gloves—he would need to go to the supply room for a set of refills soon—Gil let himself into the musty garage. The ten-year-old Catera was still in the same spot. Gil couldn't help wondering who would take the car, or would it be left here to molder away?

The oil was exactly where Gil remembered seeing it—on a wooden shelf over the workbench. It was in a cardboard box that had been cut off so that the bottles stood half exposed above their cardboard container. Reaching up, Gil pulled the first one out of its corner spot. The heft of it, the play of the heavy liquid inside the plastic, told Gil that he was wrong. What was in his hand was, as advertised, a bottle of premium motor oil with, according to the buzz on the bottle, an engine-cleaning chemical additive.

There were a dozen bottles in the box—four wide and three

deep. And all of the bottles in the front row clearly contained oil. The same held true for three of the bottles in the second row. When he picked up the fourth one, however, it seemed lighter than air, and instead of ponderous liquid, there was something or maybe two somethings inside the bottle that rattled when Gil shook the container. At first glance, the bottle appeared to be unopened. There was still a manufacturer's seal over the cap, but the bottle had clearly been tampered with.

Gil returned that bottle to its place and tried the first bottle in the back row. Like the one with the rattle, this one weighed considerably less than the bottles filled with oil, and whatever was inside this one wasn't liquid. It rustled when Gil shook it. Something inside went up and down with a kind of thump, but the noise didn't resemble the rattle in the other bottle. Whatever was inside this one took up far more space.

The second bottle in the back row was similarly loaded. The last two were entirely empty. No rattle, no thump.

Gil returned all the bottles to the cardboard container, then he lifted it down from the shelf. Because the load wasn't evenly distributed, he almost spilled it out onto the workbench. Then he lugged it out the door and down the driveway to his Camry, where he loaded it into the trunk.

He drove straight home and carried the box of bottles into the garage, where he placed them on his own workbench. After switching on his overhead work light, he examined the bottles from the back two rows. Under the rays of the lamp, it was easy to see that the bottoms of some of the bottles had been tampered with—cut through with something sharp and then glued back together.

Gil started with the one that had rattled. The glue, probably some of Richard's model airplane building epoxy, had created a bond, but not enough of one that it was impervious. Gil fastened the bottle upside down in a vise. Then, using a well sharpened wood chisel and an ordinary hammer, he gave the glued surface a sharp whack. The bottom gave way and disappeared into the bottle. Reaching inside, Gil pulled out the plastic bottom as well as two small items. Gil didn't regard himself as any kind of technical genius, but he recognized a pair of computer thumb drives when he saw them.

Setting those aside, Gil performed the same operation with one of the two thumper bottles. When the bottom gave way, it fell into the bottle, but only an inch or two, not nearly as far as the one with the thumb drives. It took some effort on Gil's part to coax the bottom piece back out of the bottle. Then, removing the bottle from the vise, Gil whacked the open end several times on the top surface of his workbench. On the third try, a sheaf of money came shooting out through the opening—a stack of hundred-dollar bills.

For a moment all Gil could do was stare. The pile of money lying there on his workbench was more cash in one place than he had ever seen before. He performed the same operation on the next bottle with similar results, and with a stack of money that was almost equal in size to the first one. Of the two remaining bottles, both empty, both had been cut open but not glued back together.

Standing and looking at the cash as well as the empty bottles, Detective Morris was able to draw several interesting conclusions. Richard Lowensdale had been involved in some kind of illicit behavior for which he was being paid in cash. His killer had come to the house expecting to find it and had, presumably, gone away empty-handed. That was what the missing fingers were all about. The killer had tortured Lowensdale expecting him to reveal his hiding place, and he had not.

So what was Brenda Riley's role in all this? Was she an active participant in what Richard had been doing? Had they been part-ners of some kind, and Brenda had betrayed him? Or had Brenda somehow stumbled upon what was going on and ended up in jeopardy right along with Richard? And did Brenda's part in this whole puzzle have anything to do with the key that she had kept hidden in her tampon container?

Thoughtfully, Gil put the two thumb drives in the front pocket of his jeans. He didn't have a computer at home. The family desktop had decamped to Mt. Shasta City with Linda and the kids. As for the money? Gil returned that to the applicable bottles and put the bottles back in the box. Then, he hefted the loaded box of oil up to the top shelf over his own workbench.

From where Gil was standing, it looked for the world like a perfectly innocent case of oil. He really was the kind of guy who still did his own oil changes.

45

Salton City, California

Curious, Ali followed Flossie Haywood as she trudged across the road and through the rock-strewn sandy shoreline. Flossie carried the shovel. Ali lugged the metal detector, which she found to be surprisingly heavy.

But the walk gave her some time to consider. Richard Lowensdale's murder had taken place on Friday. Mina had lit her middle-of-the-night bonfire sometime overnight between Saturday and Sunday. What if she was burning evidence? Or trying to burn evidence? If Ali encouraged Flossie to dig up the leavings—or if she even allowed it—there was a good possibility they would both be tampering with possible evidence in a criminal proceeding. Ali wanted to know what Ermina Blaylock had been burning in the worst way. That was Ali—plain Ali. But the one who was almost a cop—almost a sworn officer—didn't want to do anything that might make it easier for Mina to get away with what she had done and whatever she was hiding, regardless of what it was.

"Here, I think," Flossie said. "Hand me the metal detector."

For several long seconds she ran it a few inches above the fine sand. Eventually it started alarming. "See there?" Flossie said. "I told you so."

She reached for the shovel, but Ali held it out of reach. "We can't do this," she said.

"Yes, we can," Flossie said. "I was raised on a farm. I was shoveling manure before I learned how to read and write."

"It's not the digging," Ali said. "It's possible that this may be important evidence. If we disturb it in any way, and if Ermina Blaylock has committed a crime, our messing with the evidence might make it impossible for a district attorney to convict her."

Flossie stood stock-still. "Are you saying you think she's done something wrong? I mean something really wrong, not just disrespecting her husband. You mean like something against the law?"

"Yes," Ali said, "that's exactly what I mean, and I don't want to be responsible for letting her get away with it."

"Neither do I," Flossie said. "So what do we do?"

"Get a rock," Ali said. "A big rock that you can use to mark the spot so we can find it again."

Flossie nodded. "Okay," she said, but she seemed disappointed.

It took some time for her to find a suitable rock. Then Ali helped carry the equipment back across the road.

"So what am I supposed to do now?" Flossie asked. "Just forget about it?"

"No," Ali said. "Not at all. It may take some time, but I'll call it in."

"Are you some kind of a cop?"

There were times when telling the truth was the only option.

"No," Ali said thoughtfully. "I'm no kind of a cop at all. I have a friend named Brenda Riley, at least I had a friend named Brenda. She may be dead, and I have reason to believe that Ermina is responsible for what happened to her. If that turns out to be the case, I want her caught and convicted."

"All right," Flossie said in grudging agreement.

"But there is something you can do," Ali offered.

"What?"

"If I can make this work, a little later on tonight, a bunch of cops are going to show up here with a search warrant, and you can do them a big favor."

"What's that?"

"Show them where to find that clicker. It'll be a lot easier for them to get inside the Blaylocks' house if they can raise or lower the shutters."

"You think there's a chance that bitch will go to jail?"

"Yes," Ali said. "I certainly do."

"Then you can count on me," declared Flossie Haywood. "I will not let you down."

Ali waited only long enough to drive out of Flossie's sight before she was on her Bluetooth and dialing Stuart Ramey. Yes, it was a holiday, but she had every confidence that Stuart would answer—which he did, once she managed to outwit the series of voice mail prompts.

"Hey, Stuart," she said. "I want you to look up a telephone number for me. The name is Gilbert Morris, Grass Valley, California. I have his cell phone and his work number. I'm looking for a home number."

"Have you tried information?"

"He's a cop," Ali said. "I'm guessing it's unlisted."

"That may take a little longer."

It turned out the number was unlisted and getting it did take a little longer. Wanting to be able to write down the number, Ali pulled over and parked in a small business park bustling with weekend campers on their way back to their respective cities at the end of the three-day weekend.

"Okay," Stuart said, "you called that shot. Here it is."

Ali jotted the home number down on the back of Ermina's background check, right along with Gilbert's office and cell phone numbers. When the phone started to ring, she held her breath.

Answer, damn it! she thought. *I don't want to give you another chance not to call me back.*

"Hello." He sounded tentative, uncertain. Before dialing his number, she had put in the code that would block her caller ID.

"Is this Detective Gilbert Morris?" Ali asked. Her tone was brisk, businesslike.

"Yes, it is," he said. "But who's calling, please?"

"My name is Alison Reynolds," she said. "I called earlier and left you two messages. You didn't call me back."

"This is an unlisted number. How did you—"

"Listen very carefully," she said. "I have important information, but since you probably won't believe me, I want you to call a third party. Do you have a pencil handy?"

"I have a pen," he said.

"Good. The guy's name is Laughlin. Detective James Laughlin. He's a retired homicide cop from Jefferson City, Missouri. I want you to call him. Ask him about Ermina Vlasic Cunningham. Once you do, I believe you'll be interested in calling me back. Here's his number."

After reading off James Laughlin's number, Ali hung up, without leaving her own number or answering any questions. When Gil Morris got around to calling her back—as she was certain he would—he could damned well go looking for her number. After all, she had already given it to him. Twice.

46

Grass Valley, California

Gilbert Morris was pissed. He had no idea who had given this pushy broad his number but he intended to find out and then there would be hell to pay. This was exactly why cops had unlisted numbers—so every crazy in the universe couldn't pick up the phone and give them pieces of their ringy-dingy minds just because they felt like it.

His first instinct was to ignore it. She'd already told him that she was a friend of Brenda Riley. Yes, he probably should have picked up the phone and called her earlier today, but he hadn't, primarily to get back at Chief Jackman more than anything else. He had told himself he'd make the call tomorrow. But now she'd had nerve enough to call him at home. On his unlisted number.

But still, something about the call rang true. Who the hell was Ermina Cunningham anyway? And who was Detective James Laughlin? And what did any of it have to do with the price of tea in China?

Finally curiosity got the better of him. He called the number. It was two o'clock in California. Four o'clock in Jefferson City,

Missouri. A woman answered with an accent so southern that it sounded like verbal honey.

"Yes, of course," she said. "He'll be right here."

"Jim here," a male voice said a minute or so later. "Who's this?"

"My name is Gilbert Morris," Gil said, feeling stupid. "I'm a homicide detective with the Grass Valley Police Department in Grass Valley, California. Someone suggested that I should give you a call and ask you about someone named Ermina Vlasic Cunningham. I'm not sure why."

"That's odd," Laughlin said. "That's the second request I've had for information about her in as many days. Someone else was asking about her six months or so ago. Long story short, Ermina lived here for a few years with her adoptive parents, Lola and Sam Cunningham. Lola died. Sam supposedly committed suicide. I didn't buy it then, and I'm not buying it now. I know, as sure as you're born, that Ermina killed her dad but I've got no way to prove it. The inquest ruled Sam's death a suicide. The daughter was never charged."

Gil knew what was coming before he ever asked the question. "How did he die?"

"He was drunk," Tom said. "Somebody put a plastic bag over his head and taped it shut."

"Holy crap!" Gil said. "And now she may have done it again!"

He ended the call, opened the earlier message—the one he had ignored—and jotted down Ali's name and phone number before calling her back.

"Okay," he said, "I talked to Laughlin. Where are you? What have you got? How did you make the connection, and are you a cop?"

Disregarding all Gil's questions, Ali asked, "Do you have a fax machine?"

Gil glanced around his clean but bare-bones living room. "Are you kidding? I'm at home. I barely have a microwave. Why?"

"An iPhone maybe?"

"Lady, look, if you're looking for high tech, I'm not your guy. There's a fax machine at the office. What do you want to send me?"

"As I told you in my earlier message, Brenda was my friend. On Friday, just before she disappeared, she sent me an e-mail, requesting that I order a background check on Ermina Blaylock. That's what led me to Detective Laughlin."

"You're not a cop?"

"No. Not for lack of trying. I made it through the academy but my department furloughed me due to budgetary considerations."

Great, Gil thought. *An unemployed almost cop.*

"So what are you, then, a glorified PI?"

"I'm not a PI, and I'm currently in Salton City, east of Palm Springs. I've just come from the home of one of Mark and Mina Blaylock's neighbors. The woman, Florence Haywood, witnessed Ermina burning something in a barbecue grill bonfire in the early hours of Sunday morning. Later on, that same woman—sort of a neighborhood busybody—saw Mark Blaylock dump the ashes into a wheelbarrow and bury them. We used a metal detector to locate the site. It's marked so we can find it again. Florence was all set to dig it up. I cautioned her that since this might be critical evidence, she needed to leave it as is."

Gil thought about that for a minute. "Salton City. What county is that, Riverside?"

"Imperial," Ali replied.

"I'm a city cop. A Grass Valley cop investigating a crime that happened inside my city limits. There's no way a judge is going to grant me a request for a search warrant in a county that's half a state away from here so I can try to figure out who killed Richard Lowensdale."

"I don't give a damn about Richard Lowensdale," Ali told him. "I want to know what happened to Brenda Riley. As far as I'm concerned, those two cases are bound together, but whatever Mark Blaylock was seen burying, it isn't on private property," Ali replied.

"It's public property?"

"Yes. It's out on the beach. No one is going to require a search warrant to dig it up, but in order to maintain the chain of evidence, I need a sworn officer in attendance. You're my first choice."

"Look," Gil said. "I appreciate the tip, I really do. And I'd like to be there, but it's not going to happen. I already got hauled into my chief's office earlier today and bitched out for all the OT I put in this weekend. I was given a direct order to stand down. Based on that, I can't very well go back to him now and say, 'By the way, I need to take a four-hundred-mile side trip in hopes of picking up some evidence.' Besides, even if he said yes, that's at least a ten-hour trip, most likely longer today. There'll be lots of people heading home after the three-day weekend.

"I'm friends with a Nevada County detective named Frank Escobar. Since Brenda Riley's effects were found in the county, he's the one assigned to her possible suicide. Maybe he has some connections down where you are."

"The more people we involve, the more cumbersome it's going to be," Ali told him. "Did I understand you to say you're off work today? That your chief sent you home?"

"Yes."

"So do me a favor," she said. "Give me the fax number for your department. There's a general store here. I already checked. They happen to have a working fax machine. I'll send you a copy of this report so you'll have it in hand. I'll also send you what I have on Richard Lowensdale. Once you read the fax, give me another call. By then maybe I'll be able to figure out what our next move should be."

Our move, he thought. *Right.*

But still, Gil had to admit he was intrigued. He had to look at one of his own business cards to come up with the fax number.

"I need to shower," he said, after giving it to her. "It'll take me half an hour or so."

"All right," she said. "Bye."

47

Salton City, California

The Salton City Pay and Tote was jammed with customers buying drinks, sandwiches, chips, snacks, and gas for their journeys home. Ali waited in line. When she turned over her stack of documents to be faxed, the harassed clerk shook her head.

"All of these? Can't you see I'm busy? This is going to take time."

Ali took a twenty from her purse and laid it on the counter. "That's for you," she said. "I'll pay for the faxes separately."

"Okay," the clerk said. "Just a minute."

It took more than a minute—lots more. The machine was balky. The first three attempts, it cut off after sending only three pages, and each time the clerk started it, she came back to the cash register to help the next person in line.

While Ali waited, she used her iPhone to scroll through her e-mail account.

During Ali's years in California, as the wife of network executive Paul Grayson in a spare-no-expense era, she had made use of his company's corporate jet connections on numerous occasions. Once the network started cutting costs and shedding "nonessential" personnel, the corporate jets as well as their pilots had been jettisoned at about the same time Ali had been kicked off the air.

The pilots, most of them former military, were a good bunch of guys. Somehow a few of them had banded together with some other pilots, pooled their resources, and purchased a couple of the network's stable of secondhand jets. They had used those aircraft to start their own charter service. In turbulent financial times and against all odds, they had started You-Go Aviation and were somehow succeeding at being the low-priced spread in California's once-thriving private jet business.

Ali wasn't sure how her e-mail address had been added to You-Go's customer mailing list, but she received frequent updates advertising their various specials, one of which was $1,995 an hour all in for charters flying anywhere in California, Arizona, and Nevada. Ali remembered from reading their corporate literature that from You-Go's home base in Fresno, most flights could be done with a mere six hours' notice where most other companies required a full twenty-four. When Ali dialed their operations center, she was hoping to take a big chunk out of the six.

The young woman who took Ali's call sounded dubious when she asked to be put through to Allen Knox, one of You-Go's cofounders and a pilot Ali had known well back in the old days.

"I'm sorry," the call center clerk named Amelia told Ali. "Mr. Knox is our CEO. He doesn't involve himself in day-to-day flight arrangements."

"This is urgent," Ali said. "My name is Ali Reynolds. Please give him this number."

"Today's a holiday. I may not be able to reach him, and even if I do, I can't guarantee he'll call you back."

"Just give him the number," Ali said. "He'll call."

And he did, less than five minutes later—just as Ali was paying off the faxing bill and reassembling her stack of paper.

"Hey, Ali," Allen said. "Good to hear from you after all this time. What's going on?"

"I'm involved in a possible kidnapping situation," she said, fudging a little. "In order to maintain the chain of evidence, I need to get a homicide cop from Grass Valley to Palm Springs ASAP. How fast can you get someone from there to Jackie Cochran?"

"Today?"

"Yes, today."

"How many passengers?"

"One."

"Luggage?"

"He'll most likely be traveling light."

"All right, Nevada County Air Park is a pretty short runway. Hold on. Let me see if we have a CJ1 available."

He put her on hold and was gone for some time. While she waited, Ali finished sorting and clipping her papers and bought herself a bag of chips. She needed something to soak up those many cups of Flossie Haywood's Folgers.

"You're in luck," Allen said brightly. "Our new CJ1+ just put down here in Fresno. The pilot's still here, so we don't even have to call him out. He can refuel, file a flight plan, and be in Grass Valley in about an hour and a half. With ten minutes or so on the ground in Grass Valley, we should be able to have your guy on the ground in Palm Springs, about an hour and a half after that. So we're talking three hours give or take. Will that work for you?"

"That works."

"Let me put you back on the line with Amelia, then. She can take the passenger information and your credit card, give you the tail number and the address of Airpark Aviation, the FBO we use in Grass Valley. You haven't flown with us since we became You-Go, have you?"

"Nope," Ali said. "This is a first."

"Well, I certainly hope it's not the last," Allen said. "Welcome aboard."

Amelia worked her way through the details in a no-nonsense fashion. Once they were ironed out, Ali called Gil back, on his cell phone.

"Are you at your office yet?" she asked.

"No, I'm still at the house. I just got out of the shower. I'll be heading out in a few minutes."

"You might want to pack a bag," Ali said. "You need to be at Airpark Aviation at the Grass Valley airport in about an hour. I'm sending a plane to pick you up."

"A plane?" Gil asked. "You mean like a Cherokee or a Piper or something—one of those little outfits?"

"It'll be a CJ1," she told him. "A jet—definitely not a Piper."

"Do you mind telling me where I'm going?"

"Jackie Cochran Airport outside of Palm Springs. I'll pick you up there. Once you read the background material, you'll understand."

"Great."

"One more thing," Ali added.

"What's that?"

"I'm assuming you're armed. Don't worry. Flying private, you'll be able to wear your weapon on board with no problem. Just be sure you show up with government-issued photo ID. And if you happen to have a couple of Kevlar vests lying around, you might want to bring them along. One for you and one for me. I wear a size large."

"You want me to bring vests?" Gil asked. "I thought the purpose of this trip was to dig up evidence with shovels. You think someone is going to be taking potshots at us?"

"You never can tell," Ali said. "Better to have vests and not need them than the other way around."

She hung up on Gil before he could say anything more, then she redialed High Noon. "What now?" Stuart Ramey asked when he picked up.

"Don't you ever take any time off?"

"Not so you'd notice."

"I need more phone info," she said.

Stuart laughed. "I guess it pays to be the boss's girlfriend. I was just talking to B. He said I should give you whatever you want."

"Cell phone numbers," she said. "For people named Mark and Ermina Blaylock."

"The people who used to live in La Jolla but who now live in Salton City."

"The very ones," Ali said.

"Okay. I'll call you back when I get something."

Ali looked at her watch. Given the holiday traffic, she estimated it would take an hour to make it from Salton City to the airport. She had flown in and out of Jackie Cochran on occasion. The general aviation terminal there would have a place where she could work while she waited for Detective Morris to arrive.

The terminal had something else that was high on Ali's current list of priorities—decent restrooms. After swilling down all those cups of coffee, restrooms were more than a priority, they were an absolute necessity.

48

Grass Valley, California

Gil got off the phone, shaking his head, convinced that this Ali Reynolds character was one pushy broad. She wanted him to "pack a bag"? Really. It wasn't like he didn't have a suitcase or two. Since the chest of drawers from Target was still in the box, his clean clothes were still in the battered old suitcases on the floor of his bedroom. He picked up the one filled with his underwear and dumped the contents of that into what he thought of as his "sock suitcase."

He gathered up a pair of socks, clean underwear, and the last of his clean shirts from the laundry and stuck those in the now-empty suitcase. He added in his shaving kit, his own Kevlar vest, and a stack of spare note cards. He put his bottle of ink in a Ziploc bag, cushioned it with some of his new paper towels, and hoped the bottle didn't leak. He put that in a side pocket so it wouldn't rattle around, but when he closed it, the suitcase was still more empty than it was full. Even adding in a second vest wouldn't make much difference. This was traveling light in the extreme.

Then he remembered he'd barely eaten all day. When he'd

first come home from shopping, he'd had a bowl of cereal from his new box and made a pot of coffee. Now though, thinking it might be a long time before he saw another square meal, he made himself another bologna sandwich with bread from the new loaf. He packed the sandwich in his suitcase as well—in yet another Ziploc bag in another side pocket.

He closed the suitcase, hefted it, and laughed when he heard things rattling around inside.

"Gilbert, Gilbert, Gilbert," he laughed to himself. "You are certainly one sophisticated son of a bitch!"

He was relieved that the parking spot reserved for the chief of police was empty when he pulled into the departmental parking lot. Leaving his suitcase in the car, he hurried inside. Sergeant Andersson looked up in surprise.

"I thought you were gone for the day."

"I am," he said. "I just stopped by to pick something up. Do you happen to have a fax for me?"

Sergeant Andersson turned her chair around and plucked a stack of papers off her credenza. "More like *War and Peace* than a fax," she said. "It came in a while ago. I hadn't gotten around to putting it in your box."

Taking the fax with him, Gil used a key to let himself into the armory, where he signed out one of the spare vests. Sergeant Andersson was talking on the phone when he headed back out. He waited in the doorway until she hung up.

"You might want to let Chief Jackman know that I won't be in tomorrow," he told her. "I've been called out of town. You can mark it down as a comp day. I understand I have several of those coming."

She was making a note of it as he hurried out the door. He doubted she noticed the extra vest. Better to explain later than to ask permission.

He drove to the Nevada County Air Park and went looking for Airpark Aviation. He found a place to park and went inside, carrying his still-rattling suitcase. A young woman seated behind a counter looked up at him and smiled.

"Flying today?" she asked.

Gil nodded.

"What's your tail number?"

"I have no idea."

"The only aircraft we have coming in in the next little while is a You-Go Aviation CJ1, flying from here to Palm Springs."

"That must be it, then."

"Do you need help with luggage?"

He held up his single suitcase. "Got it. Where do I park?"

"Wherever," she said. "Don't worry about parking. Do you want some coffee? Popcorn?"

"No, thanks," he said. "I'm fine."

I've got my very own bologna sandwich.

Gil took a seat by a window, opened his suitcase, and pulled out the stack of faxes. He was interested to see that two sections of material were devoted to Richard Lowensdale. For right now, though, he needed to know everything there was to know about Ermina Cunningham Blaylock.

He made his way through the material. Without the call to Detective Laughlin in Missouri, Ermina would have seemed entirely harmless. And understandable. Mina and her husband had overextended in order to buy Rutherford International, but they had bet on a losing horse and now they were busted. They had lost their house in La Jolla, lost their fancy cars, lost their golf course membership. They ended up living in a house in Salton City that the county tax assessor said was worth $45,000. That was a big comedown, but nothing he read did anything to explain the relationship between Richard Lowensdale and Ermina.

The only connection Gil could see had to do with the money he had found squirreled away in Richard's pristine garage. If that was what the killer was looking for—and Gil thought it was—where had it come from? Was it possible Richard had been blackmailing Ermina? Given the situation in Missouri, that wasn't such an oddball idea. Maybe Mark Blaylock didn't know about his wife's somewhat questionable past. But if Richard was blackmailing Ermina, where was she getting the money to pay him?

Gilbert wasn't long on forensic accounting, but from what he could see of the Blaylocks' financial records, it seemed unlikely that there would be fifty thousand dollars just lying around loose. It also occurred to him that there was a lot more information included in the report than he would have expected. He was so engrossed in what he was reading that he lost track of time.

"Mr. Morris?"

Gil looked up. A plane had pulled up and stopped on the tarmac just outside the door. Standing in front of him was a man in a pair of chinos and a black golf shirt with the words You-Go Aviation emblazoned in gold on the pocket.

Gil stuffed his paperwork into his suitcase and zipped it. "That's me," he said.

"I'm Phil Canby, your pilot. I understand we're on the way to Palm Springs?"

Gil nodded.

"We don't need fuel, so we'll only be on the ground here for ten minutes or so," Phil said. "It's not a long trip, an hour and a half. The weather's good except for some tailwinds going into Palm Springs. That part of the trip could be a little bumpy. Now, you'll show me your ID, I'll take you out to the aircraft and you settled in. I didn't see any catering order. Did you order ."

"No," Gil said, pulling out his ID. "No food. I'm fine."

He didn't say a word about the bologna sandwich lurking in his suitcase. He settled into the soft leather seat—a leather seat with plenty of leg room.

So this is how the other half lives, he thought as he fastened his seat belt.

The pilot came on board and pulled the steps and door shut after him. "You flown the CJ before?"

Gil shook his head.

"Okay, so let me give you the full safety briefing."

Gil listened, but only partially, to information about emergency exits, oxygen masks, etc. "Any questions?" Phil Canby asked when the briefing ended.

"How much does all this cost?"

"Our company is unusual in that we have an all-in cost of just under two thousand dollars."

"Get out. Two thousand bucks to fly from here to Palm Springs?"

Phil Canby looked at him, grinned, and shook his head. "That's two thousand an hour. So it's over three thousand, to get from here to Palm Springs plus the forty minutes it took to get from Fresno to here. I take it you're not paying the freight, then?"

Gil shook his head.

"Then I suggest you sit back and enjoy it," Phil said.

The pilot disappeared into the cockpit. The irony wasn't lost on Gilbert Morris. He had just maxed out his Visa card shopping at Target. He had no idea of who or what Ali Reynolds really was, but one thing was clear. If she could afford to blow that much money on bringing him along for no other purpose than to "maintain the chain of evidence," then the lady had to be loaded.

As his mother would have said, "More money than sense."

That reminded him, of course, of that other "chain of evidence" problem. The phony oil containers that he had removed from Richard Lowensdale's garage were still in his garage. In a court proceeding against Ermina Blaylock, that could turn into a big problem for Gil. Which reminded him of something else his mother always said: "I'll cross that bridge when I come to it."

49

Palm Springs, California

Ali spent most of her two-hour wait in the Jackie Cochran terminal talking on the phone to Stuart. Locating the needed cell phone numbers was proving more difficult than expected because they had no idea who the provider was. It was only after some unauthorized snooping through the Blaylocks' none-too-secure bill pay program that Stuart had managed to get on track with that. Ali had given Flossie Haywood her cell phone number and asked her to call if either Ermina or Mark Blaylock returned to the cabin. So far her phone had remained silent.

Despite the fact that Mina had left home with no luggage, Ali was convinced that she was about to make a run for it. So far, the only other possible address they had for her was in San Diego. Rutherford International may have ceased operations, but according to the bill pay records, they were still paying utility bills on two separate addresses in the Clairemont Mesa Business Park. That wasn't an especially promising lead, but as far as Ali knew, that was the only one they had.

When she saw the You-Go Aviation CJ touch down, Ali gathered up her paperwork, stuffed it into her purse, and went to the terminal door.

Ali recognized Phil Canby as one of the pilots she knew. He sauntered toward the terminal accompanied by a man Ali assumed to be Gil Morris. The detective looked a little older than Ali and about Ali's height, although there was a lot more muscle on his frame than there was on Ali's. His crew cut was definitely turning gray. Carrying a single battered suitcase as though it weighed nothing, he looked distinctly lowbrow. Ali liked the fact that he wasn't particularly good-looking. She'd had more than one unpleasant encounter with detectives who had very high opinions about their own special appeal and who came equipped with egos to match.

If Gil Morris considered himself a hunk, it wasn't apparent in the way he was dressed or the luggage he carried. His jeans were faded thanks to numerous washings rather than having been purchased that way. His navy blue golf shirt had a spot on it where something like olive oil hadn't quite come out in the wash, and the end of the zipper on the suitcase was held in place by a strategically located piece of duct tape.

When Ali stepped outside to greet them, she found a steady wind blowing west to east across the tarmac, leaving trails of sifting sand drifting across the runway.

"Good to see you again, Ms. Reynolds," Phil Canby said, shaking her hand. "Here's Mr. Morris, safe and sound."

"And a hell of a lot faster than I would have been here if I had driven," Gil Morris said with a grin.

Ali greeted Gil with a smile of her own as well as a handshake, then she turned back to the pilot. "It's good to see you too, Phil. Do you know if you're booked on another trip right now?"

"Not that I'm aware of," Phil said. "Why?"

"Detective Morris and I have to go back to Salton City for a while, but we may need to fly somewhere else later on today. If you could stand by until I know for sure . . ."

"No problem," Phil said. "I'll let operations know. Then I'll re-fuel. That way, once you say yea or nay, we can get off the ground immediately."

Ali nodded to Phil and then looked at the detective. "Is that all your luggage?"

"What you see is what you get."

"Come on then."

50

Salton City, California

Gil followed Ali Reynolds outside and clambered into her rented Infiniti SUV. He fastened his seat belt before he said anything. "Okay," he said, "I'm suitably impressed. Obviously you've got more money than God, but I'd like to know what the hell is going on and why the big hurry."

Ali put the SUV in gear and backed out of the parking space. "Right this minute, Ermina Blaylock probably still believes she's in the clear. As long as that doesn't change, we have a better chance of finding her."

She handed Gil a piece of paper. "There's the license information on her vehicle, a silver Lincoln Town Car. I believe she's a person of interest in your homicide. Since I'm not a sworn police officer, I can't put out a BOLO on her. You can. Do it."

Rich and pushy and issuing orders, Gil thought, *but she's also right.*

He took out his cell phone and called Grass Valley. There had been a shift change. Kathleen Andersson was now off duty. Sergeant Frieda Lawson had taken her place. The two desk sergeants were sometimes referred to as the Valkyries, but that moniker was only used behind their backs. Gil was relieved. Frieda Lawson had no way of knowing that Chief Jackman had ordered him to go home. It was nice not having to explain to her why somebody who was off duty needed a BOLO.

"So what's the situation here?" he asked, once he was off the phone. By then they were already headed south on California Highway 86, where rivulets of moving sand slithered across the asphalt in front of them. "And are we really going to get out and dig around in the sand in the middle of a windstorm?"

"Yes, we are," Ali said, "unless drifting sand has covered over our marker. According to the Blaylocks' nearest neighbor, Ermina left home bright and early this morning on her own. Mark's car is at the house, but since the shutters are closed, it's likely he isn't there. I want to do our big dig before either one of them returns."

"If they return," Gil offered.

"Exactly," Ali said.

"And how are we going to do this dig, with our bare hands?"

"I'm sure Flossie will lend us a shovel, if she hasn't already done the digging herself."

"Flossie?" Gil asked.

"Florence Haywood. The neighbor. That's what she calls herself, Flossie. She was all hot to trot to dig before I left. The only way I could dissuade her was by telling her that disturbing the evidence might result in Ermina's getting off. There's apparently not a lot of love lost between Flossie and Ermina."

"You told this woman that Ermina's a suspect in a homicide?"

Ali gave him a scathing look. "As far as Florence Haywood knows, I'm working for a creditor who's trying to repossess Ermina's Town Car. Yes, I know. It was a lie, but it would probably be in both our best interests to stick to that story."

Gil nodded. He was a visiting cop who was a long way out of his own jurisdiction. Ali Reynolds didn't have one.

In other words, he thought, *we're a match made in heaven.*

Ali turned off the highway and onto a series of meandering roads that ran along beside the lake. Gil had spent his whole life in the foothills of the Sierras. He loved the trees and the mountains and the surprising lakes and reservoirs that lay hidden in the mountain valleys. The Salton Sea, surrounded by flat, forbidding desert and distant mountain ranges, seemed like a page taken from some other planet.

The road they were on curved and changed names, becoming Heron Ridge Drive, although as far as Gil could see, there were no ridges anywhere around, and no herons either.

"That's their place," Ali said, nodding toward a small house that was totally encased in what looked like sturdy metal shutters. "And this is Flossie's."

She turned into a driveway that ended at a parked motor home. "I'll tell her we're here and see if she'll let us use her shovel."

Ali didn't come right out and say, "Wait in the car," but Gil got the message. And he didn't argue. He had napped some on the plane, but he hadn't had nearly enough sleep. He was tired, and he knew it.

Ali returned to the car a few minutes later, followed by an immense woman carrying both a shovel and a stack of boxes that were evidently discards from the local liquor store.

"She says we can park here," Ali said, leaning into the car. "Where we're going is on the beach on the other side of the road."

Gil piled out of the SUV and followed the two women across the road and onto a beach covered with treacherous powdery sand punctuated by boulders.

"I was worried about losing the rock," Flossie was saying. "I came out and dusted it off a couple of times, just in case. And here it is."

Flossie moved the rock out of the way, and Gil took charge of wielding the shovel. He had turned over only a few spadefuls of sand when the blade of the shovel struck something hard. The next time Gil raised the shovel, a squarish piece of what appeared to be melted plastic sat in the bowl of the shovel. Ali examined it as he lowered the load into one of the cardboard boxes.

"See the white plastic?" Ali asked. Gil nodded.

"I'll bet I know what that is," she said. "A Time Capsule, for a Mac."

Gil remembered all the apparently undisturbed computer gear on Richard Lowensdale's desk. He had assumed it was all there. Evidently that assumption was wrong. Without another word, Gil resumed digging. The next load of sandy dirt came up with something that was only partially burned, something light blue. It took a moment for him to realize what it was—the remains of a Tyvek surgical bootie like the ones that had left bloodied tracks all through his murder victim's house.

Yes, he decided, *Ali made the right call. We really do need to maintain a chain of evidence.*

He kept digging and found a few more bits and pieces. Finally though, when his shovel loads were yielding nothing but sand, a cell phone rang—Ali's cell phone.

She answered it, listened, and then gave the house across the street a long, appraising look. "Right," she said, finally. "Got it."

Without saying anything to Gil or Flossie, she immediately dialed a number—the pilot's, presumably. "We're flying to San Diego. Wheels up in an hour," she said. She paused and listened again. "I'm not sure which airport," she said. "Whatever's closest to the Clairemont Mesa Business Park. When you figure out what airport, call Hertz and give them my profile number. Tell them we'll need a car wherever you're taking us."

She turned to Flossie. "We need to leave now," Ali said urgently, "just as soon as we get these boxes loaded in my car. I appreciate all your help, but I'm worried about Mr. Blaylock. Do you think there's a chance he's inside the house? I know you said he wouldn't be with the shutters down that way, but after we're gone, you might want to check. You did say he gave you access to a remote, didn't you?"

"Sure," Flossie said. "I'll be glad to go check on him. It won't take but a minute, if you want to wait."

"No," Ali insisted. "We need to go. We've got a plane to catch."

Gil figured that was a fib on Ali's part because he was pretty sure the plane wouldn't go anywhere without them.

As soon as the boxes were loaded, Ali headed for the driver's side, jumped in, turned the key, and gunned the engine. Gil clambered into the passenger seat, slammed the door, and fastened his seat belt. The whole vehicle reeked of wood smoke and burned plastic.

"What's the big hurry now?" he asked as she pulled out of the driveway and then accelerated down Heron Ridge Drive.

"My phone guy just called," she said. "Stuart got a hit on Mina's phone. According to cell phone towers, she's somewhere in downtown San Diego. Since there's been no activity on Blaylock's phone, Stuart tried calling that one."

"How can your guy be doing all this tracing without a court order?"

"Don't ask," she said.

"And?"

"Nobody answered Mark Blaylock's phone, but it looks like it's right here in Salton City, most likely in the Blaylocks' shuttered house. I'm willing to bet Mark Blaylock is inside there too."

"And in no condition to answer the phone," Gil concluded.

Ali nodded.

"How come Flossie would have access to the shutter controls?"

"I'm not sure they were actually given to her. Let's just say she knows where the controller is located, but if she walks in and

finds what I think she's going to find, we don't want to be anywhere around. If we were to get caught up in another homicide
investigation right now, it would really slow us down. We need to
be in San Diego."

They weren't even on the highway yet when a set of flashing
red lights appeared in front of them. Ali pulled over and stopped.
Moments later a speeding Imperial County Sheriff's Department
patrol car swept past them and sped toward Heron Ridge Drive,
the way they had come.

Gil looked at Ali. "Guess you called that shot," he said.

Nodding, she pulled back into traffic, leaving Gil to recon-
sider his initial impression of her.

Yes, he thought, *rich and pushy, but also smart—very, very smart.*

"Of course, the fact that we put out a BOLO on the wife's car
before Flossie called nine-one-one is probably going to raise a
few eyebrows."

Ali looked at him and grinned. "They'll have to catch us first,"
she said.

Gil was starting to like this girl.

"And what about your phone meister?"

"Don't worry," Ali said. "Stuart knows how to cover his tracks.
Let's just hope he can keep on working his telephone tracing
magic with Ermina."

"You realize I'm out of my jurisdiction and I don't have an arrest warrant."

"Don't worry," Ali said. "If we can catch her, I'm sure we'll be
able to come up with something that will work."

51

Escondido, California

Although Mina's major shopping excursion would be tomorrow, she needed to do some shopping today. First up was a lightweight mummy sleeping bag, one that zipped up completely and came in Mina's preferred design and color—desert camouflage. She purchased that for cash at an army surplus store in Escondido. Next on Mina's list for today was solving the problem of what to wear for tonight's meeting with Enrique.

Mina had left Salton City in a tracksuit that would do fine for dealing with Brenda, later in the evening, but it wouldn't do at all for her meeting at Enrique's penthouse unit in a newly opened high-rise condo tower in downtown San Diego.

In Escondido she spent some time looking before she located a small wedding boutique where, hidden in among all the pastel bridesmaid garb, she found a surprisingly suitable little black dress and a pair of pumps. Across the street Milady's Day Spa encouraged walk-ins. She opted for a relatively inexpensive mani-cure and pedicure, followed by a facial, a deep-tissue massage, a steam bath, and a shampoo/blow-dry. In the spa dressing room, she reapplied her makeup from the ground up. When she left the spa four hours after entering it, she was transformed. She returned to her Town Car in the tight-fitting little black dress with the tracksuit safely stowed in a shopping bag.

Mina was glad Enrique had invited her to dinner at his new San Diego condo rather than their usual haunt at the casino near Palm Springs. San Diego was far too close to La Jolla for Mina to be comfortable visiting one of the city's hip restaurants. Once she and Mark had been part of the social scene in town here, and she didn't want to run into any of the folks from those old days. The last thing Mina needed tonight was for some former acquaintance to rush up to her, gush over Mina, lie about how much everyone missed seeing them, and ask where was her wonderful husband, Mark. They'd all know about Mark soon enough, but not now, not tonight.

She drove to McClintock Plaza and parked her Lincoln in a compact parking place that was several inches too small. It was a source of annoyance to Mina that there were far more parking places for little cars these days than there were for big ones. Leaving the car behind, she collected several shopping bags. One contained the bedroll, one held her track suit and running shoes, while a third contained her portable GPS. Then she meandered through the mall and had coffee in Starbucks before summoning a cab to take her to the airport. Once there, she made her way to the car rental desks, where Sophia Stanhope rented a Cadillac sedan, which she would return to LAX the next afternoon, prior to her scheduled Air France flight.

In her rented Cadillac, Mina drove to Kettner Boulevard in downtown San Diego and parked in a pay lot just across the street from the condominium tower. There were precious few lit windows showing in the lower floors of the building, but the penthouse blazed with light. Other people might not have money enough to close on their new condo units, but apparently drug dealers were still doing fine financially, thank you very much.

Inside the lobby, Mina gave the concierge her name—her new name.

He checked a list on his computer. "Welcome, Ms. Stanhope. Mr. Gallegos is expecting you. Right this way, please."

The concierge led Mina to a private elevator, one with no buttons, where he used a key card to send her zooming nonstop to the penthouse floor, thirty-five stories up. When the elevator door opened in a secured lobby, Enrique was standing there waiting for her.

"Welcome, my dear," he said, brushing her cheek with his lips. "You're looking lovely this evening. Do come in."

He took Mina's elbow and ushered her inside—into a lush, glass-walled unit with the whole of San Diego's nighttime skyline gleaming in front of her. The view was enchanting. Walking over to look out the windows, Mina was filled with the sense that she was finally putting gritty Salton City behind her.

Moments later, Enrique returned to her side and handed her a chilled crystal flute filled with bubbling champagne. With everything else she needed to do later that night, Mina knew she couldn't afford to drink very much, but a champagne toast was definitely in order.

"To us," she murmured, clinking glasses. "And to making this deal happen."

San Diego, California

Brenda was awakened by the noisy rumble of another plane. She did not want to awaken. Unlike Uncle Joe, she had given up. She was choosing to die rather than choosing to live, but evidently choosing had nothing to do with it. If wishing to die worked, she would have been gone a long time ago.

Feverish and drifting in and out of consciousness, she no longer wondered where she was. That didn't matter. She no longer cared that some poor someone was bound to find her stinking, filthy body. Her condition didn't matter either. Once she was dead, she would no longer have to be embarrassed about that.

Brenda wished she could see her mother one more time and tell her that she loved her. And Valerie too. They had fought like crazy for as long as Brenda could remember, but Valerie Sandoz was her sister—her only sister. That was Brenda's only regret, that she wouldn't be able to tell her mother and sister how sorry she was. For everything.

And as for those other people—the woman who had put her here, and that man, what was his name again? Oh, yes, Richard. They were fading away. She could barely remember them, but she forgave them too. Why not? Sitting here dying, forgiveness was the only thing Brenda Riley had left to give.

52

Palm Springs, California

They were halfway back to the airport when Ali's phone rang. A glance at the caller ID window showed a number she recognized as Flossie Haywood's, but the voice on the phone wasn't Flossie's.

"My name's Jim Haywood. Are you the lady who was just here talking to my wife?" he demanded.

"Yes," Ali said.

"Flossie wanted me to call you. After you left, she went ahead and let herself into the house just up the road. You won't believe what she found!"

"Tell me."

"Poor Mr. Blaylock, dead as a doornail and lying in his bed. Flossie was so upset, she about had a heart attack. They're taking her into Indio to the hospital to be checked out, but she wanted me to let you know about it."

"Could she tell what happened to him?" Ali asked.

"Looked like he was just sleeping, until she tried waking him up. She called nine-one-one. There's a deputy there now. He went inside and said it may have been a suicide. There's a homicide detective on his way to the house from El Centro. The whole thing upset Flossie so much that she started having chest pains."

"Chest pains?" Ali asked. "Is she going to be all right?"

"I hope so. Like I said, they hauled her away in an ambulance. I'm on my way there right now too, but before they took her away, she gave me her phone and asked me to call you. I'm not sure what this is all about. She said something about digging up evidence from over across the road, which didn't make any sense to me. She said the detective will probably want to talk to you."

"I'm sure he will, Mr. Haywood," Ali said. "Feel free to give him this number."

"Blaylock?" Gil asked.

Ali nodded. "Dead in his bed, and thanks to my phone guy the body was found a whole lot sooner than Mina Blaylock wanted him to be found. According to Jim Haywood, there's a homicide detective on his way to Salton City right now."

"The local cops are going to want to talk to us."

"I know," Ali said, "and we will talk to them. We'll tell them everything we know, but after we get to San Diego, not before."

They drove for a while in silence while Gil considered how Chief Jackman was going to react to all this news once it got back to him. It wouldn't be pretty.

"How did Blaylock die?" Gil asked as Ali turned onto the airport drive. "Don't tell me she pulled another plastic bag stunt."

"Mr. Haywood didn't say—just that he was dead."

"How long will it take to get to San Diego?"

"Once we take off, only about half an hour."

"I'll call El Centro once we land," he said.

Ali nodded. "Good."

It was dark by the time they pulled into the terminal driveway. When the pilot saw them unloading several cardboard boxes, he came out with a rolling luggage cart. "Should these be in front or in back?" he asked, sniffing with distaste when he caught a whiff of the odor.

"In front and belted in," Ali said. "But in order to maintain the chain of evidence, Gil needs to sign them. Then we'll need some transparent packing tape to put over his signature and seal the boxes shut. That should help some with the smell."

After all, that was the whole point—maintaining the chain of evidence.

Once on the plane, they skipped the safety briefing because Ali's phone was ringing. It was B. "You realize that what Stuart has been doing is right on the edge," he said. "It's actually over the edge. In tracking down the Blaylocks' phone information, we've violated a whole bunch of privacy rules."

"Yes, I know," she said. "I'm sorry. But we've just uncovered another of Ermina Blaylock's victims. That makes three in all—her father in Missouri, Richard Lowensdale in Grass Valley, and now, if I'm not mistaken, Mark Blaylock too, in Salton City. Not to mention Brenda Riley. Ermina is a maniac, B. We need to catch her before she gets away or has a chance to kill anyone else."

B. sighed. "Where are you now?"

"On the plane, getting ready to fly to San Diego. I know, it's a long shot, but that's the only other address we have for her—the business park at Clairemont Mesa. Even though Rutherford International went out of business months ago, the utilities on two of their three office park units are still current. As broke as they are, there must be a reason those bills are being paid. We're hoping she'll show up there. Otherwise, we've got nowhere else to look."

B. was quiet long enough that Ali worried he might have hung up on her. She didn't blame him for being angry. When she had enlisted Stuart's help, she had been so preoccupied with her own concerns that she hadn't thought about the long-term ramifications for High Noon Enterprises if any of this came to light.

"I'm sorry, B.," she began, but he cut her off.

"I just had a thought," he said. "I don't know if it'll work or not, but call me again once you land."

"Who was that?" Gil asked, once she put her phone away.

"My boyfriend," Ali said. "He's also the technically savvy genius who's behind the guy you call my phone meister. He seemed to think that he had come up with an idea that might help us find Ermina."

"I hope so," Gil said. "I've only been to San Diego a couple of times, one of which was to take the kids to the zoo. It's a pretty big haystack, and Ermina Blaylock is a mighty small needle."

The CJ rose precipitously through the cold night air. Soon Palm Springs and the surrounding cities were narrow strings of lights crisscrossing the darkened desert. Leaning back in her seat, Ali was thinking about B. and regretting the untenable position her actions had created for him and for his company.

"I don't think they're broke," Gil said from across the aisle, interrupting her chain of self-recrimination.

"What?"

"I don't think the Blaylocks were broke," Gil said again. "At least not as broke as they led everyone to believe. First Ermina killed Richard Lowensdale. Then she went searching for something but didn't find it."

"How do you know she didn't find it?"

"Because I did. There was a stash of empty motor oil bottles out in Richard's garage. Hidden inside I found fifty thousand dollars in cash and these."

Gil reached into the pocket of his jeans and pulled out the two thumb drives and handed them over to her. "I don't have a computer at home, so I didn't try to look at them, but between these and the cash, I figure we're dealing with one of two things. Either Lowensdale had found out about Ermina's background and was trying to blackmail her, or else he was still working for her. My guess, it's the latter rather than the former. Once the guy outlived his usefulness, Ermina got rid of him. She got rid of your friend Brenda too, after planting evidence that would make us believe Brenda was responsible for Richard Lowensdale's death."

"What evidence?" Ali asked.

"Three of Richard Lowensdale's fingers were hacked off with kitchen shears before he died," Gil said quietly. "We found his thumb in Brenda's purse, which was left at the Scotts Flat Reservoir. I have no doubt that Brenda's body is there too. It's just going to take time for it to float to the surface. I know they have underwater equipment that could expedite a search, but I doubt the county can afford it."

"Brenda was a friend of mine," Ali said. "I kept hoping we'd find her alive."

"I know," Gil said. "I'm sorry. What do you think about the thumb drives?"

"I left my computer in Laguna Beach," she said. "When we get to the terminal in San Diego, I'll handle the car rental. Then while you load the car, I'll see if I can log on to one of the computers and send B. whatever's on the thumb drives. Then you can have them back."

"What's his name?" Gil asked.

"B.," Ali said. "B. Simpson. He was born Bartholomew Simpson; people used to call him Bart. He got tired of being teased about that. He changed his name to B. Period."

"I don't blame him," Gil said. "I think I would have done the same thing."

When the plane parked next to the terminal at Montgomery Field, Phil Canby came to open the door. "Clairemont Mesa's just to the right of us," he said, motioning. "Your car is here on the tarmac."

"Do you think I could use a computer in the FBO?" Ali asked.

"I don't see why not," Phil said. "It doesn't hurt to ask."

Ali hurried into the terminal, where the receptionist took her back into a computer-stocked room that was usually reserved for pilot use only. As she plugged the first of the thumb drives into the computer's USB port, she worried that Richard Lowensdale might have booby-trapped the drive so it would self-destruct if anyone else tried to open it. Rather than opening it, she simply copied the data as an attachment into an e-mail and sent it both to B. and to Stuart. She was in the process of uploading the second drive when her phone rang.

"Since you just sent me an e-mail, I'm assuming you're on the ground," B. said.

"Sorry," Ali told him. "I wanted to send these first."

"I know. Stuart and I will both take a look at them in a minute, but right now, I have some good news. That phone call Ermina made went to the local Hertz rental line. I went into their computer system. Two minutes after that call, a San Diego car rental reservation record shows up in the Hertz database in the name of Sophia Stanhope. She picked it up an hour later. A silver Cadillac DTS. She's supposed to drop it off at the rental return at LAX tomorrow."

"Who's Sophia Stanhope?"

"She's supposedly a divorcée from Sarajevo," B. said. "I'd be willing to bet she's really Ermina Blaylock, traveling with some kind of forged documents."

"Do you happen to have the tab number on that rented Caddy?" Ali asked.

B. laughed. "What do you think? Am I a full-service hacker or not?"

"Definitely full-service," Ali replied.

By the time she finished writing down the license information, Gil was standing looking over her shoulder.

"What's that?"

She gave him the note. "It's the plate number for a silver Cadillac DTS someone named Sophia Stanhope rented from a local Hertz agency earlier this evening," Ali told him. "Sophia and Ermina are most likely one and the same, and you may want to revise that BOLO to have information on both this vehicle and the other one. And you should probably expand it to include both the L.A. and San Diego metropolitan areas."

After sending the second e-mail, she removed the second thumb drive and handed both drives over to Gil. "Copied only," she assured him. "Did nothing with the data."

Nodding, he returned the two drives to his pocket. "Okay," he said. "You finish signing for the car. I'm going to call El Centro and see if they'll put me through to the detective."

Gil had pulled the rental car—a Mercury Marquis—through the airport gate and parked it in front of the terminal. When Ali opened the door, she was grateful that the cardboard boxes had been banished to the trunk. She found a Kevlar vest, size L, hanging on the steering wheel. She put it on.

There was no way to tell if Ermina Blaylock would be armed. If she was planning on traveling by air, she most likely wouldn't try to carry a weapon on board an international flight, but between then and now, all bets were off.

While Ali waited for Gil to emerge from the terminal, she called Stuart back.

"You're certainly keeping the phone lines humming today," he said. "I thought B. was going to hand me my walking papers when he found out what we'd been up to."

"He didn't, did he?" Ali asked guiltily.

"No. In fact, I think he'll be getting back to Hertz very soon to let them know that their secure rental database isn't especially secure. So what can I do for you now?"

"I need the addresses of those two locations in San Diego where Mark and Mina Blaylock are still paying the utilities."

"Easy," Stuart said. "Here you go."

By the time Gil got into the car, Ali had already loaded the address on Engineer Road into the rental's NeverLost GPS system. It turned out the two addresses in question were less than two miles from where they were currently parked.

"I thought it was something when I got on the plane in Grass Valley, but this is amazing," he said, as he picked up his own Kevlar vest and pulled it on over his golf shirt. "You fly up in your sweet little corporate jet and the car is parked right there on the tarmac waiting for you. No security lines. No baggage check. No car rental lines."

"It's fast," she said. "It's convenient."

"And expensive," he put in.

"That too."

"So what's your connection to all of this?" he asked.

"To Lowensdale's case?"

Gil nodded.

"Guilt," she said. "I'm the one who blew the whistle on Richard Lowensdale in the first place. Until I came up with that first background check, Brenda didn't even know what the man's name was, much less anything about the other women . . ."

Gil looked at his watch. "Crap," he said.

"What's wrong?"

"Janet Silvie, one of Richard's many girlfriends, is probably on her way into Grass Valley right this minute. She was flying into Sacramento today, and I'm not there to talk to her."

"What are you going to do?" Ali asked.

"Call the desk sergeant, Frieda Lawson," he said. "If anyone can pull my fat out of the fire, she's the one."

While Gil dialed a number on his cell phone, Ali added a new waypoint to the GPS and drove to the nearest Carl's Jr. It had been a very long time since breakfast. If she and Gilbert Morris were going to be stuck in a car on a long stakeout, Ali was determined not to starve in the process.

San Diego, California

While Ali pulled the Mercury into the drive-up line at Carl's Jr., Gil was busy having his ass chewed. Over strongly voiced protests, his call to the desk sergeant had been put through to the chief's office. Unfortunately Chief Jackman was in.

"Do you realize I have not just one but two hysterical women here in the department, both of them raising hell?" Jackman demanded.

"Two," Gil echoed.

"Yes, two. Someone named Dawn Carras showed up an hour or so ago with a worthless little dog that seems to want to take a piss on every chair leg in the waiting room. When Sergeant Lawson couldn't reach you, she called me instead. Thanks a lot. So I was here handling that crisis when Janet Silvie shows up. Now they're out in the lobby having a screaming match. You need to get your butt in here right now and take care of it."

"I can't," Gil said.

"Why the hell not?"

"Because I'm in San Diego."

"San Diego?" Jackman roared. "I told you to take the day off. I didn't say you could go to San Diego."

"You didn't say I couldn't," Gil said. "And if you'll look on the roster, you'll see I won't be in tomorrow either. It's a comp day. I worked eight days straight."

"Detective Morris, that sounds a lot like insubordination."

"It's sounds like time to file a grievance to me," Gil returned, and ended the call.

Pulling out of the drive-up, Ali handed him a bag with a burger, fries, and a soda. "I guess it's safe to assume that didn't go too well."

"Actually, I think it's fine," Gil said. "Leaving Randy Jackman to deal with two hysterical women and a pissy little dog is exactly what the man deserves. Now where are we?"

"That's Engineer Road right up ahead," she said, driving into a maze of streets lined with similarly constructed office buildings and warehouses. "We're going to drive around and see if we can see any sign of either the Cadillac or the Lincoln. If she traded that Lincoln of hers for a rented Cadillac, she might have left the Lincoln parked somewhere nearby."

When Gil's phone rang again a few minutes later, he expected it would be Jackman again. It wasn't.

"Detective Manuel Moreno with the Imperial County Sheriff's Department. I understand you called my department to say you might have some information in regard to my Salton City homicide. So I have two questions. Who are you and what kind of information?"

"I'm Gilbert Morris, a homicide dick with the Grass Valley Police Department. I'm investigating a homicide too, one that happened on Friday of last week. I have reason to believe you and I share a suspect. So let me ask you about Mark Blaylock. You know his death is a homicide rather than a suicide?"

There was a pause. Gil could imagine Detective Moreno staring at the cubicle wall in front of his desk, wondering if he should answer the question or tell Gil to go to hell.

"It could be suicide," Moreno said. "We found an empty bottle of Ambien in the trash and took it into evidence. What we didn't find was any kind of suicide note. At all. The coroner says the victim died sometime overnight last night, probably right around midnight. This morning his wife gets up bright and early, locks up the house, and then takes off for parts unknown without bothering to dial nine-one-one and without mentioning that her beloved husband is dead in their bed. And if it hadn't been for someone encouraging a nosy neighbor to go check on Mr. Blaylock's welfare, it could have been days or weeks before anyone found him. So what do you think, homicide or suicide?"

"I think the same thing you do," Gil said. "Only for a lot more reasons."

While Gil laid out to the Imperial County detective what they knew, what they thought they knew, and when they knew it, Ali did her best to ignore the telephone conversation and concentrate on driving.

The streets of the once-thriving business park wound around and around in seemingly never-ending circles. A lot of the buildings were tagged with graffiti. Many of the lights that should have illuminated the street addresses printed on the buildings were broken or had burned out. There were weeds in the grassy medians and trash blowing around in the gutters and up beside the buildings. The parking lots beside the buildings were mostly empty. That could have been because it was night, or it could have been because the business park was close to being a ghost town. There was no way to tell.

Driving past the two Rutherford units, Ali saw that one of them had a loading bay as well as a regular walk-in entrance. The other unit had only a single door. She drove to the end of the street, counting doors and units as she went, then she traveled up an alley on the far side of the building, counting in reverse. Both Rutherford units had back doors, which meant that both front and back entrances needed to be watched.

Before Gil finished talking to Moreno, however, Ali's phone rang. "UAVs," B. said. "I've had one of my friends take a look at the schematics. Stuart tells me that according to the background check, Rutherford International was hired to dismantle a bunch of UAVs."

"Yes," Ali said. "I remember seeing something like that. A statement, signed and sworn by some government inspector, saying that the UAVs had been properly disposed of."

"Then it's likely the inspector lied," B. returned. "According to the files on the thumb drives, someone—Richard Lowensdale, most likely—was tinkering with the guidance system files and making changes in their code as recently as two weeks ago."

"Who would want to buy UAVs?" Ali asked.

"Who wouldn't want to buy UAVs?" B. responded. "Anyone with a beef against the United States could be in the market for UAVs."

Ali had pulled over and stopped in a parking place that allowed her to see both Rutherford doors. Suddenly there was a sharp rap on the window near her head. Outside stood a uniformed rent-a-cop who had arrived silently on a bicycle.

"This is private property," he said. "You need to move along."

Gil started to respond, but Ali stopped him. "We're waiting to meet with a leasing agent," she said, glancing at her watch. "She's running late, but she's supposed to be here any minute."

"What was that all about?" B. asked into her ear.

"A security guard just paid us a visit," she said. "Trying to give us the bum's rush."

"Where are you?"

"Outside the front door of the two remaining Rutherford facilities in San Diego."

"Who's there with you?"

"The security guard is here, but he's not really with me. The other guy is Gil Morris, a homicide cop from Grass Valley," Ali answered.

"Shouldn't you have some local backup?"

"So far we don't have any grounds for backup," Ali said. "Nothing that would stand up in court."

"You can tell your friend that we don't have an arrest warrant at this point," Gil said, "but Detective Moreno from El Centro is currently en route. He says that if we can locate Ermina, he'll be able to question her as a person of interest in her husband's death. That's not an arrest as such, but if she's planning on leaving the country, that should at least slow her down, maybe long enough for arrest warrants to be forthcoming."

"All right," B. said. "I suppose that, as usual, you're armed?"

"And dangerous," Ali said with a smile. "So is Gil for that matter—armed and dangerous—and we're both wearing vests."

"Somehow that doesn't make me feel any better," B. said, "especially since you're on one side of the country and I'm on the other."

Ali could hear a lecture coming about her putting herself in harm's way. Even if it was true, Ali didn't want to hear it.

"I'm going to have to hang up now," she said. "My Carl's Junior burger is getting cold."

She ended the call and rustled open the bag, but for some reason, she discovered, she was no longer hungry. Even without the lecture, B.'s question had gotten to her. She and Gil were armed, but there was no telling if their opponent, who might or might not show up, would be armed as well.

"Do you think Ermina's carrying?" Ali asked.

Gil thought about it for a moment before he answered. "Present company excluded," he said, "most women I know don't carry weapons. Yes, Ermina was willing to get up close and personal with Richard, but only when he was hogtied, hand and foot. Someone who would stoop to using plastic bags or poison isn't going to have guts enough to use a gun." There was a pause and then he added a somewhat plaintive, "At least I hope she doesn't."

They both laughed aloud at that, and the laughter noticeably reduced the tension. It seemed odd for Ali to realize that although they had known each another for less than twelve hours, they were both operating on the same page. How was that possible?

She worried that the bike-riding security guard would come around again, but he didn't. Then, just when Ali was beginning to think she might need to go find a bush somewhere, the headlights of a vehicle came sliding slowly down the street. First the turn lights came on. Then, activated by a remote control, the rolling door in the loading bay part of the building went up. A silver Cadillac drove inside and stopped, then the door came back down behind it, closing it from sight.

"Okay," Gil said. "Here's the way I see it. There are two of us and, from what I can see, only one of her; two vehicles; and five doors altogether. I'll take the back two, you take these. If she tries to come out . . ."

Without a word, Ali restarted the Mercury's engine and put it in gear. "You need to get out," she said.

"Why?" Gil asked. "What are you doing?"

"I'm going to block the driveway," Ali said, jarring the Marquis's wheels up over the sidewalk. She waited long enough for Gil to scramble out the passenger door, then she parked so his side of the vehicle was within inches of the rolling door.

She rolled down her window as he came around to the driver's side.

"Looks like that'll work," he said.

Ali nodded. "I call it athwart parking rather than parallel parking. My Hertz profile says I take every insurance they offer. If Ermina tries to drive out of the garage, she'll have to go through this thing or over it."

"Good thinking," Gil said. "By my count that leaves only four doors to cover, and we outnumber her two to one."

"Do we wait for her to come out on her own?" Ali asked. "Or do we try to bring her out?"

"Let's try to maintain the element of surprise," Gil said. "I'll call you once I'm in position in the alley. Then as far as I'm concerned, I think we should sit tight. Ermina came here for one of two reasons—to pick something up or to drop something off. I doubt she's planning on staying here all night."

Gil had just disappeared from sight behind the end of the building when the security guard reappeared. Knowing he would most likely demand that she leave, Ali grabbed the car keys and shoved them out of sight into the crack between the two front seats. Then she punched her cell phone so it would dial Gil's number.

"Where's your friend?" the rent-a-cop asked.

"A call of nature," Ali said, nodding in the opposite direction from the one where Gil had disappeared.

"He can't do that. This is private property. You need to move your vehicle now. It's blocking the driveway."

"I'm sorry," Ali said. "He took the keys. He'll be back in a minute."

"You don't have a minute," the guard said. "Your presence here is impeding a federal investigation." He leaned toward the window holding an ID wallet. The badge inside said, very clearly, FBI. "Either you leave right now, or I'm placing you under arrest."

"I guess you'll have to arrest me then," Ali told him. "Because I'm not leaving."

"Step out of the vehicle," he said. "Place your hands on your head."

53

Clairemont Mesa Business Park, San Diego, California

After endless hours of utter darkness, when the lights came on overhead, their brilliance exploded in Brenda's head, temporarily blinding her. She heard rather than saw the key turn in the lock. When she could see again, a woman—the woman Brenda knew as Ermina Blaylock—was approaching the chair where Brenda was imprisoned. Her face was screwed up in a strange grimace, as though the stench of the place was beyond bearing.

Brenda had moved far beyond that. She had become so accustomed to the foul odors lingering around her that she could no longer smell anything at all. But then Brenda saw the bottle. Ermina was carrying a bottle of water—a large bottle of water.

"I'll bet you're thirsty," she said, forcing a smile. "I brought you something to drink."

Brenda stared at the bottle. She wanted the water inside it more than she had ever wanted anything in her life. But then she remembered Friday. Or, at least, she remembered parts of Friday, how during lunch she had suddenly begun losing track of who she was and what she was doing.

She wanted the water, yes. But what if Ermina had slipped something into it? In her terribly weakened condition, even a little bit of something extra might be too much. Something that might have induced unconsciousness on Friday might well prove fatal now.

Ermina twisted the cap off the bottle and held it up to Brenda's lips. "Here," she said. "Have a drink."

Brenda leaned back in the chair and closed her eyes. Once again, through the trailing ethers of memory, she heard Uncle Joe's voice. "Choose to live."

Yes, she would die of thirst, but she would not willingly swallow whatever poison Ermina was offering her. She waited. Only when the open end of the bottle touched her lips did she bring her head forward, swinging it from side to side. Ermina had expected compliance, and she was caught unawares. Brenda smacked the bottle with the side of her cheek and sent it flying out of Ermina's hand. It rolled across the floor, spilling precious water as it went. Finally it came to rest against the bottom of a chain-link fence.

"You stupid bitch!" Ermina exclaimed. "Why did you do that?"

She reached out and slapped Brenda's face with an open-handed blow that left Brenda seeing stars, but the pain of it was enough to jar Brenda fully out of her stupor. And even as Ermina readied another blow, Brenda realized that Uncle Joe would have been proud of her. For once in her life Brenda Riley had measured up.

Then suddenly the chair she was imprisoned in was moving. With Brenda still in it, the chair rolled out through the open gate in the chain-link fence, across the tiled floor to yet another door. She sped through the second door and into another interconnected section of the building. There was a car inside. Ermina wheeled Brenda past a tall stack of cardboard boxes and stopped next to the trunk of the car.

Without a word, Ermina opened the trunk. Then, after donning a pair of latex gloves, she reached inside and pulled out a plastic-wrapped package. Using a box cutter, she tore though the packaging and then shook out the contents. Brenda watched as a narrow bedroll unrolled. For some reason it reminded her of an uncoiling snake.

Ermina unzipped the bedroll and then she cut through the tape that had bound Brenda's legs. "Stand up," she said.

Brenda looked down at her feet. After being forced to sit for days on end, her limbs were severely swollen, distended. She understood without being told that if she ever got inside that bedroll, there would be no coming out. And she also understood that there was no point in screaming. She had already tried that once, to no avail. Besides, she didn't have the strength.

"I can't," she said.

"You can and you will," Ermina replied.

She held the opening of the bedroll over Brenda's head and slipped it down. As the thick material shut out the light—as darkness descended again—Brenda tried to struggle against it, but it was no use. She felt herself propelled up and out of the chair, which skittered away from her and banged up against a wall somewhere behind her. She landed hard inside the trunk as her head came to rest against the upright wall at the far end of the trunk. And then, although she struggled hard against it, she heard the zipper closing inevitably, shutting her in.

Brenda tried shouting then, one last time, in the vain hope that someone would hear her, but the down filling of the bedroll muffled her cries.

She heard the car's motor start. She heard a racket of some kind, like a garage door opening. She felt the car start to move, and then she heard a crash as it stopped moving. Her head smashed hard against something she couldn't see, and then another kind of blackness descended around her and carried her away.

54

Clairemont Mesa Business Park, San Diego, California

Gil heard the guy talking in the background on Ali's phone. For a moment he was torn. Did he abandon his post and go give Ali backup, or did he stay where he was in case Ermina heard the racket out front and made a break for it? Then Gil heard another sound in the background— a garage door rolling open. He turned and sprinted back the way he had come, but he was the better part of a block away.

The grinding sound of a crash—of crunching metal and breaking glass—was immediately followed by a shout of surprise that could have been from someone being hit or hurt.

A car engine revved. More than revved, it roared. There was another horrendous grinding and scraping of metal on metal. Gil made it around the corner in time to see the back of a Cadillac DTS T-boned into the side of the Marquis. The security guard's bicycle had been flung across the street. With its front wheel still spinning, it lay at an odd angle next to the gutter. In the middle of the street, next to the Marquis, lay the fallen security guard.

Gil took it all in as he ran. Then a woman in what looked like a tan tracksuit erupted out of the open garage door. She sped away from Gil with so much distance between them that he knew he'd never catch her. Just then, Ali sprang out of her car. She had to dodge around to keep from stepping on the fallen security guard, but then she caught her balance and ran too. She ran with her head down and her arms pumping; she ran like she meant it.

Gil paused briefly when he reached the security guard. He seemed to be coming around. Leaving the fallen man where he was, Gil pounded after the two fleeing women, who by then had disappeared around the far end of that same set of buildings.

As Gil rounded the corner, they were still far ahead of him, but he could see that Ali was closing the distance. She was a runner who worked at it chasing someone who didn't. Ali didn't shout out a warning that she was a police officer, because she wasn't, so Gil did it for her.

"Stop," he yelled. "Police."

Sirens sounded in the background. Pulsing lights showed that slowing police cars were converging on the area. Gil couldn't be sure if it was the shout or the sirens or neither one, but Ermina seemed to lose heart. She paused for a moment, and that moment was enough. Ali caught up with her.

"On the ground!" she shouted. "Now."

For a few seconds, the two women stood facing one another panting, out of breath, glaring at one another in animal fury. Then, as Gil watched in amazement, Ali Reynolds grabbed Ermina Blaylock by the arm and executed a flawless hip toss.

He caught up with them just then, stumbling to a stop in time to see Ermina land hard on the sidewalk. Her face was bloodied. Ali was astraddle her with one knee in the small of her back.

"I tried to warn you," Ali gasped breathlessly. "I told you to get on the ground!"

Moments later the business park was alive with men and women in windbreakers emblazoned with the letters FBI. Two agents stepped forward. One of them took charge of Ermina. The other one reached for Ali. Exhibiting his own badge, Gil waved him off.

"She's okay," he said. "She's with me, but you'd better go check on your undercover guy. He's down back there in the street. When I came by him, he seemed to be coming around. He's probably wearing a vest, but those are better for stopping bullets than cars, so he might have internal injuries."

One agent led Ermina away, while the other jogged off in the direction Gil had indicated. Once they were gone, Gil helped Ali to her feet.

"I couldn't believe it," Ali said. "The security guard was standing by the window hassling me when Ermina came screaming out of the garage without even glancing in her rearview mirror. I don't know how fast she was going when she hit my car, but it was with enough force that it slammed the driver's side of the Marquis into the guy on the bicycle. I saw him go down and the bicycle go flying, but I didn't stop to check on him. She was getting away."

"I think the guy on the ground is probably okay," Gil said. "But what about you? Are you all right?"

"Still out of breath," she managed. "But okay."

"You're fast," he said admiringly. "It's a good thing you were the one chasing her. She would have left me in the dust. Let's go check on that guard. And I hope you're right about your insurance, because that Mercury you rented is toast!"

The fallen FBI agent still lay on the ground with a group of fellow officers clustered around him. Somewhere in the distance came the shrill wail of an arriving ambulance. As Ali walked toward her car, one of the FBI agents broke away from the group around the injured officer.

"Okay," he said. "Now I want to know who you are and what you're doing here besides screwing up a major bust."

As Gil reached again for his ID packet, Ali leaned inside the open window on the driver's side of her wrecked car, looking for the rental agreement and her purse. Ali, Gil, and the agent all heard the noise at the same time—a muffled thump coming from the trunk of the wrecked Cadillac.

"What the hell is that?" the FBI agent demanded.

Ali was closest to the conjoined vehicles. She darted around the front of her car and arrived at the smashed rear end of the Cadillac just as another thump sounded from inside the crumpled trunk. The rear bumper had been smashed into the body of the vehicle, leaving the trunk lid jammed in place.

Wrenching open the driver's door, Ali reached for the trunk release. She found it at last and pulled it, but nothing happened.

"Hey," the agent called out, "somebody bring me a tire iron or a crowbar. We need to open this thing up."

Thirty seconds of prying later, the trunk lid gave way and opened. While the agents worked to open the trunk, Gil stayed front and center. Once the trunk lid finally sprang open, Gil peered inside at what appeared to be a squirming mass of bedroll—a smelly squirming mass of bedroll. Gil lifted the slithering mass of bedroll out of the trunk and placed it gently on the weedy grass next to the driveway. One of the agents dropped his crowbar and unzipped the zipper, letting a terrible stench loose into the air.

"Thank you," whispered a cracked voice that barely sounded human. "Water, please."

Ali was the one who recognized her.

"Oh, my God!" she exclaimed, falling on her knees beside the badly injured woman. "It's Brenda Riley. I don't believe it. She's alive!"

"Hey," the agent shouted. "Send those medics over here. Order another ambulance for Sinclair. Looks like this one is hurt a lot worse than he is."

55

Sharp Mary Birch Hospital, San Diego, California

A squawking ambulance whisked Brenda Riley away from the scene and took her to the Sharp Mary Birch Hospital ER, which was only minutes away. Ali and Gil rode there in a black Suburban with San Diego FBI Agent in Charge Sam Hollingshead at the wheel. They had transferred the luggage to the Suburban—Gil's single suitcase as well as the three cardboard boxes that still reeked of smoke and leaked trailing bits of sand.

While ER personnel attended to Brenda, Hollingshead commandeered a conference room and herded Ali and Gil inside.

"I don't know if I should thank you or throw the book at you," he said. "You caught Ermina, and from what she did to that poor woman in there, she surely needed catching, but you may have blown the cover off an operation we've been working on for months. The problem is, this is a white-collar crime case with overriding national security issues. Without a proper security clearance, I can't even discuss it with you."

"We know about the UAVs, if that's what you mean," Ali said.

Hollingshead looked at her sharply. "How would you know anything about that?"

Gil reached into his jeans and pulled out the two thumb drives. "From these," he said, placing the drives on the table in front of Hollingshead. "My homicide victim in Grass Valley, Richard Lowensdale, had these hidden in his garage. Ali was able to run the files past one of her computer people. They're the ones who came up with the drone angle."

Ali appreciated that creative bit of understatement. There was no mention of High Noon Enterprises in anything that had been said, and she doubted Sam Hollingshead would be terribly interested or motivated to track down the details. He seemed to be preoccupied with his own concerns.

"All right, then," Hollingshead said, "so you know about that too. We figured Richard was involved in the Blaylocks' drone project. We had court-ordered access to his computers, and we used his own CCTV to maintain surveillance on his house."

"So you know about the cyberstalking?" Ali asked.

"Yes," Hollingshead said, with a dismissive shrug. "As far as I could tell, it was just a harmless hobby. He didn't appear to be doing anything wrong."

Ali did a slow burn at that statement, which said more about SAC Hollingshead than it did about Richard Lowensdale.

"What he did to those poor women may have been legal, but it was most definitely wrong," Ali said.

"Yes," Hollingshead agreed, "I suppose it was, but that didn't concern us. It wasn't part of our investigation. We were convinced that Richard was working for Ermina, but since we haven't been able to find any record of payments, I surmised that perhaps they had some other involvement that overrode any monetary considerations."

"You mean you thought Richard and Mina were involved sexually?" Gil asked.

Hollingshead didn't bother denying it. "Look," he said, "she drove up there last weekend like she usually did every month or so. She went into Lowensdale's house in Grass Valley. She went inside for a while and then she came back out again. Maybe she stayed inside a little longer than she usually did, but we had no idea that she had killed the guy while she was there."

"So you had surveillance in place, but you didn't actually follow her?"

"The CCTV at Lowensdale's house went on the fritz while she was there."

"The video feed ended," Gil offered.

"Correct."

"What about her car? Did you attempt to follow it?" Ali asked.

"We didn't need to," Hollingshead said. "We had a GPS bug on her car. We know where she went and when right up until tonight when she ditched the car and gave us the slip."

"So you didn't know she had picked up Brenda Riley?" Ali asked.

"From what we can tell, Ermina drove to Brenda's mother's place on P Street in Sacramento. We're assuming that's when she met up with Brenda, but we don't know positively."

"But you knew she drove to the Scotts Flat Reservoir?" Gil asked.

"Yes, and we wondered about it after the fact, but she was only there for a few minutes, then she headed home. Since the spot didn't appear to have any bearing on our case, we just let it go."

"What about Ermina's background?" Ali asked. "Did you have any idea about what she's suspected of doing to her adoptive father in Missouri?"

Hollingshead paused for a moment, then he nodded. "Yes," he said. "One of our agents spoke to Detective Laughlin months ago. He sounded like an old guy all hung up on a long closed case. We learned about Lowensdale's death sometime yesterday, but you need to understand, there was nothing we could do about it. Our hands were tied. If we had acted on any of that information prematurely, we might have risked jeopardizing the mission."

"Yes," Ali said, "but if you had, maybe Mark Blaylock wouldn't be dead right now."

"He was part of this too, you know," Hollingshead said. "Ermina didn't do all of it on her own."

"You *think* he was part of it," Ali pointed out. "It's also possible that he was innocent—innocent and dead, an outcome you might have prevented."

"I agree," Hollingshead said. "It's an unfortunate outcome."

"Especially unfortunate for Mr. Blaylock," Ali insisted.

Hollingshead seemed to be running out of patience. "Look, Ms. Reynolds," he said placatingly, "I understand that you're angry. You have every right to be. At least two people are dead who probably shouldn't be, and your friend Brenda has suffered grievous harm, but we need to keep a lid on this. We *must* keep a lid on it.

"Our intelligence tells us that the drone shipment is due to be picked up sometime tomorrow. We're attaching bugs to each of those individual boxes. We're going to let them be picked up and delivered and delivered without incident. We already know that the middleman is a guy named Enrique Gallegos who has been on the FBI's watch list and also the DEA's for a very long time. Our intention is to take down the end users—whoever they are and wherever they might be.

"So don't expect to read about this in the paper tomorrow morning, because it turns out nothing at all happened at the business park tonight, understand? Your damaged car has been hauled away, and so has hers. The Rutherford garage bay has been cleaned up and buttoned up. Hertz is in the process of delivering a replacement vehicle to you here, no questions asked."

"Wait a minute," Gil said. "You're whitewashing this?"

"For the time being."

"You can't do that. I'm investigating a homicide that happened on my watch in Grass Valley. Detective Moreno down in Imperial County has one too. In both of those cases, the presumed doer is Ermina Blaylock, and I can assure you that we aren't going to shut up and go away just because you said so."

"And what about Brenda?" Ali demanded. "She came within inches of dying at Ermina Blaylock's hands. And then there's your own officer. She assaulted him with a moving vehicle, which counts as a deadly weapon in my book. You expect us to keep a lid on all that? Are you nuts?"

"Not nuts," Hollingshead countered, "but I am in charge. For right now, we've taken Ermina into custody. We intend to hold her at least until the drone delivery takes place. Longer if possible."

"Charged with what?" Gil asked.

"Falsifying a federal document. She may lawyer up, but there's also a chance she'll talk to us."

"This isn't my first day of being a cop," Gil said. "What talking to you really means is that you're going to try to make a deal with her, and your best bargaining chips will be reducing the charges against her—our charges, my charges."

"I'm not saying yes, and I'm not saying no," Hollingshead said.

"Which turn out to be standard weasel words for yes," Ali said.

Hollingshead said nothing in reply.

"And what will happen to the UAVs?"

"We'll be following the shipment. We'll also be following the money."

"With the same kind of GPS efficiency you demonstrated in following Ermina's car?" Ali asked without trying to disguise her sarcasm.

"Look, if we had known how dangerous she was—"

"I'm not buying that," Ali said. "You did know. Someone from your agency had already spoken to Detective Laughlin. You endangered any number of lives in order to protect your 'mission,' and now you're going to try to cover it up. Good luck with that. You underestimated Ermina Blaylock, and I suspect you're underestimating Gil and me too. When this is all over, I suggest you send yourself back to the academy for some remedial classes in fatal errors—you know, those ten mistakes cops make that end up getting them killed? Failure to call for backup is one of the biggies, but what if the agent in charge fails to call for backup? What then?

"You're all focused on your fancy electronic gizmos. Great, but what about your people? What about leaving Agent Sinclair on the street without any kind of backup? The only backup he had was Gil Morris and Ali Reynolds. If it hadn't been for us, Ermina might have gotten away and claimed another victim in the process."

With that, Ali pushed back her chair and stood up. "Now, if you'll excuse me, I have a phone call to make. There's a woman in Sacramento who needs to know that her supposedly dead daughter isn't dead!"

Ali stalked out of the conference room with Gil on her heels. "Remind me not to make you mad," he said.

"He deserved it," Ali replied.

Out in the lobby, a guy wearing a yellow Hertz shirt flagged Ali down and handed her a new rental agreement and a new set of keys.

"It's just like the one you had before," he said. "Another Marquis. It's parked in a loading zone just outside the hospital entrance. There's an FBI agent waiting beside the door. He told me to tell you your property has already been loaded."

"In other words, here's our hat, what's our hurry," Ali said.

Taking the keys, she walked back to the ER admitting desk. "Can you tell me anything about Ms. Riley?" Ali asked. "I'm about to call her mother."

"You're not a relative?"

"No. I'm a friend."

"Then I'm not authorized . . ."

Ali walked away without waiting for the usual speech about patient confidentiality. The whole thing seemed wrong somehow. It was due to Ali and Gil's efforts that Brenda Riley was even alive, not to mention in a hospital with a possibility of surviving. Still, by federal mandate, her rescuers weren't allowed to know anything about her condition.

"Let's go," she said.

"Where?" Gil asked. "It's almost midnight."

"I don't care how late it is," Ali said. "I've got a two-bedroom apartment waiting for me in Laguna Beach and I'm going there. I'll make my phone calls along the way. Now, are you coming along or are you staying here?"

"Oh, I'm coming along all right," Gil said, dropping into step beside her. "I just used up all my available credit buying house-hold goods at Target. You dragged me down here where I have no car, no place to stay, no money, and no way to get back home. In other words, if I don't go with you, I'm pretty much screwed."

"Not so much," Ali said. "You remember all that money Sam Hollingshead was just saying he couldn't find? Ermina couldn't find it either. You gave Hollingshead those two thumb drives, and he was ecstatic. He's not going to give a damn about that missing money. There's no one left to look for it."

"But—"

Ali stopped him with an upraised hand. "We've both just had a lesson in the FBI's high cost of doing business," she observed. "If somebody happens to die here and there along the way, so what?

Let's not 'endanger' the precious mission. And if Hollingshead has to make a plea deal in a homicide or two in order to nail their man or woman, that's no big deal either, right? What if Richard Lowensdale's missing money is part of the same thing—the high cost of their doing business? It's a lot like my wrecked car. Never happened. No questions asked. It would serve them right."

Gil didn't know her well enough to be able to tell if she was joking or not, but he assumed she was.

When they got outside, the agent they'd been told about was indeed keeping a discreet eye on Ali's newly rented Marquis. He moved away when they approached the vehicle and Ali used a button on the key fob to unlock the door.

They stopped on opposite sides of the car, looking at each other over the top of it. "Did anyone ever tell you you're a pushy broad?" Gil asked. "Smart but very pushy."

She grinned back at him. "Believe me, Detective Morris, you're not the first to tell me that, and you won't be the last."

"By the way," he added, "just for the record. That was one sweet hip toss."

"It's my specialty," she said. "Best thing I ever learned at the Arizona Police Academy."

56

Laguna Beach, California

When they arrived at Velma's condominium building at two o'clock in the morning, it seemed to Ali that the doorman leered at them a little as he let them into the building. She didn't bother explaining to him that their being together didn't mean they *were* together. If the doorman had a dirty mind, it was none of Ali's business.

Once in the unit, they took one cursory look at the nighttime ocean view from the balcony, then they disappeared into their separate bedrooms. Ali fell asleep immediately. The next morning she was up bright and early. She went for a morning stroll on the beach with Maddy Watkins and the three dogs. Two hours later, she was drinking coffee and typing an e-mail to B. when Gil finally made his tardy appearance.

He wandered over to the kitchen counter and poured himself a cup of coffee.

"There are bagels on the counter and cream cheese in the fridge," she said. "Help yourself."

Gil found what looked like a bread knife in a utility drawer.

When he sliced a sesame bagel in half, he was amazed at how much sharper the knife was than the sole remaining one in his knife block at home. Something else to put on the list for his next household goods extravaganza.

He put the sliced bagel in the toaster and pushed down the button. "How's your friend this morning?" he asked.

It had taken them close to an hour and a half to drive to Laguna Beach from the hospital in San Diego. They'd done a lot of talking on the way. In the process Ali had told Gil about her dying friend, Velma Trimble.

Ali shook her head. "Not well. I went for a walk on the beach this morning with Maddy and the dogs. She said Velma's not doing well at all, and she seems anxious about my getting the check she gave me deposited. She's evidently concerned that there might be some kind of blowback from her son about her making that donation. She wants to be certain all the t's are crossed and i's dotted."

"You'd better handle that today, then," he said. He sat down across from her and took a sip of his coffee. "Have you heard from Camilla Gastellum?"

Ali nodded. "Valerie, her other daughter, and her husband drove all night. The three of them got to the hospital in San Diego this morning about eight. Brenda is out of the ICU. Her condition has been upgraded from critical to serious. They're treating her for dehydration. There's some concern about blood clotting issues as well. She was evidently left sitting in that chair for so long that there's concern about her developing DVTs."

"What's that?"

"Deep vein thrombosis from sitting for long periods of time. Blood clots that form in your legs can break loose and travel to the heart or lung or brain."

"I'm glad her family is there," Gil said. "I'll need to talk to

Brenda once she gets back north. It sounds like the actual kidnapping took place in Sacramento, but that all needs to be sorted out. That was my chief on the phone, by the way, calling to give me hell."

Ali had heard Gil's cell phone ringing earlier. That was evidently what had propelled him out of bed.

He retrieved his toasted bagel, put it on a plate, and brought that, a butter knife, and a container of cream cheese to the table.

"Chief Jackman told me yesterday that he wanted me to take comp time to make up for all the overtime, but it turns out he didn't mean I should take it now. And the fact that you and I managed to track down Richard Lowensdale's killer on our own time and that we saved Brenda Riley's life in the process barely registers in his little bean-counting skull. I told him I'll be in tomorrow. With that in mind, I guess I'd better rent a car someplace and head north."

"No," Ali said.

"What do you mean no?"

"As you pointed out last night, I'm the one who got you down here and I'm prepared to get you back. I've called You-Go. They'll have yesterday's CJ at John Wayne Airport, KSNA as it's known in aviation circles, at one p.m. You should be back in Grass Valley, KGOO, by about two thirty."

"You can't do that," he said. "I can't *let* you do that. It's too expensive."

"You can't stop me because it's already done. Here's your tail number. They asked about catering. I told them to order you a chicken salad. Hope that's okay."

"But—"

"No buts," Ali said. "I owe you, Gil. Brenda's alive. If it hadn't been for you, she probably wouldn't be."

"All right," he said. After a moment's reflection he took the piece of paper with the tail number on it and slipped it into his pocket. "But I won't be able to pay you back anytime soon. I did a lot of thinking about the money situation last night," he said. "I'm not going to keep it."

Ali looked at him and smiled. "I never thought you would," she said. "You're not that kind of guy."

He raised his coffee cup. "You aren't either."

By noon, the kitchen was back in order. They were packed and ready to leave. "I need to stop by and see Velma one last time," Ali told him.

"You do that," Gil said. "I'll take the bags downstairs and wait for you in the lobby."

As soon as Ali rang the doorbell on the penthouse floor, there was the expected response—frantic barking from the three dogs, followed by a stern "Quiet," followed by "Get on your rug." When Maddy Watkins opened the door, the room was perfectly quiet.

"I'm not sure she's awake," Maddy said.

"Who is it?" Velma asked from her hospital bed by the window.

"It's Ali," Maddy replied. "Ali Reynolds."

"I'm awake," Velma said. "Send her over."

Ali was surprised by the difference even a single day had made. Maddy was right. Velma was losing ground, physically if not mentally.

"Have you been to the bank yet?" Velma wanted to know.

"Not yet," Ali said. "I'm on my way to the airport. I'll probably see a bank branch somewhere along the way."

"Good," Velma said. "I want you to have that money. Actually, I want your scholarship kids to have the money. If I put it as a bequest in my will, my son might figure out a way to keep it from happening. I love him, you see. I just don't trust him."

Ali went over to Velma's bed and gathered Velma's rail-thin

hand in her own. "I have to go now," Ali said, leaning over to kiss Velma's weathered cheek.

"I do too," Velma said with a slight smile. "Don't bother coming to the funeral," she added. "It's going to be what my son wants, not what I want, but it won't make a bit of difference to me. Having you here to drink Maddiccinos with Maddy and me was a lot more my speed. Goodbye, Ali. Thanks for everything."

Blinking back tears, Ali paused long enough to hug Maddy on her way out. "I'm glad you're here," she said.

Maddy nodded. "So am I," she said.

The day after a bank holiday was a busy one at the Bank of America branch Ali found on their way to the airport. Ali was halfway through the teller line waiting to deposit Velma's check when her cell phone rang. It was Chris.

"Hey, Grandma," her son said. "If you want to see your grandkids make their grand entrance, you'd better head home. We're on our way to the hospital in Flagstaff right now. Dr. Dixon said she'll meet us there."

"Did you say right now?" Ali asked.

"I said right now."

"Okay," Ali said. "I'll do my best."

Her next call was to operations at You-Go. "Do you have another CJ available this afternoon?"

"From where to where?"

"The first one is due to go from John Wayne to Grass Valley. I'd like to take that one for myself and fly from KSNA to Flagstaff, Arizona. When the second aircraft arrives, that one can take Detective Morris from KSNA back to KGOO in Grass Valley."

"The soonest I could have another aircraft at John Wayne is two thirty," the operations clerk said. "That's an hour and a half after Mr. Morris's scheduled departure. Are you sure that's all right with him?"

"It'll be fine," Ali said. "He doesn't care what time he gets home as long as it's today. My son and daughter-in-law are on their way to a hospital. They're about to have twins, and I want to be there."

"Your aircraft is about twenty minutes out," the young woman said. "I'll advise your pilot of the change in plans and that you need a very short turnaround. What about catering?"

"We'll both have chicken salad."

Gil was waiting patiently in the car when Ali emerged from the bank.

"It seems there's been a slight change in plans," Ali told him. "I'm going home to Arizona in your plane, and they're sending another one for you."

Gil looked at her anxiously. "I hope it's not some kind of emergency."

"It's not an emergency of any kind. I'm about to become a grandmother," Ali said with a smile. "And I wouldn't miss it for the world."

ABOUT THE AUTHOR

J. A. Jance is the top-ten *New York Times* best-selling author of the Joanna Brady series, the J. P. Beaumont series, four interrelated thrillers featuring the Walker family, and the Ali Reynolds series: *Trial by Fire, Cruel Intent, Hand of Evil, Web of Evil,* and *Edge of Evil.* Born in South Dakota and brought up in Bisbee, Arizona, Jance lives with her husband in Seattle, Washington, and Tucson, Arizona.